D1189509

➤ THE CORONA PROJECT

The CORONA Project

America's First Spy Satellites

Curtis Peebles

Naval Institute Press
Annapolis, Maryland

Library of Congress Cataloging-in-Publication
Data
Peebles, Curtis.
    The Corona project: America's first spy
  satellites / Curtis Peebles.
        p.   cm.
    Includes bibliographical references and
  index.
      ISBN 1-55750-688-4 (alk. paper)
      1. Project Corona (United States)—
  History.   2. Space surveillance—United
  States—History.   I. Title.
  UG1523.P44   1997
  327.1273—dc21   97-12272

04 03 02 01 00 99 98 97   9 8 7 6 5 4 3 2
First printing

There were four individuals who were primarily responsible for the success of the Corona project. Due to the extreme secrecy which surrounded the project, however, they were never able to receive the recognition they deserved in their lifetimes.

Dwight D. Eisenhower

Richard M. Bissell, Jr.

Maj. Gen. Osmond J. "Ozzie" Ritland

Arthur C. Lundahl

This is the story of what they did, and the world they made.

Contents

Introduction

➤ The events of the Cold War now seem to belong to some strange, distant past. Yet when it ended, but a moment ago, no one under the age of fifty could remember a time when that epic struggle did not rage. For many children growing up in the early 1960s, words like "fallout," "ICBM," "the Berlin Wall," and "Fail Safe" were as much a part of childhood as baseball and Saturday matinees. These were reminders that, in both the United States of America and the Union of Soviet Socialist Republics, men in missile silos stood ready to launch ICBMs against each other at a moment's notice.

The world remained on the edge of that potential abyss for decade after decade, until it seemed it always had and always would. Some hoped that in an unknown, far-distant future, the human race would no longer be under the shadow of the mushroom cloud. Others wondered how humanity could continue to survive indefinitely under the threat.

The Cold War was America's longest conflict. It lasted a fifth of the United States' existence as an independent nation. It was fought on many different battlefields: on the frozen hills of Korea, in the rice paddies and jungles of Vietnam, and across tables in ornate conference rooms. It remade American society, government, and the military. The Cold War opened technological and scientific vistas that were once the definition of the impossible. Because of the U.S.-Soviet rivalry, Americans walked on the surface of the Moon.

But even as the Space Race was very publicly waged on the front pages of the world's newspapers, there was another U.S. space program. It also faced impossible odds, but its triumphs and failures did not make the nightly news. Secrecy surrounded every aspect of the effort. Those who participated could not even tell their own families what they did—but what they did changed the world.

This is the story of the Corona reconnaissance satellite program, and of the people who were part of it. Corona began with a series of heartbreaking failures, as rockets exploded at launch and satellites malfunctioned in orbit. At times, it seemed that Corona would never work. Yet the people who worked on the project never surrendered to despair. When success finally came, it was a triumph of the human spirit.

The technology they created became operational at a critical time in history. The first years of the 1960s were the most dangerous of the Cold War. The Soviet Union, emboldened by the success of Sputnik and the perception of great missile strength this created, put pressure on the West. In Berlin, U.S. and Soviet tanks faced each other, cannons loaded. As one crisis followed another, nuclear war seemed inevitable. It was Corona that provided the information that prevented World War III or a humiliating U.S. retreat.

In the decade which followed, Corona profoundly changed the nature of intelligence operations, international relations, and military planning. The Soviet Union was laid bare by the Corona satellites. They allowed a precise inventory of Soviet nuclear and conventional forces. The unknowns of Soviet military and economic power that had generated fears of a surprise attack in the 1950s were revealed. It now became possible for the United States to base its military programs on the actual Soviet threat, rather than on estimates and guesswork. Furthermore, this coverage could be extended to any place on the Earth where it was needed, such as the Middle East and Vietnam.

It was satellites like Corona that made it possible for the United States and the USSR to begin arms control negotiations, and it was satellites that insured the treaty provisions were not being violated. The program spanned the years from the missile gap controversy to the Strategic Arms Limitation Talks. Indeed, the very last Corona satellite was launched on the eve of the signing of the SALT Treaty.

Corona was also a story of the human experience. It involved a late-night, high-speed run down a freeway, and was a tale of mice and men and cover stories. It is about how code names are *really* picked, and of "Tuna" and "mighty Oaks." The story of Corona is also about how preconceived notions can influence projections, how presidents deal with intelligence, and "greetings" in the snow.

For more than a decade, Corona served as a stabilizing influence in a dangerous world. Yet, for a quarter century after the program's end, it still remained hidden. No U.S. government official would say the word "Corona" in public. Only now, with the release of its photos, can this hidden dimension of Cold War history be fully understood—and the people who made it possible receive the recognition they deserve.

The importance of Corona continues even with the sudden end of the Cold War and the beginning of a new century. The program can serve as a study in government, military, and industrial relations. It was just such a team that made Corona possible, and it was a later struggle for control that posed the greatest danger to the program. Corona also shows the importance of determination in the face of failure, as no U.S. space project suffered more.

The photos returned from the Corona missions continue to serve as an invaluable record. They now can provide information about climatic changes, geological features, and historical events, at a much higher resolution than U.S. earth resources satellite images could provide. Only a tiny percentage of the information from Corona has yet been extracted and analyzed. A whole new world awaits discovery.

In researching the story of Corona, the author had the help of a remarkable group of people. My thanks go to Dino A. Brugioni, Walter Levison, Harold E. Mitchell, Jack R. Wilson, Thomas F. Hines, Donald G. Hard, Jim Muehlberger, C. B. Moore, Dr. Rick W. Sturdevant, R. Cargill Hall, Dr. Raymond L. Puffer, the National Reconnaissance Office (http://www.nro.odci.gov/), Keith R. Smith, Jr., the Air Force Space Operations Association, Peter Hunter, Donald E. Welzenbach, Dr. Timothy C. Hanley, Dr. Harry N. Waldron, Kendall LaMontagne, Arcwelder Films, Ltd., Do You Graphics, Joel Carpenter, the San Diego Aerospace Museum, Donald J. Prichard, Jan Merlin, Dean C. Kallander, L. E. Williamson, and Sue Henderson. I also want to recognize the contributions of the organizers and speakers at the George Washington University/Center for the Study of Intelligence seminar on Corona, held in May 1995.

One result of the secrecy which surrounded Corona was that even those who worked on the project did not know the whole story. People saw only that small segment they personally worked on; the rest was a blank. One example of this occurred at the Corona seminar. A former engineer in attendance had worked on the project, knew that it was a reconnaissance satellite, but had not had clearance to see the pictures. On display were a number of enlarged photos. Only now, in the twilight of his life, did he finally get to see what he had created a quarter century before.

There were tears in his eyes.

➤THE CORONA PROJECT

ONE

Toward a New Frontier
The Birth of the Space Age, 1945–1957

With the advent of atomic weapons . . . the military and civilian leaders of a
government must know with the greatest possible accuracy the capabilities
of any potentially hostile nation to wage atomic war.

Intelligence Review, October 1946

➤ The story of the Corona reconnaissance satellite had its
beginnings on December 7, 1941. The Japanese surprise attack on
Pearl Harbor not only brought U.S. involvement in World War II, but
had a profound effect on American attitudes. The generation that lived
through the attack was scarred by the experience.[1]

Pearl Harbor made it clear that intelligence was critical to national
survival. In November 1945, with World War II ended just two months
before, Army Air Forces (AAF) Gen. H. H. "Hap" Arnold warned Secretary of War Robert Patterson that in a future war the United States would
not have a chance to mobilize, rearm, or train reserves. To prevent future
surprises, Arnold said that the United States would need "continuous
knowledge of potential enemies" covering their "political, social, industrial, scientific, and military life" in order "to provide warning of impend-
ing danger." Such information, Arnold warned, could not come from
traditional peacetime intelligence sources, such as air attachés.[2]

What was needed was a conceptual breakthrough, the realization
that aerial reconnaissance could do more than meet a simple combat
role—that it could be the primary source of Cold War intelligence, and
the means of safeguarding U.S. security. As with other great break-
throughs, it had its origins in one man with a vision.

Richard Leghorn and the Birth of Cold War Reconnaissance

Lt. Col. Richard S. Leghorn had served as chief of the 67th Reconnaissance Group in England, with responsibility for all pre–D-Day and post–D-Day aerial reconnaissance for the Normandy invasion. After the war's end, Leghorn was named deputy commander of Task Unit 1.52, which would photograph the nuclear tests at Bikini Atoll. Working with Leghorn were Amrom H. Katz, Col. Richard W. Philbrick, Dr. Duncan Macdonald, and Walter J. Levison. All would play major roles in the development of Cold War reconnaissance.

During the long train ride to the staging area, Leghorn read a book titled *The United States Strategic Bombing Survey*. This was a report on the effectiveness of Allied bombing raids on Nazi Germany. Leghorn was shocked by how much information had been overlooked. For example, one German weak point was their electrical power system—had it been destroyed, the war could have been ended sooner. However, its importance was not recognized and no attacks were made.

The AAF had concentrated on the tactical role of photoreconnaissance. In doing so, Leghorn realized, they had missed the "big picture"—the weak points of the enemy, and how its society was functioning. Leghorn continued to mull over the report's conclusions during the tests. In late-night discussions, he argued that the only way to prevent another—nuclear—Pearl Harbor was by keeping careful watch on any potential enemy.

One of those he impressed was Dr. Macdonald, a lens designer at Boston University. Following the end of the Bikini tests, Dr. Macdonald returned home to establish, at AAF request, the Boston University Optical Research Laboratory (BUORL). He invited Leghorn to be the main speaker at BUORL's opening on Friday, December 13, 1946. This gave Leghorn the chance to present his ideas to executives of the major photographic firms and to senior AAF officers. His remarks defined the basic pattern of Cold War reconnaissance:

> The nature of atomic warfare is such that once attacks are launched against us, it will be extremely difficult, if not impossible, to recover from them and counterattack successfully. Therefore, it obviously becomes essential that we have prior knowledge of the possibility of an attack, for defensive action against it must be taken before it is launched. . . .

Aerial reconnaissance, as one of the principal information collecting agencies of military intelligence, can play an exceedingly important role in this period prior to the outbreak of hostilities. This situation is particularly true in the case of potential enemies of a totalitarian, police-state nature where the acquisition of information by the older methods of military intelligence is more successfully blocked.

Leghorn realized that, to be successful, such peacetime overflights would have to be politically and socially acceptable as a peacekeeping tool:

However, if we were to perform a military reconnaissance flight over a nation with whom relations are not too friendly, under present thinking this flight would be considered an act of military aggression. It is also probable that the attitude of the American public would reject this means of acquiring information. It is unfortunate that whereas peacetime spying is considered a normal function between nation-states, military aerial reconnaissance—which is simply another method of spying—is given more weight as an act of military aggression. Unless thinking on this subject is changed, reconnaissance flights will not be able to be performed in peace without permission of the nation-state over which the flight is being made. For these reasons, it is extraordinarily important that means of long-range aerial reconnaissance be devised which cannot be detected. Until this is done, aerial reconnaissance will not take its rightful place among the agents of military information protecting our national security prior to the launching of an atomic attack against us.[3]

Leghorn's vision of the potential of aerial reconnaissance in a nuclear world would have a central role in the winning of the emerging Cold War. But first, another conceptual leap was needed—into space.

Prelude to Space

The early U.S. interest in the possibilities of satellites was sparked by interrogations of Dr. Wernher von Braun, the German rocket scientists who had designed the V-2, during the first week of May 1945. He submitted a report on the future prospects of rocketry, including ideas about satellites.[4] This caught the interest of the U.S. Navy, which on October 3, 1945, proposed to develop a satellite.

An initial report from the Navy's Bureau of Aeronautics (BuAer) on satellites followed in December 1945. This was followed by a Navy request for a satellite feasibility study.[5] There was resistance within BuAer to guided missile programs, however. They were seen as a challenge to advanced aircraft and to the aviators who now dominated Navy ranks.

General Arnold had no such limitations. He was a visionary who saw the possibilities that missiles represented. At one point he said, "I see a manless Air Force. . . . I see no excuse for men in fighter planes to shoot down bombers."[6] In November 1945, he stated that design of a spaceship "is all but practical today." The following month, the Army Air Forces Scientific Advisory Group issued a report stating that long-range rockets were feasible and satellites were a "definite possibility." The report was written by Dr. Theodore von Karman, a professor at the California Institute of Technology, who headed the school's rocket research program. As such, he was one of the few academics with first-hand experience with rockets.[7]

Such optimistic estimates were rejected by Dr. Vannevar Bush, who had headed the National Defense Research Committee, which had overseen U.S. scientific research during World War II. In November and December 1945, he told the U.S. Senate Special Committee on Atomic Energy, "In my opinion such a thing [a long-range rocket] is impossible and will be impossible for many years." He added a slap at Arnold and von Karman:

> The people who have been writing these things that annoy me have been talking about a 3,000 mile high-angle rocket shot from one continent to another carrying an atomic bomb, and so directed as to be a precise weapon which would land on a certain target such as a city. I say technically I don't think anybody in the world knows how to do such a thing and I feel confident it will not be done for a very long period of time to come. I think we can leave that out of our thinking. I wish the American public could leave that out of their thinking.[8]

On March 7, 1946, the Navy proposed an interservice space program. The proposal was presented to the Joint Army-Navy Aeronautical

Board of Research and Development on April 9. At the request of the Army representative, the board decided to reconsider the proposal at its May 14 meeting, to allow time to consult Maj. Gen. Curtis E. LeMay, director of research and development.

RAND Satellite Studies, 1946–1947

General LeMay turned to Douglas Aircraft Company's Project RAND (Research ANd Development) for a three-week "crash" study of satellites to be ready in time for the next Aeronautical Board meeting. The report, titled "Preliminary Design of an Experimental World-Circling Spaceship," examined both the feasibility of a satellite and what activities it could perform. In addition to scientific research, the report identified such military missions as reconnaissance, weather observation, communications relay, missile guidance, and use as an orbital weapons platform. The report also noted the intangibles of a satellite:

> In making the decision as to whether or not to undertake construction of such a craft now, it is not inappropriate to view our present situation as similar to that in airplanes prior to the flight of the Wright brothers. We can see no more clearly all the utility and implications of spaceships than the Wright brothers could see fleets of B-29's bombing Japan and air transports circling the globe. . . .
>
> The achievement of a satellite craft by the United States would inflame the imagination of mankind, and would probably produce repercussions in the world comparable to the explosion of the atom bomb.[9]

The RAND report sparked AAF interest, and in July 1946 a second, six-month study was ordered. This was to provide "a design study sufficiently complete so that production contracts can be made for actual vehicles of this type." James E. Lipp, head of RAND's missile division, managed the satellite feasibility study. On February 1, 1947, RAND published a series of eleven papers on rocket and satellite design, and the potential of satellite reconnaissance.

Lipp wrote the final section of "The Time Factor in the Satellite Program," which established the basic design concept of a reconnaissance satellite:

> By installing television equipment combined with one or more Schmidt-type telescopes in a satellite, an observation and reconnaissance

tool without parallel could be established. As mentioned previously in various reports on the subject, a spaceship can be placed upon an oblique or north-south orbit so as to cover the entire surface of the Earth at frequent intervals as the Earth rotates beneath the orbit. . . .

If the satellite could accumulate information on film or wire and televise the record rapidly when interrogated by the ground station, a workable system would result. The period of revolution of the satellite is about 1½ hours, so that its successive tracks over the Earth would be about 1,500 miles apart at the equator. If it is assumed that scanning to a distance of 100 miles on each side of the track is feasible, then a complete coverage of the Earth would require about a week. . . . Obviously, scanning and recording would only be done over areas of interest in order to conserve power and space in the vehicle. . . .

In conclusion it is hardly necessary to point out that most of the reasons for beginning a satellite development program cannot be assigned values in terms of dollars and cents lost in each year of delay. It is equally clear that some of the items discussed are of sufficient importance that the probable cost of the project becomes insignificant. It is therefore desirable that a satellite development program should be put in motion at the earliest possible time.

The formal assessment of the RAND reports did not take place until September 25, 1947, a week after the U.S. Air Force was established as an independent service. The Air Staff directed the Air Materiel Command (AMC) to review the RAND proposals. AMC responded in December 1947 that it concurred that a satellite was feasible, but questioned whether it was practical. AMC proposed that continuing studies be made to establish Air Force satellite requirements and specifications.[10]

The Joint Army-Navy Aeronautical Board of Research and Development, now a policy body, decided on December 19, 1947, that the Air Force should be the only service to undertake satellite studies. On January 15, 1948, Air Force Vice Chief of Staff Gen. Hoyt S. Vandenberg stated that the U.S. Air Force had "the logical responsibility for the satellite." The next day, the Navy withdrew any claim for control of satellite development.[11]

Although the Air Force had achieved its goal of acquiring responsibility for space activities, there was no approval for such a program. The early postwar years were a time of austere military budgets.

Vannevar Bush, now chairman of the Research and Development Board, recommended that funding for military research and development in fiscal year 1949 be limited to $500 million.[12] He had also not lost his disdain for those who believed rockets were feasible—referring to them as "some eminent military men exhilarated perhaps by a short immersion in matters scientific."[13]

High-Altitude Balloon Reconnaissance

While U.S. satellite and ballistic missile activities marked time, a second element in the history of space reconnaissance was emerging. Surprisingly, the primary source for the technology later used in the Corona satellite was not reconnaissance airplanes, but high-altitude ballooning.

With the start of the Korean War in 1950, interest grew in the possibilities of using high-altitude balloons for reconnaissance. In July, C. B. Moore of the General Mills corporation flew four reconnaissance camera tests from the University of Minnesota airport for George Magnus of the Reconnaissance Laboratory at Wright-Patterson AFB. The flights proved very successful. One of the negatives from the second flight, made on July 24, 1950, was made into a ten-by-twenty-foot enlargement and mounted on a wall at Wright-Patterson AFB. The center of attention was a fisherman in a boat on the Minnesota River. The resolution was so good that, reportedly, a fishing pole could be detected in his hands—this from 91,000 feet.[14]

RAND was also becoming involved with balloons. In July 1950, members of RAND's electronics department, including William W. Kellogg (who worked on the early satellite studies) and Stanley M. Greenfield (a former New York University student who worked on balloons), prepared a brief overview of balloon reconnaissance. Kellogg and Greenfield went to the Reconnaissance Laboratory at Wright-Patterson AFB, where they learned of the earlier balloon tests. Kellogg and Greenfield decided to further explore the potential of balloon reconnaissance.[15]

In September 1950, the Air Force Scientific Advisory Board held a meeting to assess ways to extend photographic coverage of the Soviet Union's interior. The board concluded the only feasible means was by balloons. On October 3, Air Force Intelligence issued a summary, which concurred. It noted that there was almost no postwar photographic coverage of the USSR. This made it impossible to confirm or deny reports of atomic production, industrial development, railyards, and airfields. With manned aircraft ruled out for political reasons, and satellites still years away, balloons seemed the only short-term solution. The summary concluded that the hardware was available, and that the meteorological problems seemed solvable. A system could be operational by 1951.[16]

On November 6, 1950, Maj. Gen. Donald L. Putt, Director of Research and Development, gave approval for development of a reconnaissance balloon program.[17] It was given the code name "Project Gopher." The balloons would be launched from Western Europe and drift across the Soviet Union on the winter jet stream. Once they reached Japan, the camera-carrying gondolas would be cut free of the balloons and recovered.

Although it was planned that Project Gopher would begin over-flights of the Soviet Union in the winter of 1951–52, technical and management problems doomed the original schedule. The four July 1950 test flights had reached the design limits of existing balloon technology. There were no data on how to make a prolonged balloon flight in the stratosphere, and no ballast control had been developed for the ten-day flight time Project Gopher required. Another problem was a sudden rash of balloon failures. Balloons fabricated after the start of the Korean War began failing for no apparent reason. The failures were traced to low-grade polyethylene, which became brittle and shattered in the extreme cold. (High-grade polyethylene was being reserved for signal cables needed for the war.)

The relationship between the Air Force and General Mills was very poor. The Air Force demands increased, while C. B. Moore, who was in charge of General Mills Balloon Operations, opposed acceptance of contracts mandating performance requirements that could not be met. He believed that research on improved balloons was the primary need, while the Air Force wanted General Mills to concentrate on the development of high-wind launching techniques. Moore would say later that the Air Force had "completely and deliberately" ignored the limitations of current balloon technology. Moore was forced out of General Mills in 1952.[18]

In May of 1951, as Project Gopher was running into problems, Lt. Col. Paul Worthman at Air Force Headquarters wrote a directive to the Cambridge Research Center to begin a separate experimental balloon program. Known as "Project Moby Dick," these balloons were to fly at a constant altitude between 50,000 and 100,000 feet. As the balloons drifted, the tracking data would indicate the high-altitude winds.

A friend of Worthman was working on Project Gopher. When they compared notes, they realized the two programs could complement each other. The improvements in balloon technology, experience, and knowledge of high-altitude winds would aid Gopher, while Moby Dick would provide cover. Gopher would be just another "weather balloon."[19] During 1953 and 1954, a total of 640 Moby Dick balloons were launched.[20]

Development was also under way on the gondola recovery procedure. Rather than being allowed to come down at sea or on land, it was decided that the gondolas, which were the size of a refrigerator, would be caught in midair. Fairchild C-119 Flying Boxcar cargo planes would be fitted with two poles, with several nylon loops and grappling hooks strung between them. The gondola's parachute would be snagged, and the gondola winched aboard.

As with the rest of Gopher, there were problems with the recovery program. By early 1953, it seemed to be a disaster: one of the C-119s had nearly crashed during a recovery attempt. That spring, the program was transferred from the Wright Air Development Center to the Cambridge Research Center and placed under Worthman. By August of 1954, one of his colleagues, Maj. Eugene Duff, had succeeded in perfecting the midair recovery.[21]

RAND's Project Feed Back Studies

In November 1950, coincidental with the start of balloon reconnaissance development, the Air Force authorized RAND to undertake further satellite studies. In April 1951, RAND presented two studies to the Air Force. The first, "The Utility of a Satellite Vehicle for Reconnaissance" by James Lipp, Robert Salter, and Reinhart Wehner, examined ground coverage, resolution, the television system, transmission of the photos, and possible countermeasures against satellites.[22]

The second of the April 1951 studies was by Kellogg and Greenfield (who had worked on the balloon reconnaissance study). Titled "Inquiry into the Feasibility of Weather Reconnaissance from a Satellite Vehicle," it determined that if cloud types could be identified, and if broad regional weather patterns could be monitored, then a weather satellite would be practical.

The basic problem with the RAND satellite concept was photographic image resolution. This became apparent when Lipp and Salter went to the Reconnaissance Laboratory. On hand for the briefing were members of the laboratory staff, including chief physicist Amrom Katz; BUORL director Dr. Macdonald; Walter Levison, an assistant director of BUORL; and Colonel Philbrick, the Air Force liaison officer at BUORL. The proposal received a cold reception; they were not interested in resolution of 200 feet. Several of the audience gave Lipp a hard time. (He was secretly delighted—it did not matter that they thought the images would be useless; their interest was more important.)

Macdonald, Levison, Philbrick, and Katz formed an ad hoc group with the intent of showing that the satellite was a ridiculous idea. In late 1951, Katz arranged an aerial simulation of the quality of satellite imagery. A 7.5-mm lens was mounted on a modified Leica camera. This was flown at 30,000 feet, using coarse grain film, which was then processed in hot developer. (As Katz said later, "This shows what we thought of TV at the time.") Katz was confident that nothing would appear on the enlargements. He was very surprised when the photos showed the runways at Wright-Patterson AFB and the bridges and city blocks of downtown Dayton. Katz became a convert to satellite reconnaissance.

Following the two reports of April 1951, the Air Force authorized RAND to make recommendations on a reconnaissance satellite development program. This effort was called "Project Feed Back." In March 1952, RAND issued a subcontract to North American Aviation for a study of orbital guidance and control, and sensing systems. In June 1952, a similar study was made by the Radio Corporation of America (RCA) examining reconnaissance systems. Topics studied included optical and television systems, radiation detectors, recording devices, presentation techniques, and the reliability of the payload.[23]

The RAND design for the reconnaissance satellite was influenced by the available technology, and perceptions of how a satellite would have to operate. Because of the high cost of developing both the satellite and the booster, it would have to have a long operating lifetime. This effectively eliminated a film-based camera, such as a "Wirephoto" system in which the film is exposed, developed, and scanned, and the image transmitted to Earth. (A month's supply of film would weigh 1,500 pounds.) A film-return satellite was also eliminated, due to the weight of the copper heat shield and the technical unknowns of reentry. Thus, a television system was seen as required.[24]

Leghorn, the Beacon Hill Study, and the Future of Reconnaissance

In April 1951, at the same time RAND was issuing its satellite studies, Lieutenant Colonel Leghorn, now retired and working for Eastman Kodak, was recalled to active duty at Wright-Patterson AFB. Colonel Philbrick, a World War II colleague, arranged for him to be placed in charge of the Reconnaissance Systems Branch. Once there, Leghorn presided over a study that would do much to set the future of reconnaissance.

Conducted by the Massachusetts Institute of Technology (MIT) between July 1951 and June 1952, this was the "Beacon Hill" study, a review of intelligence and reconnaissance requirements for the years 1952 to 1960. As the study was being organized, Leghorn prepared a five-page analysis. He concluded that a vehicle for pre–D-day reconnaissance would need a minimal risk of detection and interception, should preferably be unmanned, and should lend itself to a "scientific" or "weather mission" cover story. Leghorn judged the Gopher reconnaissance balloon to be the preferred system, followed by a reconnaissance version of the Snark cruise missile or a drone aircraft. Manned aircraft could also be used for pre–D-day reconnaissance, he wrote, but their vulnerability and the political consequences of flying a bomber over the USSR in peacetime limited them to lightly defended areas.

The Beacon Hill study essentially transformed Leghorn's 1946 ideas from Task Unit 1.52 into guidance for Air Force planning for the 1950s. At the time, Leghorn had little knowledge of RAND's satellite studies. No RAND member served on the committee, which was drawn exclusively from New England universities and industrial firms, and none of the briefings considered satellites for reconnaissance. Leghorn said of satellites, "The Earth satellite concept does not offer sufficient promise today to justify the expenditure of development funds by the Air Force. This is particularly true in view of the great promise of Project Gopher. Although the Earth's satellite concept justifies limited and continued studies, development work does not appear justified as yet."

Not surprisingly, the final Beacon Hill report, "Problems of Air Force Intelligence and Reconnaissance," issued on June 15, 1952, did not consider satellites for either the 1952–56 period, or for 1956–60.[25]

Leghorn's efforts attracted the attention of Col. Bernard A. Schriever, the assistant for Air Force development planning. Schriever was open to unconventional ideas and in August 1951 had Leghorn transferred to the Pentagon, where his job was to write a development planning objective (DPO) for reconnaissance. In this role, Leghorn began developing new ideas for reconnaissance aircraft. He also acted as Air Force liaison with RAND.

Leghorn met with Merton E. Davies, who had been working on the RAND satellite studies for several years. Davies hoped to discuss the possibilities of satellites and possibly write a section on their use for the DPO. They met in the morning, then into the afternoon, went to dinner, and did not finish their discussions until after eleven at night. During the course of this meeting, Leghorn, like Katz, became a believer in satellite reconnaissance.

Leghorn completed his DPO in early January 1953. It proposed that high-altitude balloons—and later, satellites—be used for large area surveillance of the USSR. Specific target areas would be covered by a special lightweight single-engine reconnaissance aircraft specifically designed for peacetime overflights of the Soviet Union. With an altitude of more than 70,000 feet, this aircraft would be above the reach of Soviet radars and interceptors. Later, a second generation of satellites could take over this role. At the end of the month, Leghorn was released from active duty and returned to Eastman Kodak.

Despite the years of work and the support of Leghorn's DPO, the RAND scientists were becoming frustrated by the failure of the Air Force and the Central Intelligence Agency to take any action to begin satellite development. Leghorn observed years later that both organizations had institutional limitations.

The Air Force saw reconnaissance as supporting the strategic strike role, by providing targeting data and poststrike damage assessment. Reconnaissance aircraft in the early 1950s were converted bombers or fighters, not specialized vehicles designed for that mission. There was not yet a realization that reconnaissance could monitor deployment and numbers of enemy forces, and provide surprise-attack warning.[26]

In contrast, the CIA saw the importance of strategic intelligence and attack warning, but was limited by a traditional vision of intelligence. The management of the CIA was dominated by former World War II Office of Strategic Services (OSS) personnel. They were from old money, Eastern establishment families, who had gone to Ivy League schools and traveled abroad. They saw intelligence through their OSS experience—agents parachuting behind enemy lines, and covert action.

The photoreconnaissance unit within the CIA was small, and staffed by wartime veterans with Midwestern backgrounds.

One of the early CIA pioneers of photoreconnaissance was Dino A. Brugioni. He had flown as an AAF crewman on sixty-six bombing missions over Italy during World War II. When he joined the CIA in 1948, it was clear both that the Soviet Union was now the enemy and that the United States knew almost nothing about its industry. The initial source of reconnaissance information on the USSR was German aerial photos of the Eastern Front, which covered the whole of the western Soviet Union up to the Ural mountains. They had been captured at the end of the war, and stored in foot lockers at an old torpedo warehouse. Brugioni urged they be used, and the Air Force arranged their cataloging.

These "GX photos," as they were called, were used to create the "industrial register" of the Soviet Union. This provided the first targeting data for the Air Force. The information from the GX photos was augmented by interviews with returning German and Japanese prisoners of war who had worked on forced labor projects within the USSR, and by data from U.S. companies who had built factories within the Soviet Union during the 1930s.[27]

While Brugioni was working on the industrial register he met the man who would direct CIA photo interpretation activities for the next two decades, Arthur C. Lundahl. Lundahl had been asked, before the start of World War II, to train photo interpreters. He subsequently joined the Navy and was stationed at Adak, Alaska, where he did photo interpretation for missions over the Aleutian Islands, Japan, and the Kuriles. With the end of the war, Lundahl remained with the Navy and in 1946 helped write the charter for the Naval Photographic Interpretation Center, which was originally in the Office of Naval Intelligence but was soon transferred to the Bureau of Aeronautics. After seven years there, Lundahl concluded the Navy lacked the organizational outlook needed for effective photo interpretation.

It was at this point that he was approached by the CIA. Otto Guthe told Lundahl that the CIA was going into the photo interpretation business and was looking for someone with both the experience and credentials to run the operation. Lundahl was the person they had in mind. Lundahl joined the CIA in early 1953 as the director of the Photographic Intelligence Division (PID). Initially the PID consisted of Lundahl, Brugioni, and twelve other people. It was located in an abandoned WAVES barracks.[28]

Change in Direction: The Development of the ICBM

In January 1953, Dwight D. Eisenhower became president of the United States. The new administration brought the "New Look" defense policy, which stressed nuclear weapons as a means of both deterring the Soviets and reducing military spending. As part of an "economy drive," Secretary of Defense Charles E. Wilson on June 16, 1953, ordered a review of missile programs. The Armed Forces Policy Council formed a Guided Missiles Study Group to recommend cost-cutting measures. The group, in turn, formed a special subcommittee known as the Strategic Missiles Evaluation Committee. Better known as the "Teapot Committee," its chairman was Dr. John von Neumann.

The committee realized that the development of thermonuclear weapons had made the intercontinental ballistic missile (ICBM) practical, by allowing a smaller rocket and reducing the accuracy requirement. The committee issued a number of recommendations that the United States immediately begin development of an ICBM. These were given to Air Force Assistant Secretary for Research and Development Trevor Gardner in early 1954. He and von Neumann gained the support of Air Force Chief of Staff Gen. Nathan F. Twining and Air Force Secretary Harold E. Talbott. President Eisenhower then gave his approval.

In July 1954, the Air Force created the Western Development Division (WDD), directed by now–Brigadier General Schriever. The WDD was to develop the Atlas and Titan ICBMs, and the Thor intermediate range ballistic missile (IRBM). The latter was a shorter-range missile, which could strike Soviet targets from Western Europe. The Thor would be ready sooner than the more advanced ICBMs.[29]

For the satellite programs, the approval to develop ICBMs and IRBMs meant the RAND satellite proposals now had a booster. The effort now shifted toward hardware development.

The Start of the WS-117L Reconnaissance Satellite

Air Force Headquarters ordered the Air Research and Development Command (ARDC) to start "active direction" of the RAND Project Feed Back studies on May 22, 1953. In August, ARDC staff visited the RAND "Satellite Office," and Lt. Col. Victor L. Genez returned convinced that the Air Force should immediately begin satellite development, even if a reconnaissance payload was not ready.

On September 8, 1953, Lipp forwarded RAND's initial Project Feed Back report to ARDC. It recommended that ARDC issue a reconnaissance satellite design contract within one year, followed by full-scale development. In December 1953, ARDC established Project 409-40, "Satellite Component Study," and unofficially gave the reconnaissance satellite the designation "Weapons System 117L" (WS-117L). The work was assigned to the Wright Air Development Center.

RAND issued its Project Feed Back final report on March 1, 1954. As with the earlier RAND studies, it envisioned a television system: a 0.96-by-1.28-inch photocathode and an optical system with a 38-inch focal length. The images would be recorded on magnetic tape for transmission to ground stations. From a 300-mile orbit, the optical system would scan a 375-mile-wide strip with a resolution of 144 feet. RAND specifically recommended that the Air Force undertake "the earliest possible completion and use of an efficient satellite reconnaissance vehicle" as a matter of "vital strategic interest to the United States." RAND also urged that the satellite project be "considered and planned" at a high policy level, under tight security considerations, in order to prevent international repercussions. The total estimated cost was $165 million, although the report warned that technical uncertainties could greatly increase the costs.

In May 1954, Air Force Headquarters directed ARDC to assume responsibility for the WS-117L satellite studies. In July, the Coordinating Committee on Guided Missiles, which had been established to carry out the recommendations of the Teapot Committee, approved the reconnaissance satellite program on behalf of Defense Secretary Wilson. In August, authorization to start work reached WDD.

Despite the growing support for the WS-117L satellite, it faced conflicting demands on funding. Strategic Air Command (SAC) Commander in Chief Gen. Curtis LeMay was very interested in the project, and wanted preparation of a formal SAC requirements document covering the satellite. SAC's operations research analysis staff meanwhile argued that there was a greater need for new bombers and improved refueling techniques.

On November 27, 1954, ARDC issued System Requirement No. 5 to develop a reconnaissance satellite. Eight years after Leghorn's visionary speech at BUORL, the effort was finally moving out of the study and analysis stage, toward hardware development.

Despite the increased activities, however, there was continuing hostility toward satellites and space within the Eisenhower administration.

On December 17, 1954, Defense Secretary Wilson responded to a prediction that the Soviets might place a satellite into orbit before the United States by saying, "I wouldn't care if they did."[30]

It was not until a full year after completion of the Project Feed Back final report that the Air Force prepared a formal request. Titled "General Operational Requirement for a Reconnaissance Satellite Weapon System" (GOR No. 80), it was issued by Air Force Headquarters on March 15, 1955. The WS-117L's mission was defined as providing reconnaissance worldwide and/or of selected areas. This included:

Collection of intelligence data to satisfy national intelligence objectives

Support of U.S. emergency war plans

An aid in determining the intentions of a potential enemy and the status of his warmaking capabilities

The WS-117L satellite would carry a range of different reconnaissance payloads. In addition to the radio-transmission camera system, there would be a signals intelligence (SIGINT) package to intercept Soviet radio and radar transmissions, and a mapping camera system. (In September 1958, an infrared payload to detect Soviet ICBM launches would be added.) GOR No. 80 envisioned that the earliest versions of WS-117L should be available by mid-1960, while "a fully operational capability must be available by 1965."[31]

Surprise Attack

The austere military budgets, cutbacks in research, and failure to proceed with missile and satellite development during the early postwar years were based in large part on a belief in a prolonged U.S. atomic monopoly. The test of the first Soviet atomic bomb on August 29, 1949, therefore came as a surprise for many in the United States. The reality of U.S. military power in the wake of the Soviet test was shocking. The U.S. Air Force was hollow; the only squadron capable of carrying atomic bombs, the 509th Bomb Group, lacked the fuel, training, and equipment to carry out their emergency war plan.

There were more intelligence surprises to come. On June 25, 1950, the North Korean army launched a surprise attack on South Korea. Then, on November 26, Communist Chinese forces unexpectedly intervened in the war. Their onslaught drove U.S. ground units south in a headlong retreat. Many in the U.S. government and military believed the Korean War was the prelude to a Soviet invasion of Western Europe, and an air attack against the U.S. mainland. This was considered no more improbable than the Japanese attack on Pearl Harbor had been.

U.S. air defenses could do little to stop a Soviet attack, should one be launched. U.S. radar coverage was limited, even in such critical areas as Alaska and the Pacific Northwest, while fighters were few in number and outmoded. Soviet Tu-4 Bull bombers (copies of the U.S. B-29), flying from bases in the Arctic, could hit every major U.S. government and industrial target in a one-way attack.[32]

Several RAND studies from 1952–54 underlined the dangers of a Soviet surprise attack. The USSR had the ability, due to its closed society, to strike without warning. RAND estimated that if fifty Tu-4s, each armed with a 40- to 100-kiloton A-bomb, attacked at low altitude, they could destroy two-thirds or more of SAC's bombers on the ground. The RAND study concluded, "A substantial reduction in vulnerability would result from advanced indications of enemy activities *provided these could be translated into sufficient unambiguous states of alert;* but from the limited data now available at RAND, the probability of such action appears to be small" (emphasis in original text).[33]

In 1953, the threat facing the United States grew considerably. On August 12, the Soviets tested their first thermonuclear bomb, a mere nine months after the first U.S. H-bomb explosion. Again, the test came as a surprise to U.S. intelligence. A CIA report of June 16—only two months before—had stated, "We have no evidence that thermonuclear weapons are being developed by the USSR."[34] At the same time, the Soviets were developing the means to deliver H-bombs against the United States. In late 1953, a U.S. attaché spotted a new Soviet jet bomber at the Ramenskoye air base outside Moscow. The Mya-4 (NATO code name Bison) was estimated to have performance comparable to the U.S. B-52.

The intelligence surprises of this period had created an atmosphere of fear. The Soviets had repeatedly developed new weapons sooner than U.S. intelligence had estimated. It seemed that even the "worst-case" estimates were not bad enough. The Air Force now estimated that there would be thirty Mya-4s by the end of 1955, 500 by mid-1959, and 600–700 by 1969. This was more than the planned B-52 force, and the situation became known as the "bomber gap."[35]

The twin problems of the threat of Soviet surprise attack and the inability of U.S. intelligence to reliably estimate Soviet military activities would shape policy throughout President Eisenhower's administration. Eisenhower told the National Security Council (NSC) on February 24, 1954, that it was difficult to determine the appropriate level of military preparedness when the threat was uncertain. He expanded on this in a meeting with members of the Office of Defense Mobilization's Scientific Advisory Committee on March 27, saying, "Modern weapons had made it easier for a hostile nation with a closed society to plan an attack in secrecy and thus gain an advantage denied to the nation with an open society."

To provide better warning of a possible Soviet surprise attack, Eisenhower approved establishment of the National Indications Center on July 1, 1954. It drew upon intelligence information on Soviet military, economic, social, and technical activities and issued a weekly "watch report." It was assumed that the Soviets would have to make extensive preparations before launching a nuclear attack on the United States. These would include dispersing its industry and population, and such military moves as deploying bombers to Arctic bases near the United States. These "indicators" would signal that an attack was about to be made.

The weakness of the National Indications Center was the poor quality of intelligence the United States had on the Soviet Union. Repeatedly, U.S. intelligence had been caught unawares. There was no guarantee that a "bolt from the blue" attack would not take place. As at Pearl Harbor, the first "indicator" could be detection of the incoming bombers on radar. And, as at Pearl Harbor, it would then be too late.

President Eisenhower saw the political consequences of this "Pearl Harbor mentality," and the fear it generated, as being as dangerous as the military ones. He later observed that, without reliable intelligence, "you would have only your fears on which to plan your own defense arrangements. . . . Now if you're going to use nothing but fear . . . you are going to make us an armed camp."

At his March meeting with the Scientific Advisory Committee, Eisenhower told the group of the Mya-4 bomber and the threat it represented. He challenged them to advise him of any new technology that could prevent a surprise attack. Dr. James R. Killian, Jr., the president of MIT, offered to organize a special group to undertake a study. Eisenhower approved his proposal on July 26. Originally called the

"Surprise Attack Panel," it was subsequently given the nondescript title "Technological Capabilities Panel" (TCP). The TCP was divided into three parts: Project One, Continental Defense; Project Two, Striking Power; and Project Three, Intelligence Capabilities.

The chairman of Project Three was Dr. Edwin H. "Din" Land, the founder of Polaroid. A dynamic, larger-than-life individual, Dr. Land insisted no committee he chaired would be larger than the number of people who could fit into a taxi (thus its unofficial name, the "Taxi-cab Committee"). The other members of Project Three were James Baker, a Harvard University optical designer; John Tukey, coauthor of the Coolley-Tukey Algorithm, which served as the basis of subsequent electronic developments; nuclear physicist and Nobel laureate Edward Purcell; Joseph W. Kennedy, the chemist who first isolated plutonium; Allan Latham, Jr., another founder of Polaroid; and Allen F. Donovan of the Cornell Aeronautical Laboratory. Several had been involved with the Beacon Hill study two years before, and were familiar with Leghorn's ideas on pre–D-day reconnaissance.[36]

The TCP began work in August 1954. The Project Three panel soon concluded that a program of overflights of the USSR was the only solution to the threat of a Soviet surprise attack. Their interest centered on a Lockheed Aircraft proposal called the CL-282. This was a very light-weight aircraft based on an XF-104 fuselage and long sailplane wings. The CL-282 was the kind of unconventional aircraft needed for so sensitive an operation.

Overflights of the Soviet Union were not a new activity. Following the start of the Korean War, short-range penetration of Soviet and Chinese airspace had been made by U.S. Air Force and Navy planes. These covered border areas, ports, and islands. It was the British Royal Air Force (RAF) that actually made the first deep overflights. On the nights of April 17, 1952, and April 28, 1954, three RAF-operated RB-45C Tornados overflew the western USSR to obtain radarscope photos of potential targets. Two of the planes covered northern areas, while the other covered targets in the south. The missions were completed without mishap.[37]

Between October 15, 1952, and May 8, 1954, U.S. Air Force RB-47 Stratojets made six overflights of the USSR (two over the Kola Inlet and four over Siberia). The flights were intended to check out reports of bomber deployments, as well as provide targeting data. These overflights were authorized by Presidents Truman and Eisenhower, with the concurrence of the Director of Central Intelligence (DCI), the chairman of the Joint Chiefs of Staff, and the secretaries of defense and state.[38] The program ended when an RB-47 was intercepted and hit by cannon fire from a MiG-17; the plane was able to reach England despite damage to a fuel tank and the left wing.

On November 24, 1954, Land and Killian met with Eisenhower to discuss the panel's tentative conclusions. Several factors made the CL-282 attractive. Its altitude of well over 70,000 feet was greater than any existing or planned reconnaissance aircraft. The Project Three scientists believed that it would fly too high for Soviet radars to detect, allowing overflights to be covert. Its design, looking like a powered sailplane, would also be less threatening than a converted bomber.

Eisenhower approved the recommendation, and development of the aircraft began. Clarence L. "Kelly" Johnson, chief designer at Lockheed's Skunk Works, promised the plane would be ready for its first test flight in eight months. It was not to be an Air Force project, however. The overflights would be a primary source of intelligence on the USSR. Eisenhower believed the project was too important to be under the control of a military service or caught up in interservice rivalries, and so he assigned the project to the CIA.

DCI Allen Dulles was reluctant to undertake the project; he was still oriented toward traditional human intelligence, rather than technical collection. It was Deputy Director of Central Intelligence (DDCI) Lt. Gen. Charles P. Cabell who pushed the project.[39] He had been director of Air Force intelligence during the Korean War, and understood photoreconnaissance.

To run the program, two individuals were selected who would have a profound impact on the future of reconnaissance. The project was headed by Richard M. Bissell, Jr. He was a Yale-trained economist who had joined the CIA in 1954 as special assistant to the director of central intelligence for planning and coordination. Although Bissell had no prior military or intelligence experience, he was brilliant at organizing projects, turning them from concept to hardware in minimal time and with maximum secrecy.[40] At six feet three inches tall, he was physically imposing and seemed to be constantly in motion, whether pacing incessantly as he dictated a memo or polishing his glasses as he sat at his desk. Bissell had the ability to absorb and retain enormous amounts of information. Lundahl later recalled that Bissell "could outwit, outspeak, out-think most of the people around him."[41]

Bissell's deputy was Air Force Col. Osmond J. "Ozzie" Ritland. In contrast to the tall, athletic Bissell, Ritland was short, balding, and heavyset. After completing AAF flight training in 1939, he had been assigned directly to Wright Field as a test pilot. The training of a new test pilot was more "casual" then: Ritland was briefed on the test procedures, made several flights in a Northrop A-17 attack plane, and wrote up the results. He was then considered ready.[42] After the war, he had served as commander of the 4925th Test Group (Atomic) based at Kirtland AFB. This unit adapted aircraft to carry nuclear weapons, made drop tests of new designs, participated in live nuclear tests in Nevada and the Pacific, and sampled the radioactive clouds after the explosions.[43] It was Ritland who provided the technological expertise and liaison with the Air Force. While the project was directed by the CIA, the Air Force was to be a partner. This would set the pattern for later reconnaissance projects. The aircraft was given the code name "Aquatone." History would know it as the U-2.

Toward Space

Independent of the RAND efforts, ideas were also taking shape for a civilian scientific satellite program. Between 1948 and 1951, British Interplanetary Society members Kenneth W. Gatland, Anthony M. Kunesch, and Alan E. Dixon privately studied the smallest possible booster that could launch a satellite. They presented their findings in the paper "Minimum Satellite Vehicles" at the second International Astronautical Federation (IAF) Congress in September 1951.

Their study came to the attention of Alexander Satin of the Office of Naval Research (ONR) in November 1952. As he read the paper, Satin realized the United States already had all the hardware to put together such a three-stage vehicle.[44]

Satin discussed the concept with Dr. Fred Singer, a physics professor at the University of Maryland. Initially, Dr. Singer was reluctant to become involved with anything as "disreputable" as space. Dr. Singer soon changed his mind, however, and at the fourth IAF Congress in 1953, he presented a paper on a small satellite design. Called "MOUSE" (Minimum Orbital Unmanned Satellite of the Earth), it was a lightweight satellite, as low as fifty pounds, equipped with a radio transmitter and simple instruments to measure cosmic rays, micrometeorites, and solar ultraviolet and X-rays. He noted that a larger satellite with more complex instruments "seems far removed from the standpoint of feasibility."[45]

During April 1954 the MOUSE proposal was discussed by the Upper Atmosphere Rocket Research Panel at White Sands, New Mexico. Later that summer, the International Scientific Radio Union and the International Union of Geodesy and Geophysics both endorsed use of satellites for scientific study.

At the same time, there was growing military interest in a scientific satellite program. On June 25, 1954, Dr. von Braun, who now worked at the Army's Redstone Arsenal, met with ONR personnel. They discussed a joint Army-ONR satellite program called "Orbiter." The booster was to be an Army Redstone rocket with three upper stages of small Loki solid-fuel rockets. The ONR would build a five-pound inert satellite and a tracking network, and provide logistics support and data analysis.

While a joint project faced the possibility of interservice rivalry, the main threat to Orbiter came from within the Navy. In July 1954 the Naval Research Laboratory (NRL), which was separate from the ONR, studied two advanced versions of the Viking sounding rocket. The NRL argued that the Viking launchers could take a heavier payload, and that Orbiter was too limited and unreliable.[46]

While the Army and Navy debated boosters, a satellite program received an important scientific endorsement. On October 4, 1954, the Special Committee for the International Geophysical Year (IGY) recommended that satellites be considered by the participating nations. Space flight, which had up to this point been associated with such "kiddy" television programs as "Tom Corbett, Space Cadet," now had the backing of some of the world's most eminent scientists.[47]

There was also secret support. When the TCP final report, "Meeting the Threat of Surprise Attack," was issued on February 14, 1955, it recommended the immediate start of a small satellite program to establish the legal principle of "freedom of space" for later military missions. This would mean a satellite could pass over the territory of another nation without violating its airspace. Assistant Secretary of Defense for Research and Development Donald Quarles realized the importance of freedom of space to the future of U.S. intelligence, and quickly set about implementing the TCP recommendations.

In late February 1955, Quarles privately urged the U.S. IGY committee to formally request a small satellite program, which it did on May 18.[48]

This request was passed to Dr. Alan T. Waterman, director of the National Science Foundation, who, as prearranged, sent it to Quarles. Quarles referred the different satellite proposals to his Advisory Group on Special Capabilities and requested they recommend a preferred project.

Quarles was instrumental in shaping early U.S. space policy. By early 1955, the United States had two emerging space projects—the proposed civilian IGY satellite and the military WS-117L reconnaissance satellite—but no national policy on space. Quarles wrote a draft statement on space policy for the NSC. Dated May 20, 1955, it was the first such document prepared for the U.S. government. It stressed that the IGY satellite "will provide a test of the principle of 'Freedom of Space.'" The satellite would be launched under international auspices "in order to emphasize its peaceful purposes." This was to be arranged so as not to "imply a requirement for prior consent by any nation over which the satellite might pass in its orbit."[49]

The NSC approved Quarles's statement on May 26. This approval was defined negatively, however: the satellite would not be launched with a military booster, nor was it to interfere with the ICBM program. The next day, "after sleeping on it," Eisenhower approved both the satellite program and policy. The NSC decision effectively eliminated both the Army-ONR Orbiter and the Air Force "World Series" proposals. (The latter was an Atlas ICBM with an Aerobee-Hi second stage.) Only the NRL's Viking-derived proposal remained.[50]

Open Skies

The fear of a surprise attack remained strong in the mid-1950s. A poll of American adults indicated that most thought it was more likely they would die in a Soviet nuclear attack than from old age.[51] This climate of fear was very much on Eisenhower's mind as he prepared for the Geneva summit meeting with First Secretary of the Communist Party Nikita Khrushchev. He assigned responsibility for developing arms control proposals to Nelson Rockefeller, who was assisted by Max Milliken and Walt Rostow of MIT, and Harold Stassen, the former governor of Kansas who now was an adviser on disarmament. Their proposal incorporated the ideas Leghorn had first described nearly a decade before.

Eisenhower delivered the proposal at the Geneva summit on July 21, 1955. He told the Soviet leadership that the lack of trust and such "terrible weapons" as hydrogen bombs created "fears and dangers of surprise attack." To remove these fears, Eisenhower proposed that the United States and USSR provide "facilities for aerial photography" of each other and conduct mutual supervised overflights. Called "Open Skies," it was the most innovative proposal of the early Cold War. But before the day was out, Khrushchev rejected it.[52]

Years later, Khrushchev's son Sergei explained that the same fear of surprise attack motivated the rejection. He had asked his father if they could accept Open Skies. His father said it was not possible because the Americans were really seeking targeting data. Once the United States learned that the USSR was defenseless against aerial attack, the pressure for a preventive war would grow.[53]

Events following the Geneva summit underlined the growing ties between Open Skies, satellite projects, and easing the fears of a Soviet attack. On July 29, soon after returning from Geneva, Eisenhower announced that the United States would launch small satellites as part of its IGY activities. The National Science Foundation would oversee the project. There was, of course, no mention of the covert role of establishing freedom of space. In early August, the NRL Viking proposal was selected (a foregone conclusion given the NSC decision of May). The program was given the name "Vanguard." In August, Leghorn became a member of the Rockefeller/Stassen study group, serving on the "aerial inspection" subcommittee. He saw Open Skies as serving two functions: warning of surprise attack and policing disarmament and nuclear test ban agreements.

Early Development of WS-117L

While the Vanguard IGY satellite program was being approved, WS-117L was moving toward the contract stage. In October 1955, the program was transferred to the WDD, which meant the ICBM and satellite programs were now under one roof. This was done at the urging of Brigadier General Schriever and Simon Ramo, executive vice president of the Ramo-Woolridge Corporation (later TRW). They had feared the satellite project would compete with the ICBMs for money, resources, and personnel unless the two were combined.

Responsibility for WS-117L was assigned to Navy captain Robert C. Truax. During World War II, Truax had worked with American rocket pioneer Dr. Robert H. Goddard.

The next phase in the WS-117L program was to organize a contract competition. By November 1955, fourteen basic technical tasks had been identified and approved, and were being studied by the WDD staff.

Contracts for satellite design studies were issued to RCA, Glenn L. Martin, and Lockheed Aircraft under the code name "Pied Piper."[54] A small group of engineers, including James W. Plummer, worked on the Lockheed draft study. The Air Force had informed them in January 1956 that the booster would be an Atlas ICBM, which had an orbital payload of 3,500 pounds. The Lockheed engineers determined that if the forward end of the Atlas was reinforced to support a second stage, the payload could be increased to between 10,000 and 15,000 pounds. Convair, the Atlas contractor, was unwilling to do this, however, as it would interfere with the ICBM program.

Lockheed submitted its Pied Piper study to the Air Force on March 1, 1956. The report proposed two different satellites: a "Pioneer" satellite weighing 3,500 pounds and an "Advanced" version weighing 7,800 pounds.[55] The report was not very thick or detailed by current standards, but in late June 1956 Lockheed was selected as the winner. Fred O'Green was named WS-117L program manager at Lockheed, while Willis Hawkins served as vice president in charge of satellites.[56]

Although U.S. space policy was designed to use Vanguard to establish freedom of space in order to permit military satellites like WS-117L, neither project flourished. When Air Force Headquarters approved the WS-117L development plan on July 24, 1956, it provided a mere $3 million in funding. Following a November 17 briefing on the WS-117L program, Quarles, now secretary of the Air Force, instructed Lieutenant General Putt, now the deputy chief of staff for research and development, to halt construction on the vehicle. Quarles explicitly banned the fabrication of the actual WS-117L satellite or even a mockup without his personal permission. Vanguard was to be the first satellite in space, while WS-117L would mark time.

There were basic doubts about WS-117L. Quarles did not believe that satellite reconnaissance would be practical for another decade or more. Dr. Killian, who had organized the TCP study, thought the RAND satellite was a "peripheral project" and refused to give it active support. For 1957, WS-117L was given only $10 million, with the restriction that this money could not be used for systems development.

The Eisenhower administration also wanted to prevent any discussion of possible military space activities. When Brigadier General

Schriever said in a February 1957 speech that the Air Force was ready to "move forward rapidly in space," he was ordered the next day never to use the word "space" in a public speech again.[57] The reasoning behind U.S. space policy was closely held, and it was not thought necessary to explain it to Schriever and other military officials.

Vanguard was to be a "stalking horse" to establish freedom of space, but with satellite reconnaissance still thought to be a faraway possibility, it had no priority. Nor did Vanguard enjoy the complete support of the scientific community. During early discussions of an IGY satellite, fears were expressed that it would divert funding from other research.[58] The scientific establishment's hostility was expressed in January 1956 by the new Astronomer Royal, Dr. Richard van der Riet Woolley: "Space travel is utter bilge."

It is also apparent that there was no deep commitment to space within the Eisenhower administration. Defense Secretary Wilson continued to dismiss Vanguard as "a 'damn orange' up in the air." By May 1957, Vanguard costs had grown from $20 million to $100 million. At an NSC meeting to discuss the overruns, President Eisenhower complained that the satellite's scientific instruments had become "gold-plated." Treasury Secretary George Humphrey asked if Vanguard would be followed by "another tremendous program to launch additional satellites." Both Eisenhower and Wilson said without enthusiasm this was probably true.[59]

The funding problems were not limited to Vanguard. An economic downturn during 1957 had also caused a scaling back of the ICBM program. In July, Quarles imposed sharp spending limits on WS-117L, reducing it to the study level. Not surprisingly, physical progress on WS-117L was limited. Yet despite the "stop-and-go situation," Plummer later recalled, the small group of engineers in a small division of Lockheed had determined the basic features needed for a reconnaissance satellite.[60]

The WS-117L satellite was to be built around the Agena second stage, which would boost the payload into its final orbit, then stabilize it so the camera stayed pointed toward the Earth. As envisioned in a decade of RAND studies, the camera was to be a television system. Although resolution would be poor, this was not considered as important as timeliness. One of the satellite's main missions was post-strike reconnaissance, which would involve locating the impact points and assessing the damage from U.S. nuclear strikes. As this would be a fast-developing situation, it would require near real-time transmission of photos.[61]

New Concepts in Satellite Reconnaissance

In early 1956, as the WS-117L studies were under way, Richard C. Raymond, a physicist with RAND's Electronics Division, proposed a reexamination of a film-return satellite. He based this on a comparison of the rates of data recovery between a television and a film-recovery satellite. Raymond, who had a background in information theory, calculated that the film-return satellite would provide at least two orders of magnitude more information. Based on his concept, in March 1956 RAND's president, Frank Collbohm, wrote "Photographic Reconnaissance Satellites," a Top Secret recommendation to the Air Staff to develop a film-return satellite.

The document did not receive a warm welcome at the Air Staff. The Air Force was committed to the concept of near real-time reconnaissance. A film-return satellite would involve long delays between taking the pictures and their analysis. More important, the feasibility of returning a capsule from space was still not clear. RAND withdrew the report.

During the summer of 1956, the development of ICBM warheads finally provided a workable reentry system. The warhead was covered with an ablative material. During reentry, it would slowly melt, carrying away the heat. RAND's John H. Huntzicker and Hans A. Lieske investigated the recovery of "such heat-sensitive items as photographic film," presenting their results in a memorandum titled "Physical Recovery of Satellite Payloads," dated June 26, 1956 (concurrent with the awarding of the WS-117L contract to Lockheed). Although the Air Force was committed to real-time reconnaissance, RAND saw that with development of ICBMs and the solution of the reentry problem, economics now favored the film-return design.

This realization led to a merger of RAND's research on balloon and satellite reconnaissance, which in turn created a partnership between two individuals who would become the "founding fathers" of Corona: Merton Davies and Amrom Katz.[62]

The two men had taken very different roads to space. Davies had become interested in space as a teenager in the 1930s when he read the book *Rockets Through Space* by P. E. Cleator, the founder of the

British Interplanetary Society. Davies began to build a collection of space books. Following his 1938 graduation from Stanford with a degree in mathematics, Davies had wanted to become an AAF pilot. At six feet eight inches tall, however, he exceeded the maximum height. He subsequently joined Douglas Aircraft Company's El Segundo facility, where he spent World War II designing Navy aircraft. He joined RAND soon after the initial 1946 satellite studies.

Katz came to the space field by sheer chance. Following graduation from the University of Wisconsin, Katz had taken the civil service examination in optics, ending up with a job in the photo lab at Wright Field. There, he began with evaluation of film, then lenses and shutters, and ultimately moved into the field of photo interpretation, developing special slide rules for calculating the size of objects in photographs. Katz had been skeptical when the reconnaissance satellite had first been proposed, but eventually became a believer. After fifteen years at Wright-Patterson AFB, he joined RAND in 1954. Katz brought an understanding of the photo interpretation process, and the relationship between resolution and the ability to discover intelligence data.[63]

Together at RAND in early 1957, Davies and Katz began to look at advanced camera designs. On February 19, they attended a meeting at BUORL to discuss possible future balloon cameras. On hand were Dr. Duncan Macdonald, Dow Smith, James Baker, and Walter Levison. Levison described an advanced concept for a night camera. It was based on a "spherical shell camera," which Baker had designed during World War II. Baker proposed that a very fast lens be focused onto a glass hemisphere covered with emulsion. (Kodak actually made test hemispheres.) Because it was not practical to change the "film," Levison's design proposed taking a narrow "slab" of the hemisphere and bending the 70-mm film to match the curvature. This would provide 120-degree coverage.

Three weeks later, Davies and Katz went to the annual meeting of the American Society of Photogrammetry. At a social meeting, they talked to Fred Willcox, vice president of the Fairchild Camera and Instrument Corporation. Willcox described a design for a rotating panoramic camera to be carried in fighter wing pods. It used a 45-degree mirror in front of a 12-inch focal length lens. The entire camera and film assembly rotated around the optical axis to provide the panoramic coverage. A slit acted as a shutter, while the film was moved past the slit to compensate for the rotation.

Davies's first reaction was, "What a terrible design to be moving all that mass within a drum." As he mulled it over, however, Davies recalled that most of the RAND satellite designs (the reconnaissance vehicles were the exception) were *spin*-stabilized. He realized that in a spinning reconnaissance satellite, the camera could be fixed. It would look out at a right angle to the spin axis. While the satellite camera design was still being formulated, Katz telephoned Levison to describe the beauty of a panoramic camera. It combined two qualities which seemed to be contradictory—wide-angle coverage *and* high resolution. Katz told Levison about the spinning camera design and suggested it might be useful.

At the same time, the various ideas for an advanced balloon camera came together in the "HYAC" camera (so named by Katz for "high acuity"). Levison served as program manager, and the camera was designed by Frank Madden, who was chief engineer at BUORL. A number of ideas were contributed by Dow Smith. The 12-inch focal length, f/5 lens was pivoted so it swung like a pendulum through a 120-degree arc. During each pass, it "painted" the image across a strip of film 2 inches wide and about 25 inches long. As the lens swung back, the film was advanced, and the next frame could then be taken. The exposures were timed so there was a 10 percent overlap, to prevent gaps appearing. (This was not a sufficient overlap to provide stereo photos; that requires about a 60 percent overlap.)

The balloon was limited in the weight it could carry, so electrical power requirements had to be kept small. Temperature was controlled by putting water bottles in the camera case. These stabilized the camera at 32 degrees Fahrenheit, with no use of power and minimal weight. Another problem was azimuth stabilization: the camera package rotated around its suspension point. If not corrected, the film strips would not be parallel. An oil-filled compass was used. Several holes were drilled in the compass card and lights and photo cells were placed on either side of the card. These were connected to a stepper motor between the camera case and the balloon, which stabilized the camera within a couple of degrees.

The importance of the HYAC camera was that it produced a resolution of 100 lines/mm. This was an order of magnitude improvement over World War II camera technology, which had only 10 lines/mm, and allowed the HYAC camera to produce 100 times the information of the earlier cameras. Levison later compared it to going from a pinhole camera to a modern single-lens reflex camera.

While Levison was working on the HYAC camera for balloon reconnaissance, Davies and Katz refined their ideas for a spinning recoverable satellite. During the summer of 1957 they developed a strategy for accelerating the reconnaissance satellite program, taking into account the increasingly critical issue of timing. By September 10, they had developed the concept of a satellite boosted into polar orbit by a Thor Able rocket—a Thor IRBM with a Vanguard second stage. The small, spin-stabilized satellite would carry a 12-inch focal length panoramic camera and 5-inch-wide film. When the mission was over, a solid-fuel rocket would fire to deorbit the satellite. It would splash down in the Pacific, and be picked up by recovery forces guided by a radio beacon. Davies and Katz believed that this design was better than WS-117L, and would be ready much sooner than the more complex satellite. They set about preparing briefings on the design.

Despite the advances in optical design these activities represented, the summer of 1957 brought devastating news. The government had decided that research was too expensive, as it led to costly production of new ideas. A number of university research contracts were being cancelled. BUORL had been receiving about $1 million per year to develop new ideas in reconnaissance systems. Now it was in danger of closing. Levison later called this "the low point in government/industry relations."

In September 1957, Leghorn founded the Itek (for "information technology") Corporation with five or six employees. Leghorn soon gained the financial backing of Laurance Rockefeller, who had long supported aviation and scientific activities. With his support, Itek could assume the payroll of the BUORL staff. Itek would then continue the BUORL research efforts, including the HYAC camera. On January 1, 1958, the one hundred or so employees of BUORL became part of Itek.[64]

The WS-117L program had also undergone a change in camera design in the summer of 1957. An RCA study recommended the Air Force abandon the television system, as the resolution would be too poor. It was replaced with a film-scanning system. The film would be exposed and processed, then scanned with a light beam that would transform the photos into electronic signals that were radioed to a ground station. It was not real-time, but the photos would still be in the hands of interpreters sooner than a film-return satellite.[65]

The Genetrix Reconnaissance Balloons

As Davies and Katz were refining their new concept of a reconnaissance satellite, Open Skies became a covert reality. In mid-1953, the reconnaissance balloon program shifted to full-scale development and was renamed "Grandson." Test flights, design work, and advanced planning for the operational campaign continued.[66] By August 1954, this was completed and the balloons were judged ready for long-range test flights. The program, now called "Grayback," would have to show the balloons were capable of crossing the huge Soviet landmass.

The first attempt was made in December 1954, when the Air Force launched eight Moby Dick balloons from Scotland. It was intended that they would float across the USSR on the winter jet stream. Instead, they ended up making lazy circles over Yugoslavia and North Africa. A second attempt, in January 1955, ended in failure when none of the balloons remained aloft.

Although this was an Air Force project, the CIA became involved. The CIA's assistant director (collection) for scientific intelligence was a retired Marine colonel named Philip G. Strong. He was also a member of several Air Force scientific advisory groups, and soon learned of Grayback's problems. Strong was aware of several projects within the CIA's Directorate for Plans that involved balloons. The most important of these to the balloon reconnaissance program was an unmanned balloon launched by CIA operatives from Scotland that had drifted across the USSR and been retrieved near South Korea. Strong passed this information along to the Air Force.[67]

During the summer of 1955, the launch and recovery units conducted practice Grayback missions over the United States. These provided not only training, but also final tests of the equipment and photos from the gondola cameras.

Operational deployment began in October 1955; the launch crews of the 1110th Air Support Group were sent to Scotland, West Germany, Norway, and Turkey, while the recovery planes were deployed in an arc from Alaska through Japan down to Okinawa. With this deployment came the final name change, to "Genetrix."

The operation was to involve the launch of twenty-five hundred Genetrix balloons. This would provide complete coverage of the Soviet landmass. Although the planned start date was December 1,

1955, Eisenhower did not give approval to begin launches until December 27.

The first nine balloons were launched from Turkey and West Germany on January 10, 1956. Three days later, three Genetrix balloons reached the recovery zone near Japan and turned on their homing beacons. The aircrews of the 456th Troop Carrier Wing were eager to make the first midair recovery. The first plane to spot a balloon was a C-119 flown by Capt. Slaughter Mimms. The crew rigged the recovery equipment—two poles hanging down from the open "beavertail" rear door with several lines between them. A radio signal transmitted from the plane released the camera gondola. As it descended under its parachutes, the C-119 made repeated passes before the drogue chute was caught by the lines. The drogue and four main chutes were reeled aboard, until the gondola was hanging just behind the aircraft. The crew then reached out and pulled it aboard. The first midair recovery had been completed. When Captain Mimms's plane landed, it was met by the wing commander, Col. James L. Daniels. He presented the crew with a case of whiskey. The two other balloons were also successfully recovered by other aircraft.

The Genetrix launches continued for twenty-eight days, from January 10 to February 6, for a total of 448 balloons. For the first three weeks, the balloons reached the recovery zones in adequate numbers, and without any Soviet protests. After this, however, Soviet, Eastern European, and Communist Chinese air defenses were able to stop the balloons. On February 4, 1956, Soviet Deputy Foreign Minister Andrei A. Gromyko gave a protest note to the U.S. ambassador over the balloons. Two days later, President Eisenhower ordered a halt. In response to the Soviet protest and the display of captured gondolas, the United States claimed they were "weather balloons." The launch and recovery crews were brought home.

Of the total of 448 balloons launched, forty-four were successfully recovered (sixteen in midair, of which three were by Mimms's crew). Of these, forty had photos, amounting to 13,813 exposures, which covered 1,116,449 square miles of the Soviet and Chinese landmasses. Because three-fourths of the recovered gondolas had been launched from Turkey, the bulk of coverage was in Siberia and northern China. There was only scattered coverage of European Russia and Central Asia.[68] The most significant target discovered was the vast nuclear refining facility at Dononovo in Siberia. The CIA's Photographic Intelligence

Division sent a photo interpreter to the Air Force Aeronautical Chart and Information Center at St. Louis to assist with the photos.

A forty-fifth Genetrix gondola was recovered about a year later when it drifted to Adak in the Aleutian Islands. It was found by Colonel Philbrick, who was then commander at Adak.[69] He had worked with Leghorn, had been involved with the early satellite studies, and was one of the few people who could have realized what the strange object was. Philbrick told an airman to keep the gondola in water, so that the film would not stick to itself. When the film was processed, it provided some of the best photos of the Genetrix program.

Five months after the Genetrix program ended, U-2 overflights began.

Aquatone over the USSR

Despite starting from scratch and having incredible performance requirements, Kelly Johnson had the Aquatone ready within the schedule. The prototype U-2 made its first hop on August 1, 1955, and a first flight three days later. Over the next eleven months, additional aircraft were produced, technical problems such as engine flameouts were solved, CIA pilots were recruited and trained, practice missions over the United States were flown, and the first unit was deployed to an airbase outside Wiesbaden, West Germany.[70]

Because an overflight of another country was a violation of international law, it would be up to President Eisenhower to give approval for the missions. Due to the risk, the program was seen as a short-term effort, lasting only a year or two. This was based on the belief that it would take that long for the Soviets to develop a radar network able to track the plane. With the tracking data, the Soviets could then make diplomatic protests, which would force an end to the overflights. For the moment, however, it was estimated that Soviet radar could detect the U-2 only on a sporadic basis.[71]

On July 2, 1956, Bissell sent a request to presidential assistant Brig. Gen. Andrew J. Goodpaster to begin overflights. The next day, Goodpaster sent word that Eisenhower had given approval for overflights of the USSR for ten days. When Bissell asked if this meant ten days of good weather, Goodpaster responded, "It means ten days from when you start."[72]

The pilot selected for the first overflight of the USSR was Hervey S. Stockman. He had been a P-51 Mustang pilot who flew combat missions over Germany during World War II. Like all the other pilots recruited for the U-2 program, he was a reserve officer on active duty, with a Top Secret clearance, exceptional pilot ratings, and extensive single-seat, single-engine jet time.

The first U-2 overflight of the Soviet Union began at five o'clock on the morning of the Fourth of July. Stockman flew over East Berlin and over northern Poland via Poznan, then crossed the Soviet border. Stockman recalled years later that he knew why he was there, and believed in the mission, but was very aware that "this is another guy's air." The flight covered a number of Soviet bomber bases in the western USSR. When Stockman reached Minsk, he turned north toward Leningrad. After making the turn, he looked at the drift sight, an inverted periscope that allowed him to see the ground. What Stockman saw came as a shock: there were Soviet MiGs following his U-2.

Despite the estimates, the Soviets were able to detect and track the U-2 on its very first flight. More than twenty intercept attempts were made. The camera package photographed the MiGs trying to "zoom-climb" up to the U-2. Each time, the MiG's engine would flame out, and the plane would fall back. Stockman continued on to Leningrad, then turned west and flew along the Baltic coast. The plane landed back at Wiesbaden after eight hours and forty-five minutes in the air.[73]

In all, five U-2 overflights were made in the first series: one on July 4 and two each on July 5 and 9.[74] The fact that the planes had been detected was deeply upsetting to President Eisenhower. The TCP had recommended the program and Eisenhower had approved it based on the belief that Soviet radars could not detect a plane flying above 70,000 feet.

Khrushchev was both surprised and angered by the overflights. While Stockman was overflying his country, Khrushchev and the Soviet leadership were at the American Embassy attending the Independence Day reception. Khrushchev had been told of the aircraft before leaving for the reception, but said nothing. He was not worried about the photos, but saw the overflight as an affront, intended to show American superiority over the Soviet Union.[75]

The Soviets lodged a protest over the incidents on July 10. It stated that a U.S. twin-engine bomber had violated Soviet airspace, and gave the flight paths of the first two missions. The United States denied it had flown a twin-engine bomber over the Soviet Union (but said nothing about a single-engine plane).

Although Eisenhower ordered a halt to the overflights, it was clear that the U-2 had created a revolution in intelligence. When the photos from the first series of overflights were analyzed, they showed that the Soviets had *not* built a large number of bombers, as had been thought. The Soviets had only a token number compared to the United States. The mass flybys had been bluffs—the same handful of planes had made repeated passes with different bort numbers to create the illusion of a large force. Because of the U-2, it was now possible to prove the negative. The end of the bomber gap was the prime example of what Leghorn had envisioned a decade before.

Eisenhower understood the value of the U-2 overflights, but feared the possible Soviet response. Accordingly, he kept a tight control on the missions. There were only three more overflights made in the next year.

Because the U-2 was a national resource, the missions were planned by the Ad Hoc Requirements Committee (ARC), headed by longtime CIA staff member James Q. Reber. Each of the military services had its own intelligence requirements: the Air Force needed information on ballistic missiles, the Navy wanted to cover naval bases, and the Army sought information on Soviet antiballistic missiles and ground forces. Once the ARC developed a consensus on a mission, James Cunningham would plot the proposed flight path, while Brugioni at the CIA's Photographic Interpretation Center (PIC) would develop lists of bonus targets that could be covered with slight changes in the flight plan. A memo on the proposed flight would be sent to the president.[76] Bissell would brief Goodpaster on the proposed mission. If Goodpaster thought Eisenhower might approve, he would arrange for Bissell and DCI Dulles to see him for presidential authorization. If Eisenhower approved, he would initial the flight map "DDE."

Soviet SS-6 ICBM Test Flights

While the U.S. long-range missile program marked time during the late 1940s and early 1950s, the corresponding Soviet effort accelerated. This was due to one man, Sergei P. Korolev. Under his direction, the original ICBM studies had been performed by the Mathematical Institute of the Soviet Academy of Sciences starting in 1949. The design was refined between 1951 and 1954, while Korolev continued to press for approval to develop the ICBM. He wanted to make the enormous leap from short-range missiles to one capable of reaching the United States. His arguments finally won out, and development of the R-7 ICBM (NATO code name SS-6 Sapwood) began in 1954.[77]

For Korolev, however, rockets had always been the means to spaceflight. Just as he had overcome the opposition to the ICBM program, he would also singlehandedly lead the Soviet Union into space. The SS-6 ICBM, he argued, could also serve as the basis of a satellite launcher. (Many in the Soviet military suspected this was his real goal when he advocated the program.) In May 1954, with the SS-6 approved, Korolev wrote to the Soviet Council of Ministers, proposing development of artificial satellites.[78] On August 29, 1955 (a month after Eisenhower announced the U.S. IGY satellite program), Korolev recommended the start of an ambitious space program to include satellites, probes to the Moon and planets, and manned spaceflights.

Korolev realized that, in a totalitarian society, approval of a new project depended on the whim of the leader. During a tour of Korolev's design bureau in early 1956, Khrushchev was taken into a separate room and shown a satellite model. Korolev told him, "If we pursue this we can go ahead of America in the International Geophysical Year." Khrushchev looked at the model and responded, "If it will not affect work on the intercontinental ballistic missile, you may do this."[79]

On January 30, 1956, Khrushchev issued a decree approving development of a heavy satellite called "Object D" and a modified version of the SS-6 to launch it. By December, however, with Object D falling behind schedule, Korolev decided to substitute a much simpler satellite design—a small sphere with a radio transmitter to allow tracking.[80]

The first SS-6 was ready for launch on May 15, 1957. The rocket lifted off successfully, but 98 seconds into the flight one of the four strap-on boosters tore away from the rocket's core stage and the missile disintegrated. The second SS-6 made three launch attempts, on June 9, 10, and 11, but it never left the pad. When the rocket was examined, a nitrogen valve was found to have been installed incorrectly. The third SS-6 proved no more successful when it was launched on July 12. After liftoff, the missile began to spin. Thirty-three seconds after launch, the four strap-ons flew away and the rocket was destroyed.[81]

In response to the SS-6 tests, Eisenhower approved an unprecedented number of U-2 overflights of Soviet Central Asia. In all, seven missions were flown during August 1957.[82]

U.S. officials knew the launch site was somewhere east of the Aral Sea, but its exact location was unknown. U-2 missions were flown following railroad lines, since any base would be rail-serviced. Flying along the rail line southeast from Aralsk, a U-2 pilot saw construction in the distance. He altered course and photographed the SS-6 launch site. The launch pad was at the end of a fifteen-mile-long spur that ran north from the main line. The site was named "Tyuratam" by the CIA, after the railroad station where the spur joined the main line. The name came from a 1939 map prepared by Mil-Geo, the geographic component of the Wehrmacht. This was the best map available of Central Asia and Siberia. (In the Kazakh language, "Tyuratam" means "arrow burial ground.")[83]

Following the intensive series of August overflights, two more were made in September 1957. These were also directed toward Soviet missile activities—one revisited Tyuratam, while another went to Kapustin Yar. The latter was the test center for shorter-range missiles, located in the western USSR near the Volga River. This brought the total number of U-2 overflights to seventeen.[84]

While the SS-6 tests during the spring and summer of 1957 attracted U.S. attention, they did not spark concern about a Soviet satellite launch. In June 1957, a private individual named V. A. Nekrassoff wrote Quarles, now deputy secretary of defense, suggesting the Soviets would launch a satellite on September 17, the 100th anniversary of the birth of Konstantin Tsiolkovsky, who was regarded by the Soviets as the "father of astronautics." Quarles passed it on to DCI Dulles, who responded on July 5, 1957, "The USSR probably is capable of launching a satellite in 1957, and may be making preparations to do so. . . . The U.S. [intelligence] community estimates that for prestige and psychological factors, the USSR would endeavor to be first to launch an Earth satellite."

Despite that possibility, no efforts were made to accelerate Vanguard to beat the Soviets into space. The only action was to prepare a statement for Dr. Detlev W. Bronk, president of the National Academy of Sciences, should the Soviets announce their intent to launch a satellite.[85] The simple fact was that the U.S. government, from Eisenhower on down, did not think it was important whether or not the Soviets launched a satellite.

After the setbacks of the spring and summer, Korolev and the SS-6 program regrouped. The fourth attempt was made on August 21 and was a partial success. The missile lifted off and flew downrange, but when the dummy warhead reentered the atmosphere over Kamchatka in the Soviet Far East, it broke up. This was also the fate of the second successful flight on September 7.[86] Although the warhead needed redesign, the SS-6 itself had been proven. The way was now clear for Korolev to accomplish his lifelong dream.

With the two successful SS-6 flights, the road to space was now open. On the night of Friday, October 4, 1957, a modified SS-6 lifted off its Tyuratam pad. Just over five minutes later, the core stage engines shut down, the nose cone separated, and a polished metal ball was released.

Sputnik 1 had become Earth's first man-made satellite.

TWO

First Spark
The Birth of Corona

Corona . . . had begun as a desperate attempt to meet a sinister threat.

A Point in Time (CIA film)

➤ The launch of *Sputnik 1* came as a deep shock to the American people. They looked to President Eisenhower for visible leadership. What they received were comments by his aides, who dismissed Sputnik as "a nice scientific trick" or "a silly bauble." Eisenhower's own comment that Sputnik "does not raise my apprehension, not one iota" did nothing to reassure the American people. Eisenhower's calm, nonpartisan leadership style, which had served him so well, was now seen as complacent.

The first man-made satellite called into question not only Eisenhower administration military and space policy, but American society itself. America was seen as indifferent to an aggressive Soviet military build-up. Critics said that society no longer valued education; few students took math or science courses, the stress now being on "togetherness" and "life adjustment." All that mattered were such materialistic concerns as the depth of carpet and the height of the tail fins on cars.[1]

With the Soviets' successful test of an ICBM, the intelligence community estimated that the first few Soviet ICBMs would be ready in 1960. By November 1957, this was moved up to 1959, when it was thought the Soviets might have ten SS-6s operational. In January 1958, a special estimate projected the Soviets might have as many as one hundred ICBMs ready by 1959. In 1960, the report estimated, the number deployed would increase to five hundred. By 1961, there would be one thousand Soviet ICBMs, with fifteen hundred by 1962 and two thousand by 1963. In contrast, the first squadron of U.S. Atlas ICBMs would not be ready until late 1959, and the total number of U.S. ICBMs planned by 1962 was a mere 130.

This difference between the *planned* number of U.S. missiles and the *estimated* number of Soviet ICBMs became known as the "missile gap." Chalmers Roberts, a reporter with the *Washington Post,* wrote in December 1957 that, in the view of experts, the United States was "in the gravest danger in its history" and was headed toward the "status of a second-class power" as it faced "cataclysmic peril" from the missile gap. On another level, the threat of such a Soviet attack could be used as political blackmail. From Eisenhower's viewpoint, the resulting controversy forced increased defense spending, which he saw as the primary danger to U.S. economic stability. For all these reasons, it became critical that the United States learn the true size of the Soviet ICBM force.[2]

One aspect of Sputnik was not realized by either the Soviets or the American people: the Soviets had not asked permission to orbit their satellite over the United States. This did not escape Eisenhower's attention, however. Four days after the launch, Deputy Secretary of Defense Quarles met with Eisenhower. Quarles observed, "The Russians have in fact done us a good turn, unintentionally, in establishing the concept of freedom of international space." Eisenhower then asked about a reconnaissance satellite.[3]

Post-Sputnik Reconnaissance Satellite Proposals

Immediately following the Soviet launch, both the Army and Navy proposed reconnaissance satellite programs separate from the ongoing Air Force WS-117L project. On October 26, 1957, the Army submitted a proposal to the Department of Defense for a three-part development program. The first step was to be the orbiting of a 20-pound satellite in January 1958, using a Redstone rocket with small solid-fuel upper stages. This would be followed with the launch of a 100-pound satellite in June 1958 by a Jupiter IRBM with small upper stages. This satellite would test photo quality and transmission systems. The final step would be a 500-pound reconnaissance satellite to be orbited in May 1959.

The operational satellite would be spherical and spin-stabilized. A television camera would scan the Earth as the satellite rotated. The expected resolution would be 100 feet, which could show missile sites, airfields, ships, factories, and other targets. The booster would be a modified Jupiter IRBM with an improved upper stage, which would place the satellite in a 300-mile-high orbit. The images would be recorded on board and transmitted to a ground station within thirty minutes. The USSR could be completely covered every three days. The satellite could also be modified to carry SIGINT equipment that could locate Soviet radar sites within twenty-five miles. By correlating this with photo coverage, the radars could be precisely located. An advanced package would intercept Soviet radio communications.[4]

Although the Army soon received permission to launch a series of small test satellites, its ambitious reconnaissance plans went nowhere. The use of television had previously been shown to be impractical, and the Army did not have the political support to usurp the Air Force role in space. The Army proposal did, however, identify the need for a reconnaissance program on a shorter time scale than WS-117L.

The Navy reconnaissance program was every bit as ambitious as that of the Army, and actually made some test flights. The early Navy space program was conducted at the Naval Ordnance Test Station at China Lake, California, with Dr. John Nicolaides as technical director. The Navy reconnaissance satellite was to use a booster similar in design to the Vanguard, but unlike the Vanguard satellite, the program was to support the Navy, rather than scientific research. Like the Army proposal (and the original RAND concept), the Navy satellite would use television.

The small infrared camera was initially flown on a pair of launches. The test satellite was a small cylinder less than a foot across, with a small final stage solid-fuel rocket in its center and the camera looking out the side. The satellite carried enough battery power for three orbits. The launch vehicle for the tests was as remarkable as the satellite—a multistage solid-fuel rocket launched from under the wing of a Douglas F4D Skyray. Of several tries, the attempts on July 25 and August 22, 1958, were thought to possibly have reached orbit. Weak signals were reported, but no pictures could be reconstructed.

The camera was subsequently tested on at least three Navy Transit navigation satellites launched in the early 1960s. The photos showed cloud cover, but lacked the resolution for strategic reconnaissance. The existence of a Navy reconnaissance program and the Transit tests were not declassified until March 1996. Other test components were also flown on Transit satellites, but these remain secret.[5] Although these early efforts would develop into operational systems for navigation and ocean surveillance, the Navy proposal for a reconnaissance satellite never left the planning stage.

The reconnaissance satellite program that was actually developed brought together the ideas from RAND, the technology from the reconnaissance balloons and WS-117L, and the CIA–Air Force teamwork that developed the U-2. It would be called "Corona."

The Start of an Interim Program

On October 24, 1957, the President's Board of Consultants on Foreign Intelligence Activities submitted its semiannual report. The board expressed concern over the WS-117L program. It felt that the program lacked focus, its schedule was unrealistic, and the film read-out technology was unproven, and they doubted that WS-117L could produce an operational system before mid-1959.[6]

The panel concluded that there was a need for an interim photoreconnaissance satellite system that could be ready on a much shorter time scale.[7] This was to be a short-term, high-risk program to determine the number and location of Soviet missiles. It was to be used only until WS-117L became operational.[8] There was no intent to change the original plan to give SAC control once WS-117L became operational. The executive secretary of the NSC informed the secretary of defense and the DCI on October 28 that Eisenhower had asked for a joint report on the interim program.

At the same time, Merton Davies and Amrom Katz of RAND were completing a report on their study of a spin-stabilized, film-return satellite. Titled "A Family of Recoverable Satellites," it concluded that this design would allow a better reconnaissance satellite much sooner and more easily than WS-117L could. RAND formally recommended to the Air Staff that the Air Force begin such a program.

In a cover letter to the report, RAND President Collbohm noted that such a spin-stabilized satellite, with 500 feet of film and a 12-inch camera, would have a resolution of 60 feet and could cover some four million square miles (almost one-quarter of the Soviet Union). This would show major targets, airfields, road and rail lines, and urban and industrial areas. The launch vehicle would be a Thor with a Vanguard second stage and a small solid-fuel third stage. Although the satellite would operate for only a single day before being deorbited, Collbohm said that it could still provide as much information as the early WS-117L would during its entire lifetime. He concluded that this simple satellite could be ready in a year.

The RAND report was submitted to the Air Force on November 12, 1957 (only nine days after the launch of the second Soviet satellite, *Sputnik 2*). On the same day, Air Force Headquarters formally requested that the Defense Department approve development of such a test vehicle.[9]

Corona

On December 5, 1957, Quarles responded to Eisenhower's request for a report on the interim satellite with a joint recommendation from DCI Allen Dulles and himself that the program be approved. They also recommended that, because of the extreme sensitivity of the project, details on the new system be given only in oral briefings. Presidential Science Adviser Dr. James Killian arranged a meeting of Eisenhower, Quarles, and Dulles on the eighth to discuss the new satellite system. Eisenhower accepted the pair's recommendation. As suggested, nothing was written down; indeed, for the first four months, the project was carried out entirely by word of mouth.[10]

Dr. Edwin Land notified Richard Bissell, who had headed the U-2 program, that Bissell was to direct the reconnaissance satellite program. The instructions were very general: the film-return system of WS-117L was to be split off and run jointly by the CIA and the Air Force as a covert program, using the pattern established by the U-2 development effort. The only specific instruction was that none of the funds for the new program could come from already-approved Air Force programs. Other than that provision, Dr. Land's instructions were not so much marching orders as "marching suggestions."[11]

Bissell put together a small staff to run the project. His deputy and the Air Force representative was again Ozzie Ritland, now a brigadier general and the vice commander of the Air Force's Ballistic Missile Division. The two worked out the division between the CIA and the Air Force as they went along, in what Bissell later called "a marvelously informal manner." The group was so small and its members were so close that decisions could be made jointly. There was not the problem of having to compromise, or of delays as decisions were thrashed out between groups. The critical need for the satellite to be operational, and the enormous challenge that it represented, overshadowed issues of control or credit.[12]

The courage of Bissell, Ritland, and the small team of contractors they assembled is difficult to appreciate today. Four decades later, manned spaceflight and probes to the farthest reaches of the Solar System are taken for granted, but when they set to work, space technology did not exist. All they had were an unproven booster and an unbuilt upper stage, a decade of RAND studies, and a few drawings. Everything they would have to do was something no one had ever done before. The questions they faced were basic: was it possible to orbit a satellite whose design was not yet decided, could this satellite take meaningful photos, could the film be returned to Earth intact? But they did have one important asset—the courage to try.[13]

Their first decision was very basic. On March 10, 1958, Bissell held a meeting with two or three people at CIA headquarters to work out the satellite concept. During the meeting, someone asked, "What are we going to call this thing?" One individual, who was sitting in front of his typewriter, looked down and said, "Let's called it 'Corona.'" Bissell responded, "That's excellent," and so Corona it became.[14]

Getting Started

Even as the Corona program was getting started, interest continued to grow in RAND's proposal for a film-return satellite. On January 6, 1958, Lockheed proposed speeding up the WS-117L program by using the Thor booster with its Agena second stage. On February 1, Air Force Secretary James H. Douglas asked Defense Secretary Neil H. McElroy to approve the RAND proposal. Assistant Secretary of the Air Force for Research and Development Richard Horner wrote several memos on the subject during the month. As yet, none of these people had been told about Corona.

On February 7, 1958, the Advanced Research Projects Agency (ARPA) was established as part of Eisenhower's post-Sputnik reorganization. ARPA had overall control of military space activities, as well as temporary control of civilian efforts, pending establishment of the National Aeronautics and Space Administration (NASA) later in the year. It was also now a participant in the Corona program.

On the same day, Eisenhower was given a verbal briefing on Corona. He was told that the satellite would orbit the Earth three times, taking pictures as it passed over the Soviet Bloc, then deorbit the film capsule. It was critical that the reconnaissance mission of the satellite be kept secret, as the camera would only have a resolution of 50 to 100 feet. Should the Soviets learn of it, they could easily build decoys to fool the camera. The next day, Eisenhower directed that the satellite should be built by ARPA, under the direction of the CIA.[15]

One of ARPA's first actions was to establish Corona's cover. On February 28, ARPA issued a directive assigning responsibility for the WS-117L program to the Air Force. The directive also ordered the cancellation of the proposed interim WS-117L Thor-launched reconnaissance satellite. This was followed by all the usual official notifications within the Air Force, and formal contract cancellations were sent out to the prospective suppliers.

The cancellation raised a furor—Air Force personnel were "thunderstruck" by the abandonment of a reconnaissance system that was both desperately needed and seemed to have the best chance of success. Davies and Katz, who had originated the idea of a quick, simple reconnaissance satellite, but who were not told about Corona, could not understand why the program was killed. Contractors were furious over the suddenness of the action; it seemed to be yet another questionable decision on space by the Eisenhower administration.

With the official cancellation of the interim WS-117L system, the way was now clear to continue the program covertly. A very few Air Force, Lockheed, Fairchild Camera, and other contractor personnel were secretly brought into the Corona program.[16]

One of them was James Plummer, a Lockheed engineer with responsibility for the WS-117L payload. In early 1958, he was called into his boss's office and told he was being selected for a new project. His initial reaction was disappointment—he liked working on the WS-117L. This changed when he was told the specifics. Plummer was told to "disappear" from Lockheed and to set up a totally covert program to build a film-return satellite on a high-risk/short-timetable basis. He was given three or four RAND drawings as reference material.

Plummer rented a hotel room to look over the drawings. Over the next several weeks, Plummer and a few other Lockheed engineers worked on possible designs. Satellites shaped like a football, a cigar, and a sphere were examined. Finally, the football-shaped satellite was selected as the initial design. The Fairchild camera (as yet unbuilt) was located in the middle, with a retrorocket at the rear and a sphere from the Atlas ICBM instrument capsule at the front.[17] The "pod," as it was called, was slightly elongated at each end to correct its center of gravity.

As with the RAND studies, the pod was spin-stabilized; as the satellite rotated, the camera would scan across the Earth. Its booster was to be the Thor Agena.[18]

The preliminary design was presented in late March 1958 at a three-day conference in San Mateo, California, between representatives of the CIA, the Ballistic Missile Division, Lockheed, General Electric, and Fairchild. It was soon clear that despite the work, the design was far from complete. Furthermore, the financing of Corona was also not certain. (Although Eisenhower had approved the work on the program, no money had been provided.) Bissell told the contractors that he was "faced with the problem at present of being broke" and would need cost estimates as soon as possible in order to obtain the necessary funding to get the project under way. The contractors agreed to furnish the requested estimates by the following week. The meeting also worked out an initial schedule. The equipment would be fabricated, assembled, and tested, and the first vehicle launched within a nineteen-week period. This meant everything had to be finished by July 1, 1958.

Change in Direction: The Itek Camera

Over the next three weeks, the design of the satellite underwent major changes. The original Fairchild spin-stabilized camera design had a focal length of 6 inches and lacked any kind of motion compensation system to cancel out the satellite's orbital motion during the exposure and prevent blurring. The camera's ground resolution was limited to 50 to 100 feet.[19]

The Itek Corporation proposed that Corona use a scaled-up HYAC scanning panoramic camera. The existing optical system would be replaced with a 24-inch focal length f/5 Tessar lens, while the scan angle would be reduced to a 70-degree-wide swath perpendicular to the satellite's flight path. (The angle was chosen because beyond 35 degrees contrast was lost and there was a serious change in scale.) The panoramic system would produce a frame 2.1 inches wide and 29.8 inches long. With the resolution maintained at 100 lines/mm, the camera would have a ground resolution of between 25 and 30 feet.[20]

The three-fold improvement in resolution of the Itek camera would come at a major price, however. The camera's lens assembly pivoted back and forth to produce the panoramic coverage; this meant the satellite would have to be kept stabilized with the camera pointed toward the Earth. While spin-stabilization was simple, three-axis sta-bilization (which was planned for WS-117L) was an unproven tech-nology. This design change would upset the preliminary schedule, pushing back the first launch to as late as June 1959.

Bissell later recalled that the camera design question was "agoniz-ing." He held meetings with four possible camera contractors to assess the possibilities. His first proposal, completed on April 9, 1958, requested approval of concurrent development of both the Fairchild and Itek cameras. The Fairchild system would become operational first, with the Itek payload serving as a follow-on system.

Two days later, Bissell made a final decision to completely abandon the Fairchild spin-stabilized camera. The rewritten proposal stressed that the Itek system would provide higher resolution, a lower overall cost, and a greater potential for growth.

A third revision was soon made, which retained the Itek camera but raised the "rather arbitrary" cost estimate. The twelve Thor boosters and Agena second stages would be paid for by ARPA through the Air Force. The CIA would fund the camera payload and the reentry capsules.[21]

Another change was in the planned cover story. Originally, the Corona launches were to be described as an experimental program within the first phase of WS-117L. Within days of the launch of *Sputnik 1,* however, articles on WS-117L began to appear. They revealed that WS-117L was to be a reconnaissance satellite, that Lockheed was the contractor, that its code name was "Pied Piper," and that it had been nicknamed "Big Brother," after the totalitarian leader in George Orwell's novel *1984.* It was also noted that a reconnaissance satellite faced legal unknowns.[22]

With WS-117L now publicly identified as a reconnaissance satel-lite, the CIA feared that any ties between Corona and the WS-117L program would result in Corona being identified (rightly) as a recon-naissance satellite. This, in turn, created the risk Corona might be can-celled if its covert role was known.

Bissell decided to change Corona's cover story to that of a scientific satellite carrying biomedical and technological experiments. To add an element of truth to the cover story, the third and fourth launches would carry mice in the reentry capsule, while the seventh launch would carry a monkey. Two more flights were kept in reserve should the monkey flight fail. ARPA also developed two infrared measure-ment payloads for launch later in the program. While the legal status of a military reconnaissance satellite was still in question, the Sputnik launches had created a precedent that overflights by scientific satellites were acceptable. The biomedical cover story would also explain why a series of satellites were being placed into polar orbits and the payloads were then being recovered.

The final Corona project proposal was reviewed by Roy Johnson and Rear Adm. John E. Clark of ARPA, Assistant Air Force Secretary Horner, Brigadier General Ritland, and Dr. Killian. The proposal was then forwarded to Brig. Gen. Andrew Goodpaster, the president's staff secretary, on April 16, 1958. Eisenhower approved the proposal, but not in writing, due to the extreme secrecy. The only original record of his approval was reportedly a handwritten note on the back of an envelope by the DDCI, General Cabell.[23]

Bissell (or as he was informally known, "Mr. B") told Lockheed to stop work on the spin-stabilized football satellite. This came as a considerable shock. Lockheed was given a page-and-a-half-long work statement on April 25, 1958. It said that they were to use as much WS-117L technology as possible; that the satellite was to carry the Itek camera, which was to have a 25-foot or better resolution, and a General Electric reentry capsule; and that the design had to accommodate the biomedical cover story. Responsibility for the camera was split between Itek, which would design and develop it, and Fairchild, who would build the actual hardware. The work statement also detailed the revised schedule: the design was to be frozen in two months, the prototype to be ready after four months, the flight hardware completed in ten months, and a first flight in eleven months.[24]

With the contractors selected, the money was released. On April 25, DCI Dulles signed a memo approving $7 million in Corona funding from the CIA reserve for contingencies. The memo, like the work statement, was short and to the point—three paragraphs long.[25] The contractors began systems development on April 28. The initial design work was ready in short order, being submitted for the first review on May 14. After modifications, the Corona design was frozen on July 26.[26]

U-2 Stand Down

While the Corona satellite was getting under way, the U-2 overflights were halted. Following the surge of flights in August and September 1957, operations were scaled back. The eighteenth overflight was made on October 13, 1957, and was a relatively brief penetration over the Kola Peninsula to cover the shipyards and Soviet naval facilities around Murmansk and Severomorsk. The pilot was Hervey Stockman, who had made the first overflight.[27] It was not until March 2, 1958, that the next overflight was made. It covered the Soviet Far East and resulted in a Soviet protest.

On March 7, Eisenhower ordered a complete halt in U-2 overflights of the USSR. This would last for the next sixteen months. On several occasions during that time Eisenhower would make clear his concerns about the overflights. During a December 1958 meeting with the President's Board of Consultants on Foreign Intelligence Activities, Eisenhower questioned the "continuation of the overflight program," asking "whether the intelligence which we receive from this source is worth the exacerbation of international tensions which results." Two months later Eisenhower told Secretary of Defense McElroy, Air Force Chief of Staff Twining, and Quarles that he considered the overflights to be "undue provocation." Eisenhower added that nothing would make him request authority to declare war more quickly than violation of U.S. airspace by Soviet aircraft.

In part, this decision was influenced by the Corona program. When McElroy urged Eisenhower to approve additional overflights, he refused. Eisenhower said that the reconnaissance satellites were "coming along nicely" and he wanted the U-2 overflights "held to a minimum depending on the availability of this new equipment." With the short time scale of the Corona schedule, it appeared that the satellite would be returning pictures within a few months.

While the U-2s were banned from Soviet skies, balloon reconnaissance made a brief return. The story actually began in the spring of 1955, nearly a year before the Genetrix balloons were launched. The Air Force's Air Weather Service discovered a shift in the jet stream. For a six-week period each May and June, the normal west-to-east flow of the jet stream went from 55,000 feet, turned upward to 110,000 feet, and started to flow east to west. Based on this discovery, the Cambridge Research Center's Atmospheric Devices Laboratory proposed a new reconnaissance balloon program called WS-461L. (The HYAC camera would grow out of this proposal.)[28]

Although test flights were made over the United States, Eisenhower had no interest in advanced balloon reconnaissance projects. In May 1958, the Air Force proposed WS-461L balloons be flown over the

Soviet Union; on May 19, Eisenhower rejected the proposal. A month later, on June 25, the Air Force again sought permission. Quarles told Eisenhower that, with the balloons flying at 110,000 feet, the chances of detection were small and the risk of identification or loss was practically nil. Based on this reassurance, Eisenhower reluctantly approved.

The WS-461L balloons were launched from the aircraft carrier USS *Windham Bay* as it sailed in the Pacific beneath the area where the jet stream reversed direction. Three camera-carrying balloons were launched on July 12, 13, and 14, 1958. The payloads carried timers that would cut the camera gondolas after 400 hours; this was deemed sufficient to cross the Soviet Union and reach Western Europe. The parachuting gondolas were then to be caught in midair. (The timers were reportedly added at the insistence of the State Department to prevent the balloons from crossing the Atlantic and entering Canadian airspace.)

By this time, however, the jet stream was weakening, and the balloons traveled more slowly than expected. On July 29, the 400 hours was up for the first balloon and the gondola was released while it was still over central Poland. The two other balloons came down on July 30 and 31, also inside Communist territory. Eisenhower was furious when he learned of the loss of the balloons. He ordered Goodpaster to tell the Air Force that WS-461L "is to be discontinued at once and every cent that has been made available as part of any project involving crossing the Iron Curtain is to be impounded and no further expenditures are to be made."[29]

Building Corona: The Art of Darkness

Bissell and Ritland ran Corona much as they had earlier managed the U-2 development. Once the contracts had been issued, they began monthly suppliers meetings, which were held at the Air Force Aeronautical Chart and Information Center in St. Louis. The two would sit at the head of the table, with Bissell acting as chairman. The group included two or three people from each of the contractors. Bissell and Ritland would hear reports about progress and problems—especially ones dealing with connections between the different contractors.

There was a major difference, however, in the management arrangement for the U-2 and that for Corona. With the U-2, the lines of authority between the CIA and the Air Force were clear-cut. Corona, on the other hand, was carried out under the jurisdiction of the CIA and ARPA, with the support and participation of the Air Force. The CIA had responsibility for technical direction, the reconnaissance equipment, and photo interpretation, while the Air Force would launch the satellites, track them in orbit, recover the capsules, and process the film. For the moment, at least, the vague division of authority did not pose a problem.[30]

The covert nature of Corona affected the lives of the program personnel in many ways. The secrecy began when they left for work. Plummer recalled being told to take different routes to work each morning, to avoid being followed. The places where Corona was designed and built also had to be separate from existing facilities. There could be nothing that would link them back to the contractors. Lockheed's Corona facility was a Hiller Helicopter Co. research and development facility in Palo Alto, California. The lease was signed on April 1, 1958. As if to underline the date, Hiller personnel were then told *never* to enter the building again. Very few at Lockheed even knew the facility existed. (Plummer could only discuss the Corona project with his two immediate bosses at Lockheed.)[31] Another contractor used a dairy farm outside Boston, while a third set up shop in an old grocery warehouse in Philadelphia.[32]

The initial Corona group at Lockheed was about thirty people, eventually growing to three hundred. Each of the contractors had fifty people directly assigned. Under the "need to know" principle, each person dealt with only his or her part of the program. Cleared personnel were never to use the word "Corona" or even the abbreviation "C" on the telephone or in front of "outsiders." Dealing with outsiders posed major problems for Corona personnel. The Lockheed Corona engineers could request information at the main facility of Lockheed's Missile and Space Division, but they could not say what they needed it for.

On occasion, Lockheed engineers who were not working on Corona would come to Plummer's office with ideas for the design of a film-return reconnaissance satellite. Plummer would then have to divert them, without raising suspicion that such a program was already under way. He would tell them that it sounded like a good idea, but that Lockheed did not have the time to work on it.

Plummer found the most difficult and disagreeable aspect of Corona's secrecy was the need to lie to senior officers. In one case, Plummer had to brief a high-ranking Army research-and-development official who had no clearance for Corona. The official knew something was going on, and pressed Plummer about what Lockheed was doing. The best Plummer could do was to give some very weak answers to some very pointed questions.[33]

By the summer of 1958, these covert aspects were also having an effect on program cost. Bissell's original estimate assumed that the cost of the twelve Thors would be absorbed by the Air Force by diverting them from the cancelled element of the WS-117L program. This assumption proved incorrect, and an alternate source of money had to be found for the boosters. Compounding this problem, the launch program was expanded with the addition of three boosters for tests of the launch, orbit, and capsule recovery sequence. The Corona cover story also required several biomedical launches. ARPA balked at diverting Defense Department money for testing or cover support when there were other military space programs that were also short of funding. Accordingly, Bissell had to return to President Eisenhower with an increased estimate.[34]

Eisenhower Space Policy, 1958–1959

The Corona and WS-117L reconnaissance satellites had, by this time, become the secret centerpiece of the Eisenhower administration's post-Sputnik space policy. On January 22, 1958, the National Security Council assigned the highest priority to development of a reconnaissance satellite. President Eisenhower followed this on February 3 by ordering the highest and equal national priority for the WS-117L satellite; the Atlas, Titan, Thor, and Jupiter missiles; and the ballistic missile early warning radar system (BMEWS).[35]

For Eisenhower, reconnaissance satellites represented the beginning and end of space technology. On February 4, 1958, he told Republican congressmen, "Our major interest in this for some years will be a defense one." He continued that the only "practical" space project for the foreseeable future was a reconnaissance satellite. When the possibility of a Moon probe was raised, Eisenhower said he was opposed to putting "unlimited funds into these costly ventures where there was nothing of value to the Nation's security."

Killian and the other members of the President's Science Advisory Committee (PSAC) also had definite ideas about the role space activities should play in overall U.S. science policy. "Space cadet stuff" and "stunts" were to be avoided. George Kistiakowsky, a Harvard chemist, bemoaned the public's interest in space, saying that they "are in the middle of a great tragedy" because of the public's willingness to spend huge sums on space, at the expense of what he saw as more valuable and important scientific research. I. I. Rabi, a Columbia University physicist and Nobel Prize winner, agreed, describing the "shoestring" funding of many scientific projects and the "distortion of moral values" in spending more on beating the Soviets to the Moon than in curing cancer. Although Killian felt that space research should not overshadow the "great importance of scientific inquiry on Earth," he believed public interest in space would "work to benefit the rest of science." Manned spaceflight was dismissed. Nobel Prize winner and Harvard physicist Edward Purcell loftily proclaimed, "All a man can do is read a meter and turn a dial—and an instrument can do that much better."

Just as Eisenhower viewed space in narrow national security terms, the PSAC wanted to limit space activities to narrow scientific and academic goals, to prevent it from interfering with "real" science. For both Eisenhower and the PSAC, there was no intent to "race" the Soviets in space. Any links between space achievements and military power on Earth were denied. The PSAC argued that space did not represent the "high ground," because it was not "up" but "out."[36]

In part, this was an effort to stop ambitious Air Force proposals for offensive military space programs. The unspoken reason was the issue of freedom of space. If the United States were to begin development of offensive space systems such as orbital weapons, this could undercut attempts to establish freedom of space and leave U.S. reconnaissance satellites at risk. A few days after the launch of Sputnik, Quarles told the Air Force it was "out of line" in presenting any thoughts about using orbital nuclear weapons. He directed that the Air Force was not to consider this in future planning.

This attitude even extended to the mere suggestion of an offensive mission. On October 20, 1958, ARPA Director Roy Johnson ordered the Air Force to stop using the "Weapons System" (WS) designation on military satellite programs. This was "to minimize the aggressive international implications of overflight. . . . It is desired to emphasize the defensive, surprise prevention aspects of the system. This change . . . should reduce the effectiveness of possible diplomatic protest against peacetime deployment." Accordingly, WS-117L lost its politically incorrect designation and was renamed first "Sentry," then "SAMOS."[37]

As with the rest of Eisenhower's Cold War defense and economic policy, post-Sputnik space policy was aimed at the long haul—specifically, making reconnaissance satellites operational and laying the political groundwork to allow their use. But this strategic outlook was overshadowed by the tactical aspects of Sputnik. The problem was a failure of imagination. Eisenhower's scientific advisers repeatedly disparaged ambitious space projects as "space cadet stuff." This missed the point: television programs such as "Tom Corbett, Space Cadet" had made spaceflight the *definition* of the future. Suddenly, the future had arrived, and it had been ushered in by a country and an ideology that most Americans saw as a mortal threat. While their leaders apparently did not, the American people saw a link between space, prestige, and military strength. They saw that the United States was being directly challenged, and that Eisenhower seemed unwilling to do anything about it or even to recognize that the challenge was being made. The result was a loss of support for the administration, while Khrushchev was able to use Soviet space achievements to create the impression of growing missile strength.

In retrospect, Eisenhower's space policy can be understood by realizing that reconnaissance satellites were the only space projects to which he was fully committed. But, as will be seen, this commitment was absolute.

The Corona Mission Profile

Corona had the most complicated mission profile of any U.S. space project of the 1950s. For other satellites, it was enough that the satellite reach orbit and the instruments work. Corona required a long string of events—from booster launch through the midair recovery of the capsule—that not only had to work, but had to work within exacting limits.

The launch site selected for Corona was Cooke AFB, renamed Vandenberg AFB in October 1958 for the late Air Force chief of staff, Hoyt S. Vandenberg. Located near Point Arguello on the California coast, Vandenberg AFB was a rugged area with rolling hills and sand dunes covered by scrub brush. Fog would roll in year-round, and the site was often cold and damp. Five Thor launch pads had been built for the 672nd Strategic Missile Squadron (Thor), which conducted training for RAF launch crews. Two of these were taken over to support Corona launches. When the first Air Force and contractor personnel arrived, they found the base facilities were left over from the old Army post. Most of the buildings were wood and tarpaper with a fresh coat of paint. The base junior high school was the former post hospital.[38]

The new launch site was needed because the Corona satellites had to be placed into a polar orbit (so named because it passes over both poles) in order to cover the width of the Soviet Union. From Vandenberg AFB, the booster could be launched to the southwest and not pass over land until it reached Antarctica. This removed the risk to people on the ground of being hit by falling debris from a malfunctioning booster.

Vandenberg AFB did have one unusual shortcoming from a launch and security standpoint: Southern Pacific railroad tracks passed through the base. The busy train schedule meant the boosters could only be fired during a series of launch windows that could be as short as several minutes. Throughout Corona operations, the launches would have to be timed to occur between passing trains.

The Thor Agena boosters were to be launched from Vandenberg AFB to the south over the Santa Barbara Channel and the Pacific Ocean. To allow photography of the USSR with the proper sun angles and a recovery during daylight in the Pacific, launches had to be made in the early afternoon. Once the Corona satellite was in orbit, the Agena would yaw 180 degrees, so the capsule was pointing backwards to the line of flight. This was done both to reduce the amount of control gas need for reentry orientation at the end of the flight and to protect the capsule's heat shield from molecular heating caused by atmospheric friction. The latter was a major concern.

The early missions would carry enough film for a 24-hour, seventeen-orbit mission. The Earth's easterly rotation would shift the ground track of the satellite about 23 degrees of longitude to the west on each orbit, causing it to pass over a different part of the Earth's surface each time. On the satellite's second orbit, it would pass north to south over the eastern coast of the Soviet Union. The third, fourth, and fifth orbits would pass over Siberia, and the sixth and seventh over the central Soviet Union. The eighth orbit would cover the western Soviet Union and the ninth would pass above Eastern Europe. The camera would be turned on automatically when each pass began, photographing a broad band of the Earth, then shut down as the satellite passed beyond the "denied area." The satellite, like the reconnaissance balloons, was designed to photograph everything that passed below it, rather than covering specific targets like the U-2.

With the satellite's photo passes complete, it would continue to circle the Earth until, on the seventeenth orbit, it would pass over the Alaska tracking station. The station would transmit a radio signal to the satellite to begin the recovery sequence. The satellite would pitch down 60 degrees and eject the capsule. Small solid-fuel spin rockets would then fire to stabilize the capsule. Next, the solid-fuel retrorocket would fire to slow the capsule down for reentry. The capsule's spin would be slowed by the firing of small solid-fuel de-spin rockets, and the now burned-out retrorocket would be jettisoned.

The heat shield would take the brunt of the reentry. When the capsule had descended to an altitude of 60,000 to 65,000 feet, the heat shield and the parachute cover would be jettisoned. A deceleration chute would then deploy, followed by the main chute at 55,000 to 60,000 feet. The capsule would descend toward a recovery zone near Hawaii.

Called the "ballpark," the recovery zone was a 200-by-60-mile area patrolled by five Fairchild C-119F Flying Boxcar cargo planes. Another four planes covered an additional 400-mile section called, logically enough, the "outfield." The nine C-119s were planes that had originally been modified for the Genetrix recoveries. As with Genetrix, the capsule's parachute would be caught by a trapeze and reeled aboard. Should the midair recovery fail, the capsule would float and broadcast a radio homing signal. It could then be picked up by a surface ship or by divers from a helicopter.

There were also provisions to prevent the capsule and its film from falling into unfriendly hands, should all recovery efforts fail. The capsule would only float for one to three days. This was controlled by a device called a "capsule sink valve," which was nothing more than a plug of compressed brown sugar. It would dissolve in seawater at a rate that could be broadly predicted. When the last of the sugar dissolved, water would enter the capsule and sink it.[39]

The midair recovery of the capsules had been proposed at a meeting with Bissell. An engineer demonstrated the procedure with a fishing rod and reel and his wife's snood. Bissell asked him what the odds of a successful recovery were, and the engineer responded, "A thousand to one." Bissell replied, "Go ahead."[40]

The 6593rd Test Squadron (Special)

In the summer of 1958, ARPA headquarters began organizing the 6593rd Test Squadron (Special) to undertake the Corona recoveries. A total of nine aircraft commanders were needed; they were required both to have flown in the Genetrix program *and* have current time in the C-119. This was difficult, because after Genetrix had been completed, the pilots had been split up to other units and many had been retrained to fly Lockheed C-130 Hercules transports. The only ex-Genetrix pilots who met the requirements were currently assigned to Pope AFB; they still flew C-119s, all held Instructor Pilot ratings, and each had about 5,000 hours flight time. There were nine of them. They were transferred as a group to the new unit.

One of these pilots, Capt. Harold E. Mitchell, was briefed by his Wing Commander in early July 1958 on the possibility of a new aerial recovery program being developed. Subsequently, Mitchell was attached to a team from Tactical Air Command headquarters, led by Col. Howard C. Rose. This team flew to Ballistic Missile Division headquarters in Los Angeles later that month and attended a concept briefing chaired by Maj. Gen. Bernard Schriever. There, the possibility of using C-119 aircraft to recover the capsules was discussed in detail. After discussion of organization, procurement of material, and personnel, each attendee was cautioned on the sensitivity of information surrounding this program and the high security of any information attached to Corona.

The C-119s would each have a crew of nine. While the pilots came from Pope AFB, the copilots were from Sewart AFB; they flew C-123 transports and had limited time, but would be trained. There was also a navigator on each crew, who was required to have overwater training, and a radio operator to home in on a beacon signal from the capsule. The rest of each crew was made up of a winch operator, who supervised recovery operations, and four pole handlers, who rigged the recovery trapeze and lines. Most of the winch operators and a few of the pole handlers were also Genetrix veterans.[41] The latter included Jim Muehlberger and William B. Cullpepper, who had both served on Capt. Slaughter Mimms's crew.

Muehlberger recalled later that he was assigned to the 6593rd Test Squadron in August 1958 and sent to Edwards AFB a month later to begin training. This involved both classroom sessions and simulated

Preflight briefing for 6593rd Test Squadron. Lt. Col. Ed Pratt (back to camera) is giving the briefing. *Left to right* in the first and second rows are Capt. Felix Moran (pilot), Capt. Walter M. Milam (aircraft commander), Capt. Thomas F. Hines (aircraft commander), 1st Lt. Paul Griswold (pilot), and Capt. Lin Upchurch (navigator). Behind Upchurch are Capt. Harold E. Mitchell (aircraft commander) and 1st Lt. Chuck Leech (pilot). Despite the smiles, the first year and a half of Discoverer flights was a time of deep frustration for the unit, due to the launch and in-orbit failures. *U.S. Air Force photo via Col. Thomas F. Hines*

air pickups, using prefabricated concrete blocks on a parachute. (It did not matter what was used, just so the weight was the same as a capsule.) Each aircrew had a specific number of successful aerial recoveries to complete before being checked out as qualified by an instructor pilot, either Mitchell or Capt. Thomas F. Hines.

In addition to the training missions, there were "hours and hours of flight time," as Mitchell later described it, dedicated to testing parachutes of varying designs that would assure a correct rate of descent and the structural strength to withstand the impact of recovery. All nine of the crews were involved in long, tedious hours of training and testing in desert temperatures often exceeding 100 degrees.[42]

Tests of the recovery techniques soon revealed problems. There were major shortcomings in the capsule parachute design. Of seventy-four drops using personnel-type chutes, only forty-nine were successfully recovered in midair. With one type of operational parachute, the results were even worse—only four were recovered out of fifteen dropped, and it took an average of one and a half passes to make the hookup. Out of eleven drops with another type of operational chute, only five were successful. This design required an average of two attempts for each recovery.

Some of the problems were traced to weak parachutes and rigging. The root source of the problems, however, was the high sink rate of the parachutes—about 33 feet per second. This was too fast to allow the C-119 to line up properly. What was needed was a parachute with a sink rate of around 20 feet per second, which would allow the C-119 to make three or four passes before the capsule descended too low. The parachute system was redesigned to allow a sink rate slow enough to allow a reasonable chance of a midair recovery.[43]

Muehlberger was assigned to a crew commanded by Captain Hines. Each crew was assigned to a specific C-119 aircraft. This improved efficiency and created esprit de corps among the hand-picked personnel. Hines's plane was 045, while Mitchell flew 037. This had been Mimms's aircraft during the Genetrix program, when he had made the first, and the most, gondola aerial recoveries.

The crews were initially skeptical about the mission. When Maj. Everett Anderson asked, "What are we going to be doing here?" he was told they would be picking up nose cones. His response was disbelief. There was a similar reaction among high-ranking Air Force officers. Col. Frank Buzard, who was chief of Corona testing, later recalled giving briefings about the mission profile. They would go well until he described how the plane would make a recovery in midair. The audience's usual response was, "Hey, you're nuts."[44]

Its training finally complete and now confident in its mission, the 6593rd Test Squadron began shipping out to Hickam AFB, Hawaii, in the first week of December 1958, with one group of aircrews being transferred each week. The complete transfer took three weeks. Once in Hawaii, the unit began conducting training exercises. By late January 1959, formations of eight C-119s could be seen in the skies above Oahu nearly every day. They would fly in tight circles and make sharp rolls as the planes caught simulated capsules.

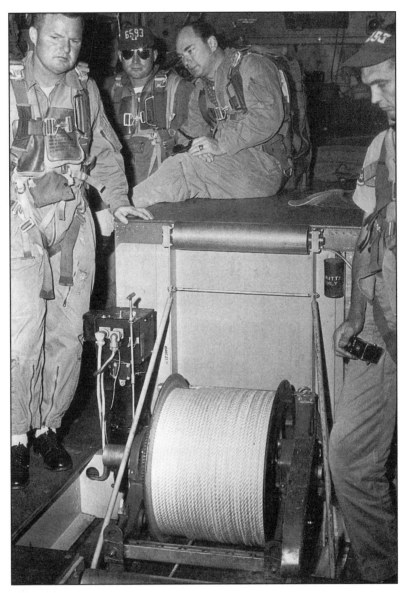

Pole handlers and winch operator aboard a C-119. A number of the original group were veterans of the Genetrix balloon recoveries. They wore parachutes, life vests, and dye markers in the event of an accident. It was a reflection of the skill, experience, and professionalism of the aircrews and ground personnel that none of the inadequate C-119s were lost. *U.S. Air Force photo via Col. Thomas F. Hines*

The 6593rd Test Squadron's unique mission required intense training. Mitchell, commander of "A" Flight, recalled that on some training missions he would have the crew deploy the poles without the nylon loops attached. After they dropped a practice capsule from 14,000 feet, the crew would bring the poles back into the aircraft, rig the nylon loops, and redeploy the system for an attempt to make the recovery. The purpose of this exercise was to train the crew to be able to rapidly re-rig the system in the event of an inversion (in which the loop flipped the parachute over rather than catching it) or any other mishap that caused a loss of the loops.

During a year of practice missions, Captain Mitchell achieved a 100 percent success rate catching the practice capsules. This string of successes came to an end following a ten-day leave. On his first training mission after his return, he misjudged the parachute position, put it through the right aircraft propeller, and missed the recovery. It required constant training to maintain a high proficiency in this very special game of "catch."[45]

Establishing Cover: The Discoverer Program

By December 1958, all the pieces were in place—the first flight hardware had been delivered, the Vandenberg launch site was finished, the tracking and control facilities were complete, and the launch and recovery crews were trained and ready. All that remained was to publicize Corona's cover story.

On December 3, 1958, ARPA Director Johnson announced the start of the "Discoverer" program, which he said would launch satellites at a rate of one per month starting in early 1959. The Discoverer satellites would carry experiments of a general nature, including biomedical payloads. These would include mice and small monkeys, and the data would be used to support research for manned spaceflight. Johnson said that the first monkey flight probably would not be made before the fifth or sixth launch. Although eight to twelve launches were initially planned, Johnson stressed that Discoverer was to be an open-ended program, lasting several years and involving heavier payloads. He added that if a third of the satellites reached orbit, "We will consider the project very successful."[46] The Discoverer satellites were, of course, the Corona program.

Just as much of the technology for Corona had come from the various balloon programs, so too did the Discoverer cover story. A balloon launch, like that of a rocket, was dramatic, and a balloon at high altitude could be seen over much of a state. Since the start of the balloon reconnaissance programs, a subtle security procedure was developed: they were hidden in plain sight. The balloon was not classified, but the *purpose* was kept secret. The same was true of Discoverer. The Thor Agena booster was not secret, nor was the fact that it would carry a capsule. But, as far as the public knew, these capsules would contain scientific experiments. The press would be allowed to watch the launches.

Behind the facade, Bissell and Ritland created a "black" Corona program office inside the Discoverer program. Col. Lee Battle was the program director who ran the day-to-day operations of Discoverer. Only Colonel Battle, his deputies, and one office worker, Kathryn Holt, knew that Discoverer really was a reconnaissance satellite. In dealing with others, special precautions had to be taken. Holt recalled that she never used words like "black" or "CIA." The Corona program was never discussed with an outsider unless he had been formally introduced: "This is so-and-so, who's been briefed on the Corona program." This applied even if she already knew he had been cleared. Within the Discoverer program office, there was not a single piece of paper with the word "Corona" on it. Literally hundreds of people worked on Discoverer without a clue that it carried a camera.[47]

The cover story was thin, however. The press was quick to note that the Discoverers were to be placed in a polar orbit from Vandenberg AFB. The *New York Times* observed that "the polar orbit is advantageous for a reconnaissance satellite." *Time* went farther, headlining the story "Polar Sky Spies" and speculating that while the early Discoverers could show cloud cover, later missions "might photograph objects as small as Russian military bases."[48] It did not take a special clearance to realize that the most important intelligence question facing the United States was the location and size of the Soviet ICBM force, and that a lot of effort was being put into orbiting mere "biomedical payloads."

Due to the many technological unknowns connected with the Corona program, the initial plan envisioned step-by-step testing of the major elements. The first Discoverer launch would test the Thor Agena booster. On subsequent launches, the capsule would be added to test the deorbit/reentry/recovery profile. These would also include cover launches, to maintain the story that Discoverer was a scientific satellite. Finally, the Discoverer satellite would be equipped with a camera for a full Corona systems test. In this way, Corona could be brought to full operational status in a short time.[49]

That was the plan. Reality would be very different.

THREE

The Hard Road to Space
The Flights of *Discoverers 1* to *13*

We were a small army in the first place, and we were an army banded
against a common enemy, namely the apparent impossibility of doing what
we were about to try to do. . . . We were all operating in those days in a field
in which we didn't really believe it could be done, we were just going to try.

John Wolfe, Itek camera program manager, *A Point in Time*

▶ In just nine months, Corona had gone from a page-and-
a-half work statement to hardware on the pad at Vandenberg AFB.
The test plan was aimed at getting the system operational as soon as
possible. No one connected with the program could have known how
very, very hard the road to space would really be. The Discoverer satellites went through the worst streak of failures and technical problems
of any space project. Colonel Buzard later observed, "Any failure that
occurred in space . . . we did first. We failed in a marvelous bunch of
different ways." This only served to make Discoverer's final success
so much sweeter, and its accomplishments all the greater.

First Tries: *Discoverers 1* and *2*

The first hints of the problems that were to plague Discoverer came
with the first launch attempt on January 21, 1959. This was to be a
flight test of the new Thor Agena booster combination, and did not
carry a capsule. The booster was very carefully checked out, and the
countdown seemed to be going well.

As the countdown reached the T-60 minute point, the automatic
sequencer button was pressed, and power was applied to test the Agena's

hydraulic system. Thirty seconds later, the explosive bolts between the Agena and the Thor unexpectedly detonated and the ullage rockets on the Agena fired. (These should not have fired until the Thor had completed its burn and the Agena had separated from the Thor.)[1] The fairing at the forward end of the Thor collapsed as the Agena settled on to it. Corrosive red fuming nitric acid oxidizer spilled from the Agena and ran down the side of the Thor. The Thor's guidance system in the forward end of the booster was damaged by the rocket firing, while the acid spill caused damage farther aft. Fortunately, the Agena did not fall from the booster, and no explosion occurred.[2]

Two days after the failure, a review meeting was held in Palo Alto. The cause of the failure was quickly identified as a "sneak circuit." This was easily solved, and the review board judged Discoverer ready for launches at the rate of one per month.

At the same time, General Electric noted a new problem with stabilizing the capsule during reentry. The capsule had been designed to carry a 40-pound film payload. During the early test flights, however, only ten to twenty pounds would be carried. To restore stability, a three-pound weight would have to be added to the capsule's forward end. The program officers decided that, rather than using a lead weight, an instrument payload would be carried as ballast. This would be either diagnostic equipment or experiments as part of the biomedical cover story, thus converting dead weight into a plus for the program.[3] (This practice of carrying small experiment packages would continue throughout the Discoverer launches and after.)

Because the Thor had never lifted off, the aborted launch attempt was not given a Discoverer number (although it was commonly, if unofficially, called *Discoverer 0*). The accident pushed back the first launch by a month.

A new booster was set up on Pad 5 at Vandenberg AFB and checkout began. As with any new booster, there were problems. The next launch attempt on February 25 underwent more than four hours of holds before it was cancelled only seconds before the planned liftoff due to first stage pressurization and propellent loading problems.[4]

Discoverer 1 successfully lifted off on its second try on February 28, 1959, at 1:49 P.M. PST. As with the first attempt, the mission goal was to test the Thor Agena booster's performance and place *Discoverer 1* into orbit. A light engineering payload was carried, but no capsule. As the press watched from two miles away, the booster climbed into blue sky and flew south. The rocket was tracked for six minutes, but then, after weak signals were picked up by a tracking ship 950 miles downrange, there was only silence.

The Air Force announced *Discoverer 1* had reached orbit, but doubts soon began to grow. Tracking stations in Alaska and Hawaii failed to pick up any radio signals on what should have been its first orbit.[5] Speculation mounted that the satellite had been structurally and/or thermally damaged when the Agena reached orbit or during the first pass.[6] Thirty-two hours after launch, the Air Force announced that "sporadic" signals on *Discoverer 1*'s frequency had been picked up, indicating it was in orbit.[7] These signals were just four to six seconds long during the six-minute pass over a tracking station. It was believed that *Discoverer 1* might be tumbling, which could be causing the brief receptions. There was no radar contact on the satellite, however.[8] For three weeks, the Air Force tried to prove *Discoverer 1* had reached orbit. Eventually, Colonel Buzard signed the final report saying it went into orbit, but he and the CIA later concluded that *Discoverer 1* had in fact reentered over the Antarctic.[9]

The launch of *Discoverer 1* raised the issues of freedom of space and the program's secrecy. An East German radio broadcast accused the United States of "carrying the cold war into space," and complained that "the Americans fired it without even talking to other states over whose territories the Discoverer is to perform espionage services." The broadcast claimed that U.S. satellite reconnaissance was futile, as Soviet military facilities and industries had been camouflaged. In contrast, it said, "U.S. war industries . . . are concentrated to an extraordinary degree in various regions and are absolutely open to view." The broadcast concluded by saying, "The United States generals are thus, as in so many other fields, involving themselves in a race in which they should know from the start that they will be left far behind."[10]

In the United States, several scientists blamed the failure to track *Discoverer 1* on the "unnecessary secrecy surrounding the project." They claimed the satellite could have been tracked if the Air Force had given advance notice of the launch. Dr. J. Allen Hynek, the head of the Moonwatch tracking program, said he had no doubt that it could have been picked up, had Moonwatch been given twenty-four hours warning.[11]

These charges were denied by Secretary of Defense McElroy the next day, before the House Committee on Science and Astronautics. He said that all the tracking facilities that had had a chance to observe the satellite had been notified. It was pointed out that *Discoverer 1* would have passed over the United States during daylight hours; the Moonwatch teams could spot a satellite only at dawn or dusk.[12]

The next step in the Discoverer program was to test the recovery sequence. At the heart of *Discoverer 2*'s payload was a capsule 27 inches long, 33 inches in diameter, and weighing 160 pounds. The capsule was shaped like a gold-plated kettle; the Corona personnel referred to it as a "bucket." The bucket was inside a cone-shaped heat shield, which added another 35 pounds. Attached to the rear were the retro-rocket and spin/de-spin rocket package. The total weight of the complete assembly was 300 pounds.

Discoverer 2 was launched at 1:18 P.M. on April 13. The liftoff had been delayed 3 hours and 19 minutes due to technical problems, trains, and fog at the launch site. The Thor headed downrange, its engine burning for 159 seconds. The Agena separated, then fired its own engine for another 120 seconds.[13] Two hours after liftoff, the Air Force announced that *Discoverer 2* was in a 156-by-243-mile orbit. The satellite had correctly oriented itself tail-first, and was stabilized in all three axes—the first satellite ever to do so. Ground stations received strong signals.[14]

There was a small technical problem, however. The start of the recovery sequence was to be initiated by an onboard timer. The timer was set with the assumption that *Discoverer 2* would be in a 94-minute orbit, but it actually had a 90.5-minute period.[15] The timer could be reset by ground control simply by pressing a series of buttons in the correct order, and so, as *Discoverer 2* passed over the Kodiak, Alaska, ground station, a controller entered the sequence. The monitor—erroneously, as it turned out—showed that the command was incorrect. The controller reentered the command signal, but under the pressure of time, forgot to press the reset button before doing so. The new coded pulses were added to the original ones, nullifying the previously correct code. The error could not be corrected, as the erroneous programming now prevented contact with Earth. The timer only turned on the communications system while the satellite should be over a ground station; based on its faulty timing, this now would occur far from the stations. At all other times, the communications system was shut down to prevent the Soviets from attempting to "take over" the satellite.[16]

The erroneously programmed timer separated the capsule successfully on April 14; two tracking stations in Alaska picked up the capsule's radio beacon, while telemetry from *Discoverer 2* showed changes in weight, center of gravity, and attitude that indicated the capsule had ejected.[17] The capsule was not descending towards the warm waters off Hawaii, however, but towards the snow-covered expanse of Spitzbergen Island, north of Norway. Observers in the mining community of Longyearbyn reported seeing a "starburst" and a descending parachute.[18]

Lt. Col. Charles G. "Moose" Mathison, vice commander of the 6594th Test Wing, which oversaw orbital operations and the recovery effort, called Maj. Gen. Tufte Johnsen, head of the Royal Norwegian Air Force Northern Command, to request permission to search for the capsule. (Ironically, Mathison was not cleared to know about Corona.)[19] Colonel Mathison then headed to Norway to supervise the search. The Norwegian government gave formal approval to begin the search on April 16.[20]

Initially, the Air Force would only say that the capsule was believed down in the Arctic. The reason for both the secrecy and the haste was that the Soviets operated coal mines on Spitzbergen, and it was feared they might find the capsule. Ground parties, two helicopters, and five aircraft searched the snowy island. The planes flew as low as 600 feet as their crews tried to spot the golden bucket and its orange and silver parachute.[21]

It was all to no avail. The search was abandoned on April 22. The only traces ever found were snowshoe tracks. General Twining, chairman of the Joint Chiefs of Staff, wrote to the deputy secretary of defense, "From concentric circular tracks found in the snow at the suspected impact point and leading to one of the Soviet mining concessions on the island, we strongly suspect that the Soviets are in possession of the capsule." (The Norwegians always wore skis, while the Soviets used snowshoes.) Twining suggested the State Department approach the Soviets to request the return of the capsule and its contents.[22]

Confirmation that the Soviets had recovered the *Discoverer 2* capsule came much later from Sergei Khrushchev. At the time, he was an engineer with Vladimir Chelomay's design bureau, which specialized in cruise missiles. Khrushchev recalled that the capsule recovery was talked about within the design bureau. According to the version he heard, the capsule landed in the USSR. The story continued that two peasants found the capsule in a forest near the town of Kalinin, then chopped it up for parts. What was left was sent to Korolev's design bureau.[23]

The possibility that the capsule had (literally) fallen into unfriendly hands did not cause the Corona managers significant worry. The bucket's payload was "mechanical mice" which simulated a biomedical package.

Cover Launch: *Discoverer 3* and the Four Mice

It was now time to establish Discoverer's cover. The third launch was to carry an actual biomedical payload—four mice. The announcement was made on April 30, 1959, by Rep. Overton Brooks (D-La.), chairman of the House Committee on Science and Technology, at a dinner of the American Rocket Society.[24]

The mice were from a group of sixty being "trained" at Holloman AFB in New Mexico. They were of the C-57 strain, commonly used for pregnancy, cancer, and blood tests. All had black fur, to determine the bleaching effects of cosmic rays. They were seven to ten weeks old, and weighed about one ounce each. They were housed inside the capsule in small individual cages about twice their size. Each mouse had a tiny radio transmitter strapped to his back to record heart action, respiration, and muscular activity. A three-day food supply was carried in each cage, containing a mixture of peanuts, oatmeal, gelatin, orange juice, and water. The pure oxygen atmosphere inside the capsule would be equivalent to an altitude of 15,000 feet, with the temperature between 65 and 79 degrees Fahrenheit and humidity below 50 percent. During liftoff and reentry, the mice would be exposed to eight Gs; while in orbit, they would be weightless for the planned 26-hour duration of the flight.[25]

The *Discoverer 3* launch was beset by problems. The first attempt was cancelled on May 21 due to coastal haze, the second try on the twenty-third was halted because of a helium regulator failure, and a third try on the twenty-fourth was aborted due to a liquid oxygen switch failure.[26] These were not the only problems. During one of the attempts, the ground controllers noticed shortly before launch that the mice were not active. At first, it was thought they were merely asleep, so a technician was sent up on a cherry picker to wake them up. He banged on the side of the vehicle and yelled. When there was still no activity inside the capsule, it was opened up and the mice were found to be dead. Their cages had been spray painted, and the mice had found this more appetizing than the trail mix.

The fourth attempt was made on June 3, with the backup "crew." During the countdown, a sensor suddenly indicated 100 percent relative humidity inside the capsule. The countdown was halted and a crew was sent out to the pad. With the booster standing vertically on the pad, the humidity sensor was directly below the cages, and the mice had urinated on it. The sensor was allowed to dry out and the count resumed.[27]

Liftoff finally came at 1:09 P.M. PDT, after 190 minutes of holds due to clouds. The Thor fired normally, but the Agena's engine shut down early due to fuel exhaustion, and there was insufficient velocity to reach orbit. *Discoverer 3* reentered the atmosphere and the four mice were killed. Several hours later the Air Force confirmed that the satellite had not reached orbit.

The attempt at a cover mission was not successful at diverting scrutiny of the program. During the press conference before the launch, hard questions had been asked by reporters who suspected there was more than mice involved. The Corona personnel had to stonewall the reporters.[28] The loss of the vehicle and its cute little crew focused further attention on the thin cover story. The British Society Against Cruel Sports made a formal protest to the U.S. ambassador against the flight. There was much press criticism over the loss of the mice, and demands were made that no more launches take place with live payloads until the launch and recovery had been perfected.

The loss of *Discoverer 3* caused an apparent change in the development plan. Originally, *Discoverers 3* and *4* would have carried mice, while *Discoverer 7* would have had a monkey passenger. This plan was dropped—*Discoverer 4* would carry the first camera and the monkey flight was put off. Although design work and mockup construction continued for another year, the monkey flight was eventually cancelled.

Driving for Cover: A Comic Interlude

This change in plan forced a speedup in the development of a payload shroud. *Discoverer 4* was to have a camera port on the side of the Agena. CIA security had issued a requirement that an interim on-pad payload shroud be developed to hide the camera port from the reporters covering the launches. Should the port be seen, it would give away the purpose of the flight.[29]

The solution was to tape brown paper on the side of the Agena to cover the port. To remove the cover, two lengths of piano wire with Ping-Pong balls at the ends were fastened under the paper. As the booster lifted off, it was intended that the airflow would cause the Ping-Pong balls and wires to act as ripcords and strip the paper away.

Before its actual use, however, the design had to be tested in simulated flight. Rather than use an expensive wind tunnel, a prototype was attached to the side of a white Ford Thunderbird sports car. Very late one night, the sports car made a high-speed run to simulate launch velocity as nearly as possible. The test was made "downrange" on the Long Island Bayshore Freeway. With the car reaching speeds of 90 miles per hour, the ripcords worked, and the shroud separated. However, the mission was aborted when the test vehicle was intercepted by a hostile power: the sports car was pulled over for speeding.

The Bad Streak: *Discoverers 4* through *8*

The public objectives of the *Discoverer 4* launch were given as tests of the launch, propulsion, and communications systems, orbital performance, and recovery techniques. It was, in fact, the first true Corona flight, and was given the classified designation "Mission 9001." *Discoverer 4*'s payload was a modified HYAC camera. The "C camera," as it was designated, was mounted between the capsule and the forward end of the Agena. To keep weight down, the camera bay was not pressurized, meaning the camera and its acetate-based film would be exposed to the hard vacuum and temperature extremes of space. Only passive temperature control techniques, such as paint patterns and reflective surfaces, were used to keep the system at a constant temperature.[30]

Discoverer 4 was launched on June 25, 1959, but like the previous mission, the Agena shut down early and it did not reach orbit. This was blamed on vortexing of the fuel.[31] It also appeared that the camera cover did not release, due to a failure of the ripcords.

Nothing seemed to work on *Discoverer 5*. The first two launch attempts, on July 28 and 29, 1959, were scrubbed due to clouds. The third attempt, on the thirtieth, was aborted due to failure of the main engine igniter. The fourth and fifth attempts (August 11 and 12) ran afoul of clouds. Mission 9002 was finally launched on August 13, on the sixth try—after another hour of holds due to air conditioner problems and trains.[32]

At a time when space technology did not exist, a few men sought to do the impossible. A Discoverer satellite is prepared for launch in 1959. The capsule (and camera bay) is covered with a temperature control blanket. Due to the security surrounding Corona, few if any of the people visible around the Thor/Agena booster knew it carried a camera. *U.S. Air Force photo*

The problems followed the satellite into orbit. On the first orbit, telemetry indicated that the temperature inside the spacecraft was abnormally low, causing the camera to fail. During the seventeenth orbit, the capsule separated and the recovery sequence began, but the ships and recovery planes never picked up its radio signals or sighted it visually. The search for the capsule continued until the sixteenth before being abandoned. The Air Force and CIA assumed that the capsule had reentered but had been lost at sea.[33]

There was an unexpected postscript to the *Discoverer 5* mission. On February 1, 1960, technicians at the Navy's Sparsur tracking system noted an unknown satellite in polar orbit. It was in a 130-by-1,058-mile orbit; these elements were inconsistent with any known satellite launch. The Department of Defense announced the discovery on February 10. There was press speculation that it might be a secret Soviet reconnaissance satellite. On February 23, the mystery was solved when the Department of Defense made a further statement that it most probably was the *Discoverer 5* capsule. The radar cross section was consistent with the 2-by-3-foot capsule.

When the capsule separated, the spin rockets apparently failed. It was pointed in the wrong direction, so that when the retrorocket fired, the capsule's speed—rather than decreasing for reentry—increased by some 1,120 feet per second, placing it into the higher orbit. An analysis of tracking data indicated the capsule had been tracked (but not recognized) on August 15, 1959, on its first pass over the United States in its new orbit. The capsule finally reentered on February 11, 1961.[34]

The next Discoverer launch, Corona mission 9003, showed no more success than the first five. *Discoverer 6,* launched on August 19, 1959, reached orbit, but the camera failed on the second orbit. When the recovery was attempted, the capsule separated but the retrorocket failed, and no recovery was possible.[35]

Discoverer launches were grounded for the next three months, while an intensive series of ground tests were made to find solutions to the repeated failures. There were problems with the satellite's electrical power supply, telemetry, tracking, separation sequence, and capsule stability. In space, the capsule's batteries were exposed to temperatures far lower than their design requirements, which prevented them from powering the recovery beacon. An independent report on September 8 recommended the program be halted for further study. There was a belief that Lockheed had been overconfident, and that the Agena and capsule should be better instrumented.

In response to the report, Lockheed increased the battery output and added instrumentation.[36] GE painted geometric patterns on the capsule to control its temperature; these would absorb heat as the capsule was in sunlight, then retain it as the satellite passed into the Earth's shadow.[37]

In the meantime, Vandenberg AFB and Corona had a distinguished "visitor." On September 20, 1959, Soviet Premier Nikita Khrushchev rode a train through Vandenberg AFB en route between Los Angeles and San Francisco.[38] The train rolled past the first three operational Atlas ICBMs. For the occasion, their gantries were rolled back so the missiles were visible. Corona, as befit a spy, was more discreet; the two pads were not visible from the train, due to the hilly landscape.

After the three-month hiatus, the final two Discoverer launches of 1959 were made in November, but only continued the litany of failure. *Discoverer 7* (Mission 9004) went into orbit on the seventh. On its first orbit, the 400-cycle power supply failed. The nitrogen gas used to stabilize the satellite was exhausted prior to the second orbit. *Discoverer 7* began a slow tumble, and the capsule could not be separated.[39] In addition, telemetry indicated that the capsule batteries were too cold to power the recovery beacon. The painted patterns had failed to keep its interior sufficiently warm.[40] The Air Force recovery team was alerted, but *Discoverer 7* was left orbiting uselessly.

Discoverer 8 was launched on November 20 on the first attempt. During the Agena burn, however, its velocity integrator failed. This unit was designed to measure the satellite's speed and shut down the engine when it reached orbital velocity. *Discoverer 8*'s engine continued to burn until the fuel was exhausted. This left Mission 9005 in an eccentric orbit with an apogee of 913 miles. To make matters worse, the camera failed immediately after reaching orbit.[41]

Due to *Discoverer 8*'s faulty orbit, the recovery plan had to be changed. With its apogee twice as high as usual, a normal reentry on the seventeenth orbit would bring the capsule down too far west. Separation therefore was moved up to the fifteenth orbit, which would bring the capsule down only slightly southeast of the normal area.[42]

The capsule separation and retrofire were successful, but retrorocket separation occurred late. This meant the capsule would come down farther south, in the outfield. The C-119 recovery aircraft detected the capsule's beacon, but the signals lasted only two minutes, rather than the normal twenty to thirty minutes. The parachute had never opened, and the capsule slammed into the Pacific.[43]

Stand Down

It was now clear that Discoverer had deep design flaws. Three of the boosters had failed to reach orbit, even though the launches had seemed successful. Another had put the satellite into an eccentric orbit. Of the five C cameras launched, none had worked properly. The satellite had shown an abnormally low temperature on one mission, and tumbled on another. Of the seven capsules, one had come down early, three had not come down at all, two had been destroyed in launch failures, and the final one had had a parachute failure.

On December 15, 1959, Richard Bissell met with presidential science adviser George Kistiakowsky; Dr. Herbert F. York, the Defense Department's director of research and development; and a number of other consultants to discuss the program. They agreed that the Corona test flights should continue, as ground tests were unable to simulate the failures.[44] A panel of consultants studied the various failures and recommended that "qualification, requalification, and multiple testing of component parts" be undertaken before assembly.

The launch failures were traced to the launch profile. Ironically, its simple nature was reducing the chance of success. To save weight, the Thor booster followed a preprogrammed trajectory using its autopilot. Unlike later boosters, the Thor's engine did not shut down when the booster reached a predetermined velocity, but was allowed to burn until the fuel was exhausted. This inaccurate flight profile, along with the low altitude of the Corona orbits, meant the orbital injection burn by the Agena had to be very precise. At the typical injection altitude of 120 miles, an angular error of plus or minus 1.1 degrees, or being too slow by only 100 feet per second, would result in the Agena not completing its first orbit.

The short-term solution was a drastic weight-control program. As with the camera shroud, inventiveness came to the fore. Lockheed engineers removed excess weight from the Agena with tin snips and files. (Even a few pounds removed in this way would improve the performance margins.) In the longer term, the solution would be the more powerful Agena B, and the removal of the instrumentation needed for the test launches. This was a year or more away, however.

The repeated C camera failures were traced to the exposure of the acetate-based film to the vacuum of space in the unpressurized bay. The film had become brittle, then torn and caused the cameras to jam. The solution was to replace the acetate film with a polyester-based film called "Estar." The official CIA Corona history observed, "The importance to the reconnaissance programs of this achievement by Eastman Kodak in film technology cannot be overemphasized. It ranks on a level with the development of the film recovery capsule itself."

Control of the spacecraft's internal temperature was another continuing problem. It had varied over the different flights, on one mission being considerably below that expected. The interim solution was to vary the paint pattern on the outer skin on each launch.

The capsule recovery sequence was as critical as the launch profile. Each one-second error in the timing of the capsule ejection resulted in a five-mile shift in the landing point. Even more critical was the orientation of the capsule during the retrorocket firing. An error of more than ten degrees in the de-orbit burn would cause the capsule to miss the recovery zone entirely.[45]

To improve the chances a capsule would be recovered after reentry, a bright strobe light was added to the capsule. This would allow the capsule to be spotted if it came down at night. Surface recovery crews could then pick it up from the ocean. Packages of radar-reflecting chaff were also added to the capsule. These would be released during the descent to allow ground stations to track the capsule's flight path.[46]

The various problems would take time and money to solve. On January 22, 1960, Bissell submitted a request to DDCI Cabell to pay for work that was already under way. He apologized to General Cabell, explaining, "Although such a sequence is regrettable, there has been considerable confusion in this program as to what the amount of the overruns would be and this has made it difficult to obtain approvals in an orderly fashion in advance."[47] Years later, Bissell recalled how difficult the early Discoverer failures had been:

> It was a most heartbreaking business. If an airplane goes on a test flight and something malfunctions, and it gets back, the pilot can tell you about the malfunction, or you can look it over and find out. But in the case of a [reconnaissance] satellite, you fire the damn thing off and you've got some telemetry and you never get it back. There is no pilot, of course, and you've got no hardware, you never see it again. So you have to infer from telemetry what went wrong. Then you make a fix, and if it fails again you know you've inferred wrong. In the case of Corona it went on and on.[48]

It would get worse, much worse.

The Time of Despair: *Discoverers 9* through *11*

The stand down of Discoverer launches lasted three months. The next attempt was made on February 4, 1960. *Discoverer 9* lifted off the pad on its fourth try, but once again the Thor shut down early. The Agena separated, but attitude control was lost at engine ignition. Mission 9006 impacted about 400 miles downrange.[49]

Discoverer 10, launched on February 19, did worse. The *New York Times* article describing the mission began, "The trouble-beset Discoverer satellite series had its most spectacular failure today." As the Thor Agena lifted off at 12:16 P.M., its engine pitched back and forth, causing the rocket to fishtail. As the booster reached an altitude of several hundred feet, it trembled and wobbled, then turned to the northeast, toward the towns of Santa Maria and San Luis Obispo. The range safety office transmitted the destruct signal 56.4 seconds after launch. The booster erupted into a huge orange fireball and chunks of the rocket the size of automobiles began falling towards the ground. The base loudspeakers blared, "Take cover! Take cover! Take cover!" and people dove under tables, trucks, and cars. Others stared upwards, ready to dodge if a piece headed for them.[50]

Suddenly, mission controllers realized that the camera payload was about to be compromised. A mad dash ensued, as security personnel rushed to the impact point. The forward section came down in one piece, without the film—or its mission—being exposed. The debris from Mission 9007 landed within 2,500 feet of Pad 5.

President Eisenhower never wavered in his support of Corona. When General Goodpaster told Eisenhower about yet another Discoverer failure, the president would say, "Don't worry about it. We're going to stay with this thing. We're going to bring it through because it's something we really need."[51]

The Corona program was expanded in the spring of 1960 to a planned twenty-nine flights, with the possibility of another six being added.[52] By late summer, this had again been expanded, to thirty-seven payloads.

Launches resumed with *Discoverer 11* on April 15, 1960. Despite high winds, the countdown and launch went smoothly (except for the trains). In addition to the usual press contingent, three Kuwaiti princesses watched the liftoff of Mission 9008. The three girls, Lulua, Fatima, and Amina Al Sabah, were nieces of Kuwaiti ruler Sheik Abdullah, and were going to school in the United States.[53] The booster performed excellently, and *Discoverer 11* was placed into a 109.5-by-380-mile orbit. Its payload was a C camera and 16 pounds of film. (*Discoverers 4* through *10* had carried only a 10-pound film load.)

As *Discoverer 11* made each pass over the Soviet Union, the camera took pictures. This was the first mission in which the camera worked throughout the flight. All of the film was exposed and loaded into the capsule.[54] The other spacecraft systems had all operated extremely well; attitude control and the electronic links were both excellent. Success for Corona mission 9008 was now only a reentry away.

On the seventeenth orbit, the reentry sequence began. The Kaena Point tracking station in Hawaii confirmed the capsule had separated and the retrorocket had fired. However, the spin rocket firing was not verified. The capsule went into a higher-than-planned reentry trajectory, and could not be recovered.[55] The Air Force announced that "some unknown malfunction occurred at a critical point just after separation" and that the capsule had probably remained in orbit.[56]

The failure of *Discoverer 11* after coming so close to success sent many with the program into despair. At a program meeting, one team member speculated that there was some basic factor that had been overlooked. This factor made recovery impossible, he continued, and they would never get anything back from space.[57] On April 25, 1960, Air Force Vice Chief of Staff Gen. Curtis LeMay sent a personal message direct to the president of Lockheed urging him to undertake "extraordinary corrective actions" to solve the problems.[58]

The repeated Discoverer failures were not the last disaster to befall the U.S. reconnaissance program that spring.

May Day and the End of Aquatone

The sixteen-month stand down in U-2 overflights of the Soviet Union lasted until July 1959. Three overflights were then made through the end of the year. Their goal was to locate possible Soviet ICBM sites. The flight paths were again along major rail lines. As this was the only reliable transportation within the USSR, any ICBM site had to be nearby.

Although a number of possible sites were covered, no ICBM bases were identified. This caused a bitter dispute between the Air Force and CIA. The Air Force argued that the ICBM sites were camouflaged, while the CIA said they simply were not there. The Air Force continued to project a huge Soviet ICBM force, but the CIA's estimates were smaller. For its part, the Navy believed there was only a token force, if any.

Following the third overflight of the year on December 6, which covered Kuybyshev and the missile test center at Kapustin Yar, there was another stand down.[59] Eisenhower continued to be under great pressure to approve additional overflights. Until a Soviet ICBM site was finally identified, the missile gap issue would continue to fester. Once a site had been discovered, it would be possible to go back to the earlier film and see if any sites had been missed.[60] Eisenhower, however, had not lost his belief that the U-2 intelligence carried too high a political price. He was also worried about the upcoming Paris summit. In a discussion on February 8, 1960, Eisenhower said that his one asset at the summit meeting was his reputation for honesty; should a U-2 be lost, the wreckage could be put on display in Moscow and ruin his effectiveness.[61]

Despite his fears, Eisenhower approved two overflights for April 1960. The first was flown on April 9 by CIA pilot Bob Ericson. It covered the Sary Shagan Antimissile Test Center, the long-range bomber base at Dolon Air Field, the nuclear test site at Semipalatinsk, and finally Tyuratam.

The second planned overflight would be different from any flown before. While previous missions had covered targets on a curved flight path, this mission would fly straight across the Soviet Union. The planned route would go from Peshawar, Pakistan, to Tyuratam, then on to nuclear weapons facilities at Sverdlovsk in the Urals. Next, the plane would cover suspected ICBM complexes at Yurya, several hundred miles east of Moscow, and at Plesetsk in the northwest Soviet Union. The final targets would be the port facilities at Arkhangelsk and Murmansk. The plane would land in Bodo, Norway, after a 3,800-mile flight.[62]

The flight was delayed several days due to bad weather over the USSR. Finally, at 6:26 A.M. on May 1, the last day Eisenhower said the flight could be made due to the summit, pilot Francis Gary Powers took off. Three hours and twenty-seven minutes into the flight, as he neared Sverdlovsk, the U-2 was brought down by a volley of SA-2 Guideline surface-to-air missiles (SAMs). Powers bailed out and was captured.

The overflights were meant to have "plausible deniability"; there was a cover story ready that the U-2 was a civilian weather plane that had accidentally strayed into Soviet airspace. When Powers's plane became overdue, the cover story was released. However, when Premier Khrushchev announced on May 7 that Powers had been captured alive and had confessed to spying for the CIA, the cover story was in shreds and the U.S. government was caught in a lie. DCI Allen Dulles offered to resign, but Eisenhower refused to let him take the blame for the flight. Eisenhower made the unprecedented admission that he had personally authorized the overflights. No head of state had ever before admitted to spying in peacetime.[63]

The Paris summit, along with any hopes for a nuclear test ban and an easing of the Cold War, was destroyed along with Powers's U-2. Khrushchev demanded Eisenhower apologize for the flight and punish those responsible. Eisenhower refused.

Before the meeting broke up, however, there was an exchange between French President Gen. Charles De Gaulle and Khrushchev. De Gaulle said that Khrushchev was "making too big a fuss." De Gaulle continued, "There is probably a ton of Russian iron [i.e., satellites] coming through French space every day without my permission. I have no idea what is inside those satellites and you have not told me." After Khrushchev admitted Soviet space probes had carried cameras, De Gaulle shot back, "Aha, in that one you had cameras. But you are not sure if all of them have cameras." Khrushchev responded, "I am only concerned with what is over the Soviet Union with a man in it. That it doesn't have men in it doesn't bother me." Eisenhower arched his brow and scribbled, "Most interesting."[64]

Fixing the Capsule

An intensive examination of the capsule failures was undertaken following *Discoverer 11*. Although each failure was different, a common problem became apparent: the spin/de-spin rockets. They were not firing properly, thus causing the capsule to tumble or wobble. When the retrorocket then fired, the instability caused the capsule to miss the recovery zone or, as with *Discoverer 5*, to be sent into a higher orbit.[65] Subsequent tests indicated that the solid propellant in the spin/de-spin rockets was absorbing water from the air, which caused them to explode when fired. Several blew up during the ground tests, and it was clear that the same thing had happened during the flights.[66]

Development work began on a "cold gas" spin/de-spin system. Rather than using small rockets, a mixture of compressed nitrogen and freon gas would be released through nozzles to act as thrusters. These provided 195 pounds of thrust for 0.8 seconds. Each of the two separate systems was composed of a small black sphere to hold the gas, a manifold, a valve, and exhaust jets. The system was retrofitted to the *Discoverer 12* capsule as it was prepared for launch.

The cold gas system was tested in a series of balloon flights from Holloman AFB. The capsule was carried to 100,000 feet by a Skyhook balloon, then released by ground command. Originally these were scheduled for nine flights, but the program was extended to allow testing of the retrorocket firing and parachute deployment. The first cold gas test was made on June 23, 1960, and cleared the way for *Discoverer 12.*

Six days after the test, *Discoverer 12* was ready for launch. Due to all the problems, this was not a Corona flight, but a diagnostic mission. (Therefore it did not have a classified Mission number.) The C camera and film were not carried. The capsule was fitted with the cold gas spin/de-spin jets. It was heavily instrumented to report on capsule operations, including the cold gas jets.

The launch was made on the first attempt on June 29. The countdown went well, with only minor delays due to problems with the acid and fuel trucks, although the weather was more troublesome, causing a major hold. The Thor and Agena engine burns were normal, but *Discoverer 12* did not reach orbit. Interference from the Agena's telemetry transmitter caused its horizon scanner to operate improperly. The Agena was in a pitch-down attitude during the engine burn, which caused it to reenter the atmosphere and burn up.

While a modification was being made to prevent a recurrence, the balloon drop tests of the Discoverer capsule continued at Holloman AFB. After release, the capsule's programmer fired the spin jets, the retrorocket, and the de-spin jets in the normal reentry sequence. The parachute then deployed. The speed and loads during parachute deployment matched those of an actual recovery. The third and fourth drop tests (the second and third successes) were made on July 23 and 27, 1960. The cold gas and retrorocket operated satisfactorily, indicating the problems had been corrected.

On August 4, two drop tests of the advanced Mark IV capsule were made at Holloman AFB. This was similar to the Discoverer capsule, but used an improved programmer and other modified systems. The first balloon burst at 30,000 feet, but the capsule was recovered. The second flight went as planned and the parachute deployment was successful.

It had been a long, hard road. Yet the failures had paved the way to success. Each problem had been overcome, even though it seemed that a new problem always took its place. From President Eisenhower to the engineers and machinists who built the systems, they had kept trying. They were all about to be rewarded.

All the Way Home: *Discoverer 13*

Like its ill-fated predecessor, *Discoverer 13* was to carry an instrument payload rather than a camera. This package would monitor the capsule separation and recovery sequence. The readings would be transmitted via a five-channel telemetry system. During the blackout of reentry, the data would be tape-recorded, then transmitted after a two-minute delay.[67] The satellite did carry one piece of classified equipment—a CIA device called "SCOTOP," which picked up Soviet radar "hits." This would allow the CIA to determine if the Soviets could track the satellite.[68]

Discoverer 13 was launched on August 10, 1960. The 1:38 P.M. PDT liftoff took place through a fog bank at Vandenberg AFB. The Thor Agena was tracked by a new radar system that allowed nearly all-weather launches.[69] The booster's flight path was slightly high and to the west, but well within limits. The Agena's performance was very close to planned, and *Discoverer 13* was placed into a 155-by-429-mile orbit, inclined 82.67 degrees. After shutdown, the satellite reoriented itself into the tail-first position as planned.[70]

Moose Mathison had monitored the launch from the control center at Sunnyvale, California, known unofficially as "Moose's Mansion." For eighteen months, he had directed "the great capsule chase" without success. *Discoverer 13* was his last chance—he had been promoted to colonel and had orders transferring him to Washington, D.C. After orbit was confirmed, Colonel Mathison boarded a C-130 transport and flew to Hickam AFB, Hawaii, to oversee the recovery attempt.[71]

The onboard programmer triggered the recovery sequence 26 hours and 37 minutes after launch. The Kodiak ground station received telemetry signals as the process began. *Discoverer 13* pitched down, the capsule's explosive bolts fired, and it was pushed free by springs. The cold gas spin jets fired, followed by the retrorocket. When the retrorocket burned out, the cold gas jets fired again to halt the spin. After this, the thrust cone, containing the retrorocket, was jettisoned properly. The capsule then passed out of range of the Kodiak station. There was nothing more to do but wait.

Slowed by the retrorocket, the capsule began to descend into the thin upper atmosphere. The heat shield began to glow, and an incandescent shock wave formed around the tiny capsule. The heat shield began to melt—as designed—from the intense heat of reentry. The surrounding ionization cut off all radio communication with the ground. The capsule then began to slow, its orbital energy being carried away in the form of heat. After about two minutes, the glow faded and the final steps began. The charred heat shield, now useless weight, was jettisoned at about 65,000 feet, followed by the deployment of the parachute. A small camera inside the capsule filmed the orange and silver parachute opening against the blue-black of space. The Hawaii ground station finally picked up the capsule's signals and confirmed that heat shield jettison and parachute deployment had occurred.[72]

Down below, the recovery aircraft and ships picked up the capsule's radio beacon and tracked toward it. The capsule was over the primary recovery area, about 250 nautical miles west-northwest of Hawaii. "A" Flight was assigned to the ballpark, with Captain Mitchell covering the primary recovery position in "Pelican 1." When the first signals were received by Pelican 1, the crew was at first unable to determine a direction toward the signal. (This phenomenon was later thought to be caused by the capsule descending directly above Pelican 1 and the strong beacon signal saturating the aircraft's receiving equipment). One of the RC-121 control aircraft, also receiving the signal, gave Pelican 1 a vector of 285 degrees to the target.

After flying this vector for a number of minutes, Pelican 1's navigator, 1st Lt. Robert D. Counts, requested a 360-degree turn to check the signal direction. After completing 180 degrees of the turn, Lieutenant Counts determined that the vector given to Pelican 1 was a reciprocal and the capsule was descending behind them. Reversing course, Captain Mitchell flew the beacon track back to the area from which they had originally come. On arriving, they were met by the sight of Pelican 3, flown by Capt. Larry Shinnick of "A" Flight, flying over the floating *Discoverer 13* capsule, its orange and silver parachute half submerged beside it.[73]

The USNS *Haiti Victory* was ordered to recover the capsule. It sailed for an hour and ten minutes before its helicopter took off and flew toward the floating capsule. The two C-119s circled protectively overhead as the gold capsule bobbed in the twelve-foot-high swells, its location marked by the flashing strobe light and a yellow-green dye marker. It was three hours after splashdown, late in the afternoon and nearing sunset, when the helicopter arrived. As it hovered, Navy Boatswain's Mate Third Class Robert W. Carroll jumped into the water. He swam over to the capsule, detached the parachute, and put it into a bag. He then attached a line from the helicopter to the capsule, and both it and the parachute bag were reeled aboard. Carroll was then picked up and the helicopter headed back towards the recovery ship.[74] Soon after, Air Force Major Ralph J. Ford sent a brief, encrypted message to CIA headquarters in Washington, D.C.: "Capsule recovered undamaged."[75]

Success. The *Discoverer 13* capsule following its recovery from the Pacific Ocean. The flight did not carry a camera, but rather was to test the recovery sequence and new cold gas jets. The capsule is on display at the Smithsonian's National Air and Space Museum. This was the first object ever recovered from orbit. *U.S. Air Force photo*

When the word of the success reached Lockheed, the Corona personnel held a party at Rickie's in Palo Alto. Plummer and the other key people ended up in the pool, swimming in their suits and ties.

Cover Stories and Public Affairs

As part of the Corona cover plan, extensive publicity was given to the first recovery of a man-made object from space. (This was the first American "first" of the early space age.) Photos were released of the liftoff, the capsule floating in the water, and the USNS *Haiti Victory*. The capsule also carried an American flag that would be presented to President Eisenhower. All this was to add validity to the Discoverer cover story that it was an experimental space program, rather than a reconnaissance satellite.

Bissell and Major General Ritland, now head of the Air Force's Ballistic Missile Division, had realized early on that, given the primitive state of space technology, it was possible that the first capsule to be successfully recovered might be from an actual reconnaissance mission. As the capsule would have a take-up reel for the film and a film-entry aperture, Discoverer's real photoreconnaissance mission would be apparent. To avoid blowing the cover story, they planned to make a covert switch of the capsule after its arrival in California. A duplicate capsule would be presented to President Eisenhower, the press, and the Smithsonian Institution. However, because *Discoverer 13* was a diagnostic flight, such a switch was not needed.[76] This first recovery was, nevertheless, planned to be a dress rehearsal of the procedures for handling a real Corona capsule. Colonel Mathison had other plans.

Mathison believed that the first Discoverer capsule recovery would offer a chance to gain press attention for the Air Force space program and the efforts of his friend, Lt. Gen. Bernard Schriever, head of ARDC. (He also led the Air Force Corona effort.) On August 12, Mathison flew out to the *Haiti Victory* in a helicopter and took charge. The ship's captain thought it would be safer for the ship to carry the capsule into port, rather than flying it to Hawaii on a helicopter. Mathison, however, insisted on taking it with him. (Legend has it the argument became quite heated, with Mathison unhooking his .45 holster; in reality, it was not so colorful.)[77]

As Mathison flew back with the capsule, he arranged to have the commander of Pacific Air Forces meet him for a photo session.[78] Mathison then had the capsule, which was packed in a 3-by-2.5-foot metal container, loaded aboard a C-130 transport for the flight to the West Coast. The radio beacon was still transmitting.[79] During the flight to Moffett Naval Air Station, near Sunnyvale, he sent messages to Ritland and to the president of Lockheed to meet him for another photo shoot.

The capsule stayed overnight at Sunnyvale, so "classified instruments" (presumably SCOTOP) could be removed before it was placed on public display. (Mathison did not know about the SCOTOP package.) Mathison and the capsule then flew to Andrews AFB, outside Washington, D.C. Appropriately, "Lucky 13" arrived on August 13th. They were met by General Schriever and Air Force Chief of Staff Gen. Thomas D. White. The capsule was placed on a table in the Andrews AFB operations building, and the parachute was placed on the floor.[80] During the brief ceremony, General White proclaimed, "During more than 40 years in military service, I have attended many of these occasions, but none has had the significance of this one." After noting that *Discoverer 13* had been launched in bad weather, recovered in bad weather, and arrived at Andrews AFB in a drizzle, he quipped, "I think that proves that it is an all-weather satellite."[81]

Discoverer 13 went to the White House on August 15. As television and movie cameras recorded the event, President Eisenhower noted that the mission showed "how rapidly Americans forged ahead in the worthwhile exploration of space." General White reached into the capsule and pulled out a small polished metal case. It contained a 24-by-18-inch American flag, which White then presented to the president. Beside General White was Colonel Mathison.

President Eisenhower said, "I should like to think of some way that I could properly commend the people who are responsible for this remarkable achievement. I know that mere medals and ribbons don't do this. But I do think I can in a feeble way attempt to assure all of you that the American people are indeed proud of what you have done."[82]

There were only a very few people who truly knew how very, very hard it had been—or how important the success was. At Vandenberg AFB, *Discoverer 14* was being prepared for launch. It carried a C camera and a 20-pound roll of film. It would change the world.

FOUR

First Voyages into the Unknown
Discoverers 14 to *18* and the Founding of the
National Reconnaissance Office

A National Reconnaissance Office is hereby established as an operating
agency of the Department of Defense. . . . With the single exception of this
directive, no mention will be made of the following titles or their abbrevia-
tions in any documents . . . National Reconnaissance Office.

DoD Directive TS 5105.23

▶ For the U.S. reconnaissance satellite program to be effective, it was not enough to simply build and launch the satellites. It was
also necessary to create organizations to manage their development,
select targets of interest, and analyze the photos. Even as Discoverer
struggled toward success, this framework was being established. In
early 1959, concurrent with the start of Discoverer launches, Director of Central Intelligence Allen Dulles formed the Satellite Intelligence
Requirements Committee (SIRC). This was in parallel with the Ad Hoc
Requirements Committee (ARC), which directed U-2 overflights.

On August 9, 1960, Dulles established the Committee on Overhead
Reconnaissance (COMOR) to supersede both ARC and SIRC. The first
COMOR chairman was James Reber, a senior CIA staff member who
had headed ARC. COMOR's role was to target Corona operations over
the USSR and other denied areas, and to indicate the areas of interest—in particular, the suspected locations of ICBM deployment.

"Talent" Coverage

The CIA estimated that 65 percent (4,764,000 square miles) of the
Soviet landmass was compatible with ICBM deployment. This was

designated the "suitable area." (The remainder was areas of perma-frost, mountains, swamps, or cities.) Because ICBM sites would have to be serviced by rail, the most likely areas for ICBM deployment were further limited to about 24 percent of Soviet territory (2,081,000 square miles). The CIA divided this region into eight "priority areas."

On July 11, 1960, the CIA's Photographic Interpretation Center (PIC) provided an assessment of how much of the USSR had been covered by the U-2 photos. The PIC report showed that, despite the U-2's success, the Soviet Union was still largely a blank. Since January of 1959, photos (code-named "Talent") from four U-2 overflights had covered only 650,000 square miles of the suitable area. Of this, only 75,150 was within the priority areas 1, 2, and 3. Areas 4–8 were complete blanks. The report concluded:

> It is estimated that more than 85 percent of the suitable area, 95 percent of the priority areas, and 85 percent of the rail route mileage in priority areas have not been observed or covered by usable TALENT during the period. In view of the large areas still uncovered and the limited numbers of ICBMs that are likely to be deployed so early in the Soviet program, it is not surprising that none of these sites has been positively identified.

In addition to the U-2 coverage, there were also visual observations by travelers inside the Soviet Union from airliners, trains, boats, and automobiles. But these observations were limited by weather, obstacles, seat location, field of view, and harassment by the KGB (Soviet state security), thus adding only about 1 to 2 percent to the total coverage.[1]

On August 18, COMOR issued a list of the thirty-two highest priority target areas. Among the suspected areas of ICBM deployments were the Kotlas-Salekhard, Vologda-Perm, Vologda-Arkhangelsk, Petrozavodsk-Pechenga, Chelyabinsk-Ivdel, Komsomolsk-Vladivostolt, Odessa-Leningrad, and Kaliningrad/Baltiysk-Riga rail lines; the Ufa-Omsk and Novosibirsk-Irkutsk segments of the Trans-Siberian railroad; and the Berezovka and Tiksi areas. Most of the sites were "supported by considerable firm evidence." Some targets, however, were included "because, on a basis of deductive reasoning, they appear to be the most likely of all known targets to bear upon missile deployment." Other priority areas were the missile test centers at Kapustin Yar, Tyuratam, Caspian Sea, and Sary Shagan.[2]

The possible sites for ICBM deployment had been located by classic intelligence techniques. Soviet émigrés were interviewed by the CIA after they reached the West. They would say that they thought something sinister was going on in a certain area because, for example, they were no longer allowed to collect honey. This was combined with the few reports from human sources inside the Soviet Union, and with SIGINT data.[3] It was imprecise, but some sites were considered more likely than others.[4]

The lack of solid information was reflected in the varying estimates of the Soviet ICBM force. A February 1960 estimate gave the probable mid-1961 force level as 140 to 200 ICBMs on launchers. An August 1960 estimate used a different approach. Because of insufficient evidence, three different programs were laid out, based on differing assumptions about Soviet production capability. Assuming the maximum rate of production, this report calculated there could be between fifty and two hundred Soviet ICBMs deployed by mid-1961.[5]

It was not possible to make decisions on the size of U.S. nuclear forces when the estimate of the current size of the Soviet ICBM deployment varied by a factor of four and there was no information about location or future production. The United States simply *had* to find out the true state of Soviet ICBM capabilities.

The same day COMOR issued its list of Soviet target areas, *Discoverer 14* was launched.

Discoverer 14's Voyage of Exploration

Discoverer 14 lifted off from Pad 4 at 12:57 P.M. PDT on August 18, 1960, through a thin fog bank. During the countdown, there were minor problems with the pad's water deluge system and the fuel truck. There was also a fifteen-minute hold to allow the empty Agena stage from *Discoverer 13* to pass through the projected flight path. The engineers were concerned that its signals might confuse the tracking equipment.[6]

The Thor Agena booster worked nearly perfectly, and *Discoverer 14* was placed into a 111-by-500-mile orbit, inclined 79.6 degrees with a period of 94.5 minutes. As the satellite made its first pass over the Kodiak ground station, however, trouble appeared. Telemetry indicated the Agena was in an abnormal attitude and was using control gas at an excessive rate.[7] For the first few orbits, *Discoverer 14* was on the verge of tumbling. The satellite's attitude did not stabilize until midway through the flight.[8]

On its second orbit, *Discoverer 14* passed over the Soviet Far East and the C camera began to take pictures. The third through eighth orbits also passed over the USSR, each farther west than the last. The ninth orbit was over Eastern Europe. The C camera functioned perfectly on each pass, and the full twenty pounds of film was exposed and loaded into the capsule.[9]

On the seventeenth orbit, the timer automatically started the reentry sequence. Separation and retrofire were normal, but the capsule came down long, overshooting the recovery zone. Below, the recovery planes and ships waited.

On each recovery mission, the "A" and "B" Flights switched locations. For *Discoverer 14*, "A" Flight covered the outfield. At the far end of the outfield was Captain Mitchell, call sign "Pelican 9." Mitchell had individualistic recovery techniques. He always set the pilot's seat the same way, to better judge the parachute descent rate. He climbed to 18,000 feet, higher than the standard 14,000 feet. This allowed him to trade altitude for speed, should the capsule be out of position. Mitchell also had the crew set the poles at a 30-degree angle, rather than the 45 degrees used by the other crews. He felt this made the recoveries easier.[10]

As Pelican 9 orbited a race track pattern some four hundred miles downrange of the primary recovery zone, the capsule's beacon signal was picked up by the navigator, Lieutenant Counts, at 12:53 P.M. His eyes watching the oscilloscope, Counts determined that the capsule was on a bearing of 255 degrees from the position Pelican 9 was orbiting. Flying a heading of 255 degrees and picking up air speed, Pelican 9 flew thirty miles and descended 4,000 feet before sighting *Discoverer 14* at a position of 12 o'clock at approximately 14,000 feet.

Orbiting the descending capsule, the recovery crew made ready to open the beavertail door and deploy the recovery gear, once the plane had slowed to the desired air speed. The weather in the immediate area was clear, with towering cumulus in the distance and a cloud layer at approximately 8,000 feet. As the plane started its first pass, a whispered admonition came over the intercom from winch operator TSgt. Louis F. Bannick, "For God's sake, don't invert it." Inverting the parachute would mean losing the entire rig.

On the first pass, the nylon loops strung between the two poles missed the parachute by about six inches. Mitchell banked the plane and made a 180-degree turn to line up for a second pass. At the same time, in the primary recovery zone, three C-119s were chasing the wrong radar blip, and were unaware that Mitchell's plane had the capsule in sight. Pelican 9 was on its own.

The second pass missed by two or three feet, and Mitchell turned for a final attempt. Time was running out, as the capsule descended towards the cloud deck at 8,000 feet, and would soon be enveloped by the mist. As the C-119 flew at 8,500 feet, just above the clouds, the parachute rolled in off the right pole and was snared by the loop and bronze hooks. Over the intercom came the welcome message, "Good pick up." The time from the first signal to the successful catch was eight minutes. The *Discoverer 14* capsule was reeled aboard, and the capsule and parachute were placed into a gray metal container.[11] The first midair recovery of a film capsule had been achieved, and with it, the first successful Corona mission.

Captain Mitchell tried to report the successful midair recovery, but was told to stay off the air so as not to interfere with the recovery attempt. The rest of the recovery force was still chasing a false target, and was not aware the capsule had already been retrieved. Finally, Pelican 9 was contacted to report its status, and it was only then that the unit knew the long, frustrating quest had ended.[12]

On the flight back, the crew's mood was jubilant, with talk of the "beer bust" that awaited their return. Pelican 9 arrived back at Hickam AFB at 3:30 P.M. Hawaiian time, but Captain Mitchell was told to wait until the rest of the squadron's planes arrived. Pelican 9 then landed and taxied up to a place of honor in front of Hangar 4. On hand was Gen. Emmett O'Donnell, commander of Pacific Air Forces, two hundred Air Force personnel, and the crew members' wives. The crew removed the container from the plane and placed it on a table before General O'Donnell and other senior officers. O'Donnell then presented Mitchell with the Distinguished Flying Cross and the other crew members with Air Medals. Air Force Chief of Staff White had authorized the immediate awards as soon as he learned of the recovery.[13]

After the ceremony, the capsule was loaded on a C-130 transport and flown to the Lockheed facility at Sunnyvale. It would be examined there, according to the statement given to the press, rather than being sent to Washington, D.C.[14] The film cassette was removed from the capsule and shipped under maximum security to Westover AFB, Massachusetts, for processing, then on to PIC in Washington, D.C.[15]

Three of Pelican 9's crew—Mitchell, Counts, and Bannick—attended a press conference in New York City, then flew to Washington, D.C., to report to ARPA about the recovery.[16]

The same day Mitchell recovered *Discoverer 14*, in Moscow, Francis Gary Powers was sentenced to ten years for espionage. His three-day show trial allowed the Soviets to again humiliate both the United States and the Eisenhower administration. The Soviets had finally put an end to a decade of U.S. Air Force, RAF, and CIA overflights. But the newspaper headlines announcing the recovery of *Discoverer 14* made it clear that it was too late—the Soviets had won the battle, but lost the war.

First Views of an Unknown Land

The arrival of the *Discoverer 14* film at PIC was marked by a special presentation. During the U-2 overflights, the practice had been established that the photo interpreters would have nighttime briefings in the PIC auditorium. They were shown a map of the Soviet Union, with a squiggly line showing the route of the U-2, and were briefed on the important targets. When they assembled for the briefing on Mission 9009, PIC Director Arthur Lundahl told the photo interpreters that it was "something new and great we've got here." Jack Gardner opened the curtain over the map of the Soviet Union. Instead of a single squiggle covering only a tiny part of the USSR, there were eight broad bands running north to south across the whole width of the Soviet landmass. The photo interpreters began to cheer.[17]

The mood was later described as "joy . . . sheer joy." Powers's U-2 mission had been intended to finally settle the question of Soviet ICBM deployment, but it had been lost and the U-2 overflight program over the USSR had ended. For the past year, the Discoverer program had been an endless series of heartbreaking failures. Now, at long last, here was the success they had dreamed of.[18]

The Mission 9009 film covered 1,650,000 square miles of the Soviet Union. This was more coverage than all twenty-four U-2 overflights combined. Many of the areas in the film, such as central Siberia, had never been reached by the U-2. The resolution was between 35 and 40 feet, much less than the U-2 had provided,[19] but despite this, large-scale facilities were readily apparent. The very first frame taken from

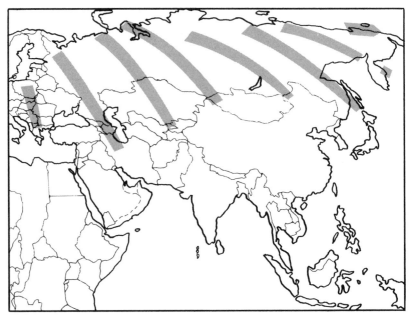

The *Discoverer 14* coverage of the Soviet Union and Eastern Europe. Like the balloon reconnaissance missions, the early Corona flights photographed everything that passed below the camera. *Map by Joel Carpenter*

space showed the Mys Shmidta Air Field. The runway and the shorter parking apron were visible as white lines against the darker ground. It was located a mere 400 miles from Nome, Alaska, and was a bomber staging base.

Cloud cover was a problem in some northern areas, but most areas in the central and southern Soviet Union were clear. Eastern Europe had heavy cloud cover.[20] Among the targets covered were the Kapustin Yar Missile Test Range and part of its downrange impact area. Twenty new SA-2 SAM sites were identified, along with another six possible SA-2 sites under construction. The Sarova Nuclear Weapons Research and Development Center, several new airfields, and numerous urban areas were also photographed. Among the military targets covered were a probable chemical weapons storage site at Arys, a chemical weapons training site at Gorokhovyyskiy Lager, numerous ammunition and explosives storage sites across the USSR, armor training areas, and railroad construction sites. In Eastern Europe, oil

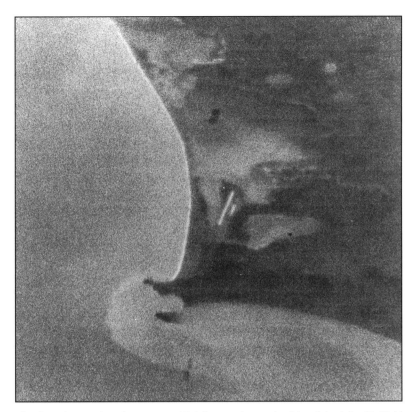

The first photo taken from space. This image shows the Mya Schmidta Air Field on the Chukchi Sea. Located close to Alaska, it was one of a number of advance bases for Soviet bombers which could be used for an attack on the United States. Due to the low resolution of the C camera, only the main runway and parking apron are visible. *National Archives*

storage facilities were spotted in Czechoslovakia, Romania, and Yugoslavia.[21] One of the few disappointments was that no Soviet ICBM complexes were observed in the *Discoverer 14* film; the ground tracks of passes 7 and 8 were on either side of the suspected site at Plesetsk.[22]

Despite the much lower resolution, 30 feet compared to 2 feet from the U-2, the quality of the film was good; photo interpreters called it "terrific" and "stupendous," and said they were "flabbergasted."[23] The only significant problem was light and dark bars running diagonally across the film. Some were due to minor light leaks, while others were caused by a type of electrostatic discharge known, ironically enough, as a "corona discharge."[24] Just as the U-2 photos were given the code name "Talent," the Corona photos were also given a special designation: "Keyhole."

Discoverer 14's voyage of exploration profoundly changed the Cold War struggle between the United States and the Soviet Union. Corona's coverage of vast geographic areas would make it possible to finally locate ICBM sites and other military installations. No longer would there be only the brief glimpse the U-2 provided; now the blanks could be filled, and the United States could *know* the size of Soviet military forces. It would take another year—and more problems—before this success was achieved, but it was finally in sight. The world had been fundamentally altered.

The Founding of the National Reconnaissance Office

While COMOR was being organized and Discoverer finally achieved success, a review of both SAMOS (the former WS-117L) and Corona was under way at the White House. On May 26, 1960, President Eisenhower met with science adviser Kistiakowsky, national security adviser Gordon Gray, and General Goodpaster to discuss the reconnaissance satellite effort. With the downing of Powers's U-2, the United States had lost its primary source of intelligence, and the reconnaissance satellite programs were not ready to take its place. It did not take Eisenhower long to decide that action was needed.

On June 10, 1960, Eisenhower directed Defense Secretary Thomas S. Gates, Jr., to form a small group to look into Corona and SAMOS, assess their ability to meet national intelligence requirements, and recommend any necessary improvements. Gates selected Kistiakowsky to make the study. During the spring and summer of 1960, Kistiakowsky and two PSAC staff members, Harry G. Waters and George W. Rathjens, worked part-time on the evaluation.

Kistiakowsky went into the study believing that SAMOS's film read-out system was too complicated to be practical. Both he and Eisenhower also shared a distrust of the Air Force. The original plan was for SAMOS to be turned over to SAC once it became operational. This would have placed the Air Force in control of both the satellite *and* interpretation of the photos. One intent of the study was to prevent the Air Force from gaining such a monopoly.

This possibility raised concerns within the Air Force, and on August 1, Kistiakowsky received calls from Undersecretary of the Air Force Joseph Charyk, Aerospace Corporation President Ivan Getting, and others. They had heard a rumor that the study group intended to recommend that SAMOS be transferred to the CIA. Kistiakowsky denied the rumor, but told Charyk that the organization should be national, and not Air Force alone. Kistiakowsky privately blamed the Air Force for the rumors, and believed they had been started to prevent any changes in the original plan.[25]

The study group's recommendations were finalized during an August 18 meeting at Cambridge, Massachusetts. (This was the same day as the launch of *Discoverer 14.*) Kistiakowsky, Waters, and Rathjens reviewed their findings with Charyk, Carl F. G. Overhage (director of MIT's Lincoln Laboratory), and Edwin Land. They agreed that reconnaissance satellites, like the U-2, were a national resource, and were too important to be controlled by a single military service or even an existing civilian intelligence agency. The group also concluded that SAMOS was suffering from management and technical problems.

The group recommended that all responsibility for Corona and SAMOS management, policy, plans, priorities, and space operations be transferred to a new office within the Defense Department. This office would have a simple and direct chain of command from the secretary of defense, through the undersecretary of the Air Force, to the general in charge of the project. The general would no longer report to or be directed by his uniformed superior. This recommendation ended satellite reconnaissance as an Air Force space mission. Its role would henceforth be limited to support—launch, orbital tracking, capsule recovery, and film processing.

A National Security Council meeting was scheduled to consider the recommendations. Bissell was briefed by the group on August 22, and Kistiakowsky discussed the recommendations with Defense Secretary Gates on the twenty-fourth. Gates gave his approval to the idea.

At 8:15 A.M. on August 25, 1960, President Eisenhower met with Kistiakowsky, Gray, Land, and George Killian. Upon entering the Oval Office, Land unrolled a duplicate reel of the *Discoverer 14* film across the carpet and announced, "Here's your pictures, Mr. President." After viewing the photos, Eisenhower directed that no satellite photo *ever* be declassified to avoid provoking the Soviets into taking countermeasures.

With the support of Eisenhower and Gates, approval of the group's recommendations by the NSC was a foregone conclusion. Air Force Secretary Dudley C. Sharp issued the organizational directives on August 31 to establish the Office of Missile and Satellite Systems. The first director was Air Force Undersecretary Charyk, while Brig. Gen. Robert E. Greer was selected as SAMOS project director. The SAMOS Project Office at the Air Force's Ballistic Missile Division in El Segundo, California, was a field extension of the Office of the Secretary of the Air Force. General Greer was to report directly to the secretary—there was to be no intermediate review within the Air Force, nor was SAC involved.[26]

The name of the new organization was soon changed to the National Reconnaissance Office (NRO). Its existence was considered so secret that even in classified documents outside the special security controls established for satellite photos and data, the words "National Reconnaissance Office" and "National Reconnaissance Program" were not to be used. Instead, the phrase "Matters under the purview of DoD TS 5105.23" would be given. (This was the directive which established the NRO.) It would be thirty-two years before the initials "NRO" were spoken in public by a U.S. government official.[27]

Not long after establishment of the NRO froze the Air Force out of reconnaissance satellite management, a second reorganization of U.S. intelligence lessened its involvement with analysis. A second study group had been established to review U.S. intelligence activities. One of the recommendations in its report, issued on December 15, 1960, was that photo interpretation activities be centralized. Eisenhower accepted the recommendation and ordered the photo interpretation sections of the Air Force, Navy, and Army be combined with the CIA's PIC. The new National Photographic Interpretation Center (NPIC) would have responsibility for analysis and distribution of the photos and the intelligence derived from them. Although run by the CIA, NPIC was to serve as a national center and draw its staff and resources from the military services. NPIC was formally established on January 18, 1961. Lundahl was named NPIC director, a role he would continue to play until the end of the Corona program.

With the founding of the NRO and NPIC, Eisenhower had completed the organizational framework of the U.S. reconnaissance satellite effort. The patterns he established have continued to this day.

Hard Times: *Discoverers 15* to *17*

During the fall of 1960, the missile gap was looming large. It was a presidential election year, and the Democratic candidate, John F. Kennedy, used the issue to attack the Eisenhower administration's defense policy. In an August speech to the Veterans of Foreign Wars, Kennedy declared, "The missile lag looms larger and larger ahead." During campaign appearances in September, he called for a step-up in ICBM production and warned that the risk of a Soviet surprise attack would grow as their missile lead increased. In November, Kennedy was the winner by a razor-thin margin.[28]

Khrushchev continued to exploit concerns over the missile gap. While at the United Nations in early October, his speeches had been a mixture of boasts and threats. His shoe-banging became a symbol of Soviet aggressiveness. Soon after his return, he claimed, "We have put missile manufacturing on a production line basis. Recently, I was at one plant and saw that missiles were being churned out like sausages from a machine."[29]

The Soviets also made explicit threats against U.S. military satellites. In an October 1960 article, Dr. G. P. Zhukov claimed, "American plans of space espionage directed against the security of the USSR and the other socialist countries are incompatible with the generally recognized principles and rules of international law, designed to protect the security of states against encroachments from outside, including outer space." He quoted Khrushchev as saying that satellite reconnaissance was "solely for a state which contemplates aggression and intends to strike the first blow. . . . The Soviet Union has everything necessary to paralyze U.S. military espionage, both in the air and outer space. . . . They will also be paralyzed and rebuffed."[30]

If the success of *Discoverer 14* showed the promise of satellite reconnaissance, the next several flights made clear that problems remained. *Discoverer 15* was launched on September 13, 1960, and went into orbit. The C camera operated properly, but while in orbit the satellite used an excessive amount of control gas. By the time the capsule was separated on the seventeenth orbit, the supply of control gas was below the minimum amount needed for the 60-degree pitch-down orientation. Reentry was successful, but the capsule came down 900 miles south of the recovery zone.[31]

Hope of finding the capsule had almost been abandoned when two search planes spotted the capsule's strobe light as it floated in rough seas near Christmas Island.[32] An amphibious plane was sent to the area, but it was unable to land and the crew dropped a floating marker. A fierce rain squall swept through the area during the night, and the next morning only the marker could be seen.[33] The sink valve had soaked through and sent the film to the depths.

The *Discoverer 16* mission carried a new payload: the C Prime camera. This was nearly identical in design to the C camera carried on the previous ten Discoverer missions, but the resolution had been improved from the 40 feet of the *Discoverer 14* photos to 30 feet.[34] *Discoverer 16* was launched on October 26, 1960, but failed to go into orbit. At liftoff, a momentary loss of power caused the "D" timer, which controlled events during launch, to stop. Due to the failure, the first and second stages did not separate, and the booster fell into the Pacific.[35]

Discoverer 17 (Mission 9012) was successfully launched through a heavy overcast on November 12, 1960. The only problem was a longer than predicted burn by the Agena's engine, resulting in an elliptical orbit.

Mission 9012 marked the start of the second phase of the Corona program. It was the first to use the Agena B second stage. It had a longer tank and a heavier payload capability.[36] This meant the mission could be extended to a second or third day, rather than the one-day operations of the earlier Discoverers. Following *Discoverer 14*'s success, a recommendation had been made to COMOR that a C Prime camera be flown aboard an Agena B second stage at the earliest possible date. This would provide both improved resolution and a more complete survey of the Soviet Union.[37]

On November 14, the Air Force announced that the *Discoverer 17* flight was being extended. Major General Ritland announced, "The vehicle is performing satisfactorily. Therefore after the thirteenth pass the decision was made to extend the duration of the test. . . . We intend to keep it in orbit for another day and then attempt recovery on the thirty-first pass."[38]

The next day, as *Discoverer 17* passed over Alaska, the ground station transmitted a signal to eject the capsule. The reentry was normal and the capsule came down directly in the 250-by-50-mile "playing field." The capsule's signals were picked up by Pelican 2.[39] The plane's pilot, Capt. Gene W. Jones, had not originally been scheduled for this mission; he was a replacement for another pilot who was on temporary duty in school. Even then, he nearly missed the recovery; his plane had to return to Hawaii shortly after takeoff with a fuel leak. He said later, "We were able to push the throttle and get out there."[40]

TSgt. Wilber R. Brown spotted the descending parachute at 31,000 feet. Pelican 2 made its first pass at 11,000 feet, but the recovery gear missed "just by a tick." On the second pass, Jones snagged the capsule at 9,000 feet. By the rules of the game, if Captain Jones had missed the second try, he would have "struck out." One of the two other planes in the area would then have been "sent to bat."[41] Jones observed that the capsule "was a little bit scorched around the edges, but otherwise in good shape." The plane was met by General O'Donnell and members of the crew's families when it landed.[42]

The medals and the trip to New York City awarded to Captain Mitchell's crew had made the other recovery crews eager for their share of the glory. As the *Discoverer 17* capsule descended, they jockeyed for position. As on a baseball field, there were (radio) calls of "I've got it" and "No, I've got it, goddammit." Alas, being number two did not count, and there were no medals for second place.[43]

On the surface, the *Discoverer 17* mission had been a success. The Agena B had shown that its systems could function for two days in space. In its postflight publicity, the Air Force noted the value of the experiments *Discoverer 17* had carried. These included a radiation counter and an emulsion pack to measure the Van Allen belts. (As a bonus, the flight had been made during a time of intense sunspot activity.) The capsule also carried a number of biological samples—artificially grown human cells, plant spores, and bacteria.

For the few people cleared for *Discoverer 17*'s real mission, however, there was only disappointment. At the start of the mission, the acetate-based film leader had broken after about twenty inches had been fed through the C Prime camera, and no photos were returned.[44]

The Debut of SAMOS

The same run of ill fortune also marked the long-delayed first launch of the SAMOS reconnaissance satellite. The initial payload was a radio-transmission camera package called "E-2." The SAMOS payload was nearly twice the weight of Corona, so the more powerful Atlas Agena booster was needed. The payload was attached to the Agena's nose and pointed down toward the Earth. The exposed film was developed on board, then scanned by a narrow beam of light, which converted the photos to electronic signals that could be transmitted to a ground station.

The advantages of near real-time transmission of the photos was clear. The SAMOS photos could be processed and transmitted on a much shorter time scale. In theory, any Soviet military moves that might indicate an attack could be spotted as they occurred. This would provide the kind of early warning that Corona could not.

With 1960 technology, it was also a very challenging mission. President Eisenhower's scientific advisers repeatedly expressed doubts on its practicality. They were also concerned about the sheer number of SAMOS payloads being developed. In addition to the E-2 radio transmission system, there was an advanced film-return version called the E-5 and a high-resolution film-return system called the E-6.[45] There were also the MIDAS missile early warning payload and SIGINT payloads under development.

A more pressing problem was the lack of any kind of cover story for SAMOS. Air Force generals, Defense Department officials, and congressmen had freely discussed SAMOS's reconnaissance mission in congressional testimony.[46] Following the loss of Powers's U-2, the Senate had increased funding for SAMOS development, over the objections of Dr. Herbert York, head of research and development at the Pentagon.[47]

The *SAMOS 1* launch was made on October 11, 1960. For an espionage project, it was conducted in a very open manner. The press was given five days' notice of the launch, a press site at Vandenberg AFB to watch the launch, and pre- and postflight briefings.[48] Nor was the satellite's purpose hidden; the fact sheet said it was carrying "photographic and related equipment." Major General Ritland was even more explicit, saying, "Through SAMOS . . . we can hurdle the Iron Curtain and peer down on our planet from the watchtower heights of space."[49]

SAMOS 1 lifted off at 12:34 P.M. PST. As the reporters watched what a *New York Times* article described as "apparently . . . the first camera-carrying vehicle to fly over Communist territory since Francis G. Powers' U-2 went down," their dominant thought was, What will Soviet Premier Nikita Khrushchev have to say about this? The launch appeared to go well, but an umbilical cable failed to separate from the Agena until after the booster had lifted off. This pulled off part of the

Agena and caused the loss of all the control gas. When the Agena engine ignited, it had no roll or pitch control and *SAMOS 1* never made it into orbit.[50]

It would be the end of the year before there was a successful Discoverer mission. It would bring back the first evidence of the greatest disaster of the space age.

Death on the Pad: The Nedelin Disaster

Discoverer 18 was launched at 12:21 P.M. on December 7, 1960. Its Thor booster had 10 percent more thrust, which allowed a heavier payload. Publicly, the capsule contained algae, bone marrow, skin samples, and film plates to test the effects of radiation.[51] Air Force officers would not comment on whether it carried a camera. They would only say that other than the biomedical experiments, the payload was classified.[52]

The following day, the Air Force announced that *Discoverer 18*'s flight was being extended by twenty-four hours. On December 9, the Air Force said the flight would remain aloft for a third day, making it the first three-day flight.[53] One article noted that "the longer the capsule remains in orbit, the more valuable information it picks up."[54] This was more accurate than the reporter knew. The ground track of each orbit was shifted to the west compared to those of the previous day, allowing the C Prime camera to photograph new areas of the Soviet Union on each pass.

On December 10, after forty-eight orbits (twenty-one over the USSR), the radio command for the capsule to separate and fire its retrorocket was transmitted. The operation was successful, and twenty minutes later the descending parachute was spotted by Captain Jones aboard Pelican 3. As the first to see it, he had first try to recover it. Jones lined up on the parachute and snagged it on the first pass. This was the first time a capsule had been recovered on the first try, and Captain Jones was the first to make two midair recoveries. As with the *Discoverer 17* recovery, he was the substitute aircraft commander—the regular pilot was in the hospital.[55]

The recovery ended the year's activities for Corona on a high note. Major General Ritland said *Discoverer 18*'s flight was "the most successful we have had in the Discoverer series. . . . The recovery after three days on orbit is very gratifying."[56] In Honolulu, an Air Force officer commented, "We're damned happy . . . two in a row recovered, 48 orbits. We ought to learn a lot from this one."[57] The biological samples carried aboard the capsule were sent to the school of aviation medicine at San Antonio, Texas, for study. The film from Mission 9013 was processed and delivered to NPIC.

The CIA was also pleased about the flight. This was the first successful mission to use both the Agena B second stage and the C Prime camera. The camera worked well and exposed the full 39 pounds of film. The image quality was as good as the best of *Discoverer 14.* The only problem was fogging on the first, second, and last frame of each pass due to minor light leaks.[58] The winter weather was a bigger problem; as with the *Discoverer 14* photos, most of the areas west of the Urals were cloud-covered.[59]

One area that did have clear weather was Tyuratam. When the NPIC photo analysts examined the Mission 9013 photos, what they saw was stunning. At the "Area C" launch complex, one of the pads was now a huge scorched area from an exploded rocket. The photos also showed there had been casualties. A close examination revealed new graves in the cemetery. This allowed a rough estimate of the number killed in the blast.[60]

What the photo analysts had seen was the aftermath of the greatest single disaster of the space age: the "Nedelin Disaster." The events had occurred nearly two months before *Discoverer 18's* launch.

On the morning of October 23, 1960, the prototype SS-7 Saddler ICBM had been rolled out to the pad. The SS-7 was a second-generation ICBM that used nitric acid and unsymmetrical dimethyl hydrazine (UDMH) as propellants. (These were storable fuels, which meant the missiles could remain on alert, ready for launch in a crisis.) On hand were Marshal Mitrofan I. Nedelin, commander of Soviet Strategic Rocket Forces; chief designer Mikhail K. Yangel; and a host of government officials, engineers, technicians, and soldiers.

As the day wore on, the highly corrosive nitric acid (which some Soviet engineers called "devil's venom") began to leak from the first stage engines. Nedelin ordered repair work to begin on the fully fueled rocket. Engineers removed the panels and began resoldering the pipe joints. It was a gross violation of the most elementary safety standards, and reflected the intense pressure Nedelin was under to get the missile launched.

The problems continued through the night and into the next day, October 24. The launch was rescheduled for 7:15 P.M. Moscow time. However, the SS-7 could only be kept fueled for forty-eight hours before the tanks would have to be drained. If they were not able to make the launch in the next several hours, it would be days before another attempt could be made. Time was running out, greatly increasing the pressure on all concerned. At the T–30 minute mark, all extraneous personnel were ordered clear of the pad. This still left some two hundred people close to the rocket.

At 6:45 P.M. Moscow time, Nedelin was discussing the latest series of problems with L. A. Grishin, a defense industry representative. They were standing only ten to fifteen meters (about thirty to fifty feet) from the missile. At that moment, a technician sent a command to reset the control system. The cable's distribution system failed, and an erroneous command ignited the second stage engines. The flames burned through the first stage tank bulkhead and ignited the fuel. The top of the rocket was engulfed by flames. Then the rocket collapsed and the rest of the propellant ignited in a huge fireball as it crashed to the pad.[61]

The technicians on the gantry never had a chance to escape and were consumed by the flames. A movie camera recorded the horror of the final moments of those on the ground. Tiny figures ran from the fireball, their clothing in flames. They stumbled and fell. Others tried to run to the vehicle shelter, but became trapped in a strip of tar that had melted from the heat. All that was left were human-shaped impressions in the tar, and bits of bone, teeth, keys, coins, insignia, buckles from gas mask straps, and the heels and soles of their boots. Others became tangled in the barbed wire fence around the pad and died there.

Nedelin was thrown by the blast against a building, then was caught by the flames. Grishin jumped over a high railing, ran across the molten tarmac, then jumped from a ramp, breaking both legs. Badly burned, he died soon after reaching the hospital. The final death toll was 165. This included not only Nedelin and Grishin, but senior military and government officials, designers, engineers, and soldiers, some only twenty years old.

The Soviet government announced that Nedelin had "died as the result of an aircraft accident." Fifty-four of the people whose deaths he had caused were unidentified; their fragmentary remains were placed in a single coffin and buried in a city park. Others were laid to rest at Tyuratam.[62] There, two months later, *Discoverer 18* would record both their resting place, and the evidence of how they died.

While the relatives and friends of those killed in the Tyuratam accident secretly mourned their dead, Washington, D.C., prepared for the incoming Kennedy administration. President-elect John F. Kennedy and those around him had very different ideas about military strategy and how military power should be used. They would inherit the reconnaissance satellite programs and the organizations to operate them that had been secretly created by Eisenhower. At the same time, Kennedy would also face an aggressive Khrushchev, who had been emboldened by Soviet space success and the perceptions in the West of great Soviet missile strength.

As Corona moved towards operational status, the Cold War would reach its coldest depths, and the promise shown by *Discoverers 14* and *18* would be realized.

FIVE

The Kennedy Administration and Corona
The End of the Missile Gap and the Start of Operations

Overnight, we went from famine to feast.
    Richard M. Bissell, Jr.

➤ The next Discoverer flight, the last launch of both 1960 and the Eisenhower administration, was a cover mission. *Discoverer 19* did not carry a capsule, but rather an infrared measurement experiment. It provided background readings for the Air Force's MIDAS early warning satellites, which were to detect Soviet missile launches by picking up their hot exhaust plumes. *Discoverer 19* was launched at 12:32 P.M. on December 20, 1960. The launch was successful, but the control gas was rapidly lost during the Agena burn, apparently due to a leak. *Discoverer 19* went into orbit, but the satellite was unstable. Despite this, about 90 percent of the data was usable.[1]

Kennedy Administration Reconnaissance Satellite Policy

On a bitterly cold January 20, 1961, John F. Kennedy was sworn in as president. But already, decisions had been made which would reshape reconnaissance policy, the role of the satellites, and the future of Corona.

Kennedy had selected Robert S. McNamara, the president of the Ford Motor Company, as secretary of defense. Later called "the human computer" by both friends and enemies, McNamara was a brilliant intellect. His brilliance was in the cognitive sense, however, not in the intuitive. He was devoted to numbers and statistics, but had no understanding of intangibles. McNamara was cold and almost devoid of emotion, believing that emotions destroyed the clarity of rational analysis. At the funeral of a former coworker, McNamara thumbed through notes for an upcoming meeting.[2]

As secretary of defense, McNamara drew upon a rising group of university strategists, civilian experts, and intellectuals. During the 1950s these academics had written extensively on nuclear strategy, developing such concepts as limited war, crisis management, flexible response, game theory, and escalation. Like McNamara, these defense intellectuals were devoted to disciplined reasoning, numbers, and analysis. But, as with McNamara, they had no room for the irrationality of human behavior. Their theories were a conscious, clinical abstraction from real life.[3]

McNamara took a top-down approach to the Defense Department, as he had at Ford. He and the small circle around him, dubbed the "Whiz Kids," would make all critical decisions—on policy, strategy, and budgets—based on concepts such as systems analysis and cost-effectiveness studies. Now all programs and activities would be initiated and micromanaged from above. This was a complete departure from all previous administrations. Prior to this, strategy and planning went upward from the individual services to the secretary of defense, with the Joint Chiefs of Staff providing an advisory role.

McNamara and the Whiz Kids did not bother to conceal their contempt for the military. McNamara behaved, as he had at Ford, like an intellectual bully, striking fear in those who failed to meet his standards of analysis. They saw themselves as "the best and the brightest," but there was a hollowness to their self-image. Often, their analyses were conducted to justify decisions they had already made.[4]

William Y. Smith, then an Air Force major on the White House staff, felt the attitude was, "If we could see it, we understand it, and if we could count it, we understand it." Just as those around McNamara gave little importance to human factors, the stress was now technical intelligence, such as that provided by Corona, at the expense of "nontangible" sources, such as human spies.[5]

Kennedy administration reconnaissance satellite policy began to take shape soon after the election. Dr. Jerome Weisner of MIT, Kennedy's science adviser, completed the "Report to the President-Elect of the Ad Hoc Committee on Space." It recommended that the publicity about U.S. reconnaissance satellites be ended. This would provide protection against Soviet charges about their "illegality." In

January 1961, McNamara and McGeorge Bundy, the assistant to the president for national security affairs, started a review of SAMOS information policy. They concurred with Weisner's recommendation, and President Kennedy and NRO Director Joseph Charyk gave final approval.[6]

The new policy of minimal disclosure was demonstrated with the launch of *SAMOS 2* on January 31, 1961. The press received only a single day's notice of the launch (rather than five days as with *SAMOS 1*), and the pre- and postlaunch briefings were eliminated. The press was still (for the moment) allowed to watch the launch. Similarly, whereas the press release for *Discoverer 19* (December 20, 1960) was seven pages long, the release for *Discoverer 21* (February 18, 1961) was only forty-five *words* long. The names of the contractors were also deleted from the abbreviated material.[7] This was to be only the first step in a gradual reduction in information.[8] Within the government, this effort went farther. In subsequent congressional testimony, Air Force officials could no longer refer to SAMOS by name or mission.

Unlike the first of the series, the launch of *SAMOS 2* was successful. Technical problems delayed the liftoff by two and a half hours, until 12:23 P.M. PST, but the Atlas Agena B then placed the satellite into a 295-by-343-mile orbit, inclined 95 degrees. *SAMOS 2* operated for nearly a month before it was shut down.[9] The results, however, were disappointing; the resolution of the few photos transmitted was only 100 to 150 feet and they were "not worth a damn."[10]

New Payloads and New Problems

With the new year and the new administration, the Corona program began to branch out into new payloads. Of the next five Discoverer missions, only one was a Corona flight.

The first Discoverer launch of the Kennedy administration saw the debut of a new reconnaissance camera—an Army-developed mapping camera code-named "Argon." Rather than high-resolution coverage of a narrow strip as provided by Corona's C Prime camera, the Argon was designed for wide area coverage at very low resolution.[11] The Argon camera had a 3-inch lens and a ground resolution of only 460 feet. It used 5-inch-square film, which covered an area of 300 by 300 nautical miles. It was designed to provide precise location data on Soviet targets.[12]

Even though the missile gap controversy remained unresolved, Argon was judged nearly as high a priority as Corona. With the deployment of U.S. Atlas and Titan I ICBMs, accurate mapping data had become critical. Without it, the missiles might not strike their targets. The location of Moscow was known within a mile, but for targets east of the Urals, the accuracy of location data fell to fifteen to thirty miles. The United States was still relying on pre-Revolution surveys, World War II data, and defector reports. On U-2 and early Corona photos, mapmakers looked for the old Tsarist survey towers to pinpoint locations.[13]

Following the *Discoverer 14* mission, a recommendation had been sent to COMOR that an Agena B with an Argon be flown as soon as possible after the launch of an Agena B with a C Prime camera.[14] President Eisenhower had given his approval, and the Corona schedule had been changed.

Discoverer 20 was fitted with the first Argon camera. It was also the first to attempt a four-day flight, the longest to date. The first try at a launch, on February 10, 1961, was cancelled when the Agena's pitch gyro showed excessive drift. The second, a week later on February 17, experimented with a novel approach to deal with the continuing train problem. At T–83 minutes, a hold was called and the countdown was advanced to T–15 minutes, in an attempt to launch before trains entered the hazard area. This was not successful, however, and the launch was not made until 12:25 P.M.

The satellite reached orbit, but the rest of Mission 9014A (the "A" suffix standing for Argon) was a bust. During the first several orbits, there were transient variations in the pitch and yaw, and the output from the horizon scanner was irregular. These eventually cleared up on their own. Much more serious, however, was the failure of the Argon camera; there were no shutter firings. The final blow came when the Agena's orbital timer and/or the S-band radio beacon failed on the thirty-first orbit.[15] This prevented the capsule recovery, and on February 21, the Air Force announced the attempt was being called off.[16]

The failure of *Discoverer 20* marked the start of another bad streak, which would last through the spring. The next launch, *Discoverer 21* on February 18, 1961, was another cover launch, with an infrared measurement package in place of the camera and capsule. The launch had to be held up for 195 minutes so the overlap of the orbital tracks of *Discoverer 20* (launched the day before) and *Discoverer 21* would be minimized. The launch was successful. During its first pass, *Discoverer 21* restarted the Agena's engine. The brief 1.05-second burn added 350 feet per second to the satellite's velocity. This experiment was conducted as part of the MIDAS program. A network of eight or more MIDAS satellites would be placed in polar orbits to keep watch for Soviet missile launches. Periodic engine burns would be needed to maintain the spacing of these satellites. Reconnaissance satellites could also use this method to correct for orbital decay due to atmospheric drag, or to take evasive action should the Soviets attempt to attack them.

After a promising start, the *Discoverer 21* flight came to a premature end. On the ninth pass, its 400-cycle inverter failed.[17]

The first Corona mission of 1961 was *Discoverer 22*, launched on March 30. It was fitted with a C Prime camera. The Thor booster lifted off successfully, but the Agena suffered a hydraulic failure, which caused the engine to move uncontrollably. The Agena underwent violent attitude changes and *Discoverer 22* did not reach orbit.[18]

The next two Discoverer launches, Missions 9016A and 9018A, both carried Argon cameras. *Discoverer 23* lifted off successfully on April 8, 1961. The Argon camera worked, but the Agena did not. On the ninth orbit, the control gas valve on the side opposite the Sun failed, possibly due to the extreme cold. The escaping gas caused the satellite to tumble, then spin. When the attempt was made two days later to recover the capsule, the Agena was wobbling. When the retrorocket fired, it was pointed in the wrong direction and the capsule was boosted into a higher orbit.[19]

Two months later, on June 8, the launch of *Discoverer 24* saw a singular act of courage. At T–30 seconds before launch, a light in the blockhouse indicated that one of six pins in the launch platform had failed to retract. A hold was called and two cars drove out to the pad. As amazed news reporters watched from 4,000 feet away, five men got out of the cars. Two of them, Warren Dolezal, the Douglas Aircraft pad control man, and Air Force MSgt. Robert Gillham walked to the base of the rocket. The Thor was fully fueled with 47,000 gallons of RP-1 kerosene and 7,000 gallons of liquid oxygen. Only the day before, an Atlas ICBM had exploded on the pad, and the memory of the huge fireball was in the reporters' minds as they watched. The switch was removed without mishap, and the men returned to the blockhouse.

Alas, their efforts were in vain. The Thor lifted off successfully, but at T+144 seconds, while the Thor's main engine was still burning, all telemetry from the Agena was lost. Subsequent analysis indicated the

2,000-cycle power supply had failed. Also, abnormally high temperatures were noted in the Agena's engine section, indicating a fire. The Agena separated, but its engine did not ignite and *Discoverer 24* impacted a thousand miles downrange.[20]

The Berlin Crisis

As the Corona satellites were in the midst of this bad streak, the Kennedy administration was under pressure from Khrushchev. In January 1961, shortly before Kennedy took office, Khrushchev had made a foreign policy speech in which he had reiterated a threat first made in November 1958: the Western Powers must end their occupation of West Berlin or the Soviet Union would take unilateral action. Khrushchev had also announced Soviet support for "national liberation wars" in the Third World. During the first months of the Kennedy administration, most attention was focused on such trouble spots as Laos, South Vietnam, the Congo, and Cuba.[21]

Meanwhile, the missile gap controversy continued to dog the intelligence community. One of the first things McNamara did after being sworn in as defense secretary was to look at the Corona photos. For several hours a day for several weeks, he and Deputy Secretary Roswell L. Gilpatric went over the photos. Although the data from *Discoverers 14* and *18* were limited, what they saw convinced them, like Eisenhower before them, that the Soviets did not have nuclear superiority.

McNamara's conclusion became public at his first press conference on February 6, 1961, which he thought was to be off the record. The first question asked was whether there was a missile gap. McNamara responded that "there were no signs of a Soviet crash effort to build ICBMs" and that no missile gap existed. This offhand remark sent the reporters running for the telephones. The *Washington Evening Star* headlined the story, "McNamara Says No Missile Gap." Two days later, Kennedy denied that any conclusion had been reached, as the issue was still under study.[22]

While American efforts in early 1961 were directed toward Soviet surrogates in the Third World, Khrushchev was laying the political groundwork for moves against West Berlin. East German leader Walter Ulbricht had been pressuring Khrushchev for years to take stronger action on West Berlin. Ulbricht was a difficult ally—more Marxist than Khrushchev, and with an attitude of superiority that endlessly irritated the Soviets. At one point he asked that Soviet workers be sent to East Germany to replace the workers fleeing to the West. Khrushchev bluntly told him that considering the horrors inflicted on the USSR by Nazi Germany during World War II, he was not going to send Soviet workers to clean East German toilets.[23]

In early 1961, facing a new U.S. administration, Khrushchev felt the time was right to force the issue of West Berlin. He told Ulbricht that the Soviet Union would soon put a man into space. This would give the Soviets a position of unchallenged strength and prestige, he said, and force the West to give in to its demands.[24] This was accomplished with the launch of *Vostok 1* on April 12, 1961. Aboard was Maj. Yuri Gagarin, who made one orbit of the Earth before landing safely. The shock in the West rivaled that of the launch of *Sputnik 1* four years before.

Five days later, a brigade of Cuban exiles sponsored by the CIA landed at the Bay of Pigs. The total failure of the Cuban invasion further worsened relations between the Joint Chiefs of Staff and the Kennedy White House. Kennedy's advisers blamed the military for the failure, while the Joint Chiefs felt that Kennedy's last-minute changes to the plan were the cause. Dulles and Bissell were soon forced to resign, the U.S. government was in disarray, and Khrushchev saw Kennedy as weak and indecisive.

On June 3 and 4, Kennedy and Khrushchev held a summit meeting in Vienna, Austria. Kennedy was given a virtual ultimatum over West Berlin: the Soviet Union would sign a unilateral peace treaty with East Germany by December 31, 1961. This would end the legal status of the Allied forces in the city and threaten the independence of West Berlin itself.

Since the start of the Cold War, defense of West Berlin had been the symbol of the U.S. commitment to Europe. It was widely believed that if the United States backed down on the issue of West Berlin, then its commitment to defend Western Europe would no longer be of any value. But if the United States and NATO tried to use force to open the road to Berlin, Khrushchev made clear, it would be considered an attack on the Soviet Union. The West was faced with either an ignominious retreat or nuclear war.[25]

Central to the Berlin crisis was the question of Soviet missile forces. On June 7, 1961 (three days after the Vienna summit ended), the CIA issued another National Intelligence Estimate on Soviet missile forces. As before, it showed deep divisions and uncertainties in the intelligence community. The CIA estimated that there were fifty to one hundred operational Soviet ICBMs; the Navy said there were only ten or fewer, while the Air Force estimated three hundred. With the failure of the Discoverer satellites during the first half of the year, there remained no way to settle the question.[26]

Throughout the summer of 1961, the threats and pressure continued. Khrushchev announced a one-third increase in Soviet defense spending on July 8. The United States responded on July 18 by formally warning the Soviets that it would defend its rights in Berlin.

President Kennedy followed this on July 25 with a televised speech. He called Berlin "the great testing place of Western courage and will. . . . We cannot separate its safety from ours." Kennedy also announced an expansion of U.S. forces, a $3.5 billion budget increase, and a larger civil defense program.[27] Many Americans were not waiting—the morning after Kennedy's speech, phones at bomb shelter companies began ringing. Nobel Prize winner Linus Pauling declared it futile: "A full-scale nuclear attack would probably kill everybody, whether or not fallout shelters had been built."[28]

On August 6, the Soviets underlined their lead in space by launching Maj. Gherman Titov aboard *Vostok 2*. He spent a full day in space before returning to Earth. At the Moscow reception on the ninth, the Soviets explicitly linked the flight and their Berlin ultimatum. Titov said that the Soviet Union had the power to "crush an aggressor should the enemies of peace launch another war," while Khrushchev spoke of 100-megaton nuclear weapons and the rockets to carry them.[29]

This was followed, on August 13, by the building of the Berlin Wall. This barrier halted the flood of refugees traveling from East Germany into West Berlin—thirty thousand in July and another twenty thousand in the first twelve days of August. "The Wall" became the brutal symbol of the division of Europe, and transformed West Berlin into an isolated enclave. The United States was powerless to halt its construction.

Two weeks after the wall went up, on August 31, the Soviets announced that they were breaking the three-year moratorium on nuclear testing. Bombs of 20 to 100 megatons were to be tested. The statement blamed the West's "threatening attitude" over Berlin, while Khrushchev said he wanted to shock the West into negotiating on Berlin and disarmament.[30] The following day the first nuclear test was made.

On September 8 and 9, 1961, Khrushchev demanded that the West accept the German peace treaty and complete East-West disarmament as the price for ending the Berlin crisis. On the tenth, the Soviets increased the pressure by announcing they would begin ICBM tests into the Pacific. The first ICBM test, on September 13, coincided with two nuclear tests. The second ICBM test, on the eighteenth, was also orchestrated with a megaton-yield nuclear test on the Arctic island of Novaya Zemlya.[31]

As the Soviet testing continued, newspapers began carrying radiation readings along with the weather report. As the summer ended and children returned to school, it was clear they were also being affected by the fear of nuclear war. An Atlanta elementary school teacher noted that children were now drawing pictures of mushroom clouds and burning cities.[32]

By early September it seemed that the West was on the defensive. Khrushchev seemed in control of events. But perceptions can be wrong, and things are not always as they seem.

The End of the Missile Gap

At 4:03 P.M. on June 16, *Discoverer 25* was successfully launched from Pad 1 at Vandenberg AFB, breaking the string of problems which had plagued the program since the start of the year. It went into an orbit of 140 by 250 miles, inclined 82.1 degrees. The Air Force announcement said that it carried radiation experiments, micrometeorite counters, and samples of common and rare metals to study the effects of space flight. It also carried a C Prime camera, which operated successfully throughout the thirty-three orbit mission, exposing the entire load of film.[33]

The capsule was deorbited on June 18, but the reentry was inaccurate and the capsule came down north of the recovery zone. One of the C-119s spotted the floating capsule about 350 miles northeast of Hawaii and radioed for divers. Three men from the 76th Air Rescue Squadron, TSgt. Leote M. Vigare and SSgts. William V. Vargas and Ray E. McClure, parachuted from an SC-54 search plane. They pulled the capsule into a twenty-man life raft to await rescue. An amphibious plane tried to fly out to them, but darkness fell before it could reach them, and the plane had to turn back. The three divers and the capsule were forced to remain on the open ocean overnight. They were finally picked up the

The SS-7 ICBM complex at Yurya. It consists of four sites with two pads each. The complex was built in a forested area for security against ground observation. The SS-7 made up the majority of the early Soviet missile force, most in soft, above-ground sites such as these. *National Archives*

next morning by the USS *Radford*.[34] The three divers were presented with Air Medals the following day by General O'Donnell.[35]

The film from Mission 9017 was processed and sent to NPIC for analysis. As the photo interpreters examined the film, it was clear how valuable a cargo the three divers had protected. The weather over the Soviet Union had been perfect. The Trans-Siberian railroad and areas west of the Urals were free of cloud cover. The photo interpreters found the first Soviet ICBM sites—still under construction. Also discovered were a number of medium range ballistic missile (MRBM) sites.

The *Discoverer 25* flight had finally brought the four-year quest to an end. At long last, the U.S. *knew* the size of the Soviet missile force. David S. Doyle, one of those involved in analyzing the *Discoverer 25* film, said years later, "It was an exciting time. . . . Every pass in those days was a new event."[36]

A revised National Intelligence Estimate, "Strength and Deployment of Soviet Long Range Ballistic Missile Forces," was issued on September 21, 1961. The second paragraph of the conclusions announced the official end of the missile gap:

We now estimate that the present Soviet ICBM strength is in the range of 10–25 launchers from which missiles can be fired against the U.S., and that this force level will not increase markedly during the months immediately ahead. We also estimate that the USSR now has about 250–300 operational launchers equipped with 700 and 1,100 n.m. ballistic missiles. The bulk of these MRBM launchers are in the western USSR, within range of NATO targets in Europe; others are in southern USSR and in the Soviet Far East. ICBM and MRBM launchers probably have sufficient missiles to provide a reload capability and to fire additional missiles after a period of some hours, assuming that the launching facilities are not damaged by accident or attack.

The Corona photos had shown three Soviet ICBM complexes under construction. They were at Yurya and Yoshkar-Ola, several hundred miles northeast of Moscow, and at Verkhnyaya Salda in the Urals. A fourth site at Kostroma, also in the Urals, showed clearings that might indicate the start of construction of a pair of pads.

The Yurya site, which was the most complete, consisted of eight pads in four pairs at various states of completion. Each of the four launch complexes was identical to those at Area C at Tyuratam, used for tests of the SS-7 ICBM. The sites were concealed from ground observation by locating them in remote forested areas and surrounding each complex with a double fence. Although defended by SA-2 SAMs, the complexes were judged highly vulnerable to attack, as the pads were above ground and separated by only three or four miles. A single large nuclear blast could damage all four complexes.

The satellite photos also indicated the probable history of the ICBM deployment effort. The Yurya complex was started in the fall of 1959, at the same time as Area C at Tyuratam (a full year before the first SS-7 test launch). The CIA's best estimate was that Yurya would be completed in early 1962. The complex at Yoshkar-Ola was many months behind Yurya, while both Kostroma and Verkhnyaya Salda were still in the early stages of construction. The CIA believed that each SS-7 complex took about two years to build.

The evidence on the suspected SS-6 ICBM site at Plesetsk was still limited. Although the CIA had evidence dating back to 1957 that Plesetsk was an ICBM site, the area was still poorly covered by the Corona photos. The Plesetsk complex was larger than Yurya, with SAM sites, several large support areas, and housing for between five thousand and fifteen thousand personnel. The presence of ICBM launch pads had not been confirmed, however.

In all, the CIA estimated that more than half the probable areas of Soviet ICBM deployment had been covered by the Corona photos. The coverage also gave an indication of the reliability of defector reports and other sources. Of the five sites, Yurya, Plesetsk, and Verkhnyaya Salda had been previously suspected as ICBM sites; Yoshkar-Ola and Kostroma had not. Conversely, a number of suspected ICBM sites had been shown by the Corona photos *not* to contain sites. (This included an area thought to be the most likely.)

By the summer of 1961, only four suspected ICBM deployment areas had still not been covered by Corona photos. Based on the experience with the five confirmed ICBM sites, it was believed that some or all of these areas might prove negative, while other, unsuspected ICBM sites might still be undiscovered. The National Intelligence Estimate concluded, "It is extremely unlikely, however, that undiscovered ICBM complexes exist in areas on which there is recent KEYHOLE photography of good quality."

The Corona photos also clarified the deployment of Soviet MRBMs. About fifty fixed sites with a total of about two hundred pads were spotted in a belt stretching from the Baltic to the southern Ukraine. These covered NATO targets from Norway to Turkey. Because the sites were always paired, another ten sites hidden by scattered clouds were known to exist. Allowing for areas not covered, the CIA estimated that there were about seventy-five MRBM sites with three hundred pads in this western belt. Approximately three-quarters were operational; some were still under construction, while the status of others was ambiguous.

On less firm information, another fifty MRBM launchers were believed to be operational in the Transcaucasus and Turkestan, where they could hit targets from Suez to Pakistan, and in the Soviet Far East within range of Japan, South Korea, and Okinawa. The estimate noted that "very recent KEYHOLE photography confirmed several sites in Turkestan and north of Vladivostok in the Soviet Far East." The MRBM sites were located in wooded areas, protected by fences and SA-2 SAMs, and were "soft" above-ground targets. The three different site configurations resembled launch areas at the Kapustin Yar test center.

Given the "strong if not fixed views" over Soviet ICBM forces, it was not surprising that there were disagreements over the new estimate. The Air Force assistant chief of staff for intelligence believed that the Soviets had about fifty ICBMs operational. The assistant chief of naval operations (intelligence), on the other hand, objected that "evidence of ICBM deployment at Plesetsk is indeterminate but that, in the aggregate, it points against such deployment."[37]

One of the reasons given for the Air Force conclusion reflected a misunderstanding that had plagued the whole missile gap debate: "The USSR's current aggressive foreign policy indicates a substantial ICBM capability." The Air Force felt it could not be just a bluff. Yet that is exactly what Khrushchev had done.

The original SS-6 site at Plesetsk had fallen behind schedule and gone over budget, due to the extreme weather conditions and swamps at the site. Shortcomings in the SS-6 itself—the short range, slow reaction time, and cumbersome size—also prevented large-scale deployment. In 1958, Khrushchev ordered SS-6 deployment be limited to Plesetsk. He also gave approval to develop the SS-7 and SS-8 ICBMs, which were smaller, lighter, faster-reaction, and longer-range ICBMs that used simpler launch complexes. Until the SS-7 complexes were ready, Khrushchev used Soviet space achievements to project the image of great missile power.[38]

Khrushchev had gambled that the United States would not discover how few ICBMs the Soviets really had. Thanks to Corona, the gamble had failed. It was time to call his bluff.

Corona and the Berlin Crisis

Corona had revealed the yawning gap between Soviet and U.S. nuclear forces. In addition to their tiny ICBM force (later revealed to be a mere six missiles), the Soviets had about 190 Tu-95 and Mya-4 bombers, as well as roughly thirty Zulu, Golf, and Hotel ballistic missile submarines, carrying a total of about ninety missiles. In contrast, the United States had seventy-eight Atlas and Titan I ICBMs, eighty Polaris missiles aboard five submarines, and 1,526 B-52, B-47, and B-58 strategic bombers. While the Soviets could deliver at most some three hundred nuclear weapons against U.S. targets, the United States could strike back with nearly seven thousand weapons.[39]

As the scale of the real missile gap became apparent, so did its relationship to the Berlin crisis. Carl Kaysen, McGeorge Bundy's deputy at the NSC, wrote a memo that said the United States did not have to worry about Berlin; the disparity in nuclear forces was so great that the United States had the Soviets "over a barrel" and could do anything it wanted.[40] Although Bundy thought this was too "ferocious," there was a stiffening in the U.S. position on Berlin.

On September 25, a column by Joseph Alsop was published in the *Washington Post*. Titled "Facts about the Missile Balance," it began:

> Mixed but broadly encouraging results have been obtained by recent, exceedingly careful recalculation of the probable nuclear striking power of the Soviet Union. The most cheerful of these results is a sharp reduction in the number of intercontinental ballistic missiles with which the Soviets are credited. . . .
>
> Prior to the recent recalculation, the maximum number of ICBMs that the Soviets were thought to have at this time was on the order of two hundred—just about enough to permit the Soviets to consider a surprise attack on the United States. The maximum had now been drastically reduced, however, to less than a quarter of the former figure—well under fifty ICBMs, and therefore not nearly enough to allow the Soviets to consider a surprise attack on this country.

The Alsop column concluded with a veiled warning to the Soviets: "For the present, what is chiefly important is to make Khrushchev understand that if he pushes the Berlin crisis to the ultimate crunch, the great power that the United States still possesses will not remain unused." The column was an obvious leak intended to unofficially let the Soviets know their bluff was being called.[41]

Khrushchev soon realized it was time to fold. At the end of September, he told Belgian diplomat Paul-Henri Spaak, "I realize that contrary to what I have hoped, the Western Powers will not sign the peace treaty. . . . I'm not trying to put you in an impossible situation; I know very well that you can't let yourself be stepped on." He concluded by saying, "I am not bound by any deadline." This was made official on October 17 at the twenty-second Party Congress; Khrushchev announced, "The Western Powers are showing some understanding of the situation and are inclined to seek a solution. . . . If that is so, we shall not insist on signing a peace treaty absolutely before December 31, 1961."[42]

Although the Berlin crisis was over, the crisis atmosphere, like the Soviet nuclear fallout, lingered. Khrushchev had dropped the deadline, but he announced that the Soviets would proceed with tests of a 50-megaton superbomb. His continued bullying made it clear that the Soviets would have to be *officially* served notice that the United States had nuclear superiority, knew it had superiority, and would not be intimidated by empty bluffs. There had originally been discussions of having the U.S. ambassador actually show the Corona photos to Khrushchev, but the more traditional approach of using a high-level policy speech was eventually used. As part of the preparation of the speech, NPIC made a comparison of U.S. and Soviet nuclear forces.

On October 22, Deputy Secretary of Defense Gilpatric spoke before the Business Council of Hot Springs, Virginia. It was an obscure place for so important a message. Gilpatric bluntly warned that the United States "has a nuclear retaliatory force of such lethal power that an enemy move which brought it into play would be an act of self-destruction on his part." There was also a cryptic reference to Corona. He noted that while the Soviets had attempted to use rigid security measures as a military weapon, "their Iron Curtain is not so impenetrable as to force us to accept at face value the Kremlin boasts."[43] The following day, Secretary of State Dean Rusk appeared on the "Issues and Answers" television program. He underlined Gilpatric's message, calling it "well-considered" and adding, "We are not dealing . . . these days from a position of weakness."[44]

Although the Soviets continued a campaign of pressure on the West, it rang hollow. Now, with the bluff exposed by Corona, the Soviets were in the position of a bully trying unsuccessfully to impress others with his power. On October 23, the Soviets tested a 25-megaton nuclear weapon in the Arctic, while Soviet Defense Minister Rodion Malinovsky threatened Western Europe, "It would take really very few multimegaton nuclear bombs to wipe out your small and densely populated countries and kill you instantly in your lairs!"

On October 27, the East Germans closed the Berlin Wall at Checkpoint Charlie and for sixteen hours U.S. and Soviet tanks faced each other. They were muzzle to muzzle with cannons loaded. For those hours, World War III seemed imminent; all it would take was a single round fired in error or panic. Finally, the Soviet tanks backed off and the crisis was over for the moment.[45]

On October 30, the Soviets detonated a 58-megaton nuclear weapon. Both the pressure and the nuclear testing continued, but by December the crisis atmosphere was all but over. The Soviets had been frustrated in their attempts to force the Western Powers out of Berlin, and had lost the prestige built up over the previous four years.

Corona had played a central role in the successful end of the Berlin crisis. The photos from *Discoverers 25, 26,* and *30* provided the Kennedy administration with two things beyond price: information and confidence. The Corona data had a marked influence on the White House discussions over the Berlin crisis, and how the crisis was viewed. The photos also gave the U.S. government the confidence to stand up to Soviet demands. Even though the information was limited, without Corona the level of confidence in their actions would have been far, far less.[46]

During the Berlin crisis, Corona served a role akin to that of the Ultra project, which broke Nazi German codes during World War II. Ultra had not only told Allied political and military leaders what the Germans were going to do, but gave them the assurance the information was reliable. Similarly, Corona gave Western leaders the assurance that Khrushchev was bluffing, and that the estimates of a small Soviet ICBM force were reliable. Just as Ultra had changed the course of World War II, Corona had changed the conduct of the Cold War.

Continuing Operations: *Discoverers 26 to 31*

Discoverer 25's success was quickly followed up with the launch of *Discoverer 26* on July 7. The Air Force announcement said it carried samples of silicon, iron, bismuth, yttrium, magnesium, nickel, lead, and uranium, as well as radiation and micrometeoroid experiments.[47] The *New York Times* article on the launch said it "probably carries . . . secret gear being tested for future photographic and missile-detection satellites."[48]

Discoverer 26's C Prime camera failed on the twenty-second orbit, but not before about three-quarters of the film was exposed.[49] The radio signal from the Kodiak ground station to begin the recovery sequence was transmitted on the satellite's thirty-second orbit, and fifteen minutes later, the descending parachute was spotted by one of the C-119 recovery planes. Capt. Jack R. Wilson caught the capsule at 15,000 feet on the first try. After the capsule was aboard, Wilson went back to take a look at it before it was put into the container. The capsule was sent to Lockheed, while the Mission 9019 film was analyzed at NPIC.[50]

By mid-July 1961, a total of seventeen camera-carrying Discoverers had been launched. Only four missions—*Discoverers 14, 18, 25,* and *26*—had returned usable film, yet they had provided coverage of some thirteen million square miles of the Soviet Union—nearly half the total area of interest.

Following the twin successes, another bad streak began. On July 21, *Discoverer 27* lifted off Pad 4. Mission 9020A carried the fourth Argon camera, but it had no better luck than its predecessors. Immediately after liftoff, the flight control system experienced a pitch oscillation, which began to increase in amplitude. At T+61 seconds, the booster was enveloped by flames, and it exploded at T+79 seconds. Most of the debris impacted 13,000 feet downrange.[51]

Discoverer 28 suffered a similar fate when it was launched on August 3. As Mission 9021, it carried a C Prime camera. The Thor was successful, but at T+398 seconds, the Agena's hydraulic pressure began to drop. Hydraulic control was lost, the Agena tumbled, and its engine shut down 18.5 seconds early. The satellite did not reach orbit.[52]

The next flight saw the first major upgrade of the Corona camera system. This was the C Triple Prime camera. It was the first camera built entirely by Itek and included a number of major improvements. On the C and C Prime cameras, the lens assembly swung back and forth like a clock pendulum, which adversely affected the Discoverer's stability. On the C Triple Prime, the lens assembly made a complete circle.[53] An exposure was made during part of its rotation. It also used an f/3.5 Petzval lens, rather than the f/5 Tessar of the earlier cameras. (Focal length remained 24 inches in all the Corona cameras.) The larger lens allowed slower film to be used, resulting in twice the resolution (12 feet compared to 25 feet with the C Prime).[54] The camera also had a new film transport mechanism, greater flexibility in camera and vehicle operations, and improved image motion compensation. The last prevented blurring of the pictures from the satellite's orbital motion.

Discoverer 29 was launched on August 30 with the first C Triple Prime camera and a 39-pound roll of film. Seconds after lifting off, the booster disappeared into a low fog, but instruments soon showed that the satellite had reached orbit and was operating successfully.[55] The following day, the Air Force announced that no decision had been made on when the capsule would be brought down.[56] The capsule was finally deorbited on September 1, after two days and thirty-three orbits. It came down about 120 nautical miles north of the recovery zone, and three divers had to parachute into the water to pick it up. Within forty minutes, they had the capsule secured in a raft and were awaiting the arrival of the USS *Epperson*.[57]

When the film from Mission 9023 was examined there was disappointment—the full film load had been exposed, but every frame was out of focus. The problem was traced to the scan head.[58] While redesign work was under way, the next two Discoverer flights reverted to the C Prime camera, with mixed results.

Discoverer 30 was successfully launched on September 12. The Air Force said the primary aim was improving control of the orbital period, thereby increasing the accuracy of the reentry capsule's impact prediction.[59] As with the previous satellites, *Discoverer 30* remained aloft for two days. The capsule separated on the thirty-third orbit and was caught in midair by a JC-130B cargo plane piloted by Capt. Warren C. Schensted.[60]

This was the first use of this new plane by the recovery squadron, and represented a vast improvement in speed, range, and safety. The old C-119s, inherited from the Genetrix program, were never adequate for so demanding a mission. They were a "two-engine aircraft flying in a four-engine ocean." It was only through the experience of the aircraft commanders, each of whom had served in Korea and had over 4,000 hours of flight time in the C-119, and the outstanding maintenance work by the ground personnel that the 6593rd was able to avoid any fatal accidents.

The conversion to JC-130Bs had taken several months. Capts. Gene W. Jones (the operations officer) and Thomas F. Hines were the first to undergo training with the planes. They completed ground school and simulator training at Sewart AFB, and flew their check rides at Edwards AFB. The other pilots were then trained to fly the new planes. The first three JC-130Bs—aircraft numbers 27, 28, and 29—were transferred from Sewart (although "dumped" might be a better word, as the unit was getting new planes). Aircraft number 28 had suffered a wing fire; it was fitted with a replacement wing, but did not fly

JC-130B recovery aircraft making a practice recovery over the Pacific Ocean. Captains Gene W. Jones and Thomas F. Hines completed C-130 training in June 1960, and in September the JC-130s began to arrive. During the summer of 1961, recovery checkout was under way, with the first recovery made in September 1961. *U.S. Air Force photo via Col. Thomas F. Hines*

quite right. By October 1961, two more new JC-130Bs, numbers 62 and 63, were delivered and the nine C-119s were retired.[61]

On September 17, only three days after *Discoverer 30*'s capsule was recovered, *Discoverer 31* went into orbit. Two days later, however, the satellite did not respond to the separation command, due to the failure of the Agena's 400-cycle power supply. The following day, radio contact was lost.[62]

The Continued Problems of SAMOS

While the Discoverer satellites had finally achieved success, the SAMOS program continued to have problems. It was not until late summer that the next launch attempt could be made. The *SAMOS 3* fact sheet gave as its mission, "continued component testing to establish the feasibility of obtaining an observation capability from an orbiting satellite."[63] The launch was attempted on September 9, but the Atlas Agena B suffered an electrical failure and exploded on the pad.[64]

The fourth SAMOS launch was made under a new information policy. The satellite was "unidentified"—there was no prelaunch notification, nor was the satellite named. Twenty minutes after its launch on November 22, 1961, a brief Air Force statement was issued, saying only that an Atlas Agena B booster had been successfully launched and that it carried "a number of classified test components." The booster did not reach orbit, however. The Atlas D lost pitch control at T+244 seconds, and the Agena was pointed down and back during its burn.[65]

The fifth SAMOS launch (also unidentified) was made on December 22, 1961. The Agena reached orbit, but the E-2 camera system failed.

Fade to Black

In the wake of the Berlin crisis, the Soviets resumed their political attacks on U.S. reconnaissance. On November 6, the newspaper *Ekonomicheskaya Gazeta* denounced U.S. military activities in space. The article raged that the United States was "littering the cosmos," "not taking into account the needs of other countries," and "setting up an elaborate system of cosmic military intelligence, communications and navigation." It continued, "Actually, this is banditry on an international scale. . . . It should be dealt with as humanity has always dealt with this vice in all countries. Banditry should be outlawed."[66]

Unlike SAMOS, Discoverer launches were still identified by name (although the "scientific satellite" cover story was still used). Discoverer was also undergoing a cutback in public information, however.

The continued Soviet propaganda attacks, as well as the Kennedy administration policy of restricting information about military space activities, meant Discoverer would soon fade into the shadows.

Corona in the Shadows
The End of Discoverer and the Politics of Secrecy

A satellite employing a Thor Agena B booster combination was launched today by the Air Force from Vandenberg Air Force Base. The satellite is carrying a number of classified test components.

Text of the Air Force statement on the launch of Corona mission 9032, April 17, 1962

➤ Despite the *Discoverer 3* mouse flight, the material and biological tests, and the infrared experiments of *Discoverers 19* and *21*, the CIA knew that the "scientific satellite" cover story was worn out. The continuing failures of the SAMOS radio-transmission satellites also meant that the "interim" Corona had been transformed into an operational system. There were plans for between eighteen and twenty-four launches per year into the indefinite future. This, along with the Kennedy administration's policy of increasing secrecy on military launches, meant the end of the Discoverer program was near.[1]

The End of Discoverer

Discoverer launches continued through the fall of 1961. *Discoverer 32* was orbited on October 13 and was successfully recovered in midair the following day by a JC-130 flown by Captain Schensted (his second in a row).[2] The redesigned C Triple Prime camera functioned properly, and Mission 9025 was judged a success.

Discoverer's erratic history continued with the next two missions. *Discoverer 33* was launched on October 23, 1961, but when the Agena's engine ignited, the hydraulic pressure fell to an abnormally low value.

For 11 seconds, the Agena was violently unstable, but then the hydraulic pressure rose back to normal, stabilizing the vehicle. After 160 seconds, however, hydraulic pressure was lost again, the Agena began tumbling, and the engine shut down. The Agena, carrying the last C Prime camera, reentered over the Pacific without reaching orbit.[3]

Discoverer 34 and its C Triple Prime camera payload were successfully placed in orbit on November 5. During the launch, the Agena engine burned too long, placing it into a higher-than-normal orbit. On the ninth pass, it suffered a complete loss of control gas, which prevented a recovery attempt.[4]

While the camera problems that had beset Corona in the early years of the program had largely been solved, it was now the Agena that was the source of failures. Of the Discoverer missions of 1961, three (*Discoverers 21, 24,* and *31*) had suffered Agena power supply problems, three (*Discoverers 22, 28,* and *33*) had hydraulic failures during launch, and two more (*Discoverers 23* and *34*) had lost their control gas. Several of the failures were traced to the static electronic inverters, which converted the battery's direct current into the various alternating current voltages to power the subsystems. Although half the weight and double the efficiency of rotary inverters, they had a high failure rate in ground tests. An intense development effort was started to solve the problems.

Despite the continued difficulties, there was a lighter side to Corona operations in 1961. When a quality assurance inspector was removing the film from one of the recovered capsules, he discovered an unusual "payload": two quarters and a buffalo nickel. They had been put in the capsule by project personnel at Vandenberg AFB. The CIA headquarters program office sent a strongly worded message to the West Coast program office telling it to halt the souvenir-launching.[5]

The year ended on a positive note, with two successful flights. *Discoverer 35* was launched on November 15 and completed eighteen orbits before its capsule was recovered in midair above Tern Island in the central Hawaiian Islands chain.[6] The recovery plane was flown by Capt. James F. McCullough, but due to the cutback of information released to the press, the *New York Times* article about the flight did not list the pilot's name.

Discoverer 36, which followed on December 12, was the final attempt at a cover launch. In addition to a C Triple Prime camera, Mission 9029 carried the OSCAR I (Orbiting Satellite Carrying Amateur Radio) subsatellite. It was built by radio "hams," and transmitted a series of Morse code dots that spelled out "hi." OSCAR I was ejected from the *Discoverer 36*, and its signals were picked up by ham radio operators in Antarctica and Alaska on the first orbit.[7] The radio transmitted for eighteen days, and its signals were picked up in seventeen countries.

Discoverer 36 stayed aloft for a record four days and sixty-four orbits. The midair recovery attempt missed, and three Air Force divers parachuted into the Pacific to recover the capsule. They secured it in a raft and were picked up by the USS *Renshaw*.[8] The photos were rated the best to date.

Discoverer 37 was to have been launched on January 12, 1962, but a payload problem delayed it a day. When the satellite was launched on the thirteenth, it was yet another case of an Agena failing to reach orbit. An electrical short at separation caused a loss of power to the attitude control gyros. At Agena engine ignition, the vehicle began to tumble. The engine shut down after 10.6 seconds.

Discoverer 37 carried the last C Triple Prime camera. The Corona payload was about to undergo a major advance.[9]

The Mural Camera: Reconnaissance in Stereo

The final Discoverer mission, number 38 in the series, marked the debut of a new camera. The original C camera had been used because it was a readily available design when Corona began in early 1958. Although its basic design had been greatly improved over the three years of Discoverer flights, it had a serious shortcoming: the C-series camera could take only monoscopic (two-dimensional) photographs.

A major development effort had been under way during 1961 to develop a stereoscopic camera, designated "Mural" or "M." The contract for the M camera was formally issued on August 9, 1961, retroactive to March 20. The first production systems were ready by the first of the new year.

The M camera consisted of a pair of C Triple Prime cameras, mounted with the rear one pointed forward at a 15-degree angle, and the forward camera pointed aft, also at 15 degrees. Two 40-pound rolls of film were carried in a double spool cassette. The two film rolls were fed separately into the cameras, exposed, and then fed into a double-spool take-up reel inside the capsule. The M camera would photograph each area twice. The forward-pointing camera would take the first exposure of a specific area, then about a half-dozen frames later, the aft-facing one would again photograph the same area.

When the two frames were properly aligned in a stereoscope, the results were magical. Rather than a flat image, the photo interpreter had a three-dimensional view. Buildings towered up at the viewer, while a bridge seemed suspended above a riverbed. The image had the appearance of a finely detailed model. The first time one saw the effect, there was the urge to touch it. Although the M camera had only a slight improvement in resolution over the C Triple Prime (10 feet vs. 12 feet), its stereo imagery vastly improved the photo interpreters' ability to spot and identify new facilities.

Another improvement of the M camera was in pinpointing the location of targets on the ground. This required the photo interpreter to know what area on the Earth's surface was covered on each frame, the scale of the photos, and the angle of the exposure relative to the ground. To determine this information, the photo interpreter needed to know the location of the satellite in its orbit, and how it was oriented in space. With the C camera series, this had been provided by using the orbital path and the camera firing sequence, combined with horizon photos on every other frame taken by a pair of horizon cameras. With the M camera, an index camera was added. This took a small-scale photo of the same area covered by the two panoramic cameras. When combined with the orbital data, the index photo simplified matching the panoramic photos with the terrain. After a few flights, a stellar camera was also added. This took a photo of a star field. When combined with the images from the two horizon cameras, there was a much more precise measurement of the satellite's orientation in space.

The first M camera was launched aboard *Discoverer 38*, which lifted off on February 27 on a four-day flight. The new camera functioned properly, but the reentry on March 3 had a unique problem. The first indication was noticed by the recovery pilot, Capt. Jack R. Wilson, as the capsule descended under its parachute. He recalled later that it had a different glint. After the capsule was caught in midair and reeled aboard the JC-130, the crew discovered that the heat shield was still attached to the bucket. It should have separated before parachute deployment, but in this case it had failed.[10]

On this note, the Discoverer program ended. Out of the thirty-eight launches, twenty-five had reached orbit. Of the twenty-three attempted capsule recoveries, thirteen had been successful: eight in midair, four more from the ocean, and the Soviet recovery of the *Discoverer 2* capsule on Spitzbergen Island. Of the recovery pilots, there was a three-way tie for the most recoveries between Captains Jones (*Discoverers 17* and *18*), Wilson (*26* and *38*), and Schensted (*30* and *32*). Captains Mitchell and McCullough each had one recovery. (Although McCullough would later make a second Corona recovery, *Discoverer 14* was Mitchell's only success.)

Discoverer was no more. Corona continued, however, in the shadows.

The Politics of Secrecy

On March 23, 1962, Deputy Defense Secretary Roswell Gilpatric signed a memo that tightened the security procedures surrounding military space activities. Drawn up by NRO Director Charyk, it finalized the trend towards greater secrecy. According to the memo, all future military space activities were to be classified Secret. This extended not only to reconnaissance satellites, but also to such previously nonsensitive activities as communications or navigation satellites. No longer were specific programs to be identified by name, nor were launches to be identified, nor were any persons to be identified as being with any specific program.

Rather than names, the memo directed that program numbers be used for space projects. Discoverer became Program 162; the SAMOS radio-transmission E-2 payload, Program 101A; the SAMOS film-return E-5 camera, Program 101B; and the high-resolution E-6 film-return payload, Program 201. The Corona cameras were also retroactively given Keyhole numbers. The C camera was renamed the KH-1; the C Prime, KH-2; the C Triple Prime, KH-3; and the new M camera, KH-4. The Argon mapping camera was designated the KH-5. (The KH-1 through -3 cameras were no longer being flown.)[11]

The public information policy was spelled out by Arthur Sylvester, the assistant secretary of defense for public affairs, on November 21, 1962. Launches and the booster used would be announced, but the payload would not. If the booster exploded on the pad or within sight of land, this would be announced, along with a statement that "an investigation is under way to determine the cause." If the failure occurred out of sight, no statement would be made. Later, after the mission was over, the orbital parameters would be registered with the United Nations.[12] The U.S. government ceased to officially acknowledge that it undertook space reconnaissance.

The new policy sparked opposition both within and without the U.S. government. The State Department believed that openness would serve to legitimize satellite reconnaissance better than secrecy. The newly created Arms Control and Disarmament Agency (ACDA) was also pushing proposals for advance notification of both satellite and missile launches, and an inspection of all satellite payloads to enforce a ban on orbital nuclear weapons. ACDA Director William C. Foster argued that secrecy made the U.S. activities look bad, and that advance notification would build confidence and be an important step in arms control.[13]

The press also objected to the secrecy. *Rockets and Missiles* magazine noted that the Soviets had the ability to track military satellites.[14] A *Flight International* editorial complained, "This secrecy prevents world scientists from studying the orbits and so learning new facts about the structure of the high atmosphere."[15]

Such objections had no impact on President Kennedy, the NRO, or the military. Blanket secrecy on military satellites would deny the Soviets information on the capabilities and limitations of the satellites, as well as preventing them from realizing how open they were to satellite reconnaissance. They also believed that flaunting the satellites' ability to cover the whole of the Soviet Bloc from space, or even acknowledging they were doing so, could provoke the Soviets into attacking them.

Corona in the Shadows

The thirty-ninth Corona was the first launched under the new secrecy policy. Mission 9032 went into orbit on April 17, 1962, but ran into problems. The telemetry link was lost, forcing an early return of the capsule on the thirty-fifth orbit. The bucket was successfully air-recovered on April 19 by Maj. James A. Brewton.

Corona flight 40 (Mission 9033), launched on April 28, was a success until literally the last moment. The reentry was successful, but the parachute failed to eject and the capsule was lost.

A pair of successful missions came next. The first of these, Corona flight 41 (Mission 9034A), was particularly significant. Launched on May 15, it was the first successful Argon/KH-5 flight. Over the previous fifteen months, four of the mapping cameras had been flown without success. This time, the satellite remained aloft four days before the capsule was successfully recovered by Captain Hines.

Hines later noted the recovery was a fluke. His plane had originally been scheduled to be the backup recovery plane (number 2). After takeoff, a crewman reported a problem with a door, which prevented pressurization. Due to this malfunction, another plane was given the more critical number 2 position, and Hines was switched to number 5, in the outfield. As it turned out, however, the capsule came down long, right over Hines's plane. As the parachute descended, it "slipped" around, moving erratically from side to side. Hines's first two tries were unsuccessful, meaning he had struck out, but due to his location, he had no backup. He caught it on the third attempt. After the capsule was aboard, Hines went back to take a look. He found the crew cutting off pieces of the parachute as souvenirs. He stopped them and told them that the chute must be returned with the capsule and would be examined.

This successful flight was followed on May 30 by a KH-4 Corona flight (Mission 9035), which remained in orbit for two days, ending with a midair recovery by Major Brewton. This was his second successful recovery, and he was now in a four-way tie for most recoveries with Jones, Wilson, and Schensted.

The forty-third Corona flight (Mission 9036), launched on June 2, was not so fortunate. After its June 5 reentry, the capsule parachute was torn during the midair recovery attempt, and it was lost at sea.

Having suffered several runs of failures, Corona now began a string of successes. Between June and August, Corona flights 44 through 49 were launched. All six carried KH-4 cameras, and all six were successfully recovered in midair.

Corona flight 45 (Mission 9038), a three-day flight launched on June 28, was the first to use the Agena D. It was more powerful than the Agena B, and unlike the earlier model, the Agena D was built on a production line, rather than by hand. The Agena D would go on to serve both civilian and military space missions for the next quarter of a century. The Agena D would be phased in over the next several months.

The string of successful flights was broken by Argon mission 9042A, the fiftieth Corona flight (launched September 1). After four days in orbit, its capsule sank in the Pacific.

Despite this setback, Corona regrouped and the next six missions were all successes. The first two, Corona flights 51 and 52, carried KH-4 cameras. Corona flight 53 (Mission 9046A) was the year's third KH-5 mapping flight, launched on October 9, 1962. Corona flight 54, launched on October 26, did not carry a capsule, but rather was an engineering flight to measure radiation from a July 9, 1962, high-altitude U.S. nuclear test.

The next two flights carried KH-4 cameras. The fifty-fifth Corona was orbited on November 5, 1962. Corona flight 56 (November 24) had two distinctions: it was the last Corona flight to use an Agena B, and it was the first to stay aloft for five days.

The successful streak was broken by Corona flight 57 (Mission 9049), launched on December 4, 1962. Yet again, it ended with another lost capsule. The final Corona launch of 1962 ended the year on an upbeat note, however; Mission 9050 (December 14) was a success.

During 1962, a total of twenty-one Corona missions had been launched—one with a KH-3 camera, three with KH-5s, and the rest with KH-4s. There were only five failures: *Discoverer 37* did not reach orbit, and the capsules from Corona flights 40, 43, 53, and 57 were lost. Despite the problems, the trend of the program was encouraging. Now it was the failures that were the exceptions, not the successes.[16]

By the end of the year, the success of the secrecy policy was clear. Reports of the launches diminished in number and size. A *New York Times* article on the December 4, 1962, launch of Mission 9049 read: "A secret satellite, believed to be a Discoverer, was launched today. The Air Force gave no details as to the type or mission."[17] Observers were reduced to a guessing game, attempting to identify flights based on the boosters and the satellites' orbits. The attempt was made more complicated by the belief that the radio-transmission SAMOS flights were continuing.

Attention now shifted to giving the Corona a high-resolution capability that would rival that of the U-2.

Lanyard, the High-Resolution Corona

The history of the Corona program was interwoven with that of the WS-117L/SAMOS. The program was started because the WS-117L would not be ready in time to deal with the emerging missile gap. The continued problems with the SAMOS radio-transmission E-2/Program 101A camera transformed Corona from an interim stopgap into an operational system. Program 101A was cancelled in 1961, with the sixth and final E-2 launch made on March 7, 1962. Although the Atlas Agena B reached orbit, the camera payload failed yet again.

Launch of Corona flight 59 on January 7, 1963. The Agena carried a KH-4 camera payload. Unlike the Discoverers and early Corona flights, the larger KH-4 required a cylindrical camera bay. (The KH-1 through KH-3 cameras were mounted in a conical fairing behind the capsule.) *U.S. Air Force photo*

The cancellation of Program 101A was not the end of SAMOS, however. It was a multirole satellite, with the E-6/Program 201 intended to provide high-resolution photos. Rather than using radio transmission, the photos would be returned to Earth in a capsule. Unlike Corona, it did not have a separate retrorocket on the capsule. Instead, the Agena B's engine would restart to deorbit the capsule. The E-6 camera was apparently a panoramic design with a 24- to 36-inch focal length lens and a resolution of 8 feet.[18] Six Program 201 launches were made between April and November 1962. The capsules from the first and last were (reportedly) successfully recovered, but Program 201 was cancelled in 1962.[19]

As the Program 201 satellite was running into problems, there was a pressing need for a higher-resolution satellite. Starting in 1960, construction of suspected antiballistic missile (ABM) sites had been observed around Leningrad. By 1962, there were thirty sites, complete with hardened bunkers for the launchers.[20] To settle the issue of whether these were part of an ABM system, the U.S. intelligence community needed photos with better resolution than Corona could provide.

To fill this short-term need, there would not be time to develop a new camera system. The only possibility was to adapt the SAMOS E-5 film-return camera for use on Corona. This interim high-resolution system was approved and work began. The SAMOS E-5 camera was given the code name "Lanyard" and the designation KH-6. Lanyard had a 66-inch focal length lens and used a mirror that swung through a 30-degree angle to provide stereo panoramic coverage. The KH-6 had an 8,000-foot supply of 5-inch-wide film. The expected resolution was 2 feet—comparable to that of the U-2.[21]

Because of the Lanyard camera's greater weight, a new booster was required. The Thor was refitted with three small solid-fuel boosters. The first mission to use the Thrust Augmented Thor (TAT) Agena D booster was the sixtieth Corona launch. The satellite was equipped with a KH-4 camera. The first launch attempt was made on February 27, 1963, but had to be cancelled due to a problem with the solid booster circuitry. Mission 9052 was pushed back a day, lifting off at 1:48 P.M. on February 28 from Pad 5. The flight was in trouble from the start. Solid motor number 2 did not ignite at liftoff and did not separate as planned at T+70 seconds. The added dead weight caused a loss of control at T+100 seconds, followed by vehicle break-up at T+127 seconds.[22]

Launch of Corona flight 60 on the first TAT/Agena D. The three solid rocket boosters increased the orbital payload for later launches. The TAT/Agena became standard for the middle years of Corona operations. The payload for this unsuccessful flight was a KH-4 package. *U.S. Air Force photo*

Despite the loss of the booster, the first Lanyard launch was scheduled for the next flight. Due to the new payload, the Lanyard flights were given mission numbers in the 8000 series (rather than 9000 as the Corona was using). The launch of the sixty-first Corona was made on March 18, 1963, but a short circuit at separation caused the Agena to lose pneumatic control. The Agena tumbled and its engine shut down. Mission 8001 impacted in the Pacific.[23]

In the wake of the Lanyard failure, the new DCI, John McCone, met with President Kennedy at Palm Beach on April 15, 1963. McCone proposed that the A-12 Oxcart aircraft make overflights of the Soviet Union to photograph the sites. With a top speed of over Mach 3 and a reduced radar signature, he said, the plane would be undetectable and unstoppable. Kennedy was unwilling to authorize any overflights, however, and expressed hope that satellites could be improved instead.[24]

The second Lanyard mission, aboard Corona flight 64, was beset by problems. The first two launch attempts, on May 7 and 8, 1963, were cancelled due to high-speed upper-air winds, while the third attempt, on the seventeenth, was aborted due to questions about the primacord used to separate the Agena. It was finally launched on May 18, on the fourth try. Mission 8002 reached orbit, but the payload power was never switched on. The capsule was recovered from the ocean after thirty-two orbits on May 20, but the Lanyard camera had never been activated.[25]

The third and, as events turned out, last Lanyard launch was made on July 31. Corona flight 68 reached orbit successfully, but after thirty-two orbits, the camera failed.[26] When the photos were examined, it was found that the Lanyard camera had a serious lens focus problem, later traced to thermal factors. The resolution was also far poorer than expected—6 feet rather than the design goal of 2 feet. This was apparently due to a problem with the motion compensation system.[27]

The problems with the Lanyard could have been solved, but it would have taken considerable time and money. The Corona cameras already had a resolution of about ten feet, near to that of Lanyard, and the improvement in resolution was not significant enough to justify the effort to make Lanyard work. There was no point in duplicating what already existed.[28]

Furthermore, on July 12, 1963, shortly before the third Lanyard mission, an Atlas Agena D had orbited the first of a new generation of high-resolution satellites. This was an Air Force–developed system with the code name "Gambit." The camera had a reported resolution of 18 inches and was designated KH-7. Three more Gambit launches followed, in August, September, and December 1963. With the success of the Gambit satellite and the new KH-7 camera, Lanyard (always intended to be an interim system) became redundant.[29] At the same time, the Soviets halted construction of the Griffon missile sites around Leningrad. The Griffon was subsequently judged by U.S. intelligence to have been an ABM, but with such a marginal capability that the Soviets soon abandoned it.[30]

Corona Operations in 1963

During 1963, while the three Lanyard missions were taking place, standard Coronas continued to be flown. The first Corona launch of 1963 was the fifty-ninth flight. Launched on January 7, 1963, it carried a KH-4 camera. The capsule was brought down on January 11; the midair attempt was unsuccessful, but it was safely recovered from the ocean.

The unsuccessful first TAT and first Lanyard mission were followed by Corona flights 62 and 63. The first was a KH-4 mission launched on April Fools' Day, 1963. Despite the rather inauspicious date, the mission was a success. Corona flight 63 did not fare as well, however. It carried a KH-5 mapping camera and was launched on April 26. During the Agena's burn, there were problems with the horizon sensor and it did not reach orbit.

Following the second Lanyard launch (flight 64), there were three more KH-4 missions. Corona flights 65 through 67 were all successful. Corona flight 68 was the third and final Lanyard launch, while flights 69 and 71 were the first flights of the standardized, definitive Corona spacecraft using the new KH-4A/B cameras. (These flights and the new system will be described in the next chapter.)

Of the remaining five flights of 1963, Corona flights 70 and 72 were KH-5 missions launched on August 29 and October 29, respectively. Both were successfully recovered in midair: one by Captain Walter M. Milam and the other by Capt. Richmond A. Apaka, his first of three recoveries. (Apaka had also been Mitchell's copilot on the *Discoverer 14* recovery.)

Corona flights 73 and 74 both carried KH-4 cameras and both were failures. The first, launched on November 9, lost its main engine flame shield at liftoff. This exposed the control system wiring to excessive heat, resulting in the Thor going out of control at T+134 seconds. The failure of Corona 74, launched on November 27, was reminiscent of some of the early Discoverer problems. When the separation command was sent on its eighty-third orbit on December 1, the capsule did not eject.

The year 1963 ended on an upbeat note with Corona flight 75. It was orbited on December 21, and remained aloft for eighty-one orbits. The capsule was recovered in midair the day after Christmas.[31] Corona 75 was the last flight of a KH-4 camera.

There had been a total of seventeen Corona missions in 1963, of which six were failures. The year saw a proliferation of payloads, with nine KH-4s, three KH-5s and KH-6s, and two advanced camera systems. In the future, the Corona payloads would be standardized with the new cameras; the KH-4 and KH-6 cameras had been phased out, and only two more KH-5s would be launched.

Despite some problems, like the launch of the second Lanyard, the countdowns and midair recoveries were becoming more "clock-like" during 1962 and 1963. This was not to say the program had become boring; one of the KH-4 water recoveries was an adventure. The capsule had come down a thousand miles from the planned impact point. It then turned upside down in the water, which blocked the beacon signal. The capsule was only recovered thanks to an alert observer who spotted the reflection of the Sun on the gold-plated bucket.[32]

The Corona and Gambit operations of 1963 established the basic pattern of U.S. satellite operations for the next decade and beyond. The area-survey Corona would spot new targets, then the high-resolution Gambit would be launched to provide a detailed examination.

The success of Corona made it clear the future of strategic reconnaissance was with satellites, rather than with aircraft. By February 1964, McCone had abandoned any remaining hopes that the A-12 could be used for overflights of the Soviet Union. The Soviets had deployed a new radar code-named "Tall King." This radar was equipped with a computer that could identify the weak, fast-moving return from the A-12. Although the plane was still thought to be impossible to intercept, it was no longer undetectable.[33] This made it politically impossible for the president to authorize missions over the USSR. Although the A-12 would later make overflights of North Vietnam and North Korea, these were tactical missions, rather than the strategic role originally envisioned for it.

The Influence of Corona, 1962–1965

Corona photos continued to make their presence felt within the U.S. government following the Berlin crisis. One area where they had an effect was in sizing U.S. nuclear forces. The Kennedy administration had to decide how many Minuteman ICBMs and Polaris submarines to build. This in turn was influenced by the estimates of the future Soviet missile force. Following the end of the missile gap controversy, White House aide Carl Kaysen wrote a memo saying that McNamara's planned numbers were too high in light of the CIA estimate. A large U.S. missile force, he wrote, would cause the Soviets to build up their own forces, accelerating the arms race. The Corona photos were successfully used to limit the number of Minuteman ICBMs deployed to one thousand, and fewer Polaris submarines were funded than originally planned.[34]

Starting in 1962, the Corona photos were also used for nuclear targeting. Corona photos provided the first accurate coordinates of Soviet military facilities. This resulted in a shift in U.S. policy. During the 1950s, little was known about the location of Soviet military bases. The lack of information was reflected in the first joint SAC–RAF Bomber Command strike plan. The plan, which went into effect on October 1, 1958, assigned 106 Soviet targets to the RAF bomber force: 69 cities, 17 airfields, and 20 air defense targets. A full two-thirds of the targets were cities. This disparity was even greater with the unilateral RAF strike plan. If Great Britain should be forced to attack alone, ninety-eight Soviet cities would be bombed.[35]

On August 1, 1962, a revised joint plan went into effect. The changes, which reflected a full two years of Corona operations, were profound. The RAF Thor IRBMs and bomber force would strike forty-four "offensive capability" targets such as airfields, ten "defensive capability" targets such as air defense control centers, twenty-eight Soviet IRBM sites, and only sixteen cities. Urban targets had gone from the majority to next to last in number. The unilateral British plan also underwent a similar change.[36]

This shift toward strikes on military targets, made possible by Corona, was outlined by McNamara in a June 1962 speech at the University of Michigan. He said that, in the event of nuclear war, the "principal military objectives . . . should be the destruction of the enemy's military forces, not of his civilian population." This became known as "city avoidance."[37]

. . .

Unlike the Corona satellites' central role in the Berlin crisis of 1961, they had little involvement in the Cuban missile crisis a year later.[38] One reason for this was the sporadic nature of the Corona launches. Because of the long interval between launches, and the delay between taking the pictures and their analysis, Corona lacked the flexibility for a fast-breaking situation like Cuba. They were unable to provide daily, up-to-the-minute information. The nonmaneuvering, short-lived Corona satellites would also have had difficulty covering a specific small area on the island. The Cuban missile crisis was the first indication of the limitations of satellite reconnaissance.

The Cuban missile crisis grew out of the Soviet failure in Berlin, Khrushchev's perception that Kennedy was weak, and the continued U.S. sabotage operations against Cuba, which the Soviets convinced themselves were the build-up to a U.S. invasion of Cuba. A *nuclear* defense of Cuba, Khrushchev believed, was the only way to prevent a U.S. attack.

The forty thousand Soviet troops sent to defend Cuba in "Operation Anadyr" were equipped with tactical nuclear weapons—twelve 2-kiloton warheads for Frog short-range artillery rockets; eighty SS-C-1 Samlet antiship missiles, each with a 5- to 12-kiloton warhead; and six Il-28 light jet bombers, each with a 6-kiloton bomb. The Frog missiles could be used to strike troops on the invasion beaches, the SS-C-1 missiles to destroy the invasion fleet at sea, and the Il-28s to attack embarkation ports in Florida. The local Soviet commander, Gen. Issa Pliyev, was initially given authority to use them as a last resort if Cuba was invaded.

Khrushchev came to see Cuba as a quick solution to his other problems. The Cuban missile force consisted of twenty-four SS-4 launchers with thirty-six missiles, and sixteen SS-5 pads with twenty-four missiles. The SS-4 could strike targets throughout the eastern and southern United States with 200- to 700-kiloton warheads, while the SS-5s could deliver slightly larger 200- to 800-kiloton weapons to the rest of the continental United States. This tripled the number of missiles the Soviets could deliver against U.S. targets, potentially limiting the ability of the United States to retaliate.

Khrushchev intended to announce the missiles' existence, with Fidel Castro by his side, during a triumphant visit to Cuba in mid-November. In that stunning moment, Khrushchev believed he would gain back all that had been lost. The U.S. lead in missiles and bombers would be countered, Cuba would be secure, and the island could then serve as a base for sparking communist revolutions throughout South and Central America.

The plan was bold, aggressive, and ill-conceived. It required the missile sites to be built in secret. Soviet Presidium member Sharaf R. Rashidov assured Khrushchev that palm trees would make the missiles undetectable, but he had no military background and no understanding of the large amount of equipment needed for each site. Although hidden from ground observation, they were totally exposed to aerial reconnaissance. On October 14, 1962, a U-2 overflight was made over an area of suspected missile deployments. The photos showed several SS-4 sites under construction.

The discovery of the missiles led to a split between the Joint Chiefs of Staff and the White House over how to deal with them. The JCS saw both the missiles and Castro as military threats that had to be removed. From Corona, they knew the United States had overwhelming nuclear superiority, and could force a successful outcome. They did not believe that the USSR would go to war over Cuba. Accordingly, the JCS recommended massive air strikes and an invasion of Cuba.

McNamara, Bundy, and many of Kennedy's civilian advisers dismissed the missiles as militarily unimportant. However, they were seen as a *political* threat, both to U.S. stature and to the administration's domestic standing. They agreed the missiles had to go, but Castro was another matter. The main danger, they believed, was not the missiles themselves, but that the situation could get out of hand, leading to nuclear war. The advisers recommended a blockade of Cuba, renamed for political reasons a "quarantine." McNamara made it clear to Chief of Naval Operations Adm. George W. Anderson, Jr., that this was "not a blockade but a means of communication between Kennedy and Khrushchev." No ship was to be fired on without his specific permission, and that would not be given without discussions with President Kennedy.

The Cuban missile crisis ended with a face-saving compromise. If the missiles were removed, the Soviets were told, the United States would promise not to invade Cuba. This was coupled with a secret understanding that the United States would remove its Thor and Jupiter IRBMs from England, Italy, and Turkey. Although Castro's survival was now protected, Khrushchev's irresponsible adventure sealed his own doom. Two years later, he would be forced from power.

The failure of the JCS and Kennedy's advisers to understand their differences in perceptions had a lasting impact. The stature of the JCS fell further. Kennedy listened to his civilian advisers and ignored the military. The Cuban missile crisis cemented the administration's belief that military force was a means of sending "signals." As such, the actions had to be tightly controlled, with approval for each step coming from the president himself. It was the logical extension of McNamara's management style and the Whiz Kids' theories. These would soon be put to the test in Vietnam.[39]

Improvements in U.S.-Soviet relations such as the "hot line" and the Limited Nuclear Test Ban Treaty influenced U.S. perceptions of future Soviet missile force levels. McNamara and Rusk became convinced that the Soviets had accepted the "rational" idea of a "finite deterrent."[40] This belief was reinforced by the continued lag in Soviet missile forces.

At the end of 1962, Corona photos showed between eighty and eighty-five missiles at about seventeen Soviet ICBM complexes. More than a dozen of the sites were for SS-7s, with as many as sixteen pads per complex. The single SS-6 complex at Plesetsk had four pads, while the few remaining sites were for the SS-8 ICBM.[41] In contrast, the United States had 294 ICBMs. In 1964 most of the twenty-six Soviet ICBM complexes were "soft" above-ground facilities, which could be destroyed by a single nuclear warhead. Less than 20 percent were "coffin" pads, in which the missile was stored horizontally within a concrete bin, giving limited protection against a nuclear blast. It was not until 1964 that construction of the first hardened underground silos was observed at Soviet missile fields.[42]

The long lead time needed for deployment reinforced the perception that the Soviets had chosen to deploy only a limited nuclear force. From the Corona photos, U.S. intelligence analysts knew it took up to two years to build an ICBM complex. Thus, as soon as the first excavation was spotted in the Corona photos, the photo interpreters could predict when the new complex would be operational. The analysts could count how many ICBMs were now operational, estimate how many there would be in the future, and detect any sudden changes. This only served to bolster the idea that because the United States could count the Soviet missiles, it understood the Soviet Union. Disillusionment would come by degrees.

The National Intelligence Estimates (NIEs) issued between 1963 and 1965 reflected the belief in a limited Soviet missile force. NIE 11-8-63 said flatly that the Soviets had "no well-defined strategic concept," were "willing to tolerate a condition of limited intercontinental capabilities and considerable vulnerability over a long period of time," and were not "seeking to match the United States in numbers of delivery vehicles." It concluded that "the Soviets will continue improving their capabilities, but at a moderate pace."[43] NIE 11-4-63 added, "The Soviets would almost certainly reason that the US would detect an effort of such magnitude, and that they could have no assurance of winning the intensified race that would ensue."[44]

The authors of NIE 11-8-64 stated, "We do not believe that the USSR aims at matching the United States in numbers of intercontinental delivery vehicles." The estimate "ruled out this option" based on economic limitations, fears over provoking the United States into a new arms race, and the lack of any Soviet mid- to long-range strategic goals. Despite the start of test flights in December 1963 of a large third-generation ICBM, the SS-9 Scarp, and construction of a new class of ballistic missile submarines, the estimate concluded that there would not be any large-scale or determined build-up of Soviet forces.[45]

The authors of NIE 11-4-65 added, "We think that the Soviets probably will continue to seek ways to curtail the arms race in a moderate degree by 'mutual example.'" These mutual examples were "unilateral, uninspected moves by both sides."[46] NIE 11-8-65 warned that such "unilateral" restraint had to be mutual. The estimate proposed that "the large U.S. ICBM force almost certainly influences the USSR to increase its force, and U.S. deployment of ballistic missile defenses might incline them towards even higher numbers." Yet, at the same time, the estimate concluded that the Soviets "would probably judge that if they appeared to be acquiring as many ICBMs as the U.S. they would simply stimulate a further arms race."[47]

Although the NIEs were classified Top Secret, McNamara made numerous public statements based on their conclusions. In an April 1965 interview published in *U.S. News and World Report,* McNamara said, "The Soviets have decided that they have lost the quantitative race, and they are not seeking to engage us in that contest. It means there is no indication that the Soviets are seeking to develop a strategic nuclear force as large as ours."[48] McNamara continued that "the possibility of error is materially less than it has been at many times in the past because of the improvement of our intelligence collection methods."[49]

Corona and Space Law

Soviet objections to U.S. orbital reconnaissance continued following the Berlin crisis. On December 11, 1961, the First (Political) Committee of the U.N. General Assembly passed a resolution extending the life of the dormant Committee on the Peaceful Uses of Outer Space (COPUOS). The committee was directed to continue its efforts to establish the rules of conduct for space activities.[50]

When COPUOS met in Geneva in May and June of 1962, the Soviet delegation submitted a highly restrictive draft declaration on basic principles. It restricted space activities to states only, banning private enterprise in space, and included a paragraph which had the effect of giving the Soviets veto power over any Western space activities that might "hinder" the use of outer space. Paragraph 8 stated: "The use of artificial satellites for the collection of intelligence information in the territory of foreign States is incompatible with the objectives of mankind in its conquest of outer space."

The issues were debated before the First Committee of the General Assembly in December 1962. When Albert Gore, Sr., the U.S. representative, said that "observation from space is consistent with international law, just as is observation from the high seas," the Soviet COPUOS delegate, Planton D. Morozov, made a sweeping response:

> We cannot agree with the claim that all observation from space, including observation for the purpose of collecting intelligence data, is in conformity with international law. . . . Such observation is just as wrong as when intelligence data are obtained by other means, such as by photographs made from the air. The object to which such illegal surveillance is directed constitutes a secret guarded by a sovereign State, and regardless of the means by which such an operation is carried out, it is in all cases an intrusion into something guarded by a sovereign State in conformity with its sovereign prerogative. Thus such observations are in violation of the sovereignty of States, and no analogy exists here with principles applying to the open seas. . . . For these reasons we consider that the activities involved are incompatible with the provisions of the United Nations Charter.[51]

U.S. and Soviet delegates resumed private talks in the spring of 1963, in hopes of finding some compromise. But on April 16, the Soviets announced that they were breaking off the discussions, and would submit a new eleven-point proposal. This new draft text also included a ban on satellite reconnaissance. The COPUOS discussions were again deadlocked.

The first hint of a change in the Soviet position came in early July 1963 at a picnic on the Dnieper River between Khrushchev and Belgian Foreign Minister Paul-Henri Spaak. Khrushchev was in a jovial mood as they discussed a ban on all nuclear tests. He argued that on-site inspections were not needed to detect underground nuclear tests. Then he added, "Anyway, that function can now be assumed by satellites. Maybe I'll let you see my photographs."

What had been an off-the-cuff comment became official Soviet policy two months later. On September 9, 1963, the new Soviet COPUOS delegate, Dr. Nikolai T. Fedorenko, gave a speech that failed to make any mention of reconnaissance satellites. Soon after, the Soviets dropped their objection to private companies in space. By December, agreement had been reached on the other issues, including a ban on orbital nuclear weapons. The "Declaration of Legal Principles Governing the Activities of States in the Exploration and Use of Outer Space" established both freedom of space, and, by omission, the legality of orbital reconnaissance.

Khrushchev made another reference to satellite reconnaissance—and its role in policing arms control agreements—on May 28, 1964. He was interviewed by William B. Benton, a former U.S. senator and chairman of the board of Encyclopedia Britannica. During their discussions about Cuba, Khrushchev said that the United States should halt its "provocative" overflights of Cuba. Benton quoted Khrushchev as saying that U.S. reconnaissance satellites were adequate to determine if Soviet missiles were on the island, and that they were much less provocative. Khrushchev added, "If you wish, I can show you photos of your military bases taken from outer space." Finally Khrushchev jested, "Why don't we exchange such photos?"[52]

With the Soviets dropping their objections to satellite reconnaissance, a mutual Open Skies policy was established. The uncertainties of the 1950s were gone, and now there could be confidence and stability. This, in turn, opened new possibilities for arms control, although it would be nearly a decade, and the eve of Corona's end, before that was accomplished.

The Issue of Control: The Struggle Between the NRO and CIA

As Corona became operational, control of reconnaissance satellite activities emerged as a contentious issue. McNamara sought to centralize control of all Department of Defense (DoD) policies and activities. One symbol of this was use of Program Evaluation and Review Technique (PERT) charts. These were spiderweb-like diagrams in which each step in a development program was laid out, with details as to how much each would cost, how long it would take, and how it affected the others. They were based on the assumption that the unknown could be planned, that innovation could be scheduled, and that the process was more important than the product.[53] The PERT charts gave the Whiz Kids control.

When McNamara looked at the satellite program, he found a strange little group of a few Air Force and CIA officers. It was highly decentralized, with a great deal of personal initiative and a close partnership between the managers and contractors. They used none of the management techniques he was forcing on DoD. The management of Corona was everything McNamara opposed, did not understand, and saw as bad government. He decided it had to be brought to heel.[54]

The opening McNamara used was the power vacuum left at the CIA after the Bay of Pigs. DCI Allen Dulles, DDCI Charles Cabell, and Richard Bissell were all forced to resign following the invasion's failure. When Bissell left in February 1962, there was a major reorganization of the CIA's reconnaissance program. The Development Projects Division of the Directorate of Plans, which had responsibility for the U-2, A-12 Oxcart, and Corona, was transferred to the new Directorate of Research headed by Herbert "Pete" Scoville. Although he worked well with NRO Director Charyk, Scoville lacked the standing Bissell had from his previous work with the U-2 and Corona.[55]

McNamara made his attempt to have DoD take over the satellite programs when Charyk was replaced as NRO director by Brockway McMillian on March 1, 1963. It was McMillian's job to implement McNamara's policy. The NRO was to have control, with the CIA to take orders, rather than being an equal partner. McNamara told the new DCI, John McCone, that the CIA should only define requirements for satellites, analyze the film, and do a little research; DoD, and not the CIA, should develop the satellites.

McCone was undecided whether the CIA should actively contest McNamara and McMillian, or should go along with their efforts at control. Ultimately, Roswell Gilpatric, who had a close personal relationship with McCone, was able to convince him to concede financial responsibility for CIA programs to the Air Force undersecretary.

Scoville was astonished by the agreement. After a year of indecision and frustration, Scoville resigned in protest. McCone asked Albert D. "Bud" Wheelon to replace Scoville. Wheelon had joined the CIA in June 1962 as assistant director for scientific intelligence. This was initially an analytical position, but he had spent the previous decade as an engineer at TRW working on ICBM and satellite programs. He quickly became involved in the debate over control of satellite activities, and had served to "backstop" Scoville in the struggle with the NRO. Wheelon respected both McCone and Scoville, but had come to the conclusion that McNamara's objectives and the CIA's were incompatible. He firmly and, he later admitted, impudently told McCone, "There's no point in screwing another light bulb into a socket that's shorted out."

McCone asked Wheelon to analyze the situation and make recommendations. Wheelon talked with Scoville at length, as well as with others connected with the satellite programs. He concluded that the United States needed the benefits of competition between the NRO and CIA. In his report to McCone, Wheelon said he realized that such competition between government agencies was messy and unseemly, but the U.S. need for reconnaissance information outweighed such considerations. This was the only way to insure there would be a vigorous program. Wheelon reminded McCone that a similar decision had been made when a second nuclear weapons design laboratory was established at Livermore.

McCone thought over what Wheelon had said for a day, then agreed that the CIA should again have a strong role in satellite reconnaissance. McCone pledged his complete support to Wheelon. He also gained the backing of Dr. Weisner and Dr. Land, whom Wheelon had known from his days as a graduate student.

With McCone's decision, the Directorate of Research was reorganized and its name was changed to the Directorate of Science and Technology. The responsibility for all overhead reconnaissance projects—the CIA U-2 overflights (now code-named "Idealist"), the Nationalist Chinese U-2 operations (code-named "Tackle"), development of the A-12 Oxcart aircraft, and Corona—was assigned to the Office of Special Activities in his directorate. Wheelon was named its head and given the title assistant director for special activities.

Wheelon said later that "after a period of—how shall I say it—readjustment of expectation," the Air Force–CIA partnership resumed. The debate then briefly centered on whether the CIA ought to pursue development of new reconnaissance systems under the NRO. The struggle for control continued until McMillian was finally replaced on October 1, 1965. The new NRO director, Alexander H. Flax, saw the Air Force and CIA as complementary assets.[56]

The Final Problem: Corona Discharge

Wheelon also had to deal with the one remaining persistent problem: the corona discharges on the film. These had first appeared on the *Discoverer 14* photos, but the problem had become worse with the complex film path of the KH-4 camera system. A static electric charge would build up on the moving parts of the system, especially the rubber film rollers. As the film moved, the electrical build-up would discharge, leaving a tree-shaped pattern on the film.

The photos from Corona flight 47 (Mission 9040, launched on July 27, 1962) were badly marred by both corona discharges and radiation fogging. Itek began a major research effort into the situation. The problem was erratic in nature—it would disappear for several flights, only to crop up again later. Despite all efforts, the problem continued.[57] In the fall of 1963, Wheelon asked Sydney Drell of Stanford University to take leave and assemble a panel to look at the problem. The Drell Committee, however, made little or no contribution to finding a solution.[58]

The corona discharge was not a well-understood phenomenon. The cause was not clear, although corona discharge was known to be more likely in a vacuum. As Levison observed years later, it was a "nasty problem" that required trial and error.[59]

Itek's chief engineer, Francis J. Madden, and the people in Itek's environmental test laboratory finally developed a procedure to test the rollers for a tendency to cause corona discharges. It was not really scientific, but it was a pragmatic solution to the problem. The conductive rubber rollers were put into a steam bath until they were saturated with water vapor. Then they were put into a test camera, which was placed into a vacuum chamber and run. The rollers that suffered from corona discharges were thrown away; those that did not were flown. Although years later Madden would jokingly credit "divine intervention" for the solution to the corona problems, it was really long, hard, and painstaking work.[60]

The Race to Ace

In mid-1962, an intense competition began among the pilots to make five recoveries and become the first "ace." There were loud arguments in the club over who had the best crew. The competition was tempered by the rotation policy, in which each pilot took turns as primary recovery pilot (number 1). After his turn as number 1, the pilot would be number 2 on the next recovery, number 3 on the one after, then number 4, and finally number 5 in the outfield. The result was a good competition, which boosted unit morale.

When the race began at the end of May, there was a four-way tie between Captains Jones, Wilson, and Schensted and Major Brewton, with two each. Coming up behind them were Captains McCullough and Hines, who had each caught one capsule.

Corona flight 44 was recovered by Captain Jones, raising his total to three. Corona flight 45 was caught by Capt. Vernon W. Betteridge, while number 46 was caught by Major Hines, bringing his total to two. As Hines had lined up on the parachute, it became lost in the clouds, but he was able to spot the capsule and make the catch on the first pass. The forty-seventh Corona was caught by Brewton, who now had three.

For the Corona flight 48 recovery, McCullough was primary pilot with Hines as backup. The parachute behaved erratically, and McCullough missed his two passes. Hines's whole crew was in the cockpit watching; they began to cheer at the second miss. Hines was following McCullough's plane and was lined up perfectly. He radioed, "We're hot," and caught it on the first pass. McCullough was so mad he had missed on the two passes that he peeled off and flew back to Hawaii alone.

Corona flight 49 was caught by Jones, bringing his total to four. Jones became the first to surpass Capt. Slaughter Mimms's total of three Genetrix gondola recoveries, and he was now only one away from five recoveries and ace status. Alas, Corona flight 49 was his last recovery. With Jones out, the standings were now Brewton and Hines with three recoveries, Wilson and Schensted tied at two, followed by McCullough and Betteridge with one each.

After the fiftieth Corona was lost on reentry, Wilson caught Corona flight 51 in midair, his third catch. The recovery was made at 8,000 feet on the first pass. It was a routine recovery.

Corona flight 52 was caught in midair by Major Hines on October 2, 1962, bring his total to four. It was not routine. This is Hines's own account of this extraordinary mission:

Five JC-130 recovery aircraft departed Hickam AFB at 1030 to be in position for recovery of a Discoverer nose cone in mid-air, cone separation and chute opening at 65,000 feet. Time 1255.

I was flying number 5 position, which was located 300 miles south of expected impact point—this position, this far south, I believed I was just going along for the ride, no chance of a nose cone going this far south of computed impact point. So I continued circling my position at 25,000 feet, smoking a cigar, while the recovery crew played cards in the back of the aircraft.

At re-entry time we were headed north so my electronic operator could get contact with the capsule on re-entry. Contact was made at 1252, it was north of us as expected. The other aircraft had an electronic indication too—then the JC-130s north of us started reporting it was south of them. My electronic operator, M/Sgt Howard Anderson, reported "it's on our tail," and south of us! Crew members were alerted that it was south of us—I did a wing-over, with the aircraft and headed south. I asked my electronic operator to check again to make sure it was south of us. This was verified and south we went, increasing speed and descending at 500 feet per minute—crew was told to go on oxygen and we started our run not knowing how far south it was—all aircraft (5) were now headed south, however we were 100 miles south of the no. 4 aircraft.

In our run, we had to stay below the expected altitude of the nose cone, so we continued our descent to pick up maximum speed. Now at 425 knots indicated, direction was still steady south. We were now over the red line speed and going as fast as the aircraft would go. Now passing through 8,000 feet.

There was an overcast under us at around 6,000 feet, so we leveled until the expected altitude of the nose cone was 4,000 feet above us—we now had to descend through the overcast; weather in the area was briefed to be 1,000 to 1,200 feet, a broken cloud deck.

We broke out of the clouds at 1,200 feet, ragged ceiling with moderate turbulence and light rain. At this speed the aircraft was really shaking and we were throwing oil from all four engines. Signal was still steady ahead and south. We had been running for 25 minutes at maximum speed, on a steady heading, so it had to be directly ahead of us. My electronic operator gave me a 3 degree heading to the right followed by 5 degrees more to the right—we had to be there, then 10 degrees more to the right. We were at 1,200 feet—cut all power and started to slow down. We had seven people in the cockpit to look for the nose cone's parachute—started a circle—a crew member got a sighting at about 1,700 feet, coming through the ragged clouds.

With the nose cone at this low altitude we would have no other recovery aircraft to back us up. We would also only have time for one pass at the chute, if that, and if we missed it would be in the ocean in a little over a minute. Was having a hard time slowing the aircraft down. Told crew members on the flightdeck to keep the chute in sight. Flew under it, at 1,200 feet, below the nose cone. Started flaps down to decrease speed and headed out-bound for fifteen seconds. Speed still high, however, had to open back doors and get recovery gear out. Started inbound turn, with rear doors coming open—still too fast. At a high rate of speed could pull recovery loops off of the poles. Turning inbound at 700 feet—parachute in sight—ahead at about 800 foot altitude. Must get recovery gear out and poles down for recovery—gave crew 5 seconds out, now at 600 feet, was told poles not down yet—3 seconds out at 500 feet—crew reports poles down, ready for recovery, speed still a little high at 130 knots.

Parachute came straight under the nose of the aircraft. Contact on parachute—down center line—hit on both hooks on top and bottom loop. Parachute engaged—winch play-out—package stopped. Crew reported, capsule was in-trail, riding steady. Had already started slow climb on contact with chute, so as line played-out, nose cone would not hit the ocean. We had recovered nose cone at 475 feet, line play-out was 275 feet. Continued slow climb while nose cone was reeled in and brought on board of the aircraft. Reported to command central—capsule on board—aircraft returning to Hickam. Time 1347.

Capsule was recovered 493 miles south of expected impact point. We had run 193 miles south of our position in 29 minutes at a speed of 450 knots, or at times as fast as the aircraft would go. If the capsule had been 10 more miles to the south, it would have been impossible to have reached it before it splashed into the ocean.

The crew received a "Well done!" from command on our landing at Hickam. A party was had by all.[61]

Maj. Thomas F. Hines and his crew following the dramatic recovery of the Corona flight 52 capsule at 475 feet. *Left to right:* Thomas F. Hines (aircraft commander), Paul Griswold (pilot), Hugh McCormick (navigator), the flight engineer, Howard Anderson (electronic operator), Jim Muehlberger (winch operator), the four pole handlers, and a photographer. At the time, crew members switched from crew to crew as necessary due to leave, sickness, or new people being checked out. *Col. Thomas F. Hines photo*

The next capsule, from Corona flight 53, was successfully recovered in midair on October 13, 1962, by Captain McCullough. Major Brewton recovered Corona flight 55 on November 9. (The fifty-fourth flight had not carried a capsule.) This was his fourth recovery, tying him with Hines, but like Captain Jones, it was also his last. Corona flight 56 was recovered later in the month by Capt. Stephen G. Calder, Jr.—his first recovery.

Following the loss of the Corona flight 57 capsule, the next midair recovery (flight 58) was made on December 17, 1962, by Captain Milam. This was his first Corona recovery, and it marked the start of a remarkable career.

The capsule of Corona flight 59 eluded the recovery squadron and was picked up from the ocean, and the next two flights were both failures. Thus, it was not until April 4 that the squadron had another midair recovery. The capsule from Corona flight 62 was recovered in midair by Captain Calder on April 4. This was his second and last Corona recovery.

Neither of the next two flights resulted in midair recoveries. Flight 63 was a failure, and flight 64 ended with a water recovery. The following three each ended with a midair recovery, but none by the leaders in the ace race: Corona flight 65 was Capt. Dale M. Palmer's first recovery, flight 66 was Captain Betteridge's second and last, and flight 67 was the first catch by Capt. James E. Varnadoe. For both Palmer and Varnadoe, these were the start of a remarkable series of recoveries.

The capsule from Corona flight 68 was successfully recovered in midair by Captain Milam, his second. The next recovery, from flight 69, was made on August 28 by Captain Palmer, also his second success. Milam then recovered the seventieth Corona's capsule, for his third success. Hines, Jones, and Brewton still held the lead with four, but Wilson and the fast-moving Milam were closing in with three each.

The capsule from Mission 1002-1 (Corona flight 71) was ejected on its sixty-fourth orbit, and was recovered in midair on September 26, 1963, by Major Hines. As with his second recovery, the parachute was in and out of the clouds. There was also no backup, due to the weather. Hines was successful, catching it on his first pass at 6,000 feet. This was his fifth recovery, making him the unit's first ace.

Since the beginning of aerial combat, aces were called the "knights of the skies." Hines, and those who followed, had become aces while performing the only aerial maneuver which required them to collide with another object.

But no one knew their names.

Hines was later given a plaque with a piece of a parachute and the following inscription:

CITATION

Having been in the right place at the right time on five separate occasions, we, the "Les Miserabbles" [*sic*] of the 6593rd Test Squadron (Special) do confer the title of ace upon Thomas F. Recovery Hines and award him the ACE RECOVERY MEDAL.

Fall 1963

The year 1963 was a time of transition for the U.S. reconnaissance program, and for American society itself. The attitudes of the 1950s were fading, while what would replace them was not yet clear. Kennedy had set America on course to the Moon, and there seemed no limit to the bright future technology could bring. In music, the Beach Boys and other groups created an image of wild surf, fast cars, and endless California summers. A new group from England, the Beatles, was starting to attract attention. Domestically, the major issue was civil rights; the previous August, the Rev. Dr. Martin Luther King, Jr., led the Freedom March on Washington, D.C. At the University of California at Berkeley, student protests paralyzed the campus. As yet, few knew and fewer cared about Vietnam.

Although there had been an easing of tensions following the Cuban missile crisis, U.S. forces remained on alert. A number of nuclear-armed B-52s and B-47s were kept aloft around the clock. Other aircraft—both strategic bombers and tactical planes such as B-57s, F-100s, and F-105s—were kept on ground alert, armed with nuclear weapons. On a fall day in late 1963, at bases around the world, bells rang and the ground alert pilots rushed to their planes. It was a routine drill they had done many times before. The crews were to climb into their planes, strap in, and start the engines within five minutes. They would then shut down the engines and return to the alert building.

This time was different. As the pilots strapped in, they were told *not* to start the engines, because this was not a drill—this time it was real. For the next six hours, they waited for the final launch verification that would send them on the way to their targets. During that time, Jim Mugavero, a B-57 pilot on alert in South Korea, thought about his wife and family, about swimming in a Michigan lake as a child, about all the things he had wanted to do but never had.

Finally, they were told to come back in; the alert had been called off. When Mugavero and the other B-57 pilots and navigators walked into the building, tired, confused, and scared, they all asked, "What happened?" And they, like all the others who had just faced the unthinkable, were told. It was November 22, 1963, and President Kennedy had just been assassinated in Dallas, Texas. In the uncertainty which followed, the full-scale nuclear alert had been called, in case the killing was the start of a Soviet nuclear attack.[62]

Lyndon B. Johnson was now president. In the months to follow, he and his advisers would make decisions which would send America towards a darker future. The Sixties had begun.

The solution of the problem of the corona discharge, as well as the struggle for control, marked the end of the first, frantic years of Corona. It had gone from an impossible task to routine operation. The camera payload had been transformed from a mono system able to spot only large facilities to the KH-4 stereo package with a fourfold improvement in resolution. The struggle for control settled, by and large, the issues that had been left unanswered when the program was first established. It insured a vigorous U.S. program, and that both DoD and CIA interests would be represented.

As great and tragic events began to unfold, the original Corona was now to be replaced with a new version. This definitive Corona satellite had far greater capabilities, lifetime, and resolution than were ever envisioned when the program began. This Corona would serve for the next nine years, and would be the heart of the U.S. reconnaissance satellite effort from the mid-1960s to the end of the program in 1972.

SEVEN

The Definitive Corona
The KH-4A/B Camera Systems

By 1965, the rate of success was phenomenal. On the average three or four recoveries were made every month. The seven years of frustration and effort were paying off.

A Point in Time (CIA film)

➤ Corona had been designed in the early 1960s as an interim reconnaissance system, with low resolution, a limited film supply, and a brief orbital lifetime. But through its success (coupled with the failure of its immediate replacements), it became America's primary reconnaissance asset.

Even after such improvements as the Mural stereo camera, there was still room for growth in the Corona system. The new TAT Agena D booster, used on the Lanyard series, offered a greater payload capability for film, batteries, and attitude control gas. In the future, Corona would use this capability to increase its operating lifetime from four days to two weeks. Rather than a snapshot of the Soviet Union, it would supply prolonged coverage of targets throughout the world. A second bucket would be carried, allowing the first batch of film to be recovered even as the satellite continued to operate. This would be the definitive Corona.

The KH-4A Camera System

The KH-4A camera, also called the J-1, was built around the Mural stereo camera. The optical resolution was slightly improved, to 120 lines/mm vs. the 100 lines/mm of the KH-1 through -4. This resulted in a ground resolution of 9 feet, compared to 10 feet with the original KH-4. Each frame covered an area of 10.6 by 144 nautical miles.[1] The film supply was doubled over the KH-4, to 160 pounds. To give some idea of the increase in capability this represented, this translated to 32,000 feet of film; *Discoverer 14* had carried a mere 3,000 feet.[2]

The KH-4A's two-bucket system required a complex film path. It had to withstand the G-forces of launch, and to function in the weightlessness of space. A particular problem was keeping the film under a constant tension, to prevent breakage or jams. The film was threaded through the system at launch. The film supply, about the size of a car tire, was located at the rear of the camera assembly. The two film rolls (80 pounds each) were threaded into separate cameras. This allowed the cameras to operate separately; should one camera fail, the other could continue to operate (although stereo coverage would be lost). After exposure, the two strips of film went into the rear bucket, then back out and into the front bucket. When the front bucket's take-up reel had a full load, the film would be cut and the capsule sealed. It would then be deorbited and recovered. The rest of the film would be threaded, while weightless, onto the second bucket's take-up reel. At the end of the flight, which could last from eight to fifteen days, the second capsule would be recovered.[3]

Like the other parts of Corona, this system of rollers and cutters was built under "compartmentalized" secrecy. The different parts were fabricated by separate Lockheed machine shops. This was done so no one person saw all the pieces, and only those directly involved saw the complete assembly. Nothing was ever referred to by name. Lockheed engineers never talked about a "camera"—it was always "the payload" or "the unit." They could not, of course, call the film system by its proper name of "cut and splice," so this was abbreviated to "CS," then turned into "chicken of the sea." It was only a short step to the final code name, "Tuna."[4]

The more complex mission profile of the KH-4A system required modifications to the Agena's command and control system. The satellite could operate in a passive or "zombie" mode for up to twenty-one days. Once the first bucket was loaded with film and released, the camera could continue to operate, or be shut down again for several days.

The longer lifetime and low orbit meant that the satellite's orbit would decay from atmospheric drag. To counteract this, "drag make-up units" were also added. This was a cluster of small solid-fuel rockets, which were fired individually when the orbit dipped too low. Each firing accelerated the satellite slightly, returning it to the original orbit.

With the new design, the flights were given mission numbers in the 1000 series. Because of the two buckets, each mission (and designation) was also split into two phases. The first phase of a KH-4A Corona flight would be designated "-1." After the first capsule was deorbited and film began to be loaded into the second bucket, the flight was redesignated "-2." The documentation and analysis of the photos would retain this split.

Early KH-4A Missions, 1963–1964

The debut of the new camera came with the sixty-ninth Corona flight, launched on August 24, 1963. As with the first flights of the earlier cameras, Mission 1001 had its problems. The shutter on the master horizon camera remained open during about a thousand of the exposures, seriously fogging the adjoining panoramic photos.[5] The first bucket was successfully recovered on August 28. The Agena then suffered a current inverter failure, and the second capsule could not be separated due to the power problem. The second KH-4A launch, aboard the seventy-first Corona, was made on September 23, 1963, and met a similar fate.

The first two flights of KH-4A payloads had had several problems. On both missions, the second capsule did not separate.[6] Additionally, the KH-4A cameras suffered from a severe heat problem, which required reducing the thermal sensitivity of the camera package, improved shielding, and changing the paint pattern.

Despite the problems, the KH-4A/J-1 camera was declared operational, and the KH-4/M camera payload was retired after its final flight on the seventy-fifth Corona on December 21, 1963.

The third KH-4A launch (Mission 1004) went into orbit on February 15, 1964, and was completely successful, with both the Mission 1004-1 and 1004-2 capsules being recovered, on February 19 and 22, respectively. The pilots were Captain Milam (his fourth) and Capt. Jeremiah J. Collins (his first). Both would go on to many more.[7]

Bad luck and booster problems struck the next launch on March 24. The Agena on Mission 1003 suffered a short in the electrical converter, and the satellite lost control and did not reach orbit. (Note that the mission numbers are out of order.)[8]

The next launch, the seventy-eighth of the Corona program, was Mission 1005. It would reach orbit, but would suffer a failure of epic proportions. What goes up . . .

. . . Must Come Down

Mission 1005 was successfully launched on April 27, 1964. At Agena separation, large electrical surges were noted in the electrical system, but the mission proceeded smoothly. After 350 cycles, however, the film in one of the cameras broke. The Vandenberg AFB tracking station transmitted a recovery command on the satellite's forty-seventh orbit, on April 30. The satellite verified the reception of the signal, but nothing happened. The pyrotechnic charges used to separate the capsule had shorted out and no longer functioned.[9]

Other tracking stations repeated the command on the next twenty-six orbits, with no success. The satellite verified that the transmissions had been received, but the capsule still was not released. A new feature that had been added to the control system was a device called "Lifeboat." This was a completely redundant recovery system that could be activated if the Agena suffered a power failure. Lifeboat was designed to separate the capsule, saving the film from being marooned in space. However, commands sent to activate Mission 1005's backup Lifeboat mode did not prove any more successful than those for the normal mode.

After May 19, the satellite stopped responding, and from May 20 on, it was assumed the satellite would reenter and burn up. The derelict satellite continued to orbit the Earth for the next six days. On each orbit, atmospheric drag slowed the satellite and it dropped lower. Finally, the Agena hit the upper atmosphere on its 452nd orbit. The satellite began to glow, then broke up under the increasing heat and aerodynamic pressure. At six minutes after midnight on May 26, observers on the ground in Maracaibo, Venezuela, saw five burning objects traveling north in the night sky. The heat of reentry destroyed most of the satellite, and the five objects flickered out. But in the night sky above the lonely mountains of southwestern Venezuela, an object was falling silent and unseen. It slammed into the ground, where it lay undiscovered for the next six weeks.

On July 7, two farm workers discovered a curious object near the town of La Fría in Venezuela, a few miles from the Colombian border.

They reported the find to their employer, Facundo Albarracin, who told them to move it some 100 yards onto his own farm. The object resembled a golden kettle. It had been badly damaged by the impact; the rounded front end had been crushed, while a ring around the rim had been bent. Inside was a large spool full of charred and exposed film. It was the first bucket from Mission 1005.

Albarracin thought the strange object might be valuable, so he spread the word it was for sale. In the isolated mountains of Tachira state, there was no interest, even from the local smugglers, so he pried loose the radio transmitter and parts of the take-up assembly as household utensils or toys for the children.

Word of the strange object slowly spread, and a trickle of visitors made their way to La Fría to see it. One of the curious was Leonardo Davila, a commercial photographer. On August 1, Davila called the U.S. embassy in Caracas, Venezuela, to say he had photographed a space object. Corona officials, with a cover story that they represented the Air Force, flew to Caracas to pick up the capsule. The battered bucket was carried out of La Fría hanging on a wooden pole carried between two peasants. It was picked up by Venezuelan defense ministry officials, who flew the capsule to Caracas. The Corona officials bought the capsule from the Venezuelan government, and explained that it was from a NASA experiment gone astray.

When the capsule was examined by Corona technicians, it was found to have reentered due to orbital decay. During reentry it had separated from the instrument fairing. As the satellite broke up, the retrorocket thrust cone had been sheared off, but the harness had remained attached. This acted as a drogue chute, preventing the capsule from burning up and stabilizing it for a hard, nose-down landing.

The local press covered the story extensively; the *Diario Católico* of San Cristóbal (the nearest town of any size) carried a lengthy report. This included a photo of peasants carrying the capsule, and two of the capsule itself. The film take-up reel was clearly identifiable. The *Daily Journal* commemorated the event with poetry:

> *I shot an arrow into the air.*
> *It fell to Earth I know not where.*
> *Cape Kennedy signalled: "Where is it at you are?"*
> *Responded the rocket, "La Fría, Tachira."*[10]

U.S. coverage was more limited. The *New York Times* article was a mere fifteen lines long, at the bottom of page four. The "space-instrument package" was described as containing "cameras, radio transmitters and other scientific instruments marked secret." Its size was given as three feet long with a weight of 175 pounds. The article concluded that it might have been part of a balloon or rocket altitude test.[11]

The lack of attention by both the American press and public was understandable—the same page was taken up by reports on the attack by North Vietnamese PT boats on the USS *Maddox* and USS *C. Turner Joy.* The Tonkin Gulf incident marked the start of the large-scale commitment of U.S. forces to Vietnam.

The KH-4A System in Operation, 1964–1966

Following Mission 1005's South American adventure, the Air Force changed the cover designation for Corona from "Program 162" to "Program 241." The next launch, Corona flight 79 on June 4, 1964, was a complete success. Mission 1006 was the first KH-4A payload to provide four days of coverage for each capsule. Both capsules were recovered in midair, Mission 1006-1 on June 8 and Mission 1006-2 on June 12. Both catches were by Major Wilson, making him the second ace and the new leader with six catches. This was the first dual recovery by a single pilot—a "double header." At the ace party, the group commander gave Wilson a box of cigars.[12]

During 1964, there were thirteen Corona missions with KH-4A payloads. Of these, nine were considered successful and two partially successful. The Mission 1011-2 capsule (aboard Corona flight 86, launched on October 5) was not recovered. The eighty-eighth Corona flight, launched on November 2, suffered a major failure. On the satellite's fifty-second orbit, both cameras failed.[13] The superstitious might have expected trouble—it was, after all, Mission 1013.

The successes far outweighed these mishaps. The average coverage of each capsule during 1964 was three or four days. Introduction of the KH-4A thus represented a major increase not only in the number of missions, but a doubling in the amount of coverage per mission.

The introduction of the KH-4A system coincided with the completion of the survey of the USSR. By March 1964, following the analysis of the Mission 1004 photos, twenty-three Soviet ICBM sites had been located. By June and the flights of Missions 1006, 9063A, and the appropriately numbered 1007, all twenty-five sites had been discovered.[14] More important, it could be stated with confidence that no sites had been missed.

In addition to the thirteen KH-4A payloads, two other launches carried the final KH-5 Argon cameras. These were Corona flights 80 and 84, launched on June 13 and August 21. Missions 9063A and 9064A were both successful, bringing the total to six out of the eleven Argon launches. The program provided coverage of 40 million square nautical miles of the Soviet Bloc and another 2.8 million square nautical miles within the United States.[15] Rather than continuing to use a specialized mapping camera like Argon, the effort now shifted to adapting the reconnaissance camera to serve a secondary mapping role.

The year 1964 also saw the first recoveries by pilots who later became top scorers. Maj. Edwin R. Bayer's first catch was Corona flight 81's second capsule, Capt. Albert F. "Al" Muller caught Corona flight 83's first bucket, and Capt. James F. McDonald, Jr., snagged the second.

The Corona launches of 1965 followed the pattern of the previous year. Again, thirteen launches carried KH-4A cameras, and the satellites continued to show an increased lifetime. The first launch of 1965, the ninetieth Corona flight (Mission 1016), was the first to provide five days of coverage per bucket. Both capsules were caught in midair by Captain Varnadoe, bringing his total of Corona recoveries to five. Corona flight 92's first capsule was recovered by Capt. Douglas S. Sliger, and was the start of his drive toward ace. Major Bayer's fifth recovery was the Mission 1021-1 capsule from Corona flight 95; it had taken him less than a year to make ace. Capt. William J. "Vip" Vipraio, an ace-to-be, made his first recovery when he caught the first bucket from Corona flight 96. Another milestone was reached with Mission 1024, launched on September 22, 1965. This was the one-hundredth Corona flight. Its two capsules were recovered by Major Palmer and Captain McDonald. This raised their individual totals to five and four Corona capsules.

There were no failed KH-4A missions during 1965, and the problems remained minor. Corona flight 94 (Mission 1019) successfully operated for ten days, but when the Mission 1019-2 bucket was released on May 8, there was a failure and the capsule was boosted into a higher orbit. On the ninety-eighth Corona flight (Mission 1023, launched on August 17), the forward camera failed. (Captain Muller also made his fifth Corona recovery when he caught the Mission 1023-1 capsule.) The 103rd Corona flight (Mission 1027), launched on December 9, suffered a control gas loss, but was able to complete its mission and both capsules were recovered. (The Mission 1027-1 capsule was the first recovery by Capt. Herbert E. Bronson, who also later went on to become an ace.)[16]

The only launch failure during the year was the ninety-ninth Corona flight. This was not a photographic flight, and did not carry either a camera or capsules. The Agena was fitted with radio propagation and ionospheric experiments from the Aerospace Corporation and the Air Force's Cambridge Research Laboratory. The Thor Agena D was launched on September 2, 1965, but was destroyed at T+61 seconds by ground control. The booster's course had deviated and it had gone outside the safety limits.[17]

The increased time in orbit provided by the KH-4A camera was reflected in Corona operations in 1966. There were only nine Corona launches during the year, four fewer than each of the previous two years. One of these, Mission 1032, failed during launch on May 3, 1966, when the Agena D did not separate from the Thor and the booster impacted about six hundred nautical miles downrange. Other than this setback, the year was distinguished by the routine nature of Corona operations. The satellites were launched, they operated successfully in orbit, the capsules were recovered in midair, and the film was processed and analyzed. It had become rare that two launch attempts had to be made, and adventures such as the Mission 1005 flight were not repeated.

As with previous years, the Corona satellites' operating lifetimes continued to expand, as did the ace list. The 107th Corona flight was the first to have a bucket achieve seven days of operation. The Mission 1031-1 capsule was recovered on April 14, 1966, by Captain Milam (his sixth Corona recovery). The Mission 1031-2 capsule followed after another four days aloft, and was caught by Capt. John E. Cahoon, Jr. (This was the first of three Corona recoveries Cahoon made.) The first bucket from Corona flight 110 (Mission 1035) was caught by Capt. Joseph Modicut, who would later make ace.

Corona flight 111 was the first to use a new version of the Thor booster. This was the Long-Tank Thrust Augmented Thor (LTTAT)

The Soviet Long-Range Aviation Air Field at Dolon in Soviet Central Asia on August 20, 1966. The photo was taken by a KH-4A camera on Mission 1036. Comparing it to the first Corona picture of the Mys Schmidta Air Field shows the huge improvement in Corona systems in six years of operations. *National Archives*

Agena D. As the name implies, the first stage was stretched to increase the orbital payload and lifetime. Mission 1036 was launched on August 9, 1966, and returned its first bucket after seven days. It was caught by Maj. Jack H. Wenning, another pilot who would become an ace. The Mission 1036-2 capsule followed six days later on August 22, bringing the total duration to thirteen days. (The recovery pilot was Captain Cahoon.)

This became the pattern for U.S. reconnaissance satellite operations in the decades to come. It was cheaper to extend the lifetime of each satellite by adding batteries, film, and another capsule—even though this required a more powerful booster—than to build and launch two or more less-capable satellites with smaller boosters. U.S. reconnaissance satellites would become fewer in number, but individually more capable.

Corona-Launched SIGINT Subsatellites

One aspect of the Corona program that still remains secret is its use in collecting SIGINT (signals intelligence). Part of the LTTAT Agena's added payload was used to carry small SIGINT subsatellites, which picked up Soviet air defense radar signals. The subsatellites were attached to the Agena's aft rack for launch. Once the Corona satellite had reached orbit, the subsatellite would be released. It would then fire an onboard rocket engine, which would boost it into a three-hundred-mile-high orbit.

The first supplementary payload carried by a Corona was the OSCAR I ham-radio transmitter satellite aboard *Discoverer 36* in December 1961. (As noted earlier, this was a cover launch.) The first KH-6 Lanyard launch, on Corona flight 61 in March 1963, was the next test of the procedure using a scientific subsatellite. It was lost along with the Corona satellite due to booster failure.

On June 27, 1963, Corona flight 66 (Mission 9056) successfully carried the Hitch-hiker I scientific subsatellite into orbit. After separation, its onboard rocket engine placed it into a highly elliptical orbit. Hitch-hiker I returned radiation data for three months.[18] This was followed by three test SIGINT subsatellites in 1963, carried on Mission 9058A (an Argon mission launched on August 29), a TAT Agena launch on October 29 (Mission 9059A; another Argon flight), and Mission 9062 (the last KH-4 payload, launched on December 21).

The SIGINT subsatellites were first flown operationally on the Atlas Agena–launched Gambit high-resolution satellites between 1964 and 1966. Reportedly, these were called "P-11" satellites and were built by Lockheed. Two or three of the subsatellites were launched per year.[19]

With the introduction of the LTTAT Agena D booster, the subsatellites were switched over to the Corona launches. The first to carry the subsatellites was Corona flight 117 (Mission 1041), launched on May 9, 1967. Two more were launched by the end of the year (Missions 1042 on June 16 and 1044 on November 2).

The year 1968 saw a sudden upsurge in the subsatellites, with a total of five. One of these, launched on the 130th Corona flight (Mission 1049 on December 12, 1968), was boosted into an orbit of about nine hundred miles. It is believed that this higher orbit was used to pick up signals from Soviet ABM radars around Moscow. Because their signals extend thousands of miles into space, a higher orbit was used for better coverage.[20]

The subsatellites were not the only SIGINT payloads orbited by the United States, and may not have been the only involvement of Corona. When the WS-117L program was started, it was planned to launch some satellites with SIGINT packages. This eventually became "Program 102," with the first launch by a Thor Agena on February 21, 1962. (Although the Agena reached orbit, a second engine burn to circularize the orbit did not take place, leaving it in an elliptical orbit.) During the next two years, seven Program 102 satellites were launched.

The next mission was different. The previous payloads had been nonrecoverable; the signals were recorded on board and transmitted to ground stations. The eighth Program 102 satellite, launched on December 21, 1964, carried a capsule. It is believed this was a Corona satellite modified for a "one-off" SIGINT mission. The KH-4 camera was replaced by a receiver package, and the magnetic tapes were loaded aboard the capsule and deorbited. Reportedly the mission was successful and lasted four days. This was similar to the lifetimes of Corona missions of that time.[21]

KH-4A Operations, 1967–1969

The successes of the KH-4A system would continue during its final three years of operations. Between 1967 and the final flight in 1969, fifteen Corona satellites with KH-4A payloads would be launched; all would reach orbit, and all thirty capsules would be recovered successfully (twenty-nine from midair, and one from the Pacific).

During this period, the Corona changed its booster. The last Corona satellite to use the TAT Agena D (the 116th of the program) was Mission 1040, orbited on March 30, 1967. The next twelve used the LTTAT Agena D. The satellites also showed a continued increase in orbital lifetime. The 118th Corona flight set a new duration record for both a satellite and an individual bucket. Launched on June 16, 1967, the Mission 1042-1 bucket was recovered in midair six days later. The recovery pilot was Major Wenning (his third Corona recovery). The Mission 1042-2 capsule then operated for a record nine days until July 1, giving Mission 1042 a final total of fifteen days of operation. This was the only capsule which was not recovered in midair; it was picked up after it splashed down in the Pacific.[22]

Only four of the satellites suffered problems. Mission 1048 (the 128th Corona, launched on September 18, 1968) had a failure of the forward camera, while Missions 1049 and 1051 (launched on December 12, 1968, and May 2, 1969, respectively) both suffered degraded film. Mission 1050, the 132nd Corona, orbited on March 19, 1969, but suffered an Agena failure, which terminated the flight on March 24. Its two capsules were successfully recovered, by Majors Ralph A. Gauthier and Miller A. Peeler. (They were Gauthier's third and final Corona recovery, and Peeler's first of three Corona successes.)[23]

In the six years of KH-4A operations, a total of fifty-two payloads were launched. Of these, two (Coronas 77 and 108) ended as launch failures, while another (Corona 78) suffered an Agena failure in orbit and reentered over South America. Four other capsules could not be recovered. Thus, of the 104 buckets launched, 94 were successfully recovered, after three to nine days of operation each. The KH-4A made up the largest number of payloads in the Corona program, and provided the bulk of coverage during its busiest years.

The increase in recoveries resulted in a number of pilots making ace status. Maj. Jack H. Wenning, Capt. Albert R. Kaiser, Maj. Robert B. Miller, Capt. Herbert E. Bronson, and Maj. Warren C. Schensted all became aces during this period. Major Schensted took the longest of the recovery pilots to make ace. His first two recoveries were Discoverers 30 and 32 in 1961. It was not until January 1967 that he made his third Corona recovery, the second bucket from Corona 114. Two more midair recoveries raised his personal total to five.

While the KH-4A payloads were being flown, there was a similar upgrading of the Gambit high-resolution satellites. A total of thirty-eight of the KH-7 payloads were launched between July 1963 and the final launch on June 4, 1967. (Two ended in booster failures.) They each operated for about a week before the Agena engine restarted to deorbit the capsule.

At the same time the KH-4A was introduced, an improved Gambit high-resolution satellite was under development. The new camera was designated the KH-8. Due to the heavier payload, which presumably included two buckets like the KH-4A Corona satellites, a new booster was required. This was the Titan IIIB Agena D. It was the Titan IIIC core stages, but without the two solid-fuel strap-on boosters or the transtage.

The first KH-8 Gambit (and the 31st flight of the Gambit program) was launched on July 29, 1966. Two more of the Titan IIIB satellites were launched by the end of the year. The KH-8 Gambit satellites initially showed a lifetime of between seven and ten days. By 1968, this had been increased to two weeks or more.[24]

The Final Corona Payload: The KH-4B System

Even with the KH-4A's success, it was clear to both the CIA and NRO that there was little room left for growth within the design. It was, after all, only a modified version of the KH-4/M camera first introduced in 1962, which was based on the KH-3/C Triple Prime camera of 1961. The early KH-4A flights showed several technical problems and operational shortcomings. Correcting these, as well as incorporating technical advances, would require a whole new system.

The camera improvement program began in the spring of 1965 with a series of meetings between representatives of Lockheed, General Electric, Itek, and the Corona program offices. They examined various ways of improving both the panoramic and stellar/index cameras, providing a more versatile command system, and adapting the camera to produce imagery suitable for mapping. From these discussions, a list of design goals was established for the new camera system:

Reduction of camera system vibration

Reduced image smear by better velocity/height match

Elimination of camera failures due to the film pulling out of the guide rails

Improved exposure control by a variable slit selection

The ability to operate at orbital altitudes as low as 80 nautical miles, rather than the minimum of 100 nautical miles of the KH-4A

Capability to handle different film types and split film loads, and the addition of inflight-changeable filters and a film change detector

The capability to use ultra-thin base (UTB) films[25]

Although it was a completely new design, the payload was given the designations KH-4B and J-3. In the new system, all oscillating parts were either eliminated or counterbalanced. In the C Triple Prime and M cameras, the lens assembly had rotated constantly during the photographic run, while the shutter unit and slit had oscillated. This design created vibrations as the shutter unit and slit came to a full stop, then reversed direction, adversely affecting image quality and satellite sta-

Artist's conception of the KH-4B camera payload and the Agena D satellite. By use of an innovative Itek camera design, the Corona was able to provide both high resolution and panoramic stereo coverage. The KH-4A/B payloads were fitted with a pair of capsules, which greatly increased the amount of coverage each satellite could provide. *Drawing by Joel Carpenter*

bility. In the "constant rotator" design, the lens assembly, shutter unit, and slit were placed in a rotating drum. The film was exposed during a 70 degree arc of the rotation.[26]

Just prior to each photographic run, the two rolls of film were rotated in opposite directions, as were the lens assemblies, shutters, and slit drums. To compensate for the orbital motion, the two camera assemblies would also rock back and forth during the exposure, again in opposite directions. Thus, despite the mass of the cameras (the drums were about five feet across and more than seven inches thick), the inertial effects on the satellite balanced out.[27]

The optical system was also improved. While the lens assembly remained an f/3.5 Petzval with a 24-inch focal length (the latter was the same in all the Corona cameras), the lens/film resolution was improved to 160 lines/mm. The combination of improved lens/film resolution and the elimination of vibration increased the ground resolution to 6 feet, compared to the 9 feet of the KH-4A. (The results of the KH-4B were thus comparable to that of the high-resolution KH-6 Lanyard.) As with the KH-4A system, the film supply was 32,000 feet and two buckets were carried.[28] Each camera also had two changeable filters and four different exposure slits. The latter allowed correct exposures under different lighting conditions. (The KH-4A had only one slit, which resulted in poor photos under low sun angles, such as during the morning or early evening, or during the winter.)

The stellar/index camera used on the KH-4As was also modified, to correct a history of erratic performance. The 1.5-inch focal length lens was replaced by a 3-inch lens, the same as on the old KH-5/Argon. This was designated the Dual Improved Stellar Index Camera (DISIC). As with the earlier cameras, the DISIC was used to locate targets on the ground in relation to large geographic features. It was located behind the second bucket. The optical package was completed by a pair of horizon cameras, to show the satellite's precise orientation in space.

The optical package also allowed the KH-4B to be used to produce maps. This was the end result of a design process dating back to the specialized KH-5/Argon mapping camera. Although few of the Argon missions were successful, the results were phenomenal: the position of an object could be located to a 30-foot accuracy horizontally and 164 feet vertically, while the distance between any two points on the opposite sides of the Earth could be measured to within 1,000 feet. Because of Argon, it was finally possible to accurately target ICBMs against a facility on the other side of the world.

The stereo capability of the KH-4 series opened new possibilities for satellite mapping. The flexibility of the Corona program was such that within a month of the proposal that the system be fitted with index cameras to allow mapping, approval was given. By 1965, the KH-4A photos were producing maps of the USSR that were more accurate than those of the contiguous United States and Alaska then in use. (These had been produced by the Army between World War II and 1950.) The relative location of any place on Earth could be measured with an accuracy of 450 feet horizontally and better than 300 feet vertically.

With the success of the KH-4A, COMOR was influenced to provide both the equipment and satellite coverage to meet mapmaking requirements. The mapping role also began to shape the design of the new KH-4B camera that was then emerging. The mapping capability of the KH-4A had been added on; with the KH-4B, all the "bells and whistles" for precision mapping would be included from the start.

The mapping requirements placed severe demands on the camera systems. Walter Levison was reluctant to call the KH-4B a mapping camera, referring to it as a "rubbery" camera with all kinds of distortions. These distortions had to be measured so they could be corrected for when the maps were created.

The index and stellar cameras recorded the satellite's orientation in space to an accuracy of 3 to 5 arc-seconds. To measure the errors in the camera lenses, they were taken to an observatory at Cloudcroft, New Mexico, and used to photograph stars. When the positions of the stars in their pictures were compared to precisely measured star positions, the minute distortions in the lenses could be measured. On aerial mapping cameras, film shrinkage and distortions of as much as 20 microns were acceptable. For the KH-4B, the limit was 1 to 2 microns. The film was very thin base and was under tension, so it stretched. It was held in place by "holy rails," which put reference marks on the edge of the film. This allowed measurements of distortions, which could then be removed from the mapping measurements.

By the time the KH-4B went into operation, there were also improved models of the Earth's true shape and the slight variations of the Earth's gravity, and better measurements of the atmospheric drag on the satellite. Because panoramic photos were different than the images previously used for mapping, new generations of measuring and plotting equipment had to be developed. The calculation requirements also pushed the state of the art in computers. In the 1960s and early 1970s, slide rules and trigonometric tables were standard tools; pocket calculators did not exist, and the only computers were large, slow mainframes that used punch cards and paper tape.

The results of the design process were phenomenal—while the KH-4A had an accuracy of 450 feet horizontally and 300 feet vertically, the KH-4B could locate an object with an accuracy of 100 feet or better.[29]

The new camera also resulted in a change in mission profile. Since the original Discoverer launches, the Agena had orbited tail first. This was done to protect the capsule's heat shield against the effects of molecular heating from the thin upper atmosphere, and to reduce the amount of control gas needed to orient the satellite for separation. This procedure had remained the same for all the subsequent cameras, including the two-bucket KH-4A. By the time the new design was under development, these concerns had diminished, so the Corona satellite would now be flown nose first.

KH-4B Operations, 1967–1969

It took more than two years of work to transform the ideas from the meetings into hardware on the pad at Vandenberg AFB. The first KH-4B payload was launched on September 15, 1967, aboard the 120th Corona. The mission number sequence was restarted at 1101 to reflect the new system. The satellite operated for ten days, both capsules were recovered, and it was a complete success. (The first KH-4B bucket recovery was by Maj. Lester S. McChristian, his first.) There were none of the problems that had marred the first flights of the earlier cameras.

The results were such that on December 4, 1967, a Corona J-3 Ad Hoc Committee was formally convened by NRO Director Flax. The group, which was formally constituted in February 1968, recommended that testing of color film and techniques be made against specific intelligence targets, that a special subcommittee of the Committee on Imagery Requirements and Exploitation (COMIREX, which replaced COMOR on July 1, 1967) be organized to evaluate satellite color photography, and that a color collection program be planned with the system program office, the Satellite Operations Center, the intelligence analysts, and the photo interpreters.[30]

The second KH-4B, Mission 1102, was orbited on December 9, 1967, only days after the J-3 Ad Hoc Committee was organized. This brought the total Corona launches for the year to seven KH-4A and two KH-4B payloads. The two systems continued to fly concurrently for three years. During 1968 there were eight Corona flights—five with KH-4A payloads and three carrying KH-4Bs. In 1969, the split was even, with three of each. The only obvious differences were that some of the KH-4A–equipped Coronas also carried the subsatellites, while the ones with KH-4B payloads went into lower orbits to maximize resolution.

During this time, experiments with the different film types were conducted. Samples of infrared film were flown on Mission 1104 (the 127th Corona, launched on August 7, 1968). The satellite operated for about twenty-one days. Missions 1105 and 1108, launched on November 3, 1968, and December 4, 1969, both included color film as part of their supply.[31] Several flights also successfully tested the UTB film, which offered a 50 percent increase in film load, with no increase in weight. The results with the film tests were mixed; while the UTB orbital tests were successful, ground tests indicated that there would be a reduction in reliability. For this reason, its use in the constant rotator camera was discontinued.

The situation with the color film was more complex. In one test, 800 feet of SO-242 high-resolution color film was flown at the end of Mission 1108-2. While one camera used the color film, the other used 3404 black and white film. The results were disappointing, due to the loss of resolution because of the multilayer emulsion required for the color film, and the poor color correction of the KH-4B optics. (The different wavelengths of light were not brought to a single focus.) The result was a resolution half that of the black and white film. The color film simply could not meet intelligence requirements such as order of battle and missile readiness.

The color photos did have wide-ranging economic and scientific potential, however. In the Mission 1104 infrared photos of Vandenberg AFB, the farm fields were a bright red. In areas such as hillsides and riverbeds where there were sources of water, the red hue from vegetation was also apparent. In other parts of the picture, however, where plant cover was lacking, the ground was a gray-green color. Thus it was possible to assess vegetation coverage, locate water sources, and estimate amounts. The Mission 1105 color coverage of Clinton-Sherman AFB, Oklahoma, showed a similar effect—the individual farm fields differed in color from an orange red to a dark brown. In the Mission 1108 photos of China, analysts could identify mineral deposits.[32]

Although the color coverage amounted to only a tiny percent of the total Corona photos, they showed that satellites could monitor the growth and types of crops, detect whether they were suffering from plant diseases or drought, monitor the use of local water resources, locate geological features, and show the spread of desert areas and city sprawl. These orbital surveys could be done more quickly, cheaply, and completely than was possible from the air or by ground parties. Corona had secretly created earth resources studies.

The KH-4A series cameras were not finally phased out until the fall of 1969. The final flight was Mission 1052, launched on September 22 (the 135th Corona launch). As was now the standard, both buckets were successfully recovered. The Mission 1052-2 bucket (the last KH-4A capsule) was caught by Major McChristian, who had previously caught the first KH-4B capsule. His recovery of the first bucket from Corona flight 130 (a KH-4A flight) and two other recoveries made him an ace.

Following the KH-4A's retirement, the SIGINT subsatellites were transferred to the KH-4B–carrying Corona satellites. The first KH-4B flight to carry a subsatellite was Mission 1105, launched on February 5, 1969. Three more Coronas carried subsatellites in 1970. The final Corona launch to carry a subsatellite was Mission 1115 on September 10, 1971.[33] Subsequent to this, they were transferred to a new generation of area surveillance satellites.

Breakout

The years following the introduction of the KH-4B system saw disquieting developments in the area of Soviet ICBM force levels. The United States had completed its missile construction program in 1967. This consisted of 1,000 Minuteman and 54 Titan II ICBMs in hardened silos, and 656 Polaris missiles aboard 41 submarines. The entire B-47 medium bomber force and the early model B-52s had been retired, as were the first-generation Atlas and Titan I ICBMs.

While U.S. nuclear forces were now effectively frozen, the satellite photos indicated that Soviet strategic forces were undergoing a sudden surge. On October 1, 1966, there had been 340 Soviet ICBMs operational. In addition, construction on between three hundred and four hundred new silos had begun for the heavy SS-9 Scarp and light SS-11 Sego. (The latter was a small liquid-fueled ICBM). Defense Secretary McNamara told Congress in January 1967 that there had been a "faster-than-anticipated rate of construction of hard ICBM silos." By midyear there were 570 missiles operational, with the number increasing to 720 ICBMs by October 1967, more than doubling in a year's time.

The bulk of the new Soviet missiles were the lighter SS-11s. In contrast, SS-9 deployments remained limited. Only thirty new SS-9 silos

An SS-9 ICBM silo at Imeni Gastello, photographed by Corona mission 1043 on September 8, 1967. Unlike the above-ground SS-7 pads, this missile was housed in a hardened silo able to withstand a nearby nuclear blast. The site is surrounded by several fences and is serviced by good roads with wide-radius curves (for the missile transporter). The SS-9 deployment was part of a sudden upsurge in Soviet ICBM strength in the late 1960s and early 1970s. *National Archives*

had been started in 1967, giving the Soviets some 114 operational and 78 under construction. Another 36 new SS-9 silos were started in the spring of 1968, but no more were added for several months. This brought the total to 228 SS-9s operational or under construction.

The rate of new starts slacked off during much of 1968. The total force continued to grow, however, as new silos were completed and their missiles became operational. The force went from 750 ICBMs at the end of 1967 to 858 in midyear and 900 in September 1968.

Nor were Soviet efforts limited to offensive weapons. Since 1961, Corona satellites had been watching construction of ABM test facilities at Sary Shagan in Soviet Central Asia. In August 1962, Mission 9041 had showed the possible start of an identical facility at SAM Site E33-1 outside Moscow. By Mission 1002-1 in September 1963, several buildings had been finished.

In early 1967 McNamara told Congress that there were eight ABM sites around Moscow, each about forty-five miles from the city, forming a ring. Each had above-ground launchers for sixteen ABM-1 Galosh interceptors, and two sets of Triad radars, which tracked incoming warheads and directed the missiles towards them. Six sites were under active construction; McNamara described "bulldozers clearing launch pads, excavating shovels digging trenches for cables and deep holes for launchers, concrete pourers laying out pads and access roads" (details which could only have come from satellite photos).[34]

The authors of the National Intelligence Estimates and McNamara himself seemed unmoved by these developments. NIE 11-8-66 had concluded that the Soviets "continued to adhere to the concept of a deterrent force" that was seen in terms of the U.S. idea of a retaliatory force, intended to "assure the destruction of a significant portion of U.S. industrial resources and population." A year later, when NIE 11-8-67 was issued, the sudden increase in Soviet ICBMs caused a limited shift in the view of Soviet goals. They were believed to have the objective of "narrowing the lead that the U.S. has held." Although the Soviets might seek an advantage over the United States, this was not seen as likely.

Estimates of the final Soviet ICBM force remained limited. In McNamara's 1967 congressional testimony, he estimated that by mid-1971 the Soviets would have between 805 and 1,080 ICBMs. As the new SS-9s and SS-11s were deployed, it was assumed that the older SS-6 Sapwood, SS-7 Saddler, and SS-8 Sasin ICBMs would be retired (much as the U.S. Atlas and Titan I ICBMs had been retired as the Minuteman force grew). The Soviets surpassed the lower end of McNamara's estimate for 1971 by the end of 1968. There were no moves to retire the SS-7s or SS-8s, while only the SS-6s deployed at Plesetsk were removed from service.

The 1967 NIE projected that the Soviets would deploy between one thousand and twelve hundred ICBMs, giving them a slight numerical superiority. It further assumed that the SS-9 force would be limited to between 180 and 222 missiles, while the lighter SS-11s would make up the bulk of Soviet missile forces, with 560 to 610 deployed. In the longer term, the Soviets were expected to deploy the solid-fuel SS-13 Savage ICBM. This was a missile nearly identical in design to the U.S. Minuteman. This had been long anticipated, as it was assumed that the Soviets would find the low cost of such an ICBM attractive, just as the United States had with the Minuteman. By mid-1972 the SS-13 force was expected to number between 250 and 300, both silo-based and mobile.

These beliefs continued in NIE 8-11-68, issued in October of 1968 and the final such report of the Johnson administration. The NIE predicted that "the Soviets will shortly overcome the U.S. lead in number of ICBM launchers." Despite this, it continued, the Soviets would reason that "further increments to their strategic forces would have little effect on the relationship between the U.S. and the USSR." The major change in the estimate was a downgrading of the importance of the SS-13. Only one silo complex had been built, and deployment seemed to be at a slow pace. Any growth in the Soviet ICBM force was expected to be in SS-11s, with few SS-9 or SS-13 starts.

One complicating factor was President Johnson's February 1967 proposal for Strategic Arms Limitation Talks (SALT). As with earlier NIEs, this was put in the context of the Western debate over "guns vs. butter." The report concluded that the Soviets saw arms control "as an option that could conserve economic resources."

The estimators argued that it was "highly unlikely" that the Soviets would "try for strategic superiority of such an order that it could be translated into significant political gain." The estimators believed that the Soviets would recognize that such attempts would be ineffectual, would require unacceptable economic sacrifices, and "would almost certainly provoke a strong U.S. reaction." The possibility of superiority for military advantage, such as destroying U.S. nuclear forces in a first strike to reduce U.S. retaliation to "tolerable levels," was rejected out of hand as absolutely "not feasible."[35]

The breakout of Soviet missile forces and the start of ABM deployment represented a major setback for McNamara and the Whiz Kids. They believed they could create a perfect world, based on logic, reason, and rationality. They had a basic belief in the power of technology. One strategist wrote of how "technology seems to have a levelling effect which subsumes political, ideological, and social differences in various political systems." McNamara and the Whiz Kids saw themselves as the peak of a strategic learning curve. Their "intellectual inferiors" who held less-advanced ideas—be they the U.S. military, NATO allies, or the Soviets—were to be "educated."

They had sought to create a stable arms race; they saw no possibility of "nuclear superiority" and believed nuclear weapons had no political value. Instead, they advanced the doctrine of "mutually assured destruction," better known as "MAD." This theory held that even if the Soviets attacked first, enough U.S. nuclear weapons would survive to destroy the USSR. With both sides equally vulnerable, both sides would be deterred from launching an attack. Once this capability had been achieved, there was no reason to add more weapons, as they did not significantly increase the amount of damage.

Despite the "logic" of the Whiz Kids' analysis and their efforts at "education," the Soviets had refused to accept their doctrines. The Soviets had built an ICBM force larger than McNamara had deemed necessary for their security. More perplexing for McNamara was the Soviets' insistence on deploying defensive measures. The Moscow ABM defenses were judged crude and easily penetrated. He simply could not understand why the USSR continued to spend vast sums on such "porous" defenses. He could only assume it was the result of the distraction effect of tradition, and "fanaticism" from "their strong emotional need to defend Mother Russia."

In the wake of these rebuffs, McNamara sought to present both an overall explanation for the arms race and the means of stabilizing it. McNamara delivered this in a speech on September 19, 1967. He started from the premise that each side only sought to preserve an assured destruction capability. However, both the United States and the Soviet Union had misinterpreted the defense programs of the other. The U.S. defense build-up of the early 1960s had been seen by the Soviets as an attempt to gain a first-strike capability. To counter the resulting Soviet build-up, McNamara announced, the United States would build its own ABM to defend cities and would equip missiles with multiple independently targeted reentry vehicles (MIRVs).

"It is precisely this action-reaction phenomenon that fuels an arms race," McNamara stated. The deployment of weapons gained an irrational (McNamara used the term "mad") momentum of its own. He blamed an intelligence failure for the U.S.-USSR arms race. While McNamara had, in previous years, expressed confidence in intelligence estimates, he now said "the blunt fact remains that if we had had more accurate information about planned [Soviet] strategic forces, we simply would not have needed to build as large a nuclear arsenal as we have today."[36]

In retrospect, McNamara's assessment was at best superficial and, at worst, a rewriting of history. It assumed that U.S. and Soviet strategic goals were identical. McNamara's simplified description was more akin to the naval arms race between the European powers before

World War I than the ideologically driven conflict between the United States and the USSR. More important, the U.S. missile build-up was not based on the erroneous missile gap estimates. McNamara knew, thanks to Corona, that the Soviets had only a token ICBM force by the fall of 1961. Yet, he had approved a major build-up. McNamara implied that the United States had overestimated the planned Soviet ICBM force, resulting in too large a force, which caused a Soviet response. In reality, McNamara and the NIE authors had consistently *underestimated* Soviet plans, assuming that they would not attempt to match the United States in ICBMs.[37]

Life with Corona

The March 15, 1967, meeting of Southern educators and government officials in Nashville, Tennessee, was a routine political event for President Johnson. Helped along by several Jack Daniels, he was in an expansive mood. During an informal session, Johnson said:

> I wouldn't want to be quoted on this, but we've spent $35–40 billion on the space program. And if nothing else had come out of it except the knowledge we've gained from space photography, it would be worth ten times what the whole program has cost. Because, tonight, we know how many missiles the enemy has. And, it turns out, our [previous] guesses were way off. We were doing things we didn't need to do. We were building things we didn't need to build. We were harboring fears we didn't need to harbor.[38]

There were more than a hundred people in the room who were not bound by press rules regarding "off-the-record" statements, so within days, President Johnson's comments were published. It was the first official public acknowledgment that the United States used reconnaissance satellites since the secrecy order had descended five years before. Those connected with the satellite effort were not pleased.

For those whose lives were entwined with Corona, secrecy affected everything they did, both at work and at home. The most feared and admired man in the Corona program was Henry Thomas, the CIA security officer. He was a tough individual who had "god-like" powers; he could remove a person from the program on the spot. When he conducted a security inspection of a facility, the staff had five minutes to produce the needed records.[39]

Before being allowed into the Corona program, one had to undergo a security indoctrination. The experience was traumatic for one Lockheed engineer who worked on the camera system. For a year after becoming part of the Corona program, it was physically difficult for him to say the words "film" or "cassette" in public. He was afraid he might somehow let slip his special knowledge.

Corona also placed tremendous demands on family life. Cleared personnel could not, of course, tell their own families what they did at work. They would often have to leave at a moment's notice, without telling their wives and children where they were going, how long they would be gone, or why it was so important. Secrecy fueled curiosity, and one engineer's son kept asking what his job was. The father would only give evasive answers, such as, "Well, I build airplanes." The son continued to make guesses, and the father finally admitted, "Son, everything I told you was a lie."[40]

While it was engineers at Lockheed, General Electric, and other contractors who built Corona, the program's ultimate results depended on a few skilled optical technicians at Itek who produced the multi-element lenses. The techniques they used differed little from those of the great nineteenth-century telescope makers such as Alvan Clark. Once each of the lens elements was rough-ground on a machine, the optical technicians would polish and figure them by hand. The Corona lenses had requirements far more stringent than those for astronomical telescopes. To achieve the 160 lines/mm resolution of the KH-4B cameras, the complete lens assembly could not deviate from a perfect shape by more than one-fortieth of a wavelength of light. The optical technicians were achieving precision on literally an atomic scale.[41]

The Corona launch crews at Vandenberg AFB had a reputation for being "colorful." Several of the Douglas personnel had been involved with the V-2 launches at White Sands nearly two decades before. They were known as "broomlighters," from the practice of igniting reluctant V-2 engines with kerosene-soaked brooms. With the Thor launches, that tactic was not required, but several times the "Douglas Daredevils" fixed a problem on the booster, then drove their car at high speed *in reverse* from the pad to the blockhouse, arriving just as the Thor engine ignited. The blockhouse crew could only watch in awe.[42]

In the 1960s, the act of launching a rocket was akin to a black art. Boosters would fail for the most trivial of reasons, or for no apparent reason at all. Not surprisingly, the launch crews became as superstitious as baseball players. There were "traditions" to insure a successful mission. On one launch, the liquid oxygen line to the Thor booster froze and would not release. An Air Force master sergeant had to use a sledgehammer to knock it loose so the launch could proceed. The mission was highly successful, so to avoid tempting fate, on subsequent launches, the same Air Force sergeant would give the connection a ceremonial tap with the sledgehammer.[43]

Another unusual feature of Vandenberg launches was the nicknames given to missions. A few had the kind of soaring grandeur that befit a rocket launch, such as "Flying Yankee" (*Discoverer 1*) and "High Journey" (Corona flight 102). After eighty-one Corona launches, "Old Hat" seemed appropriate for number 82, while "Bucket Factory" (Corona flight 91) was also fitting for a KH-4A flight. Quite a number were, to say the least, strange: "Bench Warrant" (*Discoverer 21*), "Chili Willie" (Corona 67), "Beagle Hound" (Corona 80), "Word Scramble" (Corona 99), and "Giant Banana" (Corona 116). Several, in retrospect, tempted fate. "Crisp Bacon" (*Discoverer 28*), suffered an Agena failure, reentered, and lived up to its nickname, while "Nice Bird" (Corona flight 78) proved anything but, when it reentered over South America.

To Catch A Falling Star

At the other end of the mission, the recovery crews awaited the capsules' return. By 1965 the 6593rd Test Squadron had been renamed the 6594th Recovery Control Group. In 1967, the unit was again redesignated, becoming the 6594th Test Group. Jim Muehlberger, who was with the unit until mid-1963, recalled there were a lot of squadron parties. The most memorable occurred about a year after they deployed to Hawaii, in the middle of the bad streak of Discoverer failures. It occurred because two of the unit's C-119s had been built by Kaiser-Fraser. When industrialist Henry Kaiser learned of this, he invited the entire squadron—125 pilots, crewmen, ground support personnel, and staff—to his Hawaiian plantation for a party. One memory that stayed with Muehlberger was that every building was pink.[44]

If the unit played hard, it was also true they worked hard, flying nearly daily practice missions. The early training flights involved four C-119s taking turns catching 120-pound cement blocks dropped from one of the other C-119s. By early December 1960, the unit had made 2,000 simulated midair recoveries, with a 95 percent success rate. (By the time the squadron was disbanded in 1987, the final total had reached over forty thousand practice and training pickups.) If a pilot should miss a drop one week, he was expected to make two tries the next.[45]

The 6593rd Test Squadron received the Mackay Trophy in recognition of the most meritorious flights of 1960. These were the recoveries of the *Discoverer 14, 17,* and *18* capsules. Soon after, the secrecy order descended and the unit's further achievements were unknown and unrecognized by outsiders.

As with the majority of the people involved with Corona, the recovery aircrews were never told the capsules contained film. Muehlberger recalled that the rumor was that they carried tissue samples, mice, and other test specimens. This was true, to a limited extent. The Discoverer reconnaissance flights had carried scientific experiments as cover, while the Corona capsules continued to carry cosmic ray experiments. The results of the experiments were published in scientific journals, without the satellites being explicitly identified.

The secrecy surrounding the program had its unusual aspects. Major Hines's crew was selected to star in a classified training film about the midair recoveries, *To Catch A Falling Star.* This film was never intended to be seen by the public, but only by those connected with the program. Even so, they could not be identified. The crew members were told to walk toward the aircraft, with their backs toward the camera. They were specifically instructed not to show their faces. In close-up shots, actors portrayed the aircrew.[46]

By the mid- and late 1960s, the unit had polished the recovery procedures into a complex ballet. It began with the launch of a Corona or Gambit satellite from Vandenberg AFB. While the satellite orbited, the unit had to be continuously ready to perform a recovery, in the event the capsule was called down early. Each day, at least one of the satellite's sixteen orbits would allow a recovery in the ballpark. An "estimated time of parachute deployment" (ETPD) would be continuously calculated for any suitable daylight pass. All activities—preflight briefings, engine start, takeoff, and arrival at the ballpark—were then calculated backward from the ETPD.

When a capsule recovery was scheduled, the 6594th Test Group began preparations hours before dawn. At the Operations Building, the crews reported for duty and were briefed on routes, weather information, approximate ballpark location, and takeoff time. In the Recovery

Section, equipment was issued, double-checked, and delivered to the JC-130s. The aircraft to be flown that day were fueled and preflighted.

The first aircraft to launch was an uprange telemetry plane, whose job was to pick up the telemetry signals from the bucket's two UHF beacons. It was followed by the weather reconnaissance plane, which was timed to arrive over the ballpark at first light. Its crew evaluated the weather conditions and decided whether the recovery attempt should proceed or be called off, or if the ballpark should be moved. These were critical recommendations, as once the capsule separated, it was committed.

Should the recovery be on, the JC-130 recovery planes would take off. When they arrived over the ballpark, the planes deployed in a specific flight pattern designed to allow triangulation on the descending capsule and provided maximum coverage.[47] Once the capsule was spotted, the aircraft commander ordered the crew to begin rigging the equipment. The plane was depressurized and the rear ramp and door were opened. (Because they were at 20,000 feet, the crew had to use oxygen masks.) The winch was turned on, the forty-foot-long carbon steel recovery poles were pushed to the aft end of the recovery dolly, and some of the recovery loops were deployed. These were loops of half-inch nylon line with several bronze four-tined grappling hooks to snare the parachute. The dolly was then moved to the ramp, the rest of the loops were deployed, and the poles were lowered until they hung down at a 45-degree angle.

The primary recovery plane made a fly-by to inspect the parachute, shroud lines, and capsule. Once the aircraft commander was satisfied, he notified the crew he was ready to make the recovery. At an altitude of 15,000 feet, he turned the plane to begin a straight-in run on the parachute. After getting a final "Ready" call from the back of the plane, the aircraft commander announced, "Ten seconds" over the intercom. The winch operator replied, "Ready winch."

As the plane passed over the parachute, the loops snagged it and pulled free of the poles. The aft pole handler yelled, "Contact," and the winch began to play out. The computer-controlled winch kept a preset tension on the collapsed parachute as it brought the capsule up to the speed of the plane. The winch brakes began to hum as they slowed the line to a stop. The aft pole handler then called out, "In trail."

The winch operator began to reel in the capsule, as the ramp operator kept him informed about its progress. The recovery loop and the tangled parachute entered the opening of the recovery dolly first, followed by the shroud lines. As the capsule neared the ramp, the winch operator lowered the forward part of the dolly so it could be brought aboard safely. The winch was then stopped, the dolly boom was raised so the capsule would not hit the cargo floor, and finally the dolly was moved forward. With the bucket now inside the plane, the poles were raised, the ramp and door were closed, and the plane was repressurized. The capsule was lowered into a container, and its lid was locked and sealed.[48]

Once the JC-130 arrived back at Hickam AFB, a truck would back up to the rear of the plane. The JC-130 crews were not allowed to meet the personnel on the truck, and had to leave the plane through the front crew door. The container would be loaded on the truck and driven to a waiting jet. The recovery crews had no idea where it was going or what was done with the capsule.

Like fighter pilots, the recovery crews kept score. Each midair recovery was recorded in a little notebook. When a pilot made his first recovery, his name would be entered with a cherry beside it. When he made his fifth recovery, an ace of spades symbol would be added. Because the pilots stayed with the unit for many years, remarkable scores were achieved. At the end of the Corona program, there was a two-way tie for first. Lt. Col. Edwin R. Bayer and Maj. Walter M. Milam each had twelve recoveries. This total included both Corona capsules (seven for Bayer and six for Milam) and other satellites. There was a three-way tie for second, with eight each for Maj. Albert F. Muller, Maj. Dale M. Palmer, and Capt. Richard M. Scofield. Third was split four ways among Lt. Col. James F. McDonald, Jr., and Captains Jeremiah J. Collins, Douglas S. Sliger, and James E. Varnadoe, each with seven. Another five pilots had six recoveries, while seven more pilots had five recoveries. These 21 pilots made a total of 141 midair recoveries. Of these, 94 were Corona capsules.

As with other aces, their achievements were made possible by the hard work of a large group of people. It was the ground crews who maintained the aircraft. Thanks to their efforts, there were no fatal accidents with the C-119s or JC-130s. Support also came from a number of technical representatives (tech reps) from the aircraft, engine, electronics, and recovery equipment contractors. Harry Conway was the tech rep with responsibility for the recovery gear. In the early 1950s, he had pioneered the concept of ground-to-air recoveries.

During the early tests, he had been picked up from the ground by low-flying aircraft. He was with the midair recovery program from the start of development to the end. If there were problems, Conway came up with a solution. Hines said later, "Without Harry we could not have had a recovery system."

The flights of the Corona satellites were only the first part of the effort. They were the tools to acquire photos of the USSR and other areas of interest. Translating the photos into usable intelligence was the job of the photo interpreters at NPIC. The next two chapters will examine that side of the Corona story.

EIGHT

Magic in Their Eyes
The Art of Satellite Photo Interpretation

Each day and each frame of film was the most rewarding adventure. . . .
We knew that our interpretation and analysis had to be precise, because
we knew we were only a few steps away from the President, his policy
makers, and Congress.

Dino A. Brugioni, Corona Seminar, May 1995

➤ Arthur Lundahl, the head of NPIC during the Corona
years, would often give new photo interpreters an example of what
could be learned from overhead photography. He would tell them to
draw a 25-mile circle on a map. Through a careful analysis of overhead photos of that circle, Lundahl would tell the new photo interpreters, one could discover what people there eat, what they wear,
their sources of water, how and where they are educated, what crops
they grow, how they make a living, what manufactured goods they
produce, their customs and religion, where they make their homes,
how they interact with nature, and, finally, where they are born and
where they are buried.

The point of this analogy is that reconnaissance photos are not simply about counting bombers or missiles. Rather, they provide a complete understanding of a *society*, without ever having visited it.

This is especially important when that circle is in a "Denied Area."

Learning to See: The Signatures

The photo interpreter's skill and understanding is the first step in trans-
forming satellite images into knowledge that can be used by political

and military leaders to guide national policy. The photo interpreter must pay attention to detail, be curious, be skilled at inductive and deductive reasoning, be able to recognize patterns, have both technical knowledge and a sense of history, and above all, have good eyesight.[1]

When the first Corona photos arrived at NPIC, the photo interpreters were looking at areas of the Soviet Union that had never been seen by Western eyes—whole cities whose existence had been reported but whose locations were uncertain, and facilities whose existence had not even been suspected.

To understand their meaning, the photo interpreters relied on specific clues, called "P. I. keys" or "signatures," which would allow them to identify many of the facilities they were seeing in the pictures.[2] These signatures range from the simple to the extremely subtle. The shape, size, tone, and texture of an object are all important signatures, as are patterns, shadows, location, and the association between objects and their location.[3] People's lives are controlled by laws, traditions, and practices. This is even truer for military organizations, where every step of a soldier's day, or the deployment of a weapon, is set by orders, safety considerations, and operational requirements.

When the film from *Discoverer 14* was recovered, the photo interpreters did not know what an operational Soviet ICBM site would look like. The major breakthrough came with the recovery of *Discoverer 25* (Mission 9017) in June 1961. Its photos showed the first Soviet ICBM sites under construction, as well as MRBM and IRBM bases. Because the deployment pattern of a particular weapon system was identical for each site, once the signature was identified, all subsequent sites could be identified.

By the fall of 1961, the signatures for SS-4, -5, -6, -7, and -8 missile sites had been identified.[4] An SS-5 MRBM site under construction, for instance, showed four long, parallel excavations for the launch pads. These were called "slash marks," and were enough to positively identify a site. An SS-7 site had four square cleared areas connected by roads.

The signatures for each type of weapon, military facility, and industrial plant had to be determined. At the start of Corona, some information was available from U.S. examples (photo interpreters visited U.S. guided missile, nuclear, and military installations for signatures), intelligence data, and the U-2 and World War II German GX photos. These data were often limited or out of date, however, so it was not

Soviet SS-5 IRBM site at Sary Ozek in the southern USSR. This KH-4B photo from Mission 1115 (taken on September 8, 1971) gives examples of the signatures used by photo interpreters. It is surrounded by five fences, indicating it is a sensitive facility. The dark grass between the fences further points it out. The four missile sheds are in a row—an identifying feature of SS-5 sites. *National Archives*

surprising that the "anomalies list" of unknown objects in the early Corona years was "tens of tens of tens" long. There were, for example, twelve or thirteen "Sensitive Operational Complexes." They all looked the same, but NPIC did not have a more descriptive term, and did not know their exact function.[5]

Because of the relatively poor quality of the early Corona photos and the fact that for the first two years of the program the interpreters had only monoscopic coverage, the photo interpreters designated many targets as "probable" or "possible." This division into probable and possible allowed the photo interpreters to give a sense of how sure they were of a specific facility. "Probable" meant the photo interpreter was 80 to 90 percent sure of its identity (depending on the picture quality and the day), while "possible" meant 50 percent sure. Above "probable" was "confirmed"; below "possible" was "unknown." In the early days, there were a lot of probables and possibles. There was an interplay with CIA headquarters analysts who often did not understand and would ask, "If that's a probable ICBM, what's an improbable ICBM?"

Fitting the Puzzle Together

In trying to assemble the puzzle, the photo interpreters were unwittingly aided by the Soviets' obsession with secrecy. They ringed their missile sites and other facilities with two or three fences, with grass planted between the fences. The purpose was to prevent ground observation; the Soviets seemed to believe the primary threat was from lurking Western spies. The result of their security efforts, however, was actually to highlight the sites in satellite photos. To even a rank amateur interpreter, the triple fences were a giveaway that a site was a sensitive facility. The grass also appeared dark in the photos, making it stand out against the often barren landscape. NPIC was quick to take advantage of such sheer stupidity.

Each day, week, month, and season provided the photo interpreters with other clues. For example, Sunday mornings were the best time for order of battle data, as all the tanks and other vehicles were parked in garrisons. Observing the spring training exercises of ground forces was the best time for assessing their capabilities. Activities in forested areas were best observed in the spring, before the trees leafed out.

The hot, dusty Russian summers allowed "track activity" to be measured. When vehicles or feet travel repeatedly over the same route, they churn up the soil. This is clearly apparent in the photos, even with the relatively low resolution of the Corona photos. The amount of traffic is shown by the size of the trail; thus it is easy to gauge the importance of facilities by the trails. Major facilities have pronounced trails between them, while those that are less used have lighter, smaller trails. When the trails change in size, it indicates a shift in the level of activity, such as a launch pad being abandoned. Even if the targets of interest are hidden under trees, the tracks would lead the photo interpreters to them, as if there were sign posts.

The snows of winter are the photo interpreters' best friend. Not only does track activity stand out in a field of newly fallen snow, but all camouflage efforts are negated. "Disruptive patterns," the large blotches of camouflage paint familiar from World War II, are covered by snow. "Nets and garnishing" used to conceal the shape of an object are also exposed by snow. Even the way snow is cleared gives clues to the importance of various facilities. At bases, headquarters buildings are the first to have the snow cleared from the sidewalks, with the latrines a close second. The melting of the snow on roofs indicates which buildings are heated, and therefore active.[6]

As the years passed, and with tens of thousands of looks at targets, the signatures became apparent. The photo interpreters were also able to see relationships in the photos. By tracing cable lines between ICBM silos, it was discovered that the missiles were being deployed in groups of six or ten. Further observations indicated the missiles had, depending on the system, a two- or three-year maintenance cycle. The Soviets would either remove the missiles from the silos or work on the missiles for a time.

With ground forces, it became possible to identify specific units. Sometimes the Soviets would be so obliging as to put the unit insignia in front of the headquarters building. Other times it was more subtle. Their equipment, for example, was one signature. If Corona photos showed new T-62 tanks, it was probably an elite Guards armored division; if only World War II T-34s were visible, it was an undermanned reserve unit. To a limited extent, the unit's readiness for combat could also be determined.

The same teams would follow the same targets for years. The Soviet facilities became as familiar as the photo interpreters' own neighborhoods. As with one's neighborhood, it was quickly apparent when something had changed. These specialized teams, and their continuity of experience, were a major reason Corona was so successful. Unlike the civilians at NPIC, military photo interpreters were transferred often and did not have the chance to develop this level of specialized experience.

At the same time, the Corona photos represented a flood of data. Each day a satellite was in orbit provided as much coverage as the whole of the U-2 overflight program. A single Corona mission could photograph half to two-thirds of the total Soviet landmass, plus other selected areas around the world. The photo interpreters had to meet the new

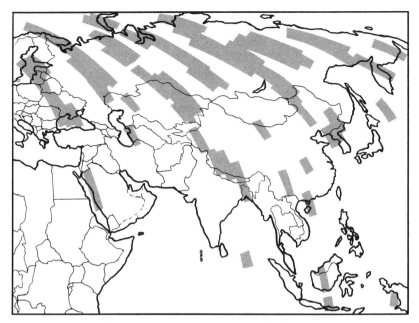

Typical coverage of a KH-4A/B payload during the first half of a mission. Unlike the blanket coverage of *Discoverer 14*, by this point the Corona satellites could be targeted on specific areas of interest. The wide area of each photo meant that many countries, such as North Korea, could be completely covered in two or three passes. *Map by Joel Carpenter*

demands this sheer abundance represented. They would have to carefully examine an area larger than the United States every few weeks.

The sheer volume of photos was reflected in missed targets and misidentifications. Whenever a new target was found in satellite footage, the photo interpreters would go back to the last time the area had been covered, to see what had been there before. Often, the "new" target was visible, usually under construction, in the earlier coverage, several months before. Eventually, just about everything was found, but often much later than it should have been. In a few cases, targets were misidentified and the original report had to be retracted.[7]

Soviet Deception Efforts

From the start of the Corona project, there had been fears of possible Soviet deception and camouflage. The "Potemkin village" was, after all, a Russian invention. With the low resolution of the initial camera, it was possible the Soviets could have built decoy airbases, factories, and missile sites that would be indistinguishable from the real thing. Lundahl and the other senior staff at NPIC all had World War II photoreconnaissance experience, and they knew the effectiveness of decoys during the war. Strategic deception had had a major role in Allied wartime success. Against Corona, similar efforts could greatly limit the satellites' effectiveness.

When the first Corona photos were analyzed, the photo interpreters saw that the Soviet Union was "wide open," with no camouflage or deception efforts. Apparently there were doubts within the Soviet government about the technical feasibility of satellite reconnaissance. However, Khrushchev himself became increasingly nervous as the Discoverer launches continued, even with the failures. When finally told the satellites could photograph the Earth, Khrushchev ordered the Ministry of Defense to begin construction of false missile sites and submarines.[8]

It was not until about four years into Corona operations that photo interpreters began to see evidence of Soviet deception and concealment efforts. During the period of Corona operations, a number of methods were observed. In 1964, the Soviets were first spotted painting their ICBM complexes with disruptive patterns. Most of the painting was done between 1966 and 1968, when Soviet ICBM deployments surged. The Soviets also used "tonal blending," which was intended to hide the missile sites using suitable colors. The efforts were not directed at the satellites, but rather to make the sites difficult to spot by bomber crews making low-level attacks on them.

Between 1966 and 1971, the Soviets built dummy roads to confuse bomber crews. Starting in 1968, dummy SAM sites started to be built at the rate of five or ten per year. In 1966, the Soviets established a satellite warning system, which notified military commanders that U.S. satellites would be in position to monitor their activities during certain times. Sensitive operations could then be halted and new equipment, such as prototype aircraft being test flown, could be hidden away. In 1967, the satellite photos began to show covers being placed over missile launchers. These may have been intended to conceal the missile underneath or to protect missiles from the cold winters. (Use of the covers was most pronounced between 1972 and 1975, after the end of the Corona program.)

With the growth of the Soviet missile submarine force in the late 1960s, major concealment efforts began to appear in this area. In 1967, the first work began on submarine tunnels. In 1970, three such tunnels were being built to provide both concealment and protection against attack. Also in 1970, the first submarine covers were seen in satellite photos. Again, it was not clear if these were meant as protection against weather or observation. (As with the missile covers, widespread use of the submarine covers did not come until 1974–75, after Corona's end.) The most ambitious, and least successful, of the submarine deception efforts began in 1971. This was the construction of dummy subs. One set of photos became legendary. A Soviet naval base was photographed shortly before a storm hit. On the next pass, a "submarine" had been bent in half by the storm. (The dummy subs were last seen in 1974.)

Those connected with the satellite programs felt such efforts had only limited success. The dummy subs and covers, it was felt, did not prevent the United States from having an accurate count of Soviet submarines. It did, however, make it difficult to know how many were in port at a given time.[9]

As with their ordinary military operations, the Soviets' deception and camouflage efforts were harmed by their own sloppiness and predictability. The rubber mockups were allowed to deflate and not pumped back up, the tail of a wooden airplane was knocked off and not replaced, a fake missile site was built without a road leading to it, and some dummy equipment was not moved for two and a half years.

Over time, the deception efforts became apparent. One of the reasons for the secrecy surrounding the photos was to prevent the Soviets from knowing the United States had detected the signatures, and to prevent them from realizing how predictable and obvious they were.[10] However, as Dave Doyle, a photo interpreter and manager at NPIC during the Corona years, observed, a successful camouflage or deception effort, by definition, cannot be detected.[11]

The threat this posed was shown by the Chinese. They were far less predictable than the Soviets. Their missile sites were very hard to find, and they were using camouflage quite early. Their gaseous-diffusion plant, used to produce nuclear bomb material, was painted with a disruptive finish. (As the building was some 2,000 feet long, this was not successful.) Sometimes it took years to identify Chinese military installations. One example was a series of mound-shaped structures surrounded by a moat. Their function was unknown until all of the sites had been spotted. Their location finally gave away their function—they had been placed along traditional invasion routes, that is, the route Soviets would take in a ground invasion. They were defensive positions.[12]

NPIC

The U-2 and Corona programs saw a major growth in CIA photo inter-pretation efforts. The original group was expanded to about one hun-dred people for the U-2 overflights. They were initially located in the Steuart Motor Company Building at 5th and K Streets, N.W., in Wash-ington, D.C. The facility, set up in June 1955, had the code name "HTAutomat," after the famed New York City restaurant. (The "HT" stood for Henry Thomas, the CIA security officer who approved the name.) At the Automat, one could get a snack, or a four-course din-ner, even in the middle of the night; Lundahl wanted the facility to be the intelligence counterpart of its namesake.

The facility itself was a "squalid building amid . . . squalid sur-roundings." NPIC occupied the fourth through the seventh floors, while cars continued to be sold in the ground floor showroom. The building lacked air conditioning and adequate heating, which made living conditions intolerable year-round. It had been built during World War II of substitute material. The ceiling was made of com-pressed seaweed, which flaked off constantly. The linoleum floor tiles curled up in the humidity of the Washington summer.

Unlike the real Automat, there were no food or cafeteria facilities in the building, and the photo interpreters had to either bring their own lunches and dinners, eat at a nearby all-night diner, or pick up food in the Center City Market. Parking was a problem, and most of the employees carpooled to work. On the ride in, the photo interpre-ters would discuss the weather and the fortunes of the Washington Redskins football team. The cars were parked in alleys or in spaces rented in backyards or from local businesses. Employees had to bribe the local children not to scratch their cars. The area was littered with broken bottles, abandoned cars, and trash.[13]

Behind the decaying facade, Lundahl had assembled a uniquely tal-ented group. What their workplace lacked in amenities was more than made up for by their skills. Lundahl established high standards, but also gave the NPIC personnel wide latitude and freedom of action. He did not set down rules, but believed that the personnel would be more successful if given the independence to be creative.[14] Like all great leaders, Lundahl understood that loyalty from below was earned by loyalty from above. The cleaning women at NPIC, for example, lacked an area to sit down during their breaks. Lundahl told them to use his office. He then saw to it that there was a pot of tea waiting for them.

By 1962, with Corona operational, it was clear the Steuart Building was no longer adequate. Members of the President's Foreign Intelligence Board had toured the building and were shocked by its condition. They recommended that a new home for NPIC be found. President Kennedy approved and told CIA Director McCone, "I want you to get them out of that structure," and asked how long it would take. McCone told him that the best possibility was a building on the grounds of the Washington Navy Yard, but that it would take a year to refurbish it. Kennedy said, "All right, you do it."

The new NPIC facility, called "Building 213," opened on January 1, 1963. It had 200,000 square feet of floor space, better facilities, air conditioning, and ample parking. There was now room for hundreds more personnel. The Steuart Building's primary security was its condition and location. (No Soviet intelligence officer would suspect that such an important facility would be located in a firetrap building amid a Washington, D.C., ghetto.) The new NPIC facility relied on physical security—most of the windows in the five-story building were bricked up to prevent eavesdropping, and it was set well away from any public areas.[15]

Besides the new facilities, NPIC also saw major advances in equipment during the Corona years. For the U-2, hand-held 7- to 13-power magnifiers, fixed 2.4- or 7-power stereoscopes, and 10- to 60-power zoom stereoscopes were used. Corona photos required an upgrade. Each KH-4B frame was 2.18 inches wide by 29.8 inches long and covered an area of 8.6 by 117 nautical miles. Looking at a print of a frame, one could see rivers and other geographic features, but only very large man-made objects, such as airfields, could be seen with the naked eye. Photos from the KH-4 series cameras, however, could be magnified as much as 100 times. At high magnification, tanks and aircraft became clear and specific types could be identified. The ability to take stereo photos was another major advance. New techniques and equipment, such as microstereoscopes and comparators, were developed to cope with the Corona photos. The chemicals and papers used for prints and briefing boards were also improved.

A few individuals had a critical role in the expansion and success of NPIC. One such person was Dr. Edwin Land. He had a major impact on intelligence operations, from the beginning of the U-2 through the development of follow-on satellites to Corona. He would often come to NPIC with suggestions and ideas for improvements to photo interpretation equipment and techniques.

Although Dr. Land's contributions to U.S. intelligence and national security were beyond price, at least one of his ideas was memorably unsuccessful. Dr. Land suggested that since the films were taken in stereo, they should be viewed in stereo. NPIC issued a contract to Bausch and Lomb to develop a stereo projection system. After the system was delivered, however, it was found that the photo interpreters felt as if their eyeballs were being jerked out of their heads after about an hour. It was like watching microfilm flash by on a viewer. The job fell to Dino Brugioni, who was in charge of the target data base, to brief Dr. Land on the machine. At the end of the presentation, Brugioni told him, "Sir, it just doesn't work. Sit down and try it." Dr. Land sat down and tried it. He finally looked up at Brugioni and said, "Well, it was only an idea."

Another individual important to NPIC's development was Gen. James H. "Jimmy" Doolittle. Although he achieved fame as a test pilot and air racer in the 1930s and as the leader of the attack on Tokyo in 1942, his role in intelligence is almost unknown. He was a member of the President's Board of Consultants on Foreign Intelligence from 1955 through 1965. As such, he was one of those responsible for the recommendation to develop a covert interim reconnaissance satellite. He would often tour NPIC with the other members of the board, then come back later to talk individually with the photo interpreters, to judge their work and learn what they needed. Both Dr. Land and General Doolittle gave unstintingly of their time, at a cost to their business activities, yet never asked for a penny in return.

A political figure who had a critical role in the development of intelligence and satellite reconnaissance was Sen. Barry Goldwater (R-Ariz.). Like Doolittle, he would come to NPIC, sit down with the interpreters, and go over their analyses. (Senator Goldwater was a skilled photographer in his own right.)

As with Dr. Land, one visit by Senator Goldwater became the stuff of NPIC legend. The NPIC staff knew Senator Goldwater liked to make models, and he was asked if he wanted to see the model shop. He said he would like to very much, so his guide said, "Sir, you go down to this corridor and you turn to your left." Goldwater looked at him and responded, "I've never turned left in my whole life." At the model shop he was shown how to use super glue. Unfortunately, Goldwater was a bit clumsy with it, and NPIC suddenly had to deal with a United States senator with his fingers glued together. Staff members were running around with solvents trying to get his hand unstuck.[16]

Mighty Oaks

The process for interpreting the Corona photos followed a certain routine at NPIC. Whenever a capsule was recovered, Brugioni would give a briefing on the targets covered and any weather that might affect the interpretation. The photo interpreters would then begin a preliminary analysis of the film, based on a three-step process developed during World War II. The initial or "flash" phase was a quick read-out of the photos, looking for critical developments. Should any be spotted, photo briefing boards would be created and Lundahl and the DCI would brief the president. Because such developments required a policy decision, a "hold" would often be placed on the information. This meant that it would not be distributed to the rest of the intelligence community until the president had seen it. The second phase was a closer analysis, leading to a written report describing activity at each facility visible in the film. The third phase was a detailed examination of specific areas of interest. This might note changes over a period of years or even decades.

Beginning in the fall of 1961, NPIC photo interpreters were organized into "search teams." Each three-man team specialized in a particular area—aviation, missiles (ICBMs, SAMs, and ABMs), nuclear energy, and so forth. Two of the team members looked at the new film through a rear projection viewer, while the third was at a 40-inch-long light table with a stereoscope. A fourth person helped out by getting maps, the "black books" containing photos and data on Soviet missiles, and other information the team needed.[17]

In analyzing the new film and preparing the second-phase written report, the photo interpreters were guided by worksheets that listed specific requirements. These were established by COMOR and would specify what targets were to be examined and what activities they were to look for. In addition to such "COMOR targets," the photo interpreters were looking for other areas of interest (non-COMOR targets) and any surprises (bonus targets). The geographic coordinates of any new targets would be fed into a computer data base.

As the photo interpreters examined each frame, they wrote their observations on the worksheets. These would be checked by an editor for style and completeness, and then passed on to the mission coordinator for approval. A keypunch operator would make an IBM card for each line of text. The cards would then be fed into a mainframe computer and a proof sheet would be printed out in subject order. This would be corrected and reviewed, then the final text would be printed. The whole process might require the photo interpreters and others to work long into the night. Finally, the finished report would be sent by low-speed secure teletype lines and in printed form to the rest of the intelligence community.[18]

The initial report produced during the second phase was called an "Oak" (referring to the phrase, "From little acorns, mighty Oaks grow"). The Oak listed the highlights of targets covered, general activity, new targets, and the quality of the photos. For example, the Oak for Mission 1042-1 of June 17–22, 1967, noted:

> Nine of the 24 deployed ICBM complexes are covered on this mission. Kostroma and Yurya are completely covered on clear photography. Drovyanaya, Imeni Gastello, Olovyannaya, Tatishchevo, Teykovo, Uzhur, and Yoshkar-Ola are observed through scattered-to-heavy clouds. Six Type IIID sites are newly identified. Five sites, including a control site, are identified at Olovyannaya. . . . At Kostroma, a possible site is identified at the transfer point.

Specific descriptions of each target would follow:

KAPUSTIN YAR LAUNCH COMPLEX D

An aerodynamic vehicle, similar to others observed previously, is on a launcher at launch area 3D.

Vehicles/pieces of equipment are on the roads behind the check-out building.

KAPUSTIN YAR LAUNCH COMPLEX G

A row of vehicles/equipment is just north of the barracks area.

No new construction, changes in facilities, or previously unreported features observed.[19]

Because of the amount of worldwide coverage a single capsule could provide, there were several Oaks per mission. Mission 1042-1 also produced a Middle East edition and a South China/North Vietnam edition. The number of targets covered by a single read-out was astonishing. The three Oaks from Mission 1042-1 covered 53 COMOR and 6 bonus targets in the USSR and China; 129 COMOR, 12 non-COMOR, and 3 bonus targets in the Middle East; and 138 COMOR and 3 non-COMOR targets in North Vietnam.[20]

The third phase produced intelligence reports on specific targets, based on specific requirements of COMOR and the rest of the U.S. intelligence community. These reports were often historically oriented. They described not only the function of a specific target, but its development over time. A December 1963 report on Soviet solid-fuel propellant test facilities and production plants used photos from twenty Corona missions between December 1960 and August 1963. (It even used captured GX photos from a July 22, 1942, German reconnaissance flight.)[21] Other reports used U-2 coverage as well. These reports included the satellite photos, line drawings of buildings, layout diagrams of plants, and maps of the area.

The procedure used in the third phase, called "comparative coverage," is a powerful tool in photo analysis. By comparing past photos of a target with new ones and with standard Soviet military practices, any changes become readily apparent. Even subtle differences in features might mean a major change in operations. (For example, during World War II, the major evidence that a German fighter base had been converted to an aircraft factory was the way the planes were being parked.) Because the clues being looked for were so subtle, considerable time was spent on these reports. A search team might spend several days or even weeks looking at just a few frames.

The Big Picture

The Corona photos, for all their importance, were only one of the elements which went into development of the intelligence "big picture." The results of the photo interpreters' efforts were sent to CIA headquarters, where they were woven together with other types of intelligence to form an "all sources" estimate of current trends and future developments.

Three broad categories formed the primary sources of U.S. intelligence, each with its particular importance, uses, and limitations. The first of these was imagery, such as the Corona photos, which gave the counts of weapons and the locations of facilities—so many bombers, the specific number of ICBMs, how many tanks or fighters or submarines Soviet factories could produce per year. Photos could provide facts—but not relationships or intentions.

The second category was signals intelligence. SIGINT covered a wide range of sources, such as intercepted radio messages between units in the field, or between those units and their higher command, up to the military and party leadership in Moscow. During the test launch of a new missile, SIGINT could provide communications and the telemetry signals from the missile to ground stations during its flight.

The role of SIGINT was to show relationships between units— which regiments were attached to which divisions, what the chain of command was from Moscow down to the individual tank commanders, and so on. SIGINT, when combined with satellite photos of training maneuvers, showed what tactics were being used. Telemetry from a missile test, when combined with satellite photos of the missile on its pad, showed the missile's capabilities, how the test program was progressing, and the threat the missile represented.

The final source of intelligence was the rarest and most fragile of all: human spies and defectors. Only the human spy could describe intentions and provide context to the other sources. If photos and SIG-INT provided a puzzle's pieces, then it was the human spy who supplied the picture on the box.[22]

The most valuable human source of the Corona era was Col. Oleg V. Penkovsky of the GRU (Soviet military intelligence). During 1961 and 1962, Penkovsky provided documents on Soviet strategy and GRU intelligence operations around the world, insights into the political and military leadership and the conflicts between them, and Khrushchev's intentions during the Berlin crisis. He indicated that Soviet missiles were few in number and had poor reliability. This information on the low numbers of Soviet missiles was confirmed by the early Corona photos.

Penkovsky also provided four photocopied plans of missile launching sites, as well as documents and manuals on the SA-2 Guideline SAM; the SS-1 Scud, SS-4 Sandal, and SS-5 Skean IRBMs; and the SS-6 Sapwood ICBM.

The SS-4 and SS-5 manuals were of critical importance during the Cuban missile crisis in determining when the sites would be operational and their refire rate. ("Ironbark," the code name for Penkovsky's missile information, appears on several CIA documents from the crisis.) The NPIC photo interpreters had access to his material; it helped to explain what they were seeing in the Corona photos, while the satellite photos illuminated the information Penkovsky had supplied.[23]

Such human sources were few in number and their usefulness was limited. During its 74 years of existence, the Soviet Union was organized as a "counterintelligence state." The KGB guards and the triple fences around military installations were specifically intended to prevent human spies from operating. There were also complicating factors within the U.S. government. McNamara and other Kennedy/Johnson administration officials disdained such material, as it did not match their numbers orientation or their preconceived notions. A more serious problem was the rampant suspicions of a Soviet "master plot" to deceive and control the CIA by use of disinformation from false Soviet defectors.[24]

The results of the all-source analysis were distilled into National Intelligence Estimates. It is instructive to compare two NIEs, one from the mid-1950s and another from the period just after Corona began operations. NIE 11-6-54, titled "Soviet Capabilities and Probable Programs in the Guided Missile Field," was issued on October 5, 1954. Its comments were very general: "The Soviets will probably devote highest priority to producing surface-to-air missiles. . . . The USSR will almost certainly have a requirement for submarine-launched missiles for nuclear attacks on U.S. and Allied coastal areas. . . . The USSR will probably give high priority to a ballistic missile for support of its field forces."

As for ICBMs (then called "IBMs") it said, "We believe that the USSR . . . will make a concerted effort to produce an IBM. In this event it probably could have ready for serial production in about 1963 (or at the earliest possible date in 1960) an IBM with a high yield nuclear warhead and [an accuracy] of roughly five nautical miles."

The report was very clear about the limitations of U.S. knowledge about Soviet missile activities. Most of the information came from German scientists who had worked for the Soviets, and had then been returned to the West. The scientists had been kept carefully isolated from Soviet development plans and activities. The NIE admitted, "Current intelligence on the particular missiles under development is almost nonexistent. . . . Our knowledge of current Soviet missile activities is so meager as to provide little basis for any firm estimate of the nature, scale—or even existence—of an actual Soviet production program."[25]

The overall impression given by this NIE about Soviet missile activities was that somehow, somewhere, something might be going on, but what it was could not be discovered. In reality, the Soviet missile program was much more advanced than the NIE indicated. Whereas the NIE said that "we have no evidence of any Soviet operational [SAMs]," the first Soviet SAM, the SA-1 Guild, was then being deployed around Moscow, while the SA-2 Guideline was beginning test launches.[26] The first Soviet submarine-launched missile was under development, and would make its first test launch about a year after the NIE was published. The SS-1b Scud short-range ballistic missile had been first launched in 1953, and would enter production in 1955. The SS-3 Shyster missile, which gave the Soviets the ability to strike U.S. bomber bases in Western Europe from Soviet territory, had begun test flights in April 1954.[27] Finally, design work for the SS-6 Sapwood ICBM had been under way since early 1951, with the design finalized in early 1954.[28]

We now jump ahead seven years, to NIE 11-8/1-61, "Strength and Deployment of Soviet Long Range Ballistic Missile Forces," dated September 21, 1961. Whereas the 1954 NIE was filled with qualifiers such as "will probably," "could also," and "we believe," the 1961 NIE included the specific numbers of ICBM and IRBM launchers, locations of ICBM sites, and drawings of both the operational bases and test centers, as well as data on the performance, range, warhead weight, accuracy, reliability rate, reaction time, and refire capability of the SS-3, -4, -5, -6, and -7 missiles.[29]

While the 1954 NIE could offer only generalities and guesses, the 1961 NIE—based on U-2 overflights, intercepted missile telemetry, Penkovsky's documents and information, and, most important of all, the film from six successful Discoverer satellites—provided specific, hard information. It was only with this kind of information that the president could make informed decisions, upon which the safety of the nation depended.

In the Halls of Power

In the final analysis, the ultimate purpose of all this effort was to guide the president of the United States, as both political leader and military commander in chief. To a real extent, the success of a president in foreign affairs depends on his use of intelligence. For any president, the most direct contact with reconnaissance is through briefings. During the Corona years, these were given by Lundahl, using notes prepared by Brugioni. Lundahl had large hands, and could hold the three-by-five-inch note cards in his open hand. During briefings, he would quickly glance down at the cards and then give detailed statistical data. This was quite impressive to the people being briefed, who did not see the cards.

Although there was a standardized format for briefing, each president had his own particular requirements, depending on his experience, background, and personality. Of the four presidents of the Corona years, the most knowledgeable about intelligence was Dwight Eisenhower. His role as supreme allied commander in Europe had given him direct contact with the most sensitive intelligence sources, including photoreconnaissance and the Ultra decoded messages. The German attacks at the Kasserine Pass in North Africa and the Battle of the Bulge also taught Eisenhower the limits of intelligence—that even with the best of sources, surprise was still possible, and with it, disaster. He understood the need for intelligence, and was a good photo interpreter in his own right.

Eisenhower wanted the briefings presented in a military manner, so Lundahl would use large briefing boards for the U-2 and Corona photos. Some briefings involved only Allen Dulles, Richard Bissell, and Lundahl. Eisenhower put great stress on secrecy. He did not discuss intelligence activities either as president or afterward. (Although he authorized the RB-47 overflights, Genetrix/WS-461L reconnaissance balloons, U-2 overflights, and Corona, he said nothing about them in his later memoirs.)[30]

John F. Kennedy was a junior naval officer in World War II, and did not have the personal experience with high-level intelligence that Eisenhower did. Soon after the election, Kennedy was tutored in aerial reconnaissance by Eisenhower, Lundahl, and Bissell. During the Kennedy administration, briefings were less formal than those for Eisenhower. Rather than using an easel, Lundahl would spread the briefing boards out on the coffee table in the Oval Office. Kennedy would sit in the famous rocking chair he used to ease his back pain and look at the prints through a magnifying glass. Lundahl, sitting at the coffee table, would explain the finer points of each photo. Kennedy became fascinated by the photo interpreting process. He would also sometimes ask for the original source material, to better judge an intelligence conclusion.[31]

Despite his close relationship with Lundahl, Kennedy still had problems understanding the specialized jargon of photo interpreting. In briefing him, Lundahl had to avoid using shorthand acronyms and technical terms as much as possible. They could not be avoided entirely, however.[32]

In contrast to his predecessors, Lyndon B. Johnson was colorless and crude in his dealings with intelligence. DCI McCone had his first meeting with Johnson on November 23, 1963. It soon became apparent that Johnson had no interest in being briefed. McCone soon stopped personally meeting with Johnson. Instead, Johnson received a written daily intelligence summary every evening at six o'clock for reading in bed that night. He insisted that it be kept to a single page in length. The only thing in which Johnson showed interest was stories of foreign leaders' sexual activities.

Johnson's main concerns were domestic, getting his Great Society programs passed. He and his advisers did not want intelligence reports that conflicted with existing policies. In early 1965, McCone confided to an aide that he could not get Johnson to read even the summaries of the CIA's annual assessment of Soviet capabilities and intentions. In April 1965, he resigned as DCI. His replacement, retired Navy Vice Adm. William F. "Red" Raborn, was selected specifically because he knew nothing about intelligence, and so could be counted on not to cause problems.

Beginning in February 1964, policymaking at the Johnson White House was concentrated within a narrow group of advisers at what became known as the "Tuesday lunches." Composed primarily of Johnson, Defense Secretary McNamara, Secretary of State Rusk, and adviser McGeorge Bundy (or, from April 1966, Bundy's successor, Walt W. Rostow), this group set Vietnam policy. They decided what targets could be bombed in North Vietnam, and even what weapons could be used. They micromanaged the war, without any significant military knowledge, advice, or experience. It was not until the summer of 1967 that military officials or the DCI was invited to the Tuesday lunches.[33]

This unwillingness to listen to outsiders, as well as the attempts to deny reality, was reflected in the briefing process for Johnson. Lundahl was never allowed to brief Johnson directly on Vietnam. McNamara said it was a wartime matter and insisted that only he should do so. NPIC prepared thousands of briefing boards on Vietnam, based on Corona photos, high-altitude A-12/SR-71 missions, low-altitude reconnaissance aircraft, and unmanned drone photos. Of these, in contrast to Lundahl's "tell it like it is" briefings, McNamara selected only the "good" pictures—the ones showing the Ho Chi Minh Trail bombed into a moonscape—because he knew that this was what Johnson wanted to see. The "bad" ones—the low-altitude photos showing arms-laden bicycles, pack animals, and humans carrying munitions wending their way through the bomb craters—were not shown to Johnson.

Johnson made it clear he did not want bad news. Whenever presented with unwelcome information, Johnson would become angry and depressed, and often flew into a profane tirade. Lundahl and Brugioni saw this side of Johnson during one such briefing. Johnson asked where they would be going next, and Lundahl said they were going to brief Sen. J. William Fulbright, the chairman of the Senate foreign relations committee and the leading congressional critic of Johnson's Vietnam policy. Johnson immediately started calling Fulbright an "S. O. B." and "piss ant."

Johnson was not a skilled photo interpreter. Having grown up in the plains of Texas, Johnson always saw the terrain in photos as flat. The NPIC model shop finally built a three-dimensional tabletop model of the area around the Marine base at Khe Sanh, South Vietnam. Johnson used it to follow the siege of the base, and even used it in planning air strikes.

The final president of the Corona years was Richard M. Nixon. He was the most knowledgeable of any American president on foreign affairs (in contrast to Johnson, who watched domestic news on three television sets in the Oval Office, but cared little for foreign information). At the same time, Nixon relied on national security affairs adviser Dr. Henry A. Kissinger's staff for intelligence information, rather than getting it directly from the CIA, which he distrusted politically and kept at arm's length.

As with other presidents, Nixon had a preferred style for briefings. He wanted them in the form of a lawyer's brief: fact 1, fact 2, fact 3, conclusion. Brugioni recalled Nixon as easy to brief, showing interest and understanding. In contrast to Nixon's wooden television image, or the dark side later revealed by Watergate, he could be quite warm in his personal relationships. When he returned from a foreign trip, Nixon would meet with the CIA watch officers who had been on duty during the trip, ask what they had done, and compliment them on their efforts.

The "Funnies"

The image so far of photo interpretation has been of painstaking, detailed work upon which the safety of the United States and its allies depended. It was all of that, but from time to time, it did have its moments of comic relief. These were known as the "funnies." Aerial photos recorded all aspects of the human experience, including the absurd. Some of the aerial and satellite photos were the source of much mirth over the years.[34]

It was one such funny that finally made the photo interpreters' jargon understandable to President Kennedy. During the Eisenhower years, Lundahl had made a number of humorous briefing boards during crisis situations, which Eisenhower had appreciated. Lundahl thought Kennedy might also like a little humor during the pressure of the Cuban missile crisis. He told the NPIC photo interpreters to be on the lookout for any comic relief. At the same time, Kennedy had several times expressed a displeasure with the use of such terms as *site* for a missile complex, *position* for the launch pads at each site, and *occupied* and *unoccupied,* indicating whether a missile was on the pad. McCone had tried to find alternatives, without success. Finally, as the missiles were being removed, a U.S. reconnaissance plane flying low over a military camp in Cuba came back with the solution to both problems.

When Lundahl's regular presidential briefing was completed, McCone asked Kennedy if he wished to see a photo of a new military site in Cuba, with three positions, one of which was occupied. Kennedy's face froze, as he knew all the Soviet missile sites discovered so far had had four positions. They then unveiled a photo of an open-topped latrine, with three holes, one of which was occupied by a soldier. Kennedy looked at the photo, smiled, then started laughing. "Why didn't I have this earlier?" Kennedy asked. "Now I understand the occupied/unoccupied problem perfectly."[35]

One regular user of the funnies was Richard Helms, the DCI between 1966 and 1973. Helms would give his regular briefing, saving the funny for the last photo. This would lighten the often grim information, and leave the president with a smile.

A prime source for Corona funnies was Tyuratam in Soviet Central Asia. Because of its use as both missile test site and space center, the Soviets knew the Corona satellites kept a regular watch on the area. During the long months of one winter, bored enlisted men stamped out a greeting in the snow:

Fuck You Spies

Each letter in the snow was 15 to 20 feet high, with the complete message stretching some 150 feet across. It was hard, cold work, requiring hours of effort and leaving the soldiers tired and wet from the melted snow.

The photo interpreters loved it, of course. The Corona satellites had laid the Soviet Union bare. The United States now knew the size, readiness, and capabilities of the Soviet military. The greetings to the satellites were monuments to the Soviets' rage at the loss of their traditional secrecy. Yet they were powerless to do anything except stamp out pointless insults in the snow.

There was no better form of official recognition for the photo interpreters' success.[36]

NINE

Top Secret Ruff
Case Studies in the Use of Satellite Photos

This document contains classified information affecting the security of the United States. . . . It is to be seen only by personnel especially indoctrinated and authorized to receive TALENT-KEYHOLE information.

Security warning printed on every document containing satellite reconnaissance data

➤ This chapter will look at several case studies to illustrate the different ways the Corona photos were used to meet the needs of the U.S. intelligence community. They ranged from simply keeping watch on regular targets and counting weapons, to early warning of new developments, supporting combat operations, and providing independent assessments. These case studies show how the various elements—GX and U-2 photos, signatures, comparative coverage, as well as covert and open sources—were brought together to create the big picture.

The Corona satellites provided a unique source of coverage. Within the limitations of their orbital paths, film supply, cloud cover, and daylight, they could photograph any part of the Soviet Union or other areas of interest, taking in huge swaths of the landscape. They could provide both a quantity and quality of information that traditional means, such as aircraft or agents, could not match. Because of the capabilities of the satellites, the photos and the information derived from them were classified Top Secret, with the code word "Ruff." All individuals with access to the reports were required to have "Talent-Keyhole" clearances.

The Tyuratam Missile Test Center, 1957–1963

A regular target of both the U-2 overflights and Corona was the Tyuratam missile test center. This facility served both to test Soviet long-range missiles and as the launch site for space missions. The first U-2 overflight to cover the area, Mission 4035, was in August 1957. This was followed in September 1957 by Mission 4058. Both showed the original SS-6 pad, called Launch Complex A or simply Area A, which served both for ICBM tests and for the first space launches.

Due to a halt in U-2 overflights, it was not until July 1959 that Mission 4125 visited Tyuratam. Its photos showed a new rail-serviced launch complex being built to the east of Area A. This facility, designated Launch Complex B, later proved to be the prototype for the four SS-6 pads at Plesetsk. It was completed the following year.

It was not until April 1960 that U-2 mission 4155 provided additional coverage of the region. Tyuratam was again being expanded, with Launch Complex C nearing completion. It was on a rail line due east of Area B and consisted of two above-ground pads for research and development flights of the SS-7 ICBM. (Tyuratam was also the destination for Francis Gary Powers's Mission 4154 of May 1, 1960, but the film, along with Powers and his U-2, were lost.)

Although the Discoverer flights quickly resumed coverage of the USSR, Tyuratam was photographed only three more times by the end of 1961 (*Discoverer 18* in December 1960, followed by *Discoverer 30* in September and *Discoverer 35* in December 1961).[1] These photos showed a second pad had been added to Launch Complex A. Little detail was available on Pad A2, but it lacked the huge flame pit of Pad A1 and the single pad at Area B. It turned out to be the research and development pad for the SS-8 ICBM tests. The *Discoverer 30* photos also showed construction was under way to support an expanded missile program. A road had been added, running some ten miles due east from Area C. At the end of the road, photo interpreters found "probable new launch area construction." At the western end of the Tyuratam complex, another road had been built to the northwest, with two areas of "unidentified construction activity" observed.[2]

During 1962, a total of eight KH-4–equipped Corona satellites photographed the Tyuratam area. This was followed in 1963 by three more KH-4 missions in April and June, two KH-4A Corona satellites in

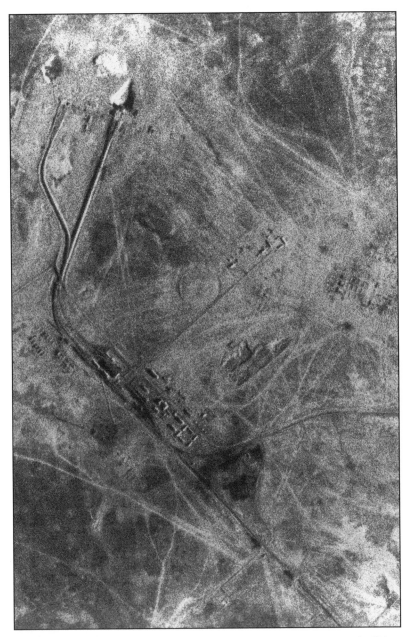

Discoverer 18 photo of Area A at Tyuratam. This shows the support facilities, assembly building, and pad area used for tests of the SS-6 Sapwood ICBM and launches of the first Sputnik and Luna space probes. *National Archives*

August and September, and the first high-resolution Gambit coverage in September 1963. These missions clarified the construction work spotted in the satellite photos of 1961.

The "probable new launch area construction" at the end of the east road was the prototype of the silo-based SS-7 ICBMs, designated Launch Complex D. Site D1 had two or three silos and was probably completed in late 1962. Site D2 was still under construction in September 1963. A third pad, C3, had also been added to Launch Complex C in mid-1962. Near Area C, a new facility was started in early 1963; this Launch Complex H had two road-serviced pads, H1 and H2, for an unknown missile system.

At the western end of the rangehead, three new launch facilities were observed. Launch Complex E was the prototype of the soft, above-ground SS-8 ICBM sites. There were three positions: Pads E1 and E2, completed in 1962, and Pad E3, finished in 1963. (They were similar to the original SS-8 Pad A2.) Farther along the west road was Launch Complex F, the prototype SS-8 silo complex. As with the SS-7 silo facility at Launch Complex D, there were two or three silos. The photo interpreters judged Launch Complex F complete by September 1963. At the end of the western road was Launch Complex G. This was a huge facility believed to be "space or ICBM related" with two pairs of rail-serviced pads. G1 and G2 were started in mid-1962 and were in the midstage of construction by September 1963. Pads G3 and G4 were judged to be at the early to midstage point.

The U-2 and Corona/Gambit coverage of Tyuratam between 1957 and 1963 illustrates several uses of satellite photos. The construction of the Area B pad was an indication that the SS-6 was nearing operational status. The A2 and Area C pads were an indication that work was beginning on a second generation of ICBMs. Examination of Launch Complexes C, D, E, and F provided signatures for detecting operational SS-7 and -8 sites elsewhere in the country. The photo interpreters could begin from the assumption that these would look like the Tyuratam test facilities.

The photos were also important for what they did not show. As of late 1963, there was no evidence of a small solid-fuel ICBM like the U.S. Minuteman. Except for Pad A1, none of the existing facilities were useful for space launches. This meant the Soviets were restricted to use of SS-6–derived boosters for space activities. In contrast, the U.S. Saturn I had been test flown, and work was under way on the Saturn IB, Saturn V Moon rocket, and Titan IIIC.

The Corona photos of 1962–63 also gave a preview of future developments. The expansion of the existing Launch Complexes C, D, and E indicated the second-generation ICBM programs were continuing. The new Launch Complex H hinted at a third-generation ICBM program.

The Launch Complex G pads indicated a major expansion of the Soviet space program. They were for the Proton booster, first flown in 1965. The Proton was comparable to the Saturn I or IB, and was capable of orbiting a manned space station or sending a manned spacecraft around the Moon. The Proton also posed the threat of a very heavy ICBM, capable of carrying a 100-megaton nuclear warhead. Within U.S. intelligence, the Proton was widely believed to have been designed for such a role, and only later adapted as a space booster. (The ICBM role was ultimately dropped.)[3]

Bad Moon Rising: The N 1 Moon Rocket

In 1963, there were only hints of what was to become the largest launch complex at Tyuratam. Over the next three and a half years, the Corona satellites watched as a sprawling facility was built only a few miles to the northwest of the original Launch Complex A. It was called Area J and was the launch site for the Soviet N 1 booster, intended to put a cosmonaut on the Moon.

There were two pads at Launch Complex J, each with a service tower that moved on a circular track, two lightning towers, and three flame deflector pits.[4] The Area J facilities were judged similar in scale to the Apollo/Saturn V pads at Merritt Island in Florida. They were estimated to be capable of supporting a booster with a first stage thrust in the range of 8 to 16 million pounds. The CIA estimated that the Area J pads could be completed by the first half of 1968 at the earliest.

The N 1 itself was an elongated cone-shaped rocket. The photo interpreters dubbed it the "J-bird." Its official U.S. intelligence designation was TT-5, signifying the fifth booster type observed at Tyuratam (TT). The thirty engines in its first stage produced 10 million pounds of thrust (compared to the 7.5 million pounds of thrust developed by the five engines of the Saturn V first stage). The N 1 booster was assembled at the "MIK" factory, moved to the pad horizontally on a huge rail transporter, and raised upright. Analysts projected a first flight in mid-1968, with man-rating by mid-1969 or 1970.

From satellite observations of the ongoing Area J construction work, U.S. intelligence was able to follow the progress of the Soviet Moon program. In 1965, the CIA believed that the Soviet lunar landing program was lagging behind the U.S. Apollo program. The first Apollo Moon landing was aimed at the 1968–69 time period; as of March 1967, the CIA did not believe a Soviet Moon landing could be accomplished before mid- to late 1969. A more likely date was thought to be 1970 or 1971.[5]

Work at Area J continued to lag behind schedule. When the Soviet lunar landing program had begun in 1964, the first landing was planned for 1968, but by late in that year the Soviets had not yet conducted even the first test launch. Corona mission 1048 photographed the facility on September 24, 1968. The photos showed the MIK assembly building with Quonset huts clustered nearby and two empty pads.

The first N 1 launch was not made until February 21, 1969, and was a failure. After liftoff, several engines shut down. Then a liquid oxygen line ruptured, sparking a fire and explosion at T+70 seconds. The debris impacted forty-five kilometers down range.[6] Remarkably, U.S. intelligence did not detect the launch. It was known a booster had been on the pad, but the analysts apparently thought it had been rolled back to the MIK for further checkout.

Another seven months passed before a second N 1 stood ready on Pad 1. The launch was scheduled for July 3, 1969; the launch of the manned Apollo 11 Moon landing mission was only thirteen days away. A half second before liftoff, the oxidizer pump for one of the N 1's first stage engines exploded when a piece of metal debris entered it. The blast damaged the cable system, and as the rocket lifted off, engine after engine began to shut down. After eleven seconds, only one engine was still firing. The N 1 climbed to an altitude of about two hundred meters and began falling. The thrust from the single engine caused the N 1 to tilt. After a flight of twenty-three seconds, the fully fueled booster hit the pad and exploded with the force of a small nuclear bomb.[7]

A month later, on August 3, 1969, Corona mission 1107 passed over Tyuratam. When its photos were recovered and processed, they captured the destruction wrought by the falling booster. A huge area had been scorched by the blast and fire. One of the lightning towers had been brought down, while the service tower had been knocked off its track. The flame deflectors had been destroyed and there was extensive damage to the pad's underground levels. Debris was scattered across a radius of a kilometer.[8]

The N 1 moon rocket pads at Tyuratam, photographed by Corona mission 1048 on September 24, 1968. At this time, final construction work was completed and preparations were under way for the first N 1 launch. *National Archives via Dwayne A. Day*

Two more N 1 launches were attempted before the program was cancelled. The third try came on June 27, 1971, and also ended with a destroyed pad. Just after liftoff from Pad 2, the N 1 booster began to rotate and the support structure between the second and third stages failed. The third stage and dummy payload fell to the pad and exploded. The first and second stages continued on some twenty kilometers before impacting. The rocket dug a crater thirty meters across and fifteen meters deep. The fourth and final try was made on November 23,

Results of the launch failure of the second N 1 booster, photographed by Corona mission 1107 on August 3, 1969. The explosion of the rocket on July 3 devastated the pad and ended Soviet hopes of landing a man on the moon. For the next twenty years, the USSR (and some in the West) would deny a Soviet moon program had ever existed. *National Archives via Dwayne A. Day*

1972 (after the end of the Corona program), and almost succeeded. Shortly before the first stage was to shut down and separate, a fire broke out. The booster was destroyed at T+108 seconds.

The failure of the N 1 program where the American Apollo program succeeded can, in retrospect, be traced to several root causes—most notably, the Soviets' much weaker industrial and economic base compared to the greater resources of the American aerospace industry, and the high-level political and financial support of Kennedy and Johnson.

The Soviet program itself did not get started until 1964 (three years after Kennedy's declaration that the United States would put a man on the Moon before the end of the decade). Once under way, the Soviet program was beset with internal squabbles, as the different design bureaus fought for control. The Soviets also underestimated the technical challenges of a lunar landing. They tried to speed up the program by skipping ground tests of the complete assembly. When the first N 1 lifted off, it was the first time the first stage had *ever* been tested as a single unit.[9]

The race to the Moon was part of the great Cold War technological, political, and economic contest between the United States and the USSR. Landing a man on the Moon was a test of the respective ideological systems. Although Corona could tell nothing about the internal disputes and decisions, it could show the results—that the Soviet Moon program was lagging behind Apollo. The United States therefore did not have to react to each Soviet space shot or propaganda statement, thanks to the objective information from Corona.

Corona also served truth. Rather than admit they had come in second, the Soviets decided to cover up their lunar failure. They destroyed the remaining N 1 boosters and rewrote history. The Soviet Moon program vanished, as the Soviets denied they had ever been in a race to the Moon. Many in the West who had opposed Apollo accepted the lie. They claimed that the Soviet Moon rocket had never existed and was only a NASA invention, while others proclaimed, "That our intelligence of the Soviet space technology was faulty is not [arguable]."[10] In the vaults at NPIC, however, every step was recorded, from the first excavations at Tyuratam to the scorched pads that marked the failure of both the N 1 and the Soviet system.

Monitoring Tyuratam was only one aspect of Corona's mission. Another was the day-to-day examination of Soviet military activities. This included counting weapons, determining the status of units, identifying new facilities, and watching for any changes. The next three case studies will provide a glimpse of this never-ending activity.

Counting SAMs

When the *Discoverer 14* photos were analyzed, they showed twenty new SA-2 SAM sites and six possible sites under construction.[11]

Soviet SA-2 SAM site near Chelyabinsk, USSR, photographed on February 8, 1969. The Corona, due to its worldwide coverage, could inventory such sites. The photo also shows the signatures associated with SA-2 sites: the six emplacements, the radar set in the center, the "star of David" road pattern, and the effects of snow. *National Archives*

Throughout the Corona program, SAM sites, both in the Soviet Union and around the world, remained a priority target. The attack routes for U.S. Air Force and RAF bombers had to be planned to avoid Soviet and Eastern European SAM sites. Where this was not possible, SAM sites would have to be attacked to clear the way for later waves. In North Vietnam, SA-2 missiles were taking a heavy toll of Air Force and Navy strike aircraft. The SA-2 was also a tool of Soviet foreign aid. SA-2s were included whenever a Third World country was supplied with Soviet weapons and advisers.

Corona had several advantages for counting SAMs, the greatest of which was its rapid area coverage. A satellite could cover the whole of Egypt or North Vietnam in two passes, while North Korea required three. Over the course of a single mission, most of the USSR and China

Table 1. Soviet-Designed SAM Deployment Worldwide

SAM	Country	Confirmed	Probable	Possible	Training
SA-1	Soviet Union	56	0	0	1
SA-2	Afghanistan	1	0	0	0
	Albania	2	0	0	0
	Bulgaria	19	0	0	0
	China	21	1	0	9
	Cuba	24	0	0	2
	Czechoslovakia	25	1	0	1
	East Germany	54	1	0	0
	Egypt	35	0	0	3
	Hungary	16	0	0	0
	India	16	0	0	1
	Indonesia	5	0	0	1
	Mongolia	2	0	0	0
	North Korea	10	1	0	0
	North Vietnam	168	1	3	2
	Poland	32	0	0	0
	Romania	18	0	0	0
	Soviet Union	1,032	2	0	35
	Yugoslavia	5	0	0	0
SA-3	Poland	0	0	1	0
	Soviet Union	110	1	0	13
SA-5	Soviet Union	32	0	0	2

could be photographed. Such rapid coverage was important, as SA-2s were designed to be mobile. They could be set up at a new location in a short time (unlike long-range ballistic missiles, which were tied to fixed sites).

The Oak for Mission 1042-1 (June 17–22, 1967) included a listing of Soviet SAM sites in the USSR and worldwide (see Table 1). These were broken down by type: the SA-1 Guild, the SA-2 Guideline, the SA-3 Goa low-altitude SAM, and the SA-5 Gammon high-altitude SAM.

As with ICBMs and other long-range missiles, it was important to watch for any new developments. The Oak provided an example of this: it listed a single possible SA-3 site in Poland. This was apparently the first SA-3 deployment outside the USSR.[12]

Soviet Nuclear Weapons Storage Facilities

Munitions storage buildings—whether used for artillery shells, conventional bombs, chemical or biological weapons, or nuclear warheads—are typically well spaced, revetted bunkers surrounded by security fences. Specific signatures were required to identify their contents. A particular type of roof and ventilators, for instance, would be a signature identifying a facility as a chemical weapons storage facility.[13]

Discoverer 14's photos showed a large number of Soviet ammunition and explosives storage sites. Over the next two years, the signatures of Soviet nuclear storage facilities were identified. In Corona photos of SS-4 and SS-5 missile sites, two different types of nuclear bunkers were observed. They were either 71 or 112 feet long, and were built of precast concrete arches eighteen and a half feet wide and tall. The bunkers were covered with a meter-thick layer of dirt, and lightning arresters were at the corners. They were enclosed by security fences and walls, guard towers, and checkpoints. A tent camp for the KGB security force was also nearby.

During the evening of October 17, 1962, precast arches were spotted by an NPIC photo interpreter in photos of an SS-5 site in Cuba. They were immediately recognized as part of a nuclear weapons storage bunker under construction.

Although bunkers were observed at nearly all the missile sites, it was not clear if the nuclear warheads were actually on the island. The NPIC photo interpreters searched for a Soviet nuclear weapons processing facility in Cuba, but they lacked the specific signatures needed to spot one. They thus had to look for such general outward signs as security fencing, new construction, or heavy guards at an isolated location.

It was not until after the end of the crisis that the question of the nuclear weapons was answered. In earlier photos, the analysts had observed four to eight large vans parked close to the SS-5 bunkers. The vans were always seen in the open, away from other vehicles. No special fences, guards, or other security measures were noted, nor any activities that would draw suspicion. Understandably, the photo interpreters paid no particular attention to them. Upon Khrushchev's agreement to remove the missiles, however, the vans were immediately driven to the Cuban port of Mariel, where the van bodies were removed from the truck chassis and loaded aboard the Soviet merchant ship *Aleksandrovsk* that evening. The ship then immediately set sail. Their importance then became apparent—they were nuclear warhead storage vans.

After the crisis was over, analysis of low-level photos of the Mariel naval air station taken on October 25 finally revealed the Soviet warhead processing site. Twenty-three coffin-shaped warhead containers were spotted under camouflage netting. Also present were warhead handling dollies, twenty storage vans, and four steel-framed buildings at the site that were apparently used for weapons checkout. It was speculated that the warheads arrived at Mariel by sea, and then were removed from the containers, placed on the dollies, and taken into the checkout buildings. The warheads would then be loaded into the vans, and driven to the missile sites.

Although the nuclear facilities were not discovered until after the fact, the photos from the Cuban missile crisis nevertheless provided signatures for identifying Soviet handling of nuclear warheads. Later satellite photos showed the same type of vans at nuclear weapons storage sites both within the USSR and in Eastern Europe. The vans were also observed during later SS-4 and SS-5 field-deployment exercises, and with Soviet tactical missiles at East German training areas.[14]

Just as the low-altitude photos taken during the Cuban missile crisis provided signatures on Soviet tactical weapon deployments, U-2 overflight photos helped identify another type of nuclear weapons storage site. U-2 mission 4155, flown on April 9, 1960 (the last successful overflight), covered the Dolon Air Field in Soviet Central Asia. This airfield was a strategic bomber base, and was west of the Soviet nuclear testing site at Semipalatinsk. The photos showed a cross-shaped building under construction at the Type III nuclear weapons storage site. When several Corona flights during 1961 and 1962 showed two similar buildings at the Berdichev regional military storage installation in the western USSR, it was possible to identify Berdichev as a regional nuclear weapons storage site.

The Berdichev site was a double-fenced area about 4,900 by 1,650 feet, with a single-fenced support area. The double-fenced area contained two cross-shaped buildings, a drive-through checkout building between them, and a small unidentified building between the two fences. The support area contained a main administrative building and four smaller buildings. In the June 1962 photos from Corona flight 44, the southeast cross-shaped building was still under construction; by

November and Corona flight 55, it had been completed. Both of the cross-shaped buildings had yet to be covered with dirt, however.

Comparing the Berdichev and Dolon sites was difficult, due to the limitations of the Corona cameras. The layout of the two sites was similar. The size of the two buildings was also similar, although measurements of the Dolon building were more precise, as this was based on high-resolution U-2 photos. Also, small details visible at Dolon were not discernible in the Corona pictures. There were differences in the location of the checkout building, the security fences, and the size and number of support buildings. The major differences were in the cross-shaped buildings themselves. They were designed so trucks carrying the nuclear weapons could be driven through them for loading and unloading. At Dolon, this drive-through section was the shorter section, while at Berdichev, it was the longer section.[15]

This case study shows the importance of location as a signature. The arched bunkers were at SS-4 and -5 missile sites, while the first cross-shaped building was located at a Type III nuclear storage site. The nuclear storage vans, in contrast, were "hidden" in plain sight, with none of the typical heavy-handed (and obvious) Soviet security procedures. (As the missile sites were secured, there was no need for added physical security around the vans themselves.) Although the vans were located at a missile site, they were nondescript, and there was nothing to separate them from the numerous other support vehicles. Once they were identified, however, the vans became a clear signature that nuclear weapons were present at a site.

The Severodvinsk Naval Base and Shipyard 402

A recurring element of both Tzarist and Soviet naval policy was the desire to build a "blue water" fleet. With the development of nuclear weapons and submarine-launched ballistic and cruise missiles, such a force could attack targets in the United States. In the late 1950s and early 1960s, it was Golf-, Zulu-, Hotel-, and Echo-class submarines that represented the largest element of Soviet long-range nuclear forces. At the same time, the growing force of Soviet November nuclear-powered attack submarines posed a threat to U.S. carriers.

U.S. knowledge of Soviet shipbuilding capabilities was very limited during this time. An example of this was the Severodvinsk naval base and its Shipyard 402, located on the White Sea in northwestern

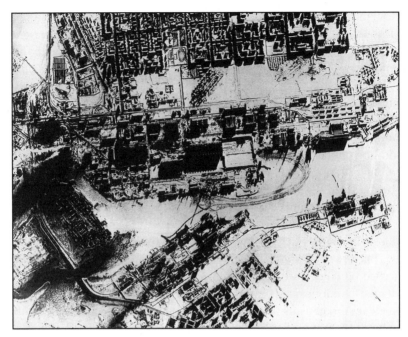

The Severodvinsk Shipyard near the White Sea. This facility was the largest producer of nuclear and diesel-powered submarines for the Soviet Union. The "fish-hook" shaped pattern was caused by icebreakers clearing the channel. Similar "track activity" in the snow is also visible on land in this February 10, 1969, photo. *National Archives*

Russia. Despite the RB-47 and U-2 overflights, the only coverage of Severodvinsk was an August 15, 1943, GX photo. This picture showed the huge assembly hall and launching basin built for the construction of battleships. It was not until *Discoverer 25* (Mission 9017) in June 1961 that new photos were taken of the complex. Over the next three years, five more Corona flights—Missions 9035 (May 1962), 9054 (June 1963), and 1006-2, 1008-1, and 1009-1 (June, July, and August 1964) —provided additional coverage.

The Corona photos showed Severodvinsk had been greatly expanded since the war. Most of the expansion was on the Yagry Island section of the base. A small shipyard, capable of handling vessels of up to 500 feet in length, had been added. Construction of this shipyard, designated Shipyard 402, was still under way in 1964, but it was believed that it would be used for maintenance and repair, possibly including the refueling of nuclear submarine reactors. (This small shipyard was similar to the Petrovka Shipyard near Vladivostok.) Several machine shops had also been built on the island. On the mainland section of the base, a fabrication/construction hall and its adjoining launching way had been completed. The excavations for the building, which could also handle ships up to 500 feet in length, had been visible in the 1943 photo.

The Severodvinsk naval base and Shipyard 402 were considered to be the largest producer of nuclear submarines in the USSR. There were several signatures leading to this conclusion. In the 1964 photos, November- and Echo-class nuclear submarines were observed. Another signature was a pair of fabrication buildings. They were T-shaped, separately secured, and had two white objects on their roofs. These were believed to be ventilating, air-conditioning, or vacuum units used to create the clean-room environment required for the welding of stainless-steel pipes used in nuclear reactors. An identical building had been spotted at the Komsomolsk Shipyard, which built the Echo-class cruise missile submarines on the Pacific coast.[16]

The expansion of Severodvinsk was an early indication of the rapid growth the Soviet navy would undergo in the 1960s. By the end of the Corona program, the Soviet surface and submarine fleet had grown into a true oceangoing force, and would directly challenge the U.S. and NATO navies.

The Dragon Armed: The Chinese Nuclear Weapons Program

In the late 1950s and early 1960s, a new threat shimmered on the horizon—the Communist Chinese nuclear weapons program. Assessing the effort was difficult because information was sparse and of uncertain validity, while photographic coverage during the early years of the program was limited. U.S. intelligence used a wide range of sources—not only U-2 and Corona photos, but also more traditional methods such as attempting to estimate the total Chinese supply of fissionable material. The outcome of this was to show how valuable Corona was.

The Chinese nuclear program began with Soviet scientific and technical help in 1957. The first indication of progress came in 1959 when a U-2 overflight of China discovered a building at Lanchou that was identified as a gaseous diffusion plant. This took ordinary uranium, turned it into a gas, and then separated the U-235 isotope. This isotope could then be used in an atomic bomb.

Despite the Western belief in a "Sino-Soviet Bloc," relations between the two Communist giants had been difficult from the start. Khrushchev finally had had enough in mid-1960, and ordered the withdrawal of all Soviet advisers from China. The Chinese nuclear program thereafter relied on native talent.

In assessing the program, the CIA believed that the Chinese—like the Americans, Soviets, and British—would use plutonium in their weapons. This required a nuclear reactor to produce the plutonium, and another facility to separate it for use in a weapon. NIE 13-2-62, "Chinese Communist Advanced Weapons Capabilities," dated April 25, 1962, estimated that enough uranium metal had been produced for a single 200-megawatt load in an as-yet undiscovered reactor. Assuming full power operations had begun in early 1962, enough plutonium would be produced in a year for a single bomb. If any problems or delays occurred, however, the estimate projected it would be several more years before a weapon could be tested. The Lanchou facility was noted, but the lack of power lines, and the belief that another building was required before the facility could produce weapons grade U-235, indicated it was not operational. Thus, an all–U-235 or composite weapon (using a mixture of plutonium and U-235) was judged not to be possible before 1966.

As one of his last acts as president, Eisenhower authorized the transfer of two U-2s to the Nationalist Chinese air force. Despite a number of training accidents and the loss of U-2s over the mainland (on September 9, 1962, and November 1, 1963), the program was highly productive. By 1963, with the Nationalist Chinese U-2 overflights under way and Corona operational, there was a greatly increased amount of information on the Communist Chinese weapons program. A U-2 overflight on March 28, 1963, showed power lines had been installed at the Lanchou facility. The only Chinese production reactor that had been discovered was a small air-cooled reactor at Pao-tou in northeast China. This was assumed to be for plutonium production.

A special national estimate, SNIE 13-2-63, "Communist China's Advanced Weapons Program," was issued on July 24, 1963, based on the new information. The report stated that the Pao-tou reactor alone could have produced sufficient plutonium for a test in early 1964.

Although difficulties could push this back to late 1964 or 1965, it was now clear that the first Chinese nuclear test was approaching. As it was probable, given the limited photographic coverage, that there was more than one plutonium facility, a Chinese test of a plutonium-based weapon at any time could not be ruled out. Although the Lanchou gaseous diffusion plant now had power, the SNIE judged the Chinese would be unable to produce weapons-grade U-235 before 1966, while 1968 or 1969 were considered more likely dates.[17]

In an effort to estimate the amount of fissionable material the Chinese might have, NPIC was requested to search for any evidence of uranium mining within a 50-nautical-mile radius of A-ko-su, in western China near the Sino-Soviet border. Photos from four missions—*Discoverer 18* (December 1960), *Discoverer 36* (December 1961), and Corona flights 56 (November 1962) and 58 (December 1962)—were examined. They showed two areas of mining 30 to 45 nautical miles northeast of A-ko-su. The lignite coal in this area was believed to contain uranium.

Various signatures were observed. The size of the coal refuse pile had grown between the December 1960 and December 1961 coverage, while track activity in the snow indicated development of the mines during the winter. The mines had security fencing and control points, which indicated they were being worked by prisoners. The stockpiling of coal at a treatment plant suggested it was being processed for the extraction of some by-product. The track activity in the November and December 1962 photos indicated the plant was operating at a low rate, however. The coal was not being mined for use in the area, as there was no accumulation of coal or ashes observed in the towns or villages of the area. Based on an estimate of the total production of coal from the mines, it was thought as much as 15 to 30 metric tons of uranium oxide could have been extracted.[18]

A similar watch was kept on the Pao-tou reactor. By September 1963, there was a better understanding of its status. The site was not operational, as construction was continuing throughout the site, including significant work around the reactor building itself. However, coverage in March 1964 showed that the major work, including service roads and security measures, had been completed.

The key to understanding the Chinese nuclear program finally came from Corona. In December 1961, construction work was observed at Lop Nor in the desert of western China. It was of a unique nature: a

4,000-meter-diameter circular road. Subsequently, barracks, an airfield, and support facilities were built. This was believed to be the Chinese nuclear testing site.

During the spring and summer of 1964, there were new developments at Lop Nor. In April 1964, a 100-meter-high tower was observed —the structure to hold the bomb. Then, between August 6 and 9, Corona flight 83's photos showed construction work on bunkers and instrumentation sites. Cable lines were being dug between the tower and electronic vans. The outward appearance and rate of construction indicated that Lop Nor would be ready for a test in two months. The layout of the site suggested that it was for both diagnostic and weapons effect experiments.

On August 26, 1964, a special estimate, "The Chances of an Imminent Communist Chinese Nuclear Test," was issued. The report was ambivalent. It stated that Lop Nor was undeniably a nuclear test site, and that it was being prepared for a test. However, it estimated that there was not enough plutonium available to the Chinese to conduct a test in the near future. The Pao-tou reactor was assessed as having gone into operation in late 1963. As it would take between eighteen months and two years to produce enough material for a bomb, the report concluded that it would be mid-1965 before a test could be made.[19]

Despite the mixed conclusions, Lundahl suggested to McCone that, to prevent the Chinese from gaining a propaganda advantage, President Johnson might want to make an announcement that a test was imminent. It was Secretary of State Rusk who made the statement on September 29, 1964. He told the press that "for some time it has been known that the Communist Chinese were approaching the point where they might be able to detonate a first nuclear device."

Corona flight 86 removed all doubts. Analysis of its photos of Lop Nor taken on October 8, 1964, showed final preparations had been completed, and workers and equipment had been removed from the test site. On October 16, the Chinese detonated a 28-kiloton atomic bomb. There was hardly a political ripple from the test.[20]

When the fallout from the test was analyzed, there was a surprise: the Chinese bomb had used U-235, not plutonium. Furthermore, analysis of the debris indicated the U-235 was unlike any produced by the Soviets since 1955, so was probably of Chinese origin. It had been the belief that plutonium would be used for the Chinese bomb that caused U.S. intelligence to overlook the importance of the Lanchou facility, to

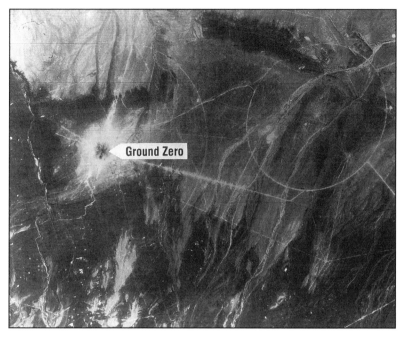

Ground Zero

The Chinese nuclear test site at Lop Nor on October 20, 1964, following the first A-bomb explosion. Corona photos provided information on Chinese uranium mining and production facilities, and identified the Lop Nor site. Corona observations of the final preparations gave warning that a test was imminent, and prevented the U.S. government from being taken by surprise. *National Archives*

misinterpret the Pao-tou reactor (which had been built for other purposes), and, as a result, to project an erroneous date for the first test.

The traditional analysis of the Chinese nuclear program started with an assumption about how the program would be organized. Then, intelligence was collected on its progress. For a nuclear program, the supply of fissionable material was critical, as it determined the speed of the program. In retrospect, trying to estimate a date based on the estimates of fissionable materials was subject to too many variables. At best, this could give orders of magnitude, and whether the program was progressing or was stalled.

It was the Corona photos of Lop Nor that provided the indication that a test was imminent. They cut through all the unknowns, and provided unmistakable evidence. The only assumption required about the Chinese nuclear program was that a test would take place once the site was ready. When the final preparations were observed, it was clear the test would be within days. The ability of Corona to survey huge areas was also valuable for the estimates of Chinese uranium mining. It would have been much more difficult to make the A-ko-su study with U-2 overflights.

It is also worth contrasting the Chinese nuclear test with the first Soviet test in 1949. In both cases, indirect evidence led to a range of estimates for the date of the first test. When the Soviet test was made, however, it came as a stunning surprise. This resulted in fears that the Soviet military was overtaking the United States, and set the stage for the bomber and missile gaps. In the case of the Chinese test, Corona was able to provide exact information. It was then possible to counter the political effects. Had the United States been forced to rely on traditional analysis, the test would have been made as much as a year earlier than estimated, and could have set the stage for a similar overreaction.

The Unidentified

The NPIC photo interpreters were trained to look for anything that seemed out of place. They never knew what the next photo would reveal. One interpreter in the late 1960s received quite a surprise. Studying a photo of East Germany, he suddenly spotted Indian tepees, covered wagons, and the gate of a cavalry fort. His first action was to check the location, as it seemed unlikely the Communist East Germans would be memorializing that most American of mythologies, the Old West. It was, in fact, a movie set of the German Film Corporation, and the East Germans did make Westerns.

Although "Dodge City on the Elbe" seems unusual, it illustrates the challenge facing the photo interpreters. By the second half of the twentieth century, the world had become a mixture of modern culture and ancient traditions. To correctly identify an unknown facility, particularly in a non-Western country, it was not enough to be knowledgeable about advanced weapons; one also had to be familiar with such factors as the customs of different societies and styles of modern architecture.

China was a prime example of this confusing mixture. When the first U-2 overflights were made of Tibet, structures were noted on mountaintop roads and trails, or in mountain passes. The structures were flanked by mounds, which suggested military strong points with bunkers and revetments. Another possibility suggested was toll booths. The answer came from a travel book. They were actually religious shrines to Chenresik, the god of travelers. A Tibetan traveler approaching a hill or pass would invoke divine protection by picking up a stone in a valley and placing it before the shrine. Over the years, large piles of such stones would build up.

A more modern example was observed in the early 1960s. At four abandoned airfields near Canton, China, new buildings were observed under construction on the old runways. The buildings appeared to be for storage, and the initial surmise was that these were military facilities. No military activities were observed, however. Again, it was an open source—a Chinese book titled *Peoples Communes*—which provided the answer. A photo in the book showed that the "military facilities" were hog pens.

U-2 overflight photos of Cuba were examined for any signs of new SIGINT facilities. Four structures resembling parabolic dish antennas were spotted at the highest point of the Sierra Maestra. Their shape suggested a missile or space tracking role, such as monitoring space activities at Cape Kennedy. In one set of photos a helicopter was observed at the site, reinforcing the suspicion it was a military installation. The power lines needed to support such a facility were not present, however, and it was carried as "unidentified" for more than a year. Then, the September 1963 issue of the Cuban magazine *Bohemia* carried photos of the buildings—they were President Fidel Castro's Museum of the Revolution. The site lacked a water source, so the dish-shaped roofs, which had attracted so much attention, were designed to catch rainwater.[21]

Any "unidentified" facility required the photo interpreters to undertake a long, painstaking analysis. Pieces of the puzzle might be supplied by a variety of collateral sources, both covert and open, and even from amateurs with special knowledge of an area. (For example, a photo of a Chinese island covered with unknown dark triangular objects was identified by a person who had lived in the Far East—they were fish nets drying in the sun.) It was not enough that an unidentified object's shape or other signatures suggested military activities; there had to be positive evidence one way or the other. What was missing was often as important as what was seen.

Historical Studies

While the U-2 and Corona were intended to monitor current Soviet military strength, and provide indications of future activities, it was soon realized they also could give insights to the past. The capability of aerial and satellite photos to reveal information about events hundreds, thousands, and even millions of years ago was discovered quite by accident, and not as part of an official research effort.

During the U-2 overflights, Dino Brugioni served as executive officer in charge of exploitation. When a U-2 mission was flown, he would be notified. While the film was being transported from Europe via the Azores to Dover, Delaware, and finally to Andrews AFB, he would make sure the interpreters were ready and that all the collateral materials had been organized. This usually left him with a few hours to kill. Once, in the late 1950s, while he was waiting for the films to arrive, he pulled out some GX photos of the Crimean region where the charge of the Light Brigade had taken place, and compared them to ground photos from the Crimean War taken by Roger Fenton. Even though the ground photos had been taken nearly a century before, he could match the specific locations, and gained a perspective the participants had lacked.[22]

Over the years to follow, he continued this unofficial historical research. In coverage of the Middle East, Brugioni saw the ruins of Roman forts. Using the same kind of analysis performed on Soviet facilities, he analyzed the military installations of the Roman empire. The design of the forts showed the Romans were in a defensive mode at the time they were built. They were held with second-line local troops and mercenaries. Brugioni also compared the location of the Roman forts with those built by the French Foreign Legion in North Africa nearly two millennia later.

Because of the huge area covered by each Corona frame, it was possible to trace the routes of many of the epic journeys of history. Brugioni followed the travels of Marco Polo on his trip to China, and was astonished to discover that many of his descriptions were still valid. On a December morning in the late 1960s, he selected a photo taken by a Corona satellite that covered the area from Nazareth to Bethlehem. Under the stereoscope, Brugioni traced Mary and Joseph's journey through each hill and valley.[23]

Remains of Fort Walls

Corona photo of a Roman fort at Lejjum, Jordan, September 29, 1971. Historical studies were undertaken at NPIC on a private basis beginning in the days of the U-2. With the release of the Corona photo archives, historians and archaeologists now have a resource of unmatched potential. *National Archives*

Other photos provided insights into World War I, the social and political consequences of which had shaped the rest of the twentieth century. A classified report was prepared at NPIC analyzing the battlefield at Verdun, where the youth of France and Germany had been slaughtered in a futile war of attrition. Brugioni also examined the site of the amphibious landing at Gallipoli, and realized how ill-conceived the attack was.[24]

The Corona photos also provided a historical record of the crises of the 1960s and early 1970s. These included the 1962 Sino-Indian border war, the 1965 and 1971 India-Pakistan wars, the build-up of Soviet forces on the Chinese border, the 1967 Six-Day War in the Middle East, and the 1968 Soviet invasion of Czechoslovakia.

And Vietnam. . . .

Corona and Vietnam

It was the Vietnam War that defined both the sixties and McNamara's style as secretary of defense. McNamara "managed" the Vietnam War the same way he had run Ford, by the collection of statistical data—weapons captured, the number of villages under South Vietnamese government control, numbers of bombing sorties flown, and the "body count"—and then used the interpretation of this information to silence critics.

This made McNamara supremely confident of success. When McNamara was asked by a reporter in May of 1962 how he could be so optimistic about a war that had barely begun, he responded without doubt or hesitation, "Every quantitative measurement we have shows that we're winning this war." As the war expanded in 1965, McNamara's display of facts and figures overwhelmed administration officials who had doubts, such as George Ball or Clark Clifford, who were made to seem ill-informed.[25]

The strategy in Vietnam was derived from academic nuclear theories, even to the use of many of the same terms, such as "escalation." The air strikes against North Vietnamese targets were centrally controlled by the White House as "signals" of U.S. "resolve." As with the Whiz Kids' nuclear strategy, there was no room for human factors—emotion, the confusion of war, morale, unit cohesion, or the determination of the North Vietnamese.

Corona had a more limited role in providing intelligence on Vietnam than on the Soviet Union. Low-altitude reconnaissance aircraft and unmanned drones could provide much better resolution than the satellites (inches vs. nine feet for Corona). An additional factor was the weather over North Vietnam. Skies were clear between May and September, but the winter monsoons of November through March produced thick clouds and heavy rain.

The advantage of Corona was in span of coverage. Low-altitude reconnaissance could cover specific targets, but their horizons were limited. A single Corona frame spanned nearly the entire width of North Vietnam, while a single pass could cover the whole length of the country. The result was literally a snapshot of North Vietnamese activities regionwide. Corona photos were also used to produce maps of the trackless jungles and hills.

Corona mission 1042-1 made two passes over Southeast Asia on June 17 and 18, 1967. The first, on orbit 6, went from southern China over central North Vietnam, eastern Laos and Cambodia, and, finally, South Vietnam. On orbit 22, southern China and northern Laos were covered.[26] The results were summarized in the Oak, "KH-4 Mission 1042-1, 17–22 June 1967, South China and North Vietnam Edition." About 45 percent of the photography was cloud-free. The Oak described missiles, air facilities, naval activities/ports, biological/chemical warfare, military activities, and complexes. No evidence was found of surface-to-surface missiles (a major concern was that the Soviets would deploy ballistic missiles in North Vietnam). There was also no significant air, naval, or ground military activity observed.

The primary information from the Mission 1042-1 photos was on SAM sites. Out of the total 172 known SA-2 sites, 144 were observed. Of these, fourteen SAM sites (Hanoi A10-2, A17A-2, A29-2, A33-2, B04-2, B12-2, B21-2, B29-2, B33-2, and C02-2; Haiphong C28-2; Hoa Binh B20-2; Vinh A36-2; and Yen Bai C10-2) were considered occupied. Another eighty-nine sites were unoccupied, while the status of the remaining forty sites was undetermined, due to the quality of the photos. The Vinh Linh B29-2 site had been bombed, and the Corona photos showed all six launch positions had been destroyed and the guidance area partially destroyed; it was therefore removed from the NPIC listing. No new sites were observed, but some changes were noted—the Thanh Hoa D04A-2 SAM site had been returned to cultivation, while Thanh Hoa D20-2 was probably unoccupied and appeared to be deteriorating.

Coverage of southern China on this mission was disappointing. It was limited to the border areas, and heavy cloud cover prevented identification of any significant activities.[27] Coverage of southern China was important, both because it was a major supply area and to provide early warning of any Chinese moves. The fear that Chinese ground forces would intervene in Vietnam (as they had during the Korean War) haunted the Johnson administration.

Ultimately, Vietnam also defined McNamara's and the Whiz Kids' failures. He complained that "You couldn't reconcile the numbers of the enemy, the level of infiltration, the body count, and the resulting figures." The pressure from above for "good numbers" corrupted the military's integrity. The body count was routinely inflated, while the number of sorties was increased by sending planes out with a partial bomb load.[28] The war destroyed the very rationality McNamara and the Whiz Kids tried to impose. The antiwar movement fractured

American society, while the establishment liberalism of McNamara was replaced by student radicalism. Unable to comprehend irrationality, McNamara and the Whiz Kids were lost. McNamara left DoD in February 1968, while many of the Whiz Kids became critics of the war and the military they had created.

The Six-Day War and the Invasion of Czechoslovakia

During the spring of 1967, tensions began to build between Israel and its Arab neighbors. By early May, Israeli troops were massing on the Syrian border, and the Egyptian air force was on alert. At 8:45 A.M. on June 5, 1967, Israeli fighter-bombers struck at several Egyptian air bases, catching the aircraft on the ground. By noon, the air forces of Egypt, Syria, Jordan, and Iraq had been effectively destroyed, and Israel had near total air superiority. At the end of the Six-Day War, Israel had taken the Sinai, all of Jerusalem, and the West Bank, and had driven deep into Syria.

The events of the Six-Day War made clear the limitations of Corona. Corona flight 117 (Mission 1041) was launched on May 9, 1967, and its two capsules were recovered on May 15 and 22, well before the war started. The day before the start of the war, the final Atlas Agena Gambit mission was launched. It remained in orbit for just over eight days, not returning to Earth until after the war was over. Corona flight 118 (Mission 1042) was not launched until June 16, 1967—five days after the war's end.[29] Reconnaissance satellites thus could play no part in U.S. intelligence operations during the Six-Day War.

Mission 1042-1 was able to provide an independent assessment of Israeli claims, however. The satellite made four passes over the Middle East from June 17 through 20, 1967, covering Syria, Jordan, Israel, and Egypt. The photos were cloud-free and showed the destruction inflicted on the airfields. At the Bir Jifjafah airfield in Egypt, twenty-two charred areas were observed. These were probably destroyed aircraft. At the Al Arish airfield in the Sinai, six probable bomb craters were observed on a runway, three charred areas at the end of another runway, and four more charred areas on a taxiway. In all, NPIC photo interpreters counted a total of 245 probable destroyed aircraft at Arab airfields—201 in Egypt, 26 in Jordan, and 18 in Syria.[30]

Fourteen months later came another lesson in the limitations of Corona. In April 1968, the new Czech Communist leader Alexander

Dubcek announced a reformism program including freedom of assembly and the abolition of censorship. Hard-line Communists, such as East Germany's Walter Ulbricht, feared "socialism with a human face" might spread, threatening their own control. As spring turned to summer, concern grew that the Soviets might crush the reforms as they had in Hungary in 1956.

A Titan IIIB–launched Gambit was placed in orbit on August 6, 1968, and operated for nine days. The next day, Corona flight 127 (Mission 1104) also went into space. When the Mission 1104-1 capsule was recovered, its photos were reassuring, showing no sign of Soviet troops massing, which might indicate an invasion.[31]

On the morning of August 21, 1968, the CIA's chief of current intelligence told DCI Helms that the Soviet Politburo was meeting in Moscow. The source was the UPI news wire. The meeting was out of the ordinary, as the Politburo members normally spent mid-August on vacation at the Black Sea. Warsaw Pact forces were also on maneuvers in East Germany. Helms discussed the situation with the chief of current intelligence, and came to the conclusion that "this was it"—the Warsaw Pact forces were about to invade Czechoslovakia.

At 12:30 P.M., Helms went to the White House for the lunch meeting. (It was only after the Six-Day War that it finally dawned on President Johnson that intelligence had a role to play. The CIA had correctly predicted the length of the war, and, as a result, Helms was finally invited to the Tuesday lunch meetings.) When President Johnson arrived, Helms told him that Warsaw Pact forces were very likely to invade Czechoslovakia—in fact the CIA was almost sure of it. Helms told the president the Politburo was meeting and gave statistics on the maneuvers. Johnson's retort was, "No, the Politburo is meeting because they are talking about us." Helms had no idea what he meant.

Once the Vietnamese bombing targets were picked and the meeting broke up, Helms took the president's note-taker aside, and asked, "What is going on around here?" He responded, "Well, if you promise not to say anything." Helms shot back, "Promise not to say anything? I don't know anything!" The note-taker said that Johnson and Rusk were planning to meet the next day with the Soviets to prepare for arms control talks, and they did not want any leaks.

Helms went to dinner, and at about eight o'clock, his pager went off. He arrived at the White House at about nine or nine-thirty, and sure enough, the Warsaw Pact forces had begun an invasion of

Czechoslovakia. The meeting was not actually about the invasion, however, but rather how to get the president "off the hook" for the meeting with the Soviets the next day about arms control.

When the film from the second bucket was finally recovered and analyzed, it showed large white crosses painted on Soviet and Warsaw Pact tanks and other vehicles. These crosses were to distinguish the invasion forces from the identical equipment of the Czech army. If U.S. intelligence had had a real-time read-out of the satellite photos, it would have known instantly what was about to happen.[32]

The Six-Day War and the invasion of Czechoslovakia clearly showed that the delays inherent in a capsule-return satellite made Corona ill-suited to the kind of dynamic crises that now posed the major threat to the United States. By the late 1960s, thoughts were turning to finding a replacement for Corona. The experiences of these two case studies showed the clear need for a real-time satellite.

TEN

Corona's Twilight
The End of Corona Operations, 1969–1972

Corona's Decade of Glory is now history. The first, the longest, and the most successful of the nation's space recovery programs, Corona explored and conquered the technological unknowns of space reconnaissance, lifted the curtain of secrecy that screened developments within the Soviet Union and Communist China, and opened the way for the even more sophisticated follow-on satellite reconnaissance systems.

Kenneth E. Greer, *Studies in Intelligence,* Spring 1973

➤ The year 1969 marked the end of a decade of Corona launches. In that time, America had undergone fundamental changes. The belief in an optimistic future had been replaced by a view that rejected science, technology, and rational thought. The innocence of the late 1950s had been replaced by the yawning gulf of the "generation gap." The Vietnam War had splintered American society, while campus riots, drugs, racial conflict, and political assassinations created an atmosphere of intolerance and violence. What divided Americans was now more important than what united them. The election of Richard Nixon by a razor-thin margin in November 1968 showed how bitter these conflicts had become. There was worse to come.

The ABM Debate

The first major defense issue facing the new Nixon administration was the U.S. ABM program. It had originally been intended for defense of American cities against a Chinese missile attack. Placement of nuclear warheads near urban areas fed a growing anti-ABM protest, and in

February 1969, President Nixon ordered a review of the program. In debating the options, which ranged from a "thick" defense to abandoning the program, a consensus emerged for a phased effort to defend Minuteman silos against a Soviet attack. Both President Nixon and his national security adviser, Dr. Kissinger, found this option both strategically and politically attractive. Nixon announced the new ABM system, called "Safeguard," on March 14, 1969.[1]

The ABM program became a symbol for a coalition of opponents of U.S. military policy. They were made up of ex–Whiz Kids, academics, intellectuals, scientists, and Vietnam War protesters. On the surface, the debate was about the technical and political merits of the Safeguard ABM, but it was really about a view of the arms race and the nature of American society. The ABM opponents took as their starting point McNamara's 1967 speech in which he had said that U.S. intelligence had routinely overestimated Soviet military activities, which resulted in huge U.S. weapons programs, that, in turn, sparked a Soviet response. Because of the assertion that the United States had been "fundamentally responsible for every major escalation of the arms race," it was up to the United States to break the "action-reaction" cycle by unilaterally showing restraint and not deploying Safeguard. The Soviets would not need to respond, the argument went, and the arms race would be controlled.

In the overheated "us versus them" political atmosphere of the late 1960s, the ABM opponents placed blame on a "virtual conspiracy" by weapons scientists, defense contractors, the military, and congressmen who all profited from the arms race, dubbing them the "military-industrial complex." Controlling the arms race, they believed, meant bringing the military-industrial complex to heel.[2] It was a continuation of McNamara's philosophy that all strategic decisions were to be controlled by a small group of "the best and the brightest." All others were uninformed or evil.

Although the Safeguard system was narrowly approved by Congress, the ABM debate was a milestone in U.S. politics. In the future, powerful and influential groups would oppose any new weapons systems. Their beliefs about the "action-reaction phenomena" and the military-industrial complex were elevated to fundamentalist dogma that was beyond question by any "right-thinking" person.

The deep divisions represented by the ABM debate extended to the U.S. government and intelligence community. Unlike the bomber and missile gap controversies, numbers were never in question. Thanks to Corona and Gambit, the United States knew how many ICBMs the Soviets had operational and under construction. The issue, rather, was the more complex one of intent.

Defense Secretary Melvin Laird believed the Soviet missile build-up was an attempt to gain a first-strike capability. Shortly after the ABM decision was announced, the Soviets began long-range testing of the SS-9 Mod 4 ICBM. This version carried three 5-megaton nuclear warheads, rather than a single 25-megaton weapon. Analysis of the tests indicated the warheads could be independently targeted, and the spacing of the impact point seemed to match the distances between Minuteman silos.

The CIA, however, believed that the SS-9 Mod 4 was intended to destroy cities. The three warheads would spread destruction across a wider area than the single larger warhead. The CIA rejected the idea of a Soviet first-strike capability. It stated in the draft text of the 1969 NIE: "We believe that the Soviets recognize the enormous difficulties of any attempt to achieve strategic superiority of such order as to significantly alter the strategic balance. Consequently, we consider it highly unlikely that they will attempt within the period of this estimate to achieve a first strike capability."

The reasons the CIA gave for this estimate were that the Soviets would conclude that the cost—added to their other military programs—would be prohibitive, that it would be impossible to deploy the offensive and defensive forces needed to counter the U.S. response, and that the Soviets would calculate the United States would detect their efforts and surpass them. This represented a continuation of the views the CIA had held of Soviet behavior since the early 1960s.

While the debate raged over the ABM and the larger issues it symbolized, Soviet ICBM deployment continued at the rapid pace of previous years. The number of operational Soviet ICBMs grew from 896 in September 1968 to 1,028 by mid-1969, 1,060 in September 1969, and 1,158 by the end of the year. In early 1970, Laird expressed his concern over the "continuing rapid expansion of Soviet strategic offensive forces" and noted that "for some time, the offensive forces becoming operational in a given year have often exceeded the previous projections for that year." The 1969 estimate had projected a total force in mid-1974 of between 1,100 and 1,500 Soviet ICBMs. However, the low end of the estimate had already been surpassed, and, while there was no indication what the ultimate force size would be, the minimum level, given the silos under construction, was 1,300 ICBMs.[3]

National Technical Means

The role of Corona expanded with the start of the Strategic Arms Limitation Talks on November 17, 1969, in Helsinki, Finland. The problems of verifying any agreement that might be reached were similar to those facing the United States at the start of Corona. The USSR was a vast police state that would not accept on-site inspectors.

The initial study of the role of satellites in policing an arms control agreement without on-site inspection was made in 1966. Lundahl gave wide latitude to his staff to pursue their own ideas. As part of this, Brugioni and Lundahl looked at what the Corona and other satellites could achieve in the way of resolution, and how this could be applied to arms control. They concluded that satellites could police a treaty limiting ICBMs, long-range bombers, ballistic missile submarines, and ABMs. All these were large objects which required large, distinctive, support facilities.

A report written by Brugioni, Ed Cates, and Kermit Gimmel was submitted to DCI Richard Helms. Helms said that it did not take into account the "Potemkin factor"—the use of decoys and false targets. In response, Helms was shown examples of Soviet deception efforts. In one example, the Soviets had built several fake ICBM silos. They had been constructed in only three months (vs. the eighteen months needed for a real silo). The roads leading to the sites lacked bridges over the gullies, and there were no support facilities. Helms was surprised at how easy it was to spot the fakes.[4]

President Nixon, his advisers, and Helms began to hold meetings on the verification issue, which continued for well over a year. The problem was particularly difficult as U.S. and Soviet strategic forces were like apples and oranges. There was, for example, no U.S. counterpart to the SS-9, while the closest Soviet missile to the Minuteman, the SS-13, was deployed in only token numbers. There was no mistaking Nixon's insistence that the treaty be verifiable, however. While he and Helms were chatting one day, President Nixon said, "Now look here, I don't want there to be any mistake about this. If you can't verify an arms control treaty, we're not going to have any arms control negotiations. Period."

Helms recalled later that no analysts would have been willing to give such an absolute guarantee.[5] Realizing that one could never be absolutely sure, the question became, as with weapons planning, How much was enough? This was not a technical or strategic question, but a political one. As SALT and later agreements would show, what was acceptable to a president might not be to Congress.

Because satellites were to be the means of verification, it was critical that they be safeguarded in the treaty. Since the start of the Corona program, there had been concerns about the possibility of Soviet attacks. Such fears were justified; as the early Discoverer launches were struggling towards success, Vladimir Chelomay's design bureau was working on an antisatellite interceptor. Khrushchev held several meetings with Chelomay to discuss how to deal with Corona. The initial tests of the Polyot (Flight) orbital interceptor were made on November 1, 1963, and April 12, 1964. Both attempts were unsuccessful.

It was four years later that the first successful Soviet space interception was actually made. On October 20, 1968, Cosmos 249, the interceptor satellite, was launched. It maneuvered, made a fast fly-by of the Cosmos 248 target satellite, and then exploded into a cloud of fragments. This was followed on November 1, 1968, when Cosmos 252 made a second interception of Cosmos 248, then also exploded. A similar dual interception was flown in 1970, while two more tests were made in 1971. The seventh and final test of this first phase of the Soviet interceptor program was conducted on December 3, 1971, when Cosmos 462 made a fly-by of the Cosmos 458 target. In this case, the target satellite was in a 250-kilometer-high, roughly circular orbit. This was similar to that of a reconnaissance satellite.[6]

The eventual target of the Soviet interceptors was made clear in an animated film about the system prepared in the 1960s. It showed the interceptor satellite as barrel-shaped with a dish antenna at the front and side-mounted thrusters. In the film, the target satellite was Corona.

While the Soviets had the means to destroy U.S. reconnaissance satellites, the interceptors were never unleashed against Corona. The reason was the political consequences of such an attack in peacetime. The Soviet leadership realized that if they shot down a U.S. satellite, then the United States would retaliate. They came to see that U.S. reconnaissance satellites were a reality of life they would simply have to live with. The interceptors were to be used only in the event of a U.S.-Soviet war.[7]

This meant, however, that the only thing protecting Corona was the Soviet leadership's state of mind, which could change without warning. During the 1960s, the United States studied several ways to counter a Soviet interception attempt, including orbital interceptors and the launch of nuclear-armed ABM missiles. One way was to fire the Agena's engine before it passed over an ABM site; the resulting orbital change would alter the timing of the pass, and foil the interception. Still another possibility that was explored was releasing decoy balloons, which would have the same radar return as the Corona. This would make it impossible to determine which target was the real satellite. There were problems, however. The decoy balloons would be affected differently by atmospheric drag than the real satellite, and could be identified. The bigger problem was that every pound of payload devoted to decoys or maneuvering fuel was one less pound of film. Given the choice, the NRO picked the extra film, and hoped the Soviets would continue to show restraint.[8]

The SALT negotiations were also an opportunity. U.N. resolutions and the 1967 Space Treaty had explicitly established freedom of space as part of international law, but had said nothing about reconnaissance from space. If protection of reconnaissance satellites could be written into the final treaty, then they would be explicitly recognized as being legitimate. No longer would their acceptance rely on an unspoken arrangement. Of course, neither the United States nor the Soviet Union acknowledged that they used reconnaissance satellites. They were referred to only as "national technical means of verification."

As the negotiations were beginning, the Soviets may have used Corona to send a signal to the United States. During late 1969 and early 1970, only ten new SS-11 and SS-13 silos were started, while SS-9 construction was halted. This sparked a debate over interpretation; some felt this was a signal of Soviet good faith, while others believed it represented problems with production and supplies. The scaling back in ICBM deployment lasted into the spring of 1970. During this time, three U.S. reconnaissance satellites were launched: Corona flights 136 on December 4, 1969, and 137 on March 4, 1970, and a Gambit high-resolution satellite on January 14, 1970.

One of the U.S. goals was to use SALT to protect the Minuteman force. In April 1970, the United States proposed "Option C" which involved a mutual ban on ICBMs with multiple independently targeted reentry vehicles (MIRVs), such as the SS-9 Mod 4 and Minuteman III.

Option D proposed that both the United States and the USSR be limited to 1,000 ICBMs by 1978. It would be possible to substitute submarine-launched ballistic missiles (SLBMs) for ICBMs, but not the reverse. The United States also proposed a sublimit on the number of SS-9s, and a ban on converting SS-11 silos to house SS-9s. The Soviets did not like the two options, and, it appeared, made their lack of interest apparent via Corona.

In May 1970, the Soviets began construction of twenty-four new SS-9 silos. Only six were in established SS-9 fields. This increased the total number of SS-9s operational or under construction from 282 to 306. Two U.S. reconnaissance satellites were launched during this period: Corona flight 138 on May 20, 1970, and a Gambit orbited on June 25. Secretary of Defense Laird announced the new SS-9 starts in July 1970, saying that "the momentum has not slowed down, it has continued."

Also in July 1970, the United States proposed Option E, which involved neither a MIRV ban nor a reduction in Soviet missile forces. Each side would be limited to a total of 1,900 missiles and bombers. The SS-9 sublimits and the SLBM/ICBM substitution and silo conversion rules remained. Some, including newspaper columnist Joseph Alsop, were concerned that Option E, because it lacked the MIRV ban, would leave the Minuteman force vulnerable should the Soviets deploy large numbers of MIRVed ICBMs. Within the U.S. government, the debate over Option E and the Minuteman vulnerability issue grew intense. It involved not only nuclear strategy, but the whole SALT process.

Over the following months, the situation remained unsettled. The SS-9 Mod 4 continued to be tested, but it was becoming clear that the missile lacked the accuracy and flexibility to destroy Minuteman silos. It was also clear that the Safeguard ABM system had deficiencies that limited its effectiveness in the face of a Soviet attack.

The Option E proposal seems to have generated a favorable Soviet signal, which was again sent via U.S. reconnaissance satellites. In October 1970, the Soviets dismantled the eighteen most recent silo starts, while work was slowed down at the two most advanced complexes. This information came from a Gambit launched on October 23, 1970, and Corona flight 140, which was orbited on November 18, 1970. Laird announced the slowdown in December. President Nixon added in his Foreign Policy Report, "The USSR could be exercising self-restraint. Its leaders may have concluded, as we have, that the number of ICBMs now deployed is sufficient for their needs."

Despite the apparent signal, 1970 had seen continued Soviet ICBM deployment. By the end of the year, the total stood at 1,440, a growth of 250 since late 1969. The situation was more ambiguous than the numbers alone would indicate. Nearly half the growth was from SS-11 ICBMs deployed in medium and intermediate range ballistic missile (M/IRBM) fields in the southwestern USSR. These missiles were aimed at Western Europe, but could still reach targets in the United States. A controversy developed over whether these missiles should be counted as part of the M/IRBM totals, as they had been in 1969, or as part of the regular ICBM force.[9]

The Twilight of Corona

During the early 1960s, Corona launches had been made at the rate of eighteen to twenty per year. In the middle years of the decade, with the introduction of the KH-4A/B cameras, the numbers began to decline. By the start of the Nixon administration, this decline was quite pronounced. In 1969, only six Corona launches were made. In 1970, a mere four flights were made: Corona flights 137 (launched on March 4), 138 (May 20), 139 (July 23), and 140 (November 18).

Although Corona had entered its twilight years, a photo taken by Corona flight 138 on the eighth day of its mission showed the kind of resolution the KH-4B camera could achieve. The photo was of Moscow; when the area of the Kremlin was enlarged, a thin black line could be seen crossing Red Square and entering Lenin's tomb. It was the line of tourists, and it was visible from orbit.

The Gambit high-resolution satellites, in contrast, had remained more stable in numbers. There had been ten in 1964, nine in 1965, fifteen in 1966, and ten in 1967. (The latter two years included both Atlas Agena D and Titan IIIB Agena D launches.) The end of the 1960s saw a relatively modest decline—eight Gambits in 1968, six in 1969, and five in 1970. Excluding the artificially high peak year of 1966, this was half the previous average rate.

The number of launches does not tell the entire story, however. With the two buckets of the KH-4A/B system, time in orbit went from two or three days to fifteen in 1967, a five-fold increase. The Gambit lifetimes were also increased from about five days to two weeks. Thus, while numbers went down, the increased lifetime balanced this out.[10]

The heart of the Empire: Moscow as viewed by a KH-4B camera. Visible are the Kremlin, a boat on the Moscow River, vehicles in the streets, and the line of tourists waiting to enter Lenin's tomb. In the decade between the *Discoverer 14* photos and this May 28, 1970, image, Corona had gone from a system limited to spotting only large facilities to one with the ability to resolve people from orbit. *National Archives*

These changes were reflected by the recovery squadron. At its peak, midair recoveries were made on a weekly basis. By the twilight of the program, this had fallen to perhaps twice a month.

In late 1969, an attempt was made to extend the recovery profile. Up to this point, all recoveries were made in daylight and clear weather to allow the JC-130B's pilot to evaluate the descending parachute. The behavior of a parachute could vary from wild swings, to "dancing" left and right, to a stable descent. A test program was begun to evaluate the feasibility of night recoveries. The JC-130 and payload were both modified for the daunting task. The transport was fitted with a "heads-up display" (HUD), which projected flight information onto a sheet of glass in front of the pilot. This allowed him to read vital data even while looking for the capsule. The capsule itself was fitted with an upward-pointing spotlight, which illuminated the parachute.

The testing was conducted at Edwards AFB. A unit was maintained there to test new equipment and procedures. Once they were proven, the Hawaii-based crews would be trained in their use. The first test was conducted just after dusk. The JC-130 pilot spotted the glowing orange parachute slightly above his plane, seeming to hang motionless in the dark sky. As the JC-130 closed on the parachute for its first pass, the spotlight failed and the orange parachute went black. The pilot immediately pulled up to avoid the now-invisible parachute. The JC-130 abandoned the attempt and flew back to Edwards. The simulated bucket and its parachute were found by Air Force personnel the next morning, snagged in a cactus.

Although a successful night midair recovery was finally achieved, the procedure was deemed too risky for operational use. The special HUD unit developed for the tests was fitted to the recovery planes, however. It proved very valuable for daylight recoveries in marginal weather, or between cloud layers where visual cues were limited and the pilot could become disoriented.[11]

One of the four Corona flights of 1970 was a special mission. This was Corona flight 139 (Mission 1111), which carried a KH-4B camera. The unusual features began with the launch of its LTTAT Agena D on July 23, 1970. Most Corona launches were made, trains permitting, between ten in the morning and two in the afternoon to optimize lighting conditions. Mission 1111, however, lifted off at 6:25 P.M. As the booster climbed, it performed a dogleg maneuver and turned west, rather than following the nearly due-south flight path normally used. The satellite was placed into a 60-degree inclination orbit; the standard Corona inclinations were between 81 and 88 degrees. This meant the satellite would not pass over any territory north or south of 60 degrees latitude. Thus the satellite could not cover the northern part of the USSR. It was, however, ideally placed for passes over the Middle East.

Mission 1111's flight was the result of events following the Six-Day War. The ceasefire between Israel and Egypt had broken down in the fall of 1967. The war of attrition that followed was marked by artillery exchanges, commando raids, and air strikes. The cycle of attacks and retaliation continued to escalate, with neither side gaining an advantage. Finally, both Israel and Egypt indicated a willingness to negotiate.

Mission 1111 was to photograph the Suez Canal area, to provide a baseline to determine compliance with the ceasefire provisions. Due to the unusual launch time, the satellite passed over the Middle East at about half past six local time each evening. This meant the late afternoon summer sun would cast long shadows. As part of the agreement, neither side was to move military equipment into a belt 50 kilometers on either side of the Suez Canal after midnight on August 8, 1970.

The standard practice for Corona coverage of the Middle East was to have one pass to the west of the canal zone to cover the deployment of Egyptian forces, and another over the Sinai to provide photos of Israeli units. The dry summer air of the desert greatly improved clarity. While the KH-4B could provide a 6-foot resolution under normal conditions, photos of the Sinai often showed 3- to $3^1/_2$ -foot resolution.

The special mission of Corona flight 139 posed unique challenges. The mission duration was extended to nineteen days. This was difficult, as the Corona satellites were powered by batteries. They did not have solar panels, which could provide power for a long-duration flight. An orbital maneuver was also required to allow the satellite to photograph the Middle East on August 10. Both capsules were recovered in midair, the first by Capt. Marshall A. Eto, the second on August 11 by Lt. Col. William Scott.

The success of the flight was praised by Dr. John McLucas, undersecretary of the Air Force and director of the NRO. On August 25, he sent a message to the CIA's director of special projects: "I extend my sincere thanks and a well done to you and your staff for your outstanding response to an urgent Intelligence Community requirement. . . . [Mission 1111] provided information which could not be obtained through any other means."[12]

The unusual flight also attracted attention from other quarters. Philip J. Klass, an editor at *Aviation Week & Space Technology,* was in the process of writing his book *Secret Sentries in Space.* This was the first book dealing with reconnaissance satellites. While doing research, he read the July 31, 1970, issue of NASA's "Satellite Situation Report," and the peculiar inclination caught his eye. He plotted the satellite's ground track, and realized it was targeted on the Middle East. Klass wrote an article on the unusual satellite, which was published in the August 31 issue of *Aviation Week.* Two days later, the *Washington Post* reported that there was now clear evidence of ceasefire violations. On September 4, *New York Times* reporter Tad Szulc tried to get official confirmation of Klass's satellite article. At a State Department brief-ing on the Middle East, Szulc asked if the United States had been con-ducting any type of reconnaissance over the Suez Canal *before* the ceasefire. The State Department official refused to comment.[13] Mission 1111 established a new role for later reconnaissance satellite operations. This was the policing of ceasefires and other agreements between com-batants. In the exchanges of charges and countercharges, reconnais-sance satellites could serve as objective witnesses.

But that was for the future. Corona was soon to become a thing of the past.

The Inheritors

On July 20, 1969, as most of the human race watched, Apollo 11 astronauts Neil Armstrong and Edwin "Buzz" Aldrin walked on the Moon. One of the questions facing President Nixon in the early months of his administration was the future of the space program for the rest of the twentieth century. NASA had mapped out an ambitious effort involving development of a space shuttle, a space station, and, finally, a manned landing on Mars in the mid-1980s, but the proposal never had a chance. The trauma of the 1960s saw American society turning inward. Rather than recognize the Moon landing as one of the great human achievements, politicians condemned and ridiculed it. Science, technology, and even rational thought were increasingly rejected. As the NASA space program began its decline, other decisions were being made to embark on a secret development effort that would rival Apollo.

By the mid-1960s, the limitations of Corona were becoming appar-ent. Dr. Albert Wheelon, who directed the CIA's overhead reconnais-sance efforts—the U-2 and A-12 as well as Corona—asked his staff to spend some time with the photo interpreters. He wanted to find out, in a precise and analytical way, what level of resolution was needed to make the discovery and identification of new targets a highly reli-able operation. The results convinced Wheelon that the physical lim-its of the Corona cameras and spacecraft systems had been reached.[14]

What Wheelon envisioned was a satellite that combined the high resolution of Gambit with a wider area of coverage than Corona. In effect, the high-resolution and area search missions would be combined in a single satellite. It would also have a lifetime measured in months rather than the two weeks of Corona. The Air Force, in contrast, proposed a series of incremental improvements to Corona called "Valley." Despite an initial rejection of Wheelon's proposal by an advisory panel, it was soon apparent that he was right—there was not enough "stretch" left in Corona. President Johnson opted for the advanced system. By the time Wheelon left the CIA in 1967, Lockheed had won the contract to build the satellite, and development was well under way.[15]

The new satellite was given the code name "Hexagon." The satellite itself dwarfed Corona. It was 9.3 feet wide, 48.3 feet long, and weighed 29,500 pounds.[16] Its payload, which was designated KH-9, had two panoramic cameras with 60-inch focal length lenses—two and a half times the focal length of the Corona cameras. Each KH-9 film frame covered an area four times that of a KH-4B frame, with a resolution of 2 feet (compared to 6 feet for Corona's KH-4B). The KH-9 cameras were also designed to use not only standard film, but also black-and-white and color infrared film. The exposed film was returned to Earth via four capsules. Some Hexagon satellites would also carry a 12-inch focal length mapping camera. Its film would be recovered with a fifth bucket. Because the satellite would orbit at a low altitude, it was fitted with a maneuvering engine, apparently based on the Agena. This would be fired periodically to raise the satellite's orbit. Due to the Hexagon's increased size and mass, a new booster, the Titan IIID, was required.

The Hexagon code name and KH-9 designation for the camera system were, like Corona and KH-4B, classified. Thus, the satellite became known by the name later given it by the press— "Big Bird."

In 1969, Hexagon became caught up in the increased funding demands of the Vietnam War, and was abruptly cancelled. As a substitute, a plan called "Higher Boy" was proposed. This involved placing Gambit high-resolution satellites into higher area-surveillance orbits. This was not acceptable to Roland S. Inlow, the chairman of the Committee on Imagery Requirements and Exploitation (COMIREX), which selected the targets for U.S. reconnaissance satellites. Inlow went to see James Schlesinger, then assistant director of the Bureau of the Budget, and told him that Hexagon was essential to verification of the SALT treaty. The program was quickly reinstated.

As Hexagon was an advanced system, it ran into the usual development problems. The first Hexagon launch was originally planned for 1970, but difficulties with the KH-9 camera system delayed the schedule until mid-1971.

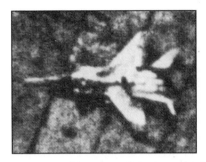 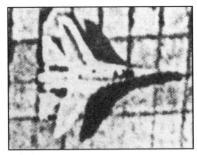

The impossible accomplished: very high resolution satellite photos of the MiG-29 Fulcrum (*left*) and the Su-27 Flanker (*right*). The black dot on the back of the MiG-29 is probably a ground crewman. The photos were part of the fiscal year 1985 DoD congressional hearings, and were released by accident. *Author's collection*

Despite its new design and remarkable capabilities, the Hexagon satellite inherited the design philosophy of Corona. It used a pair of panoramic cameras to provide stereo coverage, and multiple buckets to return the film. This also meant it shared Corona's limitations. Hexagon could not provide the near real-time coverage that was increasingly seen as necessary to meet U.S. intelligence needs. That would require a fresh philosophy, a whole new technology, and an entirely different satellite.

Real-Time Imagery

The real-time satellite traces its roots back to 1962 and the failure of the SAMOS radio-transmission satellite program. Leslie Dirks of the CIA's Directorate of Science and Technology began to consider the possibilities of a truly covert reconnaissance satellite, one that the Soviets would not know was taking pictures.

Dirks and his staff quickly realized that any satellite in a low orbit would be identified by the Soviets as a reconnaissance satellite. The alternative was to put it into a high orbit. As photoreconnaissance satellites were placed in low orbits to maximize resolution, this higher orbit would conceal its mission. When needed, the satellite would fire a rocket engine to lower its orbit and take the photos. It was possible that the Soviets would miss the maneuver. The flaw in this concept was that while the satellite was waiting, the film would degrade; by the time the satellite was needed, the film might be useless.

With any kind of film-based system out of the question, Dirks reconsidered the original RAND concept of a television reconnaissance satellite. In 1962, such a design was still not possible. Dirks realized, however, that technical advances might change this. During the 1960s, Dirks kept the idea alive, and supported research into new technologies. By the end of the 1960s, events had showed that a near real-time system was needed.

In 1969, Inlow became COMIREX chairman. As one of his first actions, he began an interagency study of the utility of a real-time reconnaissance satellite. It looked at three cases, the 1962 Cuban missile crisis, the 1967 Six-Day War, and the 1968 Soviet invasion of Czechoslovakia. The group looked at what information could have been obtained in each case, how it would have changed perceptions of the crisis, and how decision makers such as the president, military, and intelligence community could have made use of the information. In particular, they explored how different degrees of timeliness would have aided the decision-making process.

The results were stunning. In each case the advanced warning would have made many more options available. A president might have issued a warning, used diplomacy, or called a military alert. The United States would not have been caught by surprise, and been forced into taking quick, and potentially rash and risky, action. Development of a real-time system became a priority.

As before, there were two possible approaches. The Air Force Office of Special Projects proposed a modified Gambit called FROG (Film Read-Out Gambit). The basic Gambit would be equipped with a film process and transmission system similar to the old E-2/Program 101A SAMOS. Such an incremental improvement had the disadvantage that the resolution from a film-scan would be less than from the Gambit's KH-8 camera, and the area covered by each photo would be limited. Balancing this were the advantages that FROG could be ready in short order, and at a relatively low cost of $2 billion. Secretary of Defense Laird selected FROG for development.

In contrast, Carl Duckett, the CIA's deputy director for science and technology, wanted a revolutionary satellite design. It would not use film, but rather an electro-optical system. Because the satellite would not be limited by its film supply, it could operate for as long as *five years*.

In 1969, the longest a U.S. reconnaissance satellite had operated was two weeks.

Such an unconventional approach reflected Duckett's background. He did not have the Ivy League/old money background typical for senior CIA officials. Duckett had grown up in rural North Carolina. When he turned 17, his mother gave him a new pair of jeans, some money, and instructions to get a job at a local mill. Instead, he kept going and found work at a radio station. After he was drafted during World War II, his IQ tests indicated he was a genius, and he was sent to study radio at Johns Hopkins University.

After the war, Duckett worked at the White Sands Proving Ground in missile testing and telemetry analysis. He then moved to Huntsville, Alabama, to head the Army missile intelligence unit. In 1962, he so impressed DCI John McCone at a meeting of the U.S. Intelligence Board that Duckett was hired by the CIA. Within a year, Duckett was the head of the CIA's Foreign Missile and Space Intelligence Center.

Duckett began working behind the scenes to reverse the decision to develop FROG. He talked to Sen. Allen Ellender (D-La.), chairman of the Appropriations Committee, and convinced him that FROG would not meet the need for real-time intelligence. A panel headed by Dr. Eugene Fubini examined his proposal, but concluded that it was not practical. A member of the panel, Richard Garwin of IBM, disagreed strongly with this conclusion, however. Garwin was also a member of the Reconnaissance Panel, co-chaired with Dr. Edwin Land. The Reconnaissance Panel examined the proposal, and judged it was quite feasible.

The dispute would have to be settled at the White House. Dr. Land met with President Nixon to discuss the CIA proposal, while Garwin and Sidney Drell (who had worked on the KH-4 corona discharge problem several years before) saw Dr. Kissinger. Dr. Land explained to the president that the CIA proposal was actually quite simple—essentially a tube with a mirror in front of it. Dr. Land, from the days of the U-2 on, had always supported the great technological leap, even when no one else thought it could be done. The CIA proposal carried a high price tag. The satellite would cost $10 billion to develop, and could not be ready until 1976 or 1977. This was about half the total cost of the Apollo Moon landing program, and on a similar time scale. Only Dr. Land had the reputation that could have sold such a tremendous technological gamble. The proposal was further discussed at a meeting of the President's Foreign Intelligence Advisory Board. Nixon gave his approval for the new CIA system.

TRW was selected as prime contractor for the CIA satellite, which was given the code name "Kennan." This would be the first photoreconnaissance satellite not built by Lockheed. Kennan relied on a breakthrough in solid-state electronics—the charge-couple device (CCD). This had been invented at Bell Laboratories by William S. Boyd and George E. Smith in the late 1960s. The CCD had originally been developed as an improved memory device, but soon found wider uses.

The CCDs were arranged into an array of hundreds of thousands of individual units. (On the Hubble space telescope, the CCD array is 800 x 800—640,000 total—and less than a half-inch square.) When exposed to light, each of the CCDs would generate an electrical current proportional to the amount of light (much as a light meter works). This current would then be sent to an amplifier, which would convert it into a number corresponding to the range between pure white and pure black. This would then become a "pixel" (picture element).

The pixel from each CCD was used to create the final image. The pixels, each one of several hundred shades of gray, were arranged in a line. The Kennan camera system built up its pictures in thin strips. Because nothing was depleted in taking the pictures, a CCD-based system could operate indefinitely. The data were then radioed to Earth via a ground station or the Satellite Data System relay satellite.

The CCD array required a fundamentally different optical system. The SAMOS, Corona, Gambit, and Hexagon satellites had all used cameras with lenses. Kennan would be built around a telescope. Unlike an astronomical telescope, which uses a large mirror to gather light from dim stars, the Kennan would use it to maximize resolution. The larger the mirror, the smaller the angular separation between two objects that could be resolved.

The main mirror for the first Kennan was 92 inches in diameter, while slightly larger mirrors were flown on later missions. To minimize the weight of the large mirror, an unusual design was used. Rather than a solid disc of glass, the mirror used "egg-crate" construction. The front and back were thin sheets, with glass ribs between them. This design weighed a small fraction of the weight of an equivalent solid mirror. The main mirror reflected the light to a smaller secondary mirror, then back down the telescope and through a hole in the center of the main mirror to the CCD array.

Just as the Hexagon satellite became known by its press nickname of "Big Bird," the Kennan would be publicly known first by its program number, 1010, then by the designation of the telescope/camera system—KH-11.[17]

The Kennan and its KH-11 camera system represented an even greater leap into the unknown than Corona had a decade before. While Corona had at least used existing components—the HYAC camera, the WS-117L's Agena, the Thor IRBM booster, and ICBM warhead technology for the capsule—the Kennan's CCD system was still a laboratory curiosity. Like the U-2 and Corona, it was also a monument to the vision of Dr. Land. Just as the Corona had set the pattern for satellite reconnaissance for the 1960s and 1970s, the Kennan, and a later advanced version called "Crystal," would serve through the rest of the century.

The Kennan decision also marked the end of the postwar scientific, academic, and government alliance that had produced the U-2, Corona, and Hexagon. One of the "non-negotiable" demands of student radicals was an end to military research on campus. The ABM debate and the Vietnam War caused many in the scientific community to see their role not as advisers but as critics. McNamara's "action-reaction" theory gave an intellectual justification for their automatic opposition to any new weapons programs, while his management style encouraged use of analysis to support decisions already made, and the belief that decisions should be limited to a narrow academic elite.

The Last of Corona

With the approval of the Hexagon and Kennan satellite programs, the phaseout of Corona began in earnest. A large number of Corona satellites and payloads had been built in the mid-1960s and placed in storage awaiting launch. Due to program stretchouts, this lasted longer than anticipated. Concerns grew that the prolonged storage would cause the capsule heat shields to deteriorate. These fears were eased by the analysis of the reentry effects on the *Discoverer 38* capsule heat shield. It had failed to separate and was recovered in midair still attached to the capsule. (This was the last Discoverer flight, and the first KH-4/Mural camera.)[18]

The final Corona launches were to maintain coverage until the Hexagon satellite was finally ready. This presented a difficult balancing act between the dwindling supply of the older satellites and U.S. intelligence needs. There were a mere five Coronas left at the start of 1971, plus a spare Agena and KH-4B test payload. Three of them were used in 1971.

The year got off to a bad start on February 17, with the loss of Corona flight 141 due to a Thor failure. The Thor's air-conditioning system had failed, causing the turbine oil to freeze. Control was lost, and the range safety officer was forced to destroy the booster 23.25 seconds after lift-off. This was the first failure since Mission 1032 was lost on May 3, 1966. Unlucky Mission 1113 broke a string of thirty-two launch successes.

The program quickly rebounded with the successful launch of Mission 1114 on March 24, 1971. Another six months would pass before the year's final Corona launch; Mission 1115 was orbited on September 10. As in past years, all four capsules from Corona flights 142 and 143 were recovered in midair.

The recovery squadron was undergoing changes related to the expanding satellite program. In the mid-1960s, the number of recovery-qualified aircraft commanders had been limited. Between 1969 and 1973, the number increased to service the later programs. There was an influx of new pilots and aircrews. Many would find their stay with the unit to be the high point of their time in the Air Force. There was lots of flying and lots of training. The recovery procedures were as demanding as ever.

Postrecovery parties were a squadron tradition. Following each midair recovery, the successful aircraft commander would buy the first round of drinks. The parties also saw the paying off of bets and penalties for mistakes. If a navigator made an error in position, he would then buy a round. A common mistake during practice recoveries was to scrape the top of a parachute with the bottom of the plane. This could cause minor damage, such as the loss of an antenna, and cost the offending pilot a round of drinks.

The parties served to build a sense of unit cohesion. The unit undertook a difficult, demanding, and highly secret mission. The pilots flew heavy cargo planes in a manner never envisioned by Lockheed. The postrecovery party made the crews feel they were a part of something special. The result was a level of teamwork and morale not seen in most squadrons.[19]

Much of the satellite effort in 1971 was directed toward monitoring the deployment of Soviet ICBM forces. A new concern was raised by the photos from a Gambit launched on January 21, 1971. The photo interpreters spotted ten new silos in SS-9 fields across the central USSR. These new silos were much larger than normal, however. The Soviets were excavating a funnel-shaped hole for these silos—wide at the top and narrowing towards the bottom. The Gambit photos could not indicate how much the silo tapered, as the interior was in shadow.

The new silos raised concerns that the Soviets were about to begin deployment of a much larger ICBM than the SS-9. On March 4, 1971, the Senate Armed Services Committee was told of the new silos. Three days later, Sen. Henry "Scoop" Jackson (D-Wash.) announced their existence in a television interview. He described them as being for "huge new missiles . . . big or bigger than the SS-9s." He projected an estimated deployment rate of sixty to seventy per year. When President Nixon was asked about the "monster missile" claims, he commented, "[Jackson's] very close to it. He's concerned about the Soviets. We're very aware. . . . On the other hand I do not believe our expressing, as a government, trepidation about this would be helpful."

The United States reportedly expressed concern over the new silos, possibly in the "back-door" discussions being held between Kissinger and Soviet Ambassador Anatoly Dobrynin. The Soviets gave reassurances that the new silos were designed only to provide greater "hardness" against nuclear attack, rather than to house larger missiles.

This was backed up by the photos from Corona mission 1114. These indicated that the new silos could only house an ICBM no more than about twelve feet in diameter. At his April 27 news conference, Defense Secretary Laird said that "the size [of the new missile] will be along the same lines as the SS-9." In a May 10 column, Stewart Alsop gave a detailed account of the new silos:

> First they would build two fences, sometimes three, around a 100 acre site. Then they would dig a big flat hole, about 100 feet across and 25 feet deep. Inside the first hole the Russians would then dig a bigger hole, about 30 feet across and 120 feet down. They would then line the hole with concrete, put a steel liner inside that and then lower the big missile into the liner. In the remaining empty space of the first big hole, they would build a complex of workrooms, generators, fuel pumps and so on, and cover the whole thing with a thick sliding door.[20]

During the spring and summer of 1971, the watch on the new silos continued. A Gambit was orbited on April 22, 1971, and remained aloft for twenty-one days. It was followed on June 15 by the first Hexagon launch. The new satellite proved highly successful, and remained in orbit for fifty-two days. Another Gambit followed on August 12, then Corona mission 1115 in September, and still another Gambit on October 23.[21] By the end of April, there were roughly forty of the new silos under construction in six different missile fields. Laird announced that new intelligence was "confirming the sobering fact that the Soviet Union is involved in a new—and apparently extensive—ICBM construction program." There were two different types of silos, the difference being the larger silo was four feet wider than the other. In May, the number had grown to sixty, and by August it was nearly eighty. The final total in October was 91—25 in SS-9 fields and 66 in SS-11 complexes. Laird said the pace of construction had far exceeded the projections he had given Congress in March.

This continued deployment increased the pressure on the United States to conclude a SALT agreement. It was apparent that the Soviets would not accept any cuts in their strategic forces. The longer it took to reach agreement, the bigger the force the United States would have to contend with. The stalemate was finally broken with the back-door Kissinger-Dobrynin talks, and announced on May 20, 1971. The United States agreed to drop its demands for equity in nuclear forces. In effect, both sides' forces would be frozen. The present threat to the Minuteman force would only be contained until the 1980s, with a future threat not ruled out. Once the agreement was reached, the Soviets sent another signal via the satellites. Although some preliminary site preparation was observed in the fall of 1971, no actual construction was begun. At the same time, the CIA was warning that the Soviets were about to begin tests of a new generation of ICBMs, and final negotiations were being completed on the SALT treaty.

The final two Coronas were launched in 1972. The 144th Corona flight, Mission 1116, was launched from Vandenberg AFB on April 19, 1972. Both capsules were recovered in midair. The Mission 1116-1 bucket was recovered by Lieutenant Colonel McDonald. His previous Corona recovery (as a captain) was the second capsule from Corona flight 100. He had completed his tour with the squadron, been rotated out, then returned as the squadron's chief of standardization and evaluation. This was his fifth Corona recovery, and brought his total number of recoveries to seven. The Mission 1116-2 capsule was caught by Maj. Harry V. Boyd.

The 145th and final Corona satellite, Mission 1117, was launched on May 25, 1972. The following day, President Nixon and Communist Party General Secretary Leonid Brezhnev signed the SALT Treaty in Moscow. The treaty limited the Soviets to a total of 1,618 ICBMs—209 SS-7s and SS-8s, 288 SS-9s, 970 SS-11s (including 120 in M/IRBM complexes), 60 SS-13s, 25 of the larger of the two new silos, and 66 of the smaller silos. A sublimit of 313 SS-9 heavy ICBMs (288 deployed and 25 in the new silos) was also written into the treaty, as were the ban on converting SS-11 silos to house larger ICBMs and the conversion rules for SLBMs. (Under the latter, the Soviets could have up to 950 SLBMs on up to 62 submarines by "trading in" the 209 older SS-7/8 ICBMs.) Both sides were also limited to a pair of ABM sites with 100 missiles each— one to protect ICBM complexes, the other the national capital.[22]

As Mission 1117 orbited overhead, its presence was also being felt in the treaty. The Soviets had been unwilling to confirm the numbers for their missile forces. Instead, they agreed to accept the U.S. numbers for their forces. These were Corona's numbers. The treaty also included a ban on interference with "national technical means of verification."[23] Soon after, the mission's first bucket was recovered by Capt. Thomas T. Rault.

The Last Capsule

The prime recovery pilot was selected for each mission by a complicated process. Each pilot did his turn in rotation, but he had to have shown proficiency during the practice recoveries. Each training catch was "scored" according to how well the approach was flown and how the trapeze caught the parachute (much as a carrier pilot's landings are judged to assess his proficiency). Of course, if the capsule were to come down out of the recovery zone, another pilot would be ordered to catch it.

The final Corona capsule recovery was scheduled for May 31, 1972. Due to weather conditions, the ballpark for this recovery was split; four planes each were assigned to the west and east halves. The two selected as the prime recovery pilots were Captains Donald G. Hard and Donald Krump. They flipped a coin to see who went where. Captain Hard headed to the east zone.

In space, as on so many Corona flights before, the Mission 1117-2 capsule separated from the Agena, oriented itself, and fired its retrorocket.

Following reentry, the heat shield separated and the parachute deployed high above the east zone.

Captain Hard turned the JC-130 towards the parachute. His first pass was to look over the parachute. (On practice missions, the parachute often descended erratically, so pilots making their first "live" recovery expected a more difficult time than it usually turned out to be.) The parachute was coming down in a stable manner, so he prepared for a second pass. The JC-130 passed directly over the center of the parachute, and caught it between the number 7 and 8 hooks. (This was considered a good score.) The capsule was brought aboard the aircraft without incident, the door was closed, and the plane turned toward home. During the trip back, the number 2 engine had to be shut down, due to a propeller leak. This was not a major problem, and Captain Hard landed the plane successfully, bringing his first recovery to a close. The capsule was loaded on a jet, while the crew headed for the postrecovery party.[24]

And now it was over.

In twelve years of operation, 145 Corona flights had returned 165 capsules containing 866,000 frames of film. This was equivalent to one photo every ten minutes throughout the program. Laid end to end, the film would stretch for four hundred miles. The photos covered an approximate total of 99,722,000 square nautical miles (including 5,996,000 in the United States).[25]

With the conclusion of the program, the CIA began efforts to record the Corona program's achievements. A classified documentary film on Corona called *A Point in Time* was produced, and a special supplement of the CIA's internal magazine *Studies in Intelligence* was published with a history of the Corona program. The latter was classified Top Secret and carried the warning "Handle via TALENT-KEYHOLE Controls."

Efforts to develop a museum display of Corona hardware soon ran into problems, however. Very little in the way of artifacts had survived. Of the 165 capsules, the *Discoverer 13* capsule was in the Smithsonian, and the *Discoverer 14* capsule was in the Air Force Museum, while several more were in storage at Sunnyvale. The rest had been scrapped; the gold plating had been chemically removed and the platinum electrical connections were salvaged before the bucket was cut up. None of the early model cameras had survived. When the satellites reentered, the cameras always burned up. When each new camera system was built, the contract had specified that one camera—called the "floor model"—was to be built for ground testing. Each time, however, the floor model had been reconditioned and flown. The museum display was finally assembled using the floor model of the KH-4B camera, the spare Agena, and the two capsules from the Mission 1117 flight.

When the display was dedicated by DCI Richard Helms, he observed:

> It was confidence in the ability of intelligence to monitor Soviet compliance with the commitments that enabled President Nixon to enter into the Strategic Arms Limitation Talks and to sign the Arms Limitation Treaty. Much, but by no means all, of the intelligence necessary to verify Soviet compliance with SALT will come from photoreconnaissance satellites. Corona, the program which pioneered the way in satellite reconnaissance, deserves the place in history which we are preserving through this small Museum display.
>
> "A Decade of Glory," as the display is entitled, must for the present remain classified. We hope, however, that as the world grows to accept satellite reconnaissance, it can be transferred to the Smithsonian Institution. Then the American people can view this work, and then the men of Corona, like the Wright Brothers, can be recognized for the role they played in the shaping of history.[26]

ELEVEN

The View from 2001
The Continuing Importance of Corona

It can be said that without the intelligence which this program furnished,
we might have misguidedly been pressured into a World War III.

Kenneth E. Greer, *Studies in Intelligence*, Spring 1973

➤ It would be a very long time before DCI Helms's hope that
the KH-4B camera might be displayed in the Smithsonian would be
realized. For twenty-three years, it would remain hidden from public
eyes. During that interval, the world had changed dramatically.

Only a month after the end of Corona, what became known as the
Watergate scandal began. Two years later, President Nixon resigned in
disgrace. In the spring of 1975, South Vietnam, Laos, and Cambodia
fell to the Communist onslaught, bringing a humiliating end to U.S.
involvement. In the wake of military defeat and domestic turmoil,
American society turned inward and grew cynical. Jimmy Carter was
elected president and oversaw a period of U.S. decline. This culmi-
nated in the Iran hostage crisis, and the humiliation of the failed rescue attempt.

The election of Ronald Reagan as president in 1980 marked a resur-
gence of American power and determination. At the same time, the
USSR began a period of political and economic decline. A Polish shipyard worker named Lech Walesa challenged Communist control.
Although the attempt ended, for the moment, with the imposition of
martial law, the Soviet empire in Eastern Europe remained restive. In
Afghanistan, the Soviets were finding a guerrilla war against tribes-
men more difficult than they initially thought. At home, the sick and
aging Soviet leadership was increasingly detached from reality. Soviet

society had become stagnant, with a population that looked increasingly to Western ideas, rather than the state-approved Marxist ideology.

By the mid-1980s, the old leadership had finally died off, and Mikhail Gorbachev became Communist Party general secretary. Faced with resurgent American power under Reagan and the problems besetting the USSR, he realized the Communist system would have to change. He permitted free elections, reduced press censorship, withdrew Soviet forces from Afghanistan, and made it clear the Soviet Union would no longer use force to keep Eastern European Communist governments in power. In 1989, one by one, like dominoes, they toppled. In November, as the world watched on CNN, people danced atop the Berlin Wall.

The USSR was also buffeted by the winds of change. The ethnic republics wanted independence, while Communist Party hard-liners longed for a return to the old days of Stalinist control. In August 1991, the hard-liners launched a coup marked by such sheer incompetence that it collapsed before the week was out. By their actions, they brought about the very thing they had sought to prevent—the dissolution of the USSR. On December 27, 1991, the red hammer and sickle flag was lowered, and the Russian tricolor was raised in its place. The Cold War was finally over. The Russian people, and the world, had now set sail on an uncharted sea, towards the unknown future.

Corona and the Winning of the Cold War

The Cold War was fought on many fronts and in many ways. Corona and the other satellite systems played a major role in the West's victory. The Soviets' 1962 U.N. proposal was a reflection of their fear. It would not only have banned satellite reconnaissance, but would have established a doctrine of unlimited national sovereignty. This would have made it illegal to inquire about anything the Soviet Union deemed secret, by any means whatsoever. At first glance, this seems extreme, but it only reflected what had been policy since the start of the Soviet Union.

In the USSR, the number and location of ICBMs were a state secret, as were statistics about the number of airliner crashes, crime and health conditions, natural disasters such as earthquakes, and a very long list of similar forbidden subjects. Article 65 of the Soviet criminal code made it illegal for an unauthorized person to possess a state secret. There was never any definition of what exactly was a "state secret"; it was whatever the state decided to keep secret.[1] The Soviets' Cold War strategy was to keep the West (and their own people) ignorant of even the most basic military information.

The U.S. strategy was based on the policy of containment: The United States and its allies would resist Soviet attempts to expand their spheres of influence. This ceded to the Soviets the initiative in selecting the areas and level of conflict. Therefore, if containment was to be successful, the West needed information on Soviet military strengths and weaknesses. Only then would it be possible to anticipate Soviet actions, develop counters, and judge how far the Soviets could push.

It was not until Corona that such information could be provided on a reliable and complete basis. The prime example of this was the 1961 Berlin crisis. The Soviets attempted to use the perceived missile gap to force the West to accept a settlement on their terms. Corona, by giving a precise inventory of Soviet ICBM forces (or rather the lack of them), enabled President Kennedy to resist the Soviet demands. Corona also provided confidence. There was little of the uncertainty that plagued intelligence in the 1950s. Plans could be made with assurance, while the Soviets were denied the weapons of bluff and fear of the unknown.

There was also a more subtle consequence, illustrating the political power of information against a totalitarian system. Corona provided information on events the Soviets sought to keep hidden. The failure of the N 1 Moon rocket was considered a state secret by the Soviets, but reports derived from satellite photos leaked out and were published in the West.[2]

This produced an absurd situation: any high school student with an interest in the Soviet space program knew information that was officially denied Soviet citizens by their own government. The vast national security state that was the USSR—the KGB, border guards, and the legions of censors—served only to defend the Soviet Union from information available in any Western public library.

The obsessive secrecy imposed on the Soviet people was justified as protection against Western spies, but once Corona was operational, its only real function was social control. Soviet propaganda in the 1960s depicted their space program in heroic terms of technological perfection, a reflection of the USSR as a perfect society. But in a perfect society, rockets did not explode, airliners did not crash, and people did not fall victim to crime or illness or natural disasters.

The Soviet people were isolated from the reality of their own existence. By the 1980s, the unreality was untenable. Under Gorbachev, some previously blank parts of Soviet history, such as the N 1 program, were made public. If anything, official admissions that the Communist government had lied to its own people accelerated the break-up of the USSR. One of the lessons of Corona is that information and totalitarian societies are incompatible.

The Lessons of Corona

As the twenty-first century dawns, the lessons of Corona can provide guidance for an uncertain future. One is how to manage a groundbreaking program, and how not to. In looking back on Corona, those involved repeatedly refer to the "team"—the small band of CIA, Air Force, and contractor personnel—who made Corona a reality. They set aside their personal and institutional interests so that the mission could succeed. They also enjoyed the complete support of President Eisenhower. Even during the long, bad streak of Discoverer failures, he never wavered. He judged Corona to be an absolute necessity, no matter how many failures or what the final cost.

This was in marked contrast to Robert McNamara and the Whiz Kids. For them, control was an end in itself. The idea that the mission should come first was alien to their thinking. McNamara's attempt to gain control damaged the CIA–Air Force relationship. Had he succeeded, U.S. reconnaissance satellite efforts would have suffered greatly.

In retrospect, the "creative tension" between the CIA and the Air Force spurred both to do better. Both were driven to come up with better ideas that would not have been developed had they not been motivated by the rivalry.[3] Indeed, three projects under development by the CIA (Hexagon, Kennan, and the Rhyolite SIGINT satellite) later became important elements of the national reconnaissance program. Had the CIA been frozen out of satellite development, the United States would not have had the benefit of these systems.[4]

In our time, this lesson of Corona is of critical importance. Any future space activities, whether the space station, single-stage-to-orbit boosters, a return to the Moon, or a manned flight to Mars, will require teamwork and continuing political support, even in the face of failures. In the current political environment, this will be particularly difficult. Self-appointed "experts" harp on any setback, oppose any and all programs, and denigrate those with the courage to try. But in the final analysis, these new "Whiz Kids" have nothing positive to contribute.

Another lesson of Corona is to underscore the limitations of the estimation process. The "other" missile gap was the systematic under-estimating of the future Soviet ICBM force during the 1960s. A basic flaw was the lack of any recognition of the human factor in the Whiz Kids' nuclear theories. The "action-reaction" theory reduced Soviet strategic planning to the level of a single-celled organism, responding only to the outside stimulus of the U.S. nuclear effort. The larger aspect of this was "mirror imaging"—the belief that the United States and the USSR shared similar goals and nuclear doctrines. This led to unspoken assumptions about what the Soviet government wanted and its over-all goals, including the assumption that the Soviet government saw mil-itary spending as a burden, as the United States did. It was also assumed that Soviet activities were constrained by economic factors, and that the Soviet military was primarily defensive rather than offensive.[5]

The tendency toward mirror imaging was encouraged by a narrow range of viewpoint within the estimating process. Like the Whiz Kids, the Office of National Estimates (ONE), which wrote the NIEs, was staffed by an academic elite in an "ivory tower" atmosphere. Also like McNamara and the Whiz Kids, ONE had contempt for the military. An ONE official observed, "One cannot expect honest and objective intel-ligence from the military intelligence components."[6]

In retrospect, such attitudes were perhaps inevitable due to histor-ical factors. The early years of the Cold War had been marked by a series of intelligence surprises from the Berlin blockade to the Soviet H-bomb. This gave rise to a climate of fear, and the bomber and mis-sile gap controversies. When the U-2 and Corona showed these fears were unjustified, military intelligence was discredited. There was also a subtle shift in outlook. In the 1950s, the fear had been of surprise; in the 1960s, this had been replaced by a fear of overestimation. Hav-ing twice been "burned," caution became the order of the day. The result was, however, simply another kind of error.

The flaw was not in the raw intelligence—thanks to Corona and Gambit, the United States had a precise inventory of Soviet nuclear forces. The numbers of ICBMs were not in question after 1961; the United States knew exactly how many ICBMs the Soviets had opera-tional, how many silos were under construction, and when they would be completed. The NIEs were also correct in their judgment that the limited Soviet economy could not support their military efforts. The mistake was to assume the Soviets would act according to American ideas of "rational" Soviet self-interest.[7]

What the authors of the NIEs did not envision was that purely Soviet perceptions of self-interest would cause the USSR to embark on an "irrational" missile build-up. The conventional wisdom was so pervasive that the NIEs lacked the insight and imagination to consider other possibilities. This lasted long after such estimates were no longer tenable.

While the United States might not have fully understood the USSR, and in particular the mindset of the Soviet leadership, it did understand enough to succeed.

The Continuing Importance of Corona

In February 1995, nearly a quarter century after the program ended, the Corona photos finally came out from the shadow of secrecy. Their declassification was the result of their potential for a better understanding of environmental and climatic changes. The NPIC photo interpreters had long realized that only a small percentage of the data contained in the photos had ever been analyzed. As the first to see Earth from the vantage point of space, they gained an insight into the human impact on the planet.

This continuing importance of the Corona photos comes from several factors. The first is the increased span of time covered. The first NASA Landsat earth resources satellite was launched in June 1972— a month after the end of Corona. With the Corona photos, environmental studies could be extended back another twelve years, helping to separate long-term changes from normal variations in such areas as movements of sand dunes, loss of forest areas, and shifts in the courses of tropical rivers. A number of scientists, including Farouk El-Baz of Boston University and Willy Weeks of the University of Alaska, had argued since the early 1980s that the early reconnaissance satellite photos should be released for such research purposes. One example of the insights possible from this increased time span relates to the Aral Sea in Soviet Central Asia. By comparing an August 1962 Corona photo with images taken in August 1994, the shrinking of the lake due to diversion of water for farming is apparent.

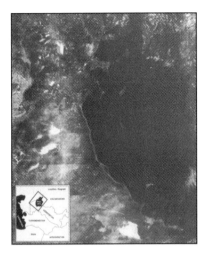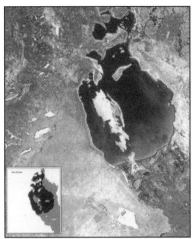

A comparison of the Aral Sea in an August 29, 1962, Corona image and a civilian earth resources image from August 1994. The sea had shrunk due to the diversion of water for irrigation (note the same white areas in each photo for reference). The Corona archives provide a record of changes due to natural and man-made causes. *National Archives*

Other advantages were the higher resolution and the stereo coverage. When Landsat was first developed, the U.S. government deliberately limited its resolution in order to avoid giving away reconnaissance technology. Even the later model Landsats had only a 100-foot resolution, while the similar French SPOT satellites could achieve 33 feet. In contrast, the KH-1 camera flown on *Discoverer 14* years earlier had resolution between 35 and 40 feet, while the KH-4B reached a 6-foot resolution. The KH-4 series cameras also took stereo photos. This allowed three-dimensional images, which could reveal changes in topography over time.[8]

By the summer of 1996, the Corona images were being used to measure the changes in the 2.5-mile-thick Antarctic ice cap. This constitutes 70 percent of the world's ice, and any significant melting due to global warming would result in the flooding of coastal areas and islands. Ken Jezek of Ohio State University headed a project to compare the Corona images with modern satellite data, such as that from the Canadian RADARSAT. He reported that there had been changes in the level of an individual crevasse. He added, "We have found remarkable changes in the ice shelf margins," but attributed this to normal causes, such as a storm breaking off part of a thin ice shelf. So far, the photos show no wide-scale melting.

The benefits of using reconnaissance satellites for earth resources studies caused the NRO in 1995 to start a program called Measurements of Earth Data for Environmental Analysis (MEDEA). In the past, the areas of photoreconnaissance coverage had been selected solely for intelligence purposes, rather than for scientific interest. Under MEDEA, specially selected areas would be photographed on a regular schedule, such as seasonally. The photos would be archived, due to the secrecy of the systems, but they would be released to a future generation of scientists for analysis.

The initial group of MEDEA subjects was made up of about two dozen areas, with plans to expand the total to five hundred. Some of these included the Mojave Desert, the Konza prairie in Kansas, forests in Russia and the Czech and Slovak republics, glaciers in Switzerland, and the slopes of Mount Kilimanjaro in Africa.[9]

Like Corona, the MEDEA program has several advantages over current civilian earth resources satellites. The "Crystal" photoreconnaissance satellite (an improved version of the KH-11 system) has higher resolution than SPOT or Landsat, as well as color and multiwavelength capability. The other current U.S. satellite (code-named at various times "Indigo," "Lacrosse," and "Vega") uses a radar system. This allows it to "see" through clouds, forests, and even into the ground. Another radar system, carried aboard several space shuttle flights, was able to detect dried-up riverbeds beneath sand dunes.

The View from 2001

The Corona program and the Cold War are both now part of history. The KH-4B camera has taken its rightful place in the Smithsonian's National Air and Space Museum, along with the Wright Flyer, the Spirit of St. Louis, and the Apollo 11 spacecraft. Its photos are now available to researchers at the National Archives and the U.S. Geological Service.

As we stand on the verge of the twenty-first century, with its new wonders and dangers, the accomplishments of Corona become apparent. It was Corona that allowed the United States to find its way in a dangerous time. Without the intelligence the satellites provided, the United States and its allies would have faced the Soviet Union without an understanding of its power, and beset by fears. Khrushchev would have had a free hand to bully and bluff. The potential for miscalculation on both sides was great, and the consequences would have been disastrous.

Corona changed all that. Where there had been only uncertainty, Corona brought confidence. Where there had been fear, it provided knowledge. Where there had been chaos, it brought a measure of stability. Corona created a revolution in both intelligence and foreign relations, and pioneered the way for the modern systems which have become an integral part of today's "Open Skies."

This is the heritage of Corona.

Appendix 1
Corona Launches, 1959–1972

This appendix lists significant data from all 145 Corona flights. It was compiled by Peter Hunter using Royal Aircraft Establishment orbital data and the Discoverer/Corona launch reports. The recovery pilot listings are from Dr. Rick Sturdevant of the Space Command History Office.

In the following statistics, launch times are given as HHMMSS.SS in Greenwich Mean Time. Orbital inclination is in degrees and the period is in minutes. Apogee and perigee data are in kilometers.

Various designations were assigned to each satellite: the USAF serial number is assigned by the U.S. Air Force, while the operational number is an internal Vandenberg AFB designation. The international designation is used for all satellites and is assigned by tracking agencies such as NORAD or NASA, consisting of the launch year and a number corresponding to the satellite's numerical order in that year's launches; the *A* signifies that it was the primary payload. The satellite numbers are a simple count of successfully orbited satellites since *Sputnik 1* on October 4, 1957. Each launch was also given a nickname, although no information is available on the nicknames or Agena numbers after Corona flight 117.

Launch pad numbers underwent changes over the thirteen years of Corona launch operations. Pad 75-1-1 became Space Launch Complex (SLC) -2E, Pad 75-3-4 became SLC-1W, Pad 75-3-5 became SLC-1E, Pad 75-1-2 became SLC-2W, and Point Arguello Launch Complex (PALC) -1-1 became SLC-3W.

Corona flight 1/*Discoverer 1* ("Flying Yankee")
Launch date (time): 28 Feb 1959 (214900.00)
Mission (payload): R&D (no reentry vehicle)
Launch vehicle (number): Thor Agena A (T163/A1022)
Launch pad: Pad 75-3-4
Orbit: Failed to orbit
USAF serial number: 58-2274
Operation number: 1003
Remarks: Agena failed.

Corona flight 2/*Discoverer 2* ("Early Time")
Launch date (time): 13 Apr 1959 (211839.00)
Mission (payload): R&D (simulated biomedical payload; no camera)
Launch vehicle (number): Thor Agena A (T170/A1018)
Launch pad: Pad 75-3-4
Orbit: Inclined 89.90, period 88.90, perigee 199, apogee 238
Decay date (flight duration): 26 Apr 1959 (13 days)
USAF serial number: 58-2274
Operation number: 1004
International designation: 1959-003A
Satellite number: 00014
Remarks: Capsule ejected on orbit 17. Lost near Spitzbergen I. due to bad
  separation timing. Recovered by the Soviets.

Corona flight 3/*Discoverer 3* ("Gold Duke")
Launch date (time): 3 Jun 1959 (201000.00)
Mission (payload): R&D/cover (biomedical: 4 mice; no camera)
Launch vehicle (number): Thor Agena A (T174/A1020)
Launch pad: Pad 75-3-4
Orbit: Failed to orbit
USAF serial number: 58-2285
Operation number: 1007
Remarks: Premature Agena burnout due to fuel exhaustion. Insufficient
  velocity to attain orbit.

Corona flight 4/*Discoverer 4* ("Long Road")
Launch date (time): 25 Jun 1959 (154800.00)
Mission (payload): 9001, reconnaissance (KH-1)
Launch vehicle (number): Thor Agena A (T179/A1023)
Launch pad: Pad 75-3-5
Orbit: Failed to orbit
USAF serial number: 58-2290
Operation number: 1010
Remarks: First Discoverer/Corona to carry a camera (KH-1 "C" camera).
  Premature Agena burnout (vortexing of fuel); insufficient velocity
  to orbit.

Corona flight 5/*Discoverer 5* ("Fly High")
Launch date (time): 13 Aug 1959 (190008.00)
Mission (payload): 9002, reconnaissance (KH-1)
Launch vehicle (number): Thor Agena A (T192/A1029)
Launch pad: Pad 75-3-4
Orbit: Inclined 79.99, period 91.91, perigee 218, apogee 518
Decay date (flight duration): 28 Sep 1959 (46 days)
USAF serial number: 58-2303
Operation number: 1012
International designation: 1959-005A
Satellite number: 00018
Remarks: Camera batteries failed on orbit 1. RV retros fired with bad
    orientation; raised orbit. RV not recovered.

Corona flight 6/*Discoverer 6* ("Hurry Up")
Launch date (time): 19 Aug 1959 (192443.91)
Mission (payload): 9003, reconnaissance (KH-1)
Launch vehicle (number): Thor Agena A (T200/A1028)
Launch pad: Pad 75-3-5
Orbit: Inclined 84.00, period 93.47, perigee 210, apogee 677
Decay date (flight duration): 20 Oct 1959 (62 days)
USAF serial number: 58-2311
Operation number: 1013
International designation: 1959-006A
Satellite number: 00019
Remarks: Camera failed on orbit 2. No RV separation; retrorocket
    malfunction. RV not recovered.

Corona flight 7/*Discoverer 7* ("Cargo Net")
Launch date (time): 7 Nov 1959 (202840.65)
Mission (payload): 9004, reconnaissance (KH-1)
Launch vehicle (number): Thor Agena A (T206/A1051)
Launch pad: Pad 75-3-4
Orbit: Inclined 81.60, period 91.50, perigee 152, apogee 542
Decay date (flight duration): 26 Nov 1959 (19 days)
USAF serial number: 58-2317
Operation number: 1017
International designation: 1959-010A
Satellite number: 00024
Remarks: Agena power supply and nitrogen gas lost prior to orbit 2.
    No RV separation. RV not recovered.

Corona flight 8/*Discoverer 8* ("Livid Lady")
Launch date (time): 20 Nov 1959 (192524.11)
Mission (payload): 9005, reconnaissance (KH-1)
Launch vehicle (number): Thor Agena A (T212/A1050)

Corona flight 8 *(continued)*
Launch pad: Pad 75-3-5
Orbit: Inclined 80.65, period 99.56, perigee 189, apogee 1,238
Decay date (flight duration): 8 Mar 1960 (109 days)
USAF serial number: 58-2323
Operation number: 1021
International designation: 1959-011A
Satellite number: 00025
Remarks: Agena guidance malfunction, high orbit. Camera failed.
    RV separation on orbit 15. Overshot/chute failed, not recovered.

Corona flight 9/*Discoverer 9* **("Hungry Eye")**
Launch date (time): 4 Feb 1960 (185200.00)
Mission (payload): 9006, reconnaissance (KH-1)
Launch vehicle (number): Thor Agena A (T218/A1052)
Launch pad: Pad 75-3-4
Orbit: Failed to orbit
USAF serial number: 59-2339
Operation number: 1026
Remarks: Thor shut down at main engine cutoff enable, 17 sec early.
    Agena attitude control lost at engine ignition.

Corona flight 10/*Discoverer 10* **("Derby Day")**
Launch date (time): 19 Feb 1960 (201500.00)
Mission (payload): 9007, reconnaissance (KH-1)
Launch vehicle (number): Thor Agena A (T223/A1054)
Launch pad: Pad 75-3-5
Orbit: Failed to orbit
USAF serial number: 59-2344
Operation number: 1027
Remarks: Thor flight control system caused pitch oscillations; destroyed
    by range safety officer at T+56.4 sec at 22,000 ft.

Corona flight 11/*Discoverer 11* **("Ram Horn")**
Launch date (time): 15 Apr 1960 (203036.73)
Mission (payload): 9008, reconnaissance (KH-1)
Launch vehicle (number): Thor Agena A (T234/A1055)
Launch pad: Pad 75-3-5
Orbit: Inclined 80.10, period 89.75, perigee 161, apogee 360
Decay date (flight duration): 26 Apr 1960 (11 days)
USAF serial number: 59-2355
Operation number: 1029
International designation: 1960-004A
Satellite number: 00032
Remarks: Camera operated. RV ejected, but spin rockets exploded.
    RV not recovered.

Corona flight 12/*Discoverer 12* ("Red Garter")
Launch date (time): 29 Jun 1960 (220100.00)
Mission (payload): R&D/diagnostic
Launch vehicle (number): Thor Agena A (T160/A1053)
Launch pad: Pad 75-3-4
Orbit: Failed to orbit
USAF serial number: 58-2271
Operation number: 1030
Remarks: No camera. Agena horizon scanner malfunctioned.
    Injection angle: –6 deg.

Corona flight 13/*Discoverer 13* ("Foggy Bottom")
Launch date (time): 10 Aug 1960 (203800.00)
Mission (payload): R&D/diagnostic (SCOTOP radar detector)
Launch vehicle (number): Thor Agena A (T231/A1057)
Launch pad: Pad 75-3-5
Orbit: Inclined 82.85, period 90.00, perigee 226, apogee 319
Decay date (flight duration): 14 Nov 1960 (96 days)
USAF serial number: 59-2352
Operation number: 1035
International designation: 1960-008A
Satellite number: 00048
Remarks: No camera. RV separated on orbit 17, water recovery on
    11 Aug —the first recovery from orbit.

Corona flight 14/*Discoverer 14* ("Limber Leg")
Launch date (time): 18 Aug 1960 (195807.85)
Mission (payload): 9009, reconnaissance (KH-1)
Launch vehicle (number): Thor Agena A (T237/A1056)
Launch pad: Pad 75-3-4
Orbit: Inclined 79.65, period 91.00, perigee 175, apogee 470
Decay date (flight duration): 16 Sep 1960 (29 days)
USAF serial number: 59-2358
Operation number: 1036
International designation: 1960-010A
Satellite number: 00054
Remarks: RV separated on orbit 17, recovered in midair on 19 Aug by
    Capt. Harold E. Mitchell in a C-119—the first midair recovery. Also the
    first recovery of Corona photos.

Corona flight 15/*Discoverer 15* ("Coffee Call")
Launch date (time): 13 Sep 1960 (221339.45)
Mission (payload): 9010, reconnaissance (KH-1)
Launch vehicle (number): Thor Agena A (T246/A1058)
Launch pad: Pad 75-3-5
Orbit: Inclined 80.90, period 90.00, perigee 180, apogee 366

Corona flight 15 *(continued)*
Decay date (flight duration): 18 Oct 1960 (35 days)
USAF serial number: 59-2367
Operation number: 1038
International designation: 1960-012A
Satellite number: 00057
Remarks: Camera operation satisfactory. Retrorocket orientation bad; RV overshot to Christmas Island. RV was sighted, but sank before being recovered.

Corona flight 16/*Discoverer 16* **("Soup Spoon")**
Launch date (time): 26 Oct 1960 (202600.00)
Mission (payload): 9011, reconnaissance (KH-2)
Launch vehicle (number): Thor Agena A (T253/A1061)
Launch pad: Pad 75-3-4
Orbit: Failed to orbit
USAF serial number: 59-2374
Operation number: 1041
Remarks: Agena "D" timer stopped at liftoff due to power interrupt, causing Agena separation failure. First Discoverer/Corona to carry a KH-2 C Prime camera.

Corona flight 17/*Discoverer 17* **("Boxing Glove")**
Launch date (time): 12 Nov 1960 (204300.00)
Mission (payload): 9012, reconnaissance (KH-2)
Launch vehicle (number): Thor Agena B (T297/A1062)
Launch pad: Pad 75-3-5
Orbit: Inclined 81.74, period 94.88, perigee 75, apogee 949
Decay date (flight duration): 29 Dec 1960 (47 days)
USAF serial number: 59-2418
Operation number: 1046
International designation: 1960-015A
Satellite number: 00061
Remarks: First use of Agena B. Agena burned too long. Payload malfunctioned. RV separated on orbit 31, midair recovery by Capt. Gene W. Jones. Transit satellite navigation beacon on board?

Corona flight 18/*Discoverer 18* **("Power Tractor")**
Launch date (time): 7 Dec 1960 (202058.50)
Mission (payload): 9013, reconnaissance (KH-2)
Launch vehicle (number): Thor Agena B (T296/A1103)
Launch pad: Pad 75-3-4
Orbit: Inclined 81.48, period 89.49, perigee 205, apogee 291
Decay date (flight duration): 2 Apr 1961 (116 days)
USAF serial number: 59-2417
Operation number: 1047

International designation: 1960-018A

Satellite number: 00067

Remarks: First successful KH-2. RV separated on orbit 48, midair recovery by Captain Jones. Transit beacon on board?

Corona flight 19/*Discoverer 19* ("Tee Bird")

Launch date (time): 20 Dec 1960 (203200.00)

Mission (payload): R&D/cover, radiometry (RM-1)

Launch vehicle (number): Thor Agena B (T258/A1101)

Launch pad: Pad 75-3-5

Orbit: Inclined 83.40, period 89.55, perigee 178, apogee 324

Decay date (flight duration): 23 Jan 1961 (34 days)

USAF serial number: 59-2379

Operation number: 1049

International designation: 1960-019A

Satellite number: 00068

Remarks: Agena control gas leaked, making satellite unstable. Measured Earth infrared radiation for Project MIDAS; data were "90% usable." No RV.

Corona flight 20/*Discoverer 20* ("Spirit Level")

Launch date (time): 17 Feb 1961 (202500.00)

Mission (payload): 9014A, mapping/geodesy (KH-5)

Launch vehicle (number): Thor Agena B (T298/A1104)

Launch pad: Pad 75-3-4

Orbit: Inclined 80.82, period 89.91, perigee 223, apogee 303

Decay date (flight duration): 28 Jul 1962 (526 days)

USAF serial number: 59-2419

Operation number: 1052

International designation: 1961-005A

Satellite number: 00083

Remarks: First KH-5 Argon camera flight; camera failed. Agena timer/ S-band beacon failed on orbit 31. RV not recovered. Transit experiment.

Corona flight 21/*Discoverer 21* ("Bench Warrant")

Launch date (time): 18 Feb 1961 (225800.00)

Mission (payload): R&D/cover, radiometry (RM-2)

Launch vehicle (number): Thor Agena B (T261/A1102)

Launch pad: Pad 75-3-5

Orbit: Inclined 80.64, period 90.19, perigee 212, apogee 344

Decay date (flight duration): 20 Apr 1962 (426 days)

USAF serial number: 59-2382

Operation number: 1053

International designation: 1961-006A

Satellite number: 00084

Remarks: Measured Earth infrared energy for Project MIDAS. First Agena orbital restart. No RV.

Corona flight 22/*Discoverer 22* ("Feather Cut")
Launch date (time): 30 Mar 1961 (203443.00)
Mission (payload): 9015, reconnaissance (KH-2)
Launch vehicle (number): Thor Agena B (T300/A1105)
Launch pad: Pad 75-3-4
Orbit: Failed to orbit
USAF serial number: 59-2421
Operation number: 1054
Remarks: Agena hydraulic pressure lost, causing "violent vehicle attitude
 changes."

Corona flight 23/*Discoverer 23* ("Running Board")
Launch date (time): 8 Apr 1961 (192100.00)
Mission (payload): 9016A, mapping/geodesy (KH-5)
Launch vehicle (number): Thor Agena B (T307/A1106)
Launch pad: Pad 75-3-5
Orbit: Inclined 82.26, period 91.68, perigee 268, apogee 443
Decay date (flight duration): 16 Apr 1962 (373 days)
USAF serial number: 59-5030
Operation number: 1055
International designation: 1961-011A
Satellite number: 00100
Remarks: Argon flight 2. Camera worked, but Agena lost control and
 spun. RV separated on orbit 32, but was boosted into higher orbit.
 RV not recovered. Transit experiment.

Corona flight 24/*Discoverer 24* ("Island Queen")
Launch date (time): 8 Jun 1961 (211600.00)
Mission (payload): 9018A, mapping/geodesy (KH-5)
Launch vehicle (number): Thor Agena B (T302/A1108)
Launch pad: Pad 75-3-4
Orbit: Failed to orbit
USAF serial number: 59-2423
Operation number: 1059
Remarks: Argon flight 3. Agena malfunction during Thor boost phase,
 telemetry lost at T+144 sec. No Agena ignition.

Corona flight 25/*Discoverer 25* ("Marked Cards")
Launch date (time): 16 Jun 1961 (230200.00)
Mission (payload): 9017, reconnaissance (KH-2)
Launch vehicle (number): Thor Agena B (T303/A1107)
Launch pad: Pad 75-1-1
Orbit: Inclined 82.11, period 88.29, perigee 175, apogee 201
Decay date (flight duration): 12 Jul 1961 (26 days)
USAF serial number: 59-2424
Operation number: 1060

International designation: 1961-014A
Satellite number: 00108
Remarks: RV separated on orbit 33, water recovery. Provided first photos
  of Soviet ICBM/IRBM sites.

Corona flight 26/*Discoverer 26* ("High Wing")

Launch date (time): 7 Jul 1961 (232900.00)
Mission (payload): 9019, reconnaissance (KH-2)
Launch vehicle (number): Thor Agena B (T308/A1109)
Launch pad: Pad 75-3-5
Orbit: Inclined 82.94, period 90.39, perigee 212, apogee 372
Decay date (flight duration): 5 Dec 1961 (151 days)
USAF serial number: 59-5031
Operation number: 1064
International designation: 1961-016A
Satellite number: 00160
Remarks: Camera failed on orbit 22. RV separated on orbit 32, midair
  recovery by Capt. Jack R. Wilson.

Corona flight 27/*Discoverer 27* ("Stacked Deck")

Launch date (time): 21 Jul 1961 (223500.00)
Mission (payload): 9020A, mapping/geodesy (KH-5)
Launch vehicle (number): Thor Agena B (T322/A1110)
Launch pad: Pad 75-3-4
Orbit: Failed to orbit
USAF serial number: 59-5045
Operation number: 1066
Remarks: Argon flight 4. Engine rate loop failed, leading to pitch oscillations
  and structural failure at T+59.5 sec.

Corona flight 28/*Discoverer 28* ("Crisp Bacon")

Launch date (time): 4 Aug 1961 (000100.00)
Mission (payload): 9021, reconnaissance (KH-2)
Launch vehicle (number): Thor Agena B (T309/A1111)
Launch pad: Pad 75-1-1
Orbit: Failed to orbit
USAF serial number: 59-5032
Operation number: 1067
Remarks: At T+398 sec Agena lost hydraulic pressure; vehicle tumbled,
  engine shut down prematurely, and Agena reentered.

Corona flight 29/*Discoverer 29* ("Full Blower")

Launch date (time): 30 Aug 1961 (200000.00)
Mission (payload): 9023, reconnaissance (KH-3)
Launch vehicle (number): Thor Agena B (T323/A1112)
Launch pad: Pad 75-3-4

Corona flight 29 *(continued)*
Orbit: Inclined 82.14, period 91.51, perigee 152, apogee 542
Decay date (flight duration): 10 Sep 1961 (11 days)
USAF serial number: 59-5046
Operation number: 1069
International designation: 1961-023A
Satellite number: 00181
Remarks: RV separated on orbit 33, water recovery on 1 Sep, 120 nm
   north of predicted area. First Discoverer/Corona to carry KH-3 C Triple
   Prime camera. Pictures out of focus.

Corona flight 30/*Discoverer 30* **("Twisted Braids")**
Launch date (time): 12 Sep 1961 (195900.00)
Mission (payload): 9022, reconnaissance (KH-2)
Launch vehicle (number): Thor Agena B (T310/A1113)
Launch pad: Pad 75-3-5
Orbit: Inclined 82.66, period 89.40, perigee 204, apogee 283
Decay date (flight duration): 11 Dec 1961 (90 days)
USAF serial number: 59-5033
Operation number: 1070
International designation: 1961-024A
Satellite number: 00182
Remarks: RV separated on orbit 33, midair recovery by Capt. Warren C.
   Schensted on 14 Sep—the first in a JC-130.

Corona flight 31/*Discoverer 31* **("Cane Pole")**
Launch date (time): 17 Sep 1961 (230000.00)
Mission (payload): 9024, reconnaissance (KH-2)
Launch vehicle (number): Thor Agena B (T324/A1114)
Launch pad: Pad 75-1-1
Orbit: Inclined 82.70, period 90.00, perigee 220, apogee 326
Decay date (flight duration): 26 Oct 1961 (39 days)
USAF serial number: 59-5047
Operation number: 1073
International designation: 1961-026A
Satellite number: 00186
Remarks: Incorrect orbit. Agena 400-cycle power supply failed in orbit.
   RV failed to separate. RV not recovered.

Corona flight 32/*Discoverer 32* **("Cap Pistol")**
Launch date (time): 13 Oct 1961 (192200.00)
Mission (payload): 9025, reconnaissance (KH-3)
Launch vehicle (number): Thor Agena B (T328/A1115)
Launch pad: Pad 75-3-4
Orbit: Inclined 82.46, period 89.91, perigee 196, apogee 332
Decay date (flight duration): 13 Nov 1961 (31 days)

USAF serial number: 60-5563
Operation number: 1075
International designation: 1961-027A
Satellite number: 00189
Remarks: RV separated on orbit 18, midair recovery by Captain Schensted on 14 Oct.

Corona flight 33/*Discoverer 33* ("Dead Heat")

Launch date (time): 23 Oct 1961 (192300.00)
Mission (payload): 9026, reconnaissance (KH-2)
Launch vehicle (number): Thor Agena B (T329/A1116)
Launch pad: Pad 75-3-5
Orbit: Failed to orbit
USAF serial number: 60-5564
Operation number: 1079
Remarks: Agena hydraulic pressure fell, causing loss of control and premature engine shutdown. Last flight of a KH-2 camera.

Corona flight 34/*Discoverer 34* ("Fog Cutter")

Launch date (time): 5 Nov 1961 (200000.00)
Mission (payload): 9027, reconnaissance (KH-3)
Launch vehicle (number): Thor Agena B (T330/A1117)
Launch pad: Pad 75-1-1
Orbit: Inclined 82.46, period 89.91, perigee 196, apogee 332
Decay date (flight duration): 7 Dec 1962 (397 days)
USAF serial number: 60-5565
Operation number: 1080
International designation: 1961-029A
Satellite number: 00197
Remarks: Agena control gas lost on orbit 9; unstable. RV recovery not attempted.

Corona flight 35/*Discoverer 35* ("Cat Fight")

Launch date (time): 15 Nov 1961 (212300.00)
Mission (payload): 9028, reconnaissance (KH-3)
Launch vehicle (number): Thor Agena B (T326/A1118)
Launch pad: Pad 75-3-4
Orbit: Inclined 81.63, period 88.20, perigee 245, apogee 310
Decay date (flight duration): 3 Dec 1961 (18 days)
USAF serial number: 60-5561
Operation number: 1081
International designation: 1961-030A
Satellite number: 00201
Remarks: RV separated on orbit 18, midair recovery by Capt. James F. McCullough on 16 Nov.

Corona flight 36/*Discoverer 36* ("Silver Strip")
Launch date (time): 12 Dec 1961 (204200.00)
Mission (payload): 9029, reconnaissance (KH-3)
Launch vehicle (number): Thor Agena B (T325/A1119)
Launch pad: Pad 75-3-4
Orbit: Inclined 81.15, period 89.60, perigee 218, apogee 298
Decay date (flight duration): 8 Mar 1962 (86 days)
USAF serial number: 60-5560
Operation number: 1088
International designation: 1961-034A
Satellite number: 00213
Remarks: RV separated on orbit 64, water recovery on 16 Dec.

Corona flight 37/*Discoverer 37* ("Candy Wrapper")
Launch date (time): 13 Jan 1962 (214100.00)
Mission (payload): 9030, reconnaissance (KH-3)
Launch vehicle (number): Thor Agena B (T327/A1120)
Launch pad: Pad 75-3-4
Orbit: Failed to orbit
USAF serial number: 60-5562
Operation number: 3201
Remarks: Power lost to Agena attitude control gyros before engine ignition;
   shut down after 10 sec. Last Discoverer/Corona to carry the KH-3 camera.

Corona flight 38/*Discoverer 38* ("Career Girl")
Launch date (time): 27 Feb 1962 (193900.00)
Mission (payload): 9031, reconnaissance (KH-4)
Launch vehicle (number): Thor Agena B (T241/A1123)
Launch pad: Pad 75-3-4
Orbit: Inclined 82.23, period 89.71, perigee 208, apogee 308
Decay date (flight duration): 21 Mar 1962 (22 days)
USAF serial number: 59-2362
Operation number: 7201
International designation: 1962-005A
Satellite number: 00247
Remarks: Last flight as "Discoverer"; renamed Program 162. First KH-4
   "M" camera. RV separated on orbit 65, midair recovery by Captain
   Wilson on 3 Mar.

Corona flight 39 ("Long Slice")
Launch date (time): 18 Apr 1962 (005400.00)
Mission (payload): 9032, reconnaissance (KH-4)
Launch vehicle (number): Thor Agena B (T331/A1124)
Launch pad: Pad 75-3-5
Orbit: Inclined 73.45, period 89.50, perigee 198, apogee 297

Decay date (flight duration): 28 May 1962 (40 days)
USAF serial number: 60-5566
Operation number: 7201
International designation: 1962-011A
Satellite number: 00276
Remarks: Agena Telemetry Link I lost. Early recovery. RV separated on
    orbit 35, midair recovery by Maj. James A. Brewton on 19 Apr.

Corona flight 40 ("Total Time")
Launch date (time): 28 Apr 1962 (233000.00)
Mission (payload): 9033, reconnaissance (KH-4)
Launch vehicle (number): Thor Agena B (T333/A1125)
Launch pad: Pad 75-3-4
Orbit: Inclined 73.07, period 88.70, perigee 166, apogee 253
Decay date (flight duration): 26 May 1962 (28 days)
USAF serial number: 60-5568
Operation number: 3201
International designation: 1962-017A
Satellite number: 00290
Remarks: RV separated on orbit 96; parachute cover failed to release.
    RV not recovered.

Corona flight 41 ("Hole Punch")
Launch date (time): 15 May 1962 (193600.00)
Mission (payload): 9034A, mapping/geodesy (KH-5)
Launch vehicle (number): Thor Agena B (T334/A1126)
Launch pad: Pad 75-3-5
Orbit: Inclined 82.32, period 90.55, perigee 248, apogee 355
Decay date (flight duration): 26 Nov 1963 (560 days)
USAF serial number: 60-5569
Operation number: 2201
International designation: 1962-018A
Satellite number: 00292
Remarks: Argon flight 5. RV separated on orbit 63, midair recovery by
    Capt. Thomas F. Hines on 19 May.

Corona flight 42 ("Leak Proof")
Launch date (time): 30 May 1962 (010000.00)
Mission (payload): 9035, reconnaissance (KH-4)
Launch vehicle (number): Thor Agena B (T336/A1128)
Launch pad: Pad 75-1-1
Orbit: Inclined 74.10, period 88.96, perigee 193, apogee 248
Decay date (flight duration): 11 Jun 1962 (12 days)
USAF serial number: 60-5571
Operation number: 6201

Corona flight 42 *(continued)*
International designation: 1962-021A
Satellite number: 00302
Remarks: RV separated on orbit 48, midair recovery by Major Brewton on 1 Jun.

Corona flight 43 ("Knotty Pine")
Launch date (time): 2 Jun 1962 (003100.00)
Mission (payload): 9036, reconnaissance (KH-4)
Launch vehicle (number): Thor Agena B (T335/A1127)
Launch pad: Pad 75-3-4
Orbit: Inclined 74.25, period 88.87, perigee 188, apogee 247
Decay date (flight duration): 28 Jun 1962 (26 days)
USAF serial number: 60-5570
Operation number: 8201
International designation: 1962-022A
Satellite number: 00304
Remarks: RV separated on orbit 64. Chute torn in aerial recovery; RV hit
  the water and sank.

Corona flight 44 ("Tight Skirt")
Launch date (time): 23 Jun 1962 (003000.00)
Mission (payload): 9037, reconnaissance (KH-4)
Launch vehicle (number): Thor Agena B (T339/A1129)
Launch pad: Pad 75-3-4
Orbit: Inclined 75.09, period 88.82, perigee 209, apogee 222
Decay date (flight duration): 7 Jul 1962 (14 days)
USAF serial number: 61-2650
Operation number: 5201
International designation: 1962-026A
Satellite number: 00315
Remarks: RV separated on orbit 48, midair recovery by Maj. Gene Jones
  on 25 Jun. Space Radio Project (cosmic noise studies).

Corona flight 45 ("Trial Track")
Launch date (time): 28 Jun 1962 (110900.00)
Mission (payload): 9038, reconnaissance (KH-4)
Launch vehicle (number): Thor Agena D (T340/A1151)
Launch pad: Pad 75-1-1
Orbit: Inclined 76.01, period 89.48, perigee 176, apogee 305
Decay date (flight duration): 14 Sep 1962 (78 days)
USAF serial number: 61-2651
Operation number: 7201
International designation: 1962-027A
Satellite number: 00316
Remarks: First Thor Agena D launch. RV separated on orbit 64, midair
  recovery by Capt. Vernon W. Betteridge on 1 Jul.

Corona flight 46 ("Adobe Home")
Launch date (time): 21 Jul 1962 (005600.00)
Mission (payload): 9039, reconnaissance (KH-4)
Launch vehicle (number): Thor Agena B (T342/A1130)
Launch pad: Pad 75-3-5
Orbit: Inclined 70.29, period 88.42, perigee 176, apogee 216
Decay date (flight duration): 14 Aug 1962 (24 days)
USAF serial number: 61-2653
Operation number: 2201
International designation: 1962-031A
Satellite number: 00344
Remarks: RV separated on orbit 48, midair recovery by Maj. Thomas Hines
    on 22 Jul.

Corona flight 47 ("Anchor Rope")
Launch date (time): 28 Jul 1962 (003000.00)
Mission (payload): 9040, reconnaissance (KH-4)
Launch vehicle (number): Thor Agena B (T347/A1131)
Launch pad: Pad 75-3-4
Orbit: Inclined 71.09, period 88.93, perigee 188, apogee 254
Decay date (flight duration): 24 Aug 1962 (27 days)
USAF serial number: 61-2658
Operation number: 8201
International designation: 1962-032A
Satellite number: 00345
Remarks: First booster using pulse duration modulation (PDM) telemetry.
    RV separated on orbit 64, midair recovery by Major Brewton on 31 Jul.

Corona flight 48 ("Apple Green")
Launch date (time): 2 Aug 1962 (001700.00)
Mission (payload): 9041, reconnaissance (KH-4)
Launch vehicle (number): Thor Agena D (T344/A1152)
Launch pad: Pad 75-1-1
Orbit: Inclined 82.25, period 88.64, perigee 179, apogee 232
Decay date (flight duration): 26 Aug 1962 (24 days)
USAF serial number: 61-2655
Operation number: 7201
International designation: 1962-034A
Satellite number: 00360
Remarks: RV separated on orbit 64, midair recovery by Major Hines on 5 Aug.

Corona flight 49 ("Apple Rind")
Launch date (time): 29 Aug 1962 (000000.00)
Mission (payload): 9044, reconnaissance (KH-4)
Launch vehicle (number): Thor Agena D (T349/A1153)
Launch pad: Pad 75-1-2

Corona flight 49 *(continued)*
Orbit: Inclined 65.21, period 89.09, perigee 170, apogee 289
Decay date (flight duration): 10 Sep 1962 (12 days)
USAF serial number: 61-2660
Operation number: 5201
International designation: 1962-042A
Satellite number: 00377
Remarks: RV separated on orbit 64, midair recovery by Major Jones on 1 Sep.

Corona flight 50 ("Beady Eye")
Launch date (time): 1 Sep 1962 (203900.00)
Mission (payload): 9042A, mapping/geodesy (KH-5)
Launch vehicle (number): Thor Agena B (T348/A1132)
Launch pad: Pad 75-3-5
Orbit: Inclined 82.79, period 90.65, perigee 266, apogee 346
Decay date (flight duration): 26 Oct 1964 (786 days)
USAF serial number: 61-2659
Operation number: 8201
International designation: 1962-044A
Satellite number: 00385
Remarks: Argon flight 6. RV separated on orbit 64; recovery attempt on
    5 Sep failed when RV sank.

Corona flight 51 ("Big Flight")
Launch date (time): 17 Sep 1962 (234600.00)
Mission (payload): 9043, reconnaissance/radiation measurement (KH-4)
Launch vehicle (number): Thor Agena B (T350/A1133)
Launch pad: Pad 75-3-4
Orbit: Inclined 81.84, period 90.09, perigee 191, apogee 363
Decay date (flight duration): 19 Nov 1962 (63 days)
USAF serial number: 61-2661
Operation number: 3201
International designation: 1962-046A
Satellite number: 00396
Remarks: TRS 1 measured radiation after Johnston Island high-altitude
    nuclear test of 2 Jul. RV separated on orbit 17, midair recovery by
    Captain Wilson on 18 Sep.

Corona flight 52 ("Arctic Zone")
Launch date (time): 29 Sep 1962 (233500.00)
Mission (payload): 9045, reconnaissance (KH-4)
Launch vehicle (number): Thor Agena D (T351/A1154)
Launch pad: Pad 75-1-2
Orbit: Inclined 65.40, period 89.08, perigee 196, apogee 262
Decay date (flight duration): 14 Oct 1962 (15 days)
USAF serial number: 61-2930

Operation number: 4201
International designation: 1962-050A
Satellite number: 00427
Remarks: RV separated on orbit 48, midair recovery by Major Hines on
    2 Oct at 475 feet.

Corona flight 53 ("Call Board")
Launch date (time): 9 Oct 1962 (183500.00)
Mission (payload): 9046A, mapping/geodesy (KH-5)
Launch vehicle (number): Thor Agena B (T352/A1134)
Launch pad: Pad 75-3-4
Orbit: Inclined 81.96, period 88.37, perigee 170, apogee 212
Decay date (flight duration): 16 Nov 1962 (38 days)
USAF serial number: 61-2931
Operation number: 4201
International designation: 1962-053A
Satellite number: 00436
Remarks: Argon flight 7. RV separated on orbit 64, midair recovery by
    Captain McCullough on 13 Oct.

Corona flight 54 ("Anchor Buoy")
Launch date (time): 26 Oct 1962 (161400.00)
Mission (payload): R&D/radiation measurement (no camera)
Launch vehicle (number): Thor Agena D (T353/A1401)
Launch pad: Pad 75-1-2
Orbit: Inclined 71.21, period 90.07, perigee 159, apogee 399
Decay date (flight duration): 5 Oct 1967 (1,805 days)
USAF serial number: 61-2932
Operation number: 1201
International designation: 1962-058A
Satellite number: 00444
Remarks: Starfish Radiation (STARAD) satellite measured radiation from
    Starfish high-altitude nuclear test (Project Fishbowl). No RV.

Corona flight 55 ("Bail Out")
Launch date (time): 5 Nov 1962 (220400.00)
Mission (payload): 9047, reconnaissance (KH-4)
Launch vehicle (number): Thor Agena B (T356/A1136)
Launch pad: Pad 75-3-4
Orbit: Inclined 74.97, period 89.02, perigee 185, apogee 265
Decay date (flight duration): 3 Dec 1962 (28 days)
USAF serial number: 61-2935
Operation number: 9201
International designation: 1962-063A
Satellite number: 00453
Remarks: RV separated on orbit 65, midair recovery by Major Brewton on 9 Nov.

Corona flight 56 ("Golden Rush")
Launch date (time): 24 Nov 1962 (220100.00)
Mission (payload): 9048, reconnaissance (KH-4)
Launch vehicle (number): Thor Agena B (T367/A1135)
Launch pad: Pad 75-3-4
Orbit: Inclined 65.13, period 89.63, perigee 204, apogee 310
Decay date (flight duration): 13 Dec 1962 (19 days)
USAF serial number: 62-3592
Operation number: 9201
International designation: 1962-065A
Satellite number: 00481
Remarks: RV separated on orbit 80, midair recovery by Capt. Stephen G.
   Calder, Jr., on 28 Nov.

Corona flight 57 ("Calamity Jane")
Launch date (time): 4 Dec 1962 (213000.00)
Mission (payload): 9049, reconnaissance (KH-4)
Launch vehicle (number): Thor Agena D (T361/A1155)
Launch pad: Pad 75-1-2
Orbit: Inclined 65.20, period 88.40, perigee 169, apogee 222
Decay date (flight duration): 8 Dec 1962 (4 days)
USAF serial number: 62-3586
Operation number: 8201
International designation: 1962-066A
Satellite number: 00490
Remarks: RV separated on orbit 34, recovery attempt on 6 Dec failed when
   RV sank.

Corona flight 58 ("Baby Doll")
Launch date (time): 14 Dec 1962 (212600.00)
Mission (payload): 9050, reconnaissance (KH-4)
Launch vehicle (number): Thor Agena D (T368/A1156)
Launch pad: Pad 75-3-5
Orbit: Inclined 70.95, period 89.08, perigee 178, apogee 274
Decay date (flight duration): 8 Jan 1963 (25 days)
USAF serial number: 62-3593
Operation number: 8201
International designation: 1962-069A
Satellite number: 00505
Remarks: RV separated on orbit 48, midair recovery by Capt. Walter M.
   Milam on 17 Dec.

Corona flight 59 ("Candy Kisses")
Launch date (time): 7 Jan 1963 (210900.00)
Mission (payload): 9051, reconnaissance (KH-4)
Launch vehicle (number): Thor Agena D (T369/A1157)

Launch pad: Pad 75-1-1
Orbit: Inclined 82.19, period 88.75, perigee 168, apogee 254
Decay date (flight duration): 24 Jan 1963 (17 days)
USAF serial number: 62-3594
Operation number: 0048
International designation: 1963-002A
Satellite number: 00525
Remarks: RV separated on orbit 32, water recovery on 11 Jan.

Corona flight 60 ("Farm Country")
Launch date (time): 28 Feb 1963 (214800.00)
Mission (payload): 9052, reconnaissance (KH-4)
Launch vehicle (number): TAT Agena D (T354/A1159)
Launch pad: Pad 75-3-5
Orbit: Failed to orbit
USAF serial number: 61-2933
Operation number: 0583
Remarks: Fault in number 2 solid rocket motor; failed to ignite or separate.
   Booster destroyed by range safety officer at T+126 sec. First launch of a
   Thrust Augmented Thor (TAT)/Agena D in Corona program.

Corona flight 61 ("Camp Out")
Launch date (time): 18 Mar 1963 (211300.00)
Mission (payload): 8001, reconnaissance (KH-6)
Launch vehicle (number): TAT Agena D (T360/A1164)
Launch pad: Pad 75-3-4
Orbit: Failed to orbit
USAF serial number: 61-2939
Operation number: 0627
Remarks: Agena lost pneumatic roll control; vehicle tumbled and engine
   shut down prematurely. First KH-6 Lanyard high-resolution camera
   payload.

Corona flight 62 ("Nickel Steel")
Launch date (time): 1 Apr 1963 (220100.00)
Mission (payload): 9053, reconnaissance (KH-4)
Launch vehicle (number): Thor Agena D (T376/A1160)
Launch pad: Pad 75-3-5
Orbit: Inclined 75.38, period 90.28, perigee 198, apogee 367
Decay date (flight duration): 26 Apr 1963 (25 days)
USAF serial number: 62-12151
Operation number: 0720
International designation: 1963-007A
Satellite number: 00562
Remarks: RV separated on orbit 48, midair recovery by Capt. Stephen G.
   Calder, Jr., on 4 Apr.

Corona flight 63 ("Fall Harvest")
Launch date (time): 26 Apr 1963 (191300.00)
Mission (payload): 9055A, mapping/geodesy (KH-5)
Launch vehicle (number): Thor Agena D (T372/A1411)
Launch pad: Pad 75-1-1
Orbit: Failed to orbit
USAF serial number: 62-3597
Operation number: 1008
Remarks: Argon flight 8. Bad Agena horizon sensor bias, inaccurate injection burn.

Corona flight 64 ("Gate Latch")
Launch date (time): 18 May 1963 (222100.00)
Mission (payload): 8002, reconnaissance (KH-6)
Launch vehicle (number): TAT Agena D (T364/A1165)
Launch pad: Pad 75-3-5
Orbit: Inclined 74.54, period 91.12, perigee 153, apogee 497
Decay date (flight duration): 27 May 1963 (9 days)
USAF serial number: 62-3589
Operation number: 0924
International designation: 1963-016A
Satellite number: 00578
Remarks: Lanyard flight 2. Camera never activated. RV separated on orbit 32, water recovery on 20 May.

Corona flight 65 ("Green Castle")
Launch date (time): 12 Jun 1963 (235800.00)
Mission (payload): 9054, reconnaissance (KH-4)
Launch vehicle (number): TAT Agena D (T362/A1161)
Launch pad: Pad 75-3-4
Orbit: Inclined 81.82, period 88.48, perigee 173, apogee 225
Decay date (flight duration): 11 Jul 1963 (29 days)
USAF serial number: 62-3587
Operation number: 0954
International designation: 1963-019A
Satellite number: 00590
Remarks: RV separated on orbit 33, midair recovery by Capt. Dale M. Palmer on 14 Jun.

Corona flight 66 ("Calico Miss")
Launch date (time): 27 Jun 1963 (003700.00)
Mission (payload): 9056, reconnaissance (KH-4)
Launch vehicle (number): TAT Agena D (T381/A1166)
Launch pad: Pad 75-1-2
Orbit: Inclined 81.60, period 88.80, perigee 168, apogee 243
Decay date (flight duration): 26 Jul 1963 (29 days)

USAF serial number: 62-12156
Operation number: 0999
International designation: 1963-025A
Satellite number: 00609
Remarks: RV separated on orbit 48, midair recovery by Captain Betteridge
on 29 Jun.

Corona flight 67 ("Chili Willie")
Launch date (time): 18 Jul 1963 (000000.00)
Mission (payload): 9057, reconnaissance (KH-4)
Launch vehicle (number): Thor Agena D (T388/A1412)
Launch pad: Pad 75-1-1
Orbit: Inclined 82.86, period 88.65, perigee 178, apogee 215
Decay date (flight duration): 13 Aug 1963 (26 days)
USAF serial number: 62-12163
Operation number: 1266
International designation: 1963-029A
Satellite number: 00621
Remarks: RV separated on orbit 64, midair recovery by Capt. James E.
Varnadoe on 22 Jul.

Corona flight 68 ("Big Talk")
Launch date (time): 31 Jul 1963 (000000.00)
Mission (payload): 8003, reconnaissance (KH-6)
Launch vehicle (number): TAT Agena D (T382/A1167)
Launch pad: Pad 75-1-2
Orbit: Inclined 74.95, period 90.40, perigee 157, apogee 411
Decay date (flight duration): 12 Aug 1963 (12 days)
USAF serial number: 62-12157
Operation number: 1370
International designation: 1963-032A
Satellite number: 00626
Remarks: Third and last KH-6 Lanyard flight. Cameras failed after 32 hr,
and photos were out of focus. RV separated on orbit 33, midair
recovery by Captain Milam on 1 Aug.

Corona flight 69 ("Ghost Dance")
Launch date (time): 25 Aug 1963 (003000.00)
Mission (payload): 1001, reconnaissance (KH-4A)
Launch vehicle (number): TAT Agena D (T377/A1162)
Launch pad: Pad 75-3-4
Orbit: Inclined 75.01, period 89.40, perigee 161, apogee 320
Decay date (flight duration): 12 Sep 1963 (18 days)
USAF serial number: 62-12152
Operation number: 1419
International designation: 1963-034A

Corona flight 69 *(continued)*
Satellite number: 00636
Remarks: First KH-4A (J-1) mission. RV-1 separated on orbit 64, midair recovery by Captain Palmer on 28 Aug. RV-2 did not separate.

Corona flight 70 ("Pelican Pete")
Launch date (time): 29 Aug 1963 (203100.00)
Mission (payload): 9058A, mapping/geodesy (KH-5)
Launch vehicle (number): Thor Agena D (T394/A1169)
Launch pad: Pad 75-3-5
Orbit: Inclined 81.86, period 90.00, perigee 261, apogee 287
Decay date (flight duration): 7 Nov 1963 (70 days)
USAF serial number: 62-12391
Operation number: 1561
International designation: 1963-035A
Satellite number: 00637
Remarks: Argon flight 9. RV separated on orbit 48, midair recovery by Captain Milam on 1 Sep. Carried the Experimental Reflector Orbital Shot (EROS).

Corona flight 71 ("Fellow King")
Launch date (time): 23 Sep 1963 (230000.00)
Mission (payload): 1002, reconnaissance (KH-4A)
Launch vehicle (number): TAT Agena D (T383/A1163)
Launch pad: Pad 75-1-2
Orbit: Inclined 74.89, period 88.64, perigee 150, apogee 282
Decay date (flight duration): 12 Oct 1963 (19 days)
USAF serial number: 62-12158
Operation number: 1353
International designation: 1963-037A
Satellite number: 00668
Remarks: RV-1 separated on orbit 64, midair recovery by Major Hines on 26 Sep, becoming the first ace. RV-2 failed to separate.

Corona flight 72 ("Mark Down")
Launch date (time): 29 Oct 1963 (211900.00)
Mission (payload): 9059A, mapping/geodesy (KH-5)
Launch vehicle (number): TAT Agena D (T386/A1601)
Launch pad: Pad 75-3-4
Orbit: Inclined 89.89, period 89.53, perigee 232, apogee 258
Decay date (flight duration): 21 Jan 1964 (84 days)
USAF serial number: 62-12161
Operation number: 2437
International designation: 1963-042A
Satellite number: 00681
Remarks: Argon flight 10. RV separated on orbit 65, midair recovery by Capt. Richmond A. Apaka on 2 Nov.

Corona flight 73 ("Jump Suit")
Launch date (time): 9 Nov 1963 (202754.51)
Mission (payload): 9060, reconnaissance (KH-4)
Launch vehicle (number): Thor Agena D (T400/A1171)
Launch pad: Pad 75-1-2
Orbit: Failed to orbit
USAF serial number: 62-12397
Operation number: 2268
Remarks: Flame shield lost at liftoff, control system tail wiring failed at
    T+134 sec, control lost.

Corona flight 74 ("Dry Dune")
Launch date (time): 27 Nov 1963 (211500.00)
Mission (payload): 9061, reconnaissance (KH-4)
Launch vehicle (number): Thor Agena D (T406/A1172)
Launch pad: Pad PALC-1-1
Orbit: Inclined 69.99, period 90.20, perigee 175, apogee 386
Decay date (flight duration): 15 Dec 1963 (18 days)
USAF serial number: 63-8479
Operation number: 2260
International designation: 1963-048A
Satellite number: 00695
Remarks: RV did not separate when ordered on orbit 83, 1 Dec. RV not
    recovered.

Corona flight 75 ("Water Spout")
Launch date (time): 21 Dec 1963 (214541.73)
Mission (payload): 9062, reconnaissance (KH-4)
Launch vehicle (number): TAT Agena D (T398/A1168)
Launch pad: Pad 75-1-2
Orbit: Inclined 64.94, period 89.96, perigee 176, apogee 355
Decay date (flight duration): 8 Jan 1964 (18 days)
USAF serial number: 62-12395
Operation number: 1388
International designation: 1963-055A
Satellite number: 00718
Remarks: RV separated on orbit 81, midair recovery by Maj. Jack Wilson
    on 26 Dec.

Corona flight 76 ("Garden Party")
Launch date (time): 15 Feb 1964 (213800.00)
Mission (payload): 1004, reconnaissance (KH-4A)
Launch vehicle (number): TAT Agena D (T389/A1174)
Launch pad: Pad 75-3-4
Orbit: Inclined 74.95, period 89.50, perigee 165, apogee 324
Decay date (flight duration): 9 Mar 1964 (23 days)

Corona flight 76 *(continued)*
USAF serial number: 62-12164
Operation number: 3444
International designation: 1964-008A
Satellite number: 00752
Remarks: RV-1 separated on orbit 49, midair recovery by Captain Milam
   on 19 Feb. RV-2 separated on orbit 112, midair recovery by Capt.
   Jeremiah J. Collins on 22 Feb.

Corona flight 77 ("Health Farm")
Launch date (time): 24 Mar 1964 (222248.58)
Mission (payload): 1003, reconnaissance (KH-4A)
Launch vehicle (number): TAT Agena D (T396/A1175)
Launch pad: Pad PALC-1-1
Orbit: Failed to orbit
USAF serial number: 62-12393
Operation number: 3467
Remarks: Agena power problem caused loss of control and premature
   engine shutdown.

Corona flight 78 ("Nice Bird")
Launch date (time): 27 Apr 1964 (232349.59)
Mission (payload): 1005, reconnaissance (KH-4A)
Launch vehicle (number): TAT Agena D (T395/A1604)
Launch pad: Pad 75-3-4
Orbit: Inclined 79.93, period 90.77, perigee 178, apogee 446
Decay date (flight duration): 26 May 1964 (29 days)
USAF serial number: 62-12392
Operation number: 2921
International designation: 1964-022A
Satellite number: 00796
Remarks: RVs failed to separate due to a short circuit on the pyrotechnic
   bus. RV-1 survived reentry and was recovered on the ground in
   Venezuela.

Corona flight 79 ("Kick Ball")
Launch date (time): 4 Jun 1964 (225922.13)
Mission (payload): 1006, reconnaissance (KH-4A)
Launch vehicle (number): TAT Agena D (T403/A1176)
Launch pad: Pad PALC-1-1
Orbit: Inclined 79.95, period 89.15, perigee 139, apogee 324
Decay date (flight duration): 18 Jun 1964 (14 days)
USAF serial number: 63-8476
Operation number: 3483
International designation: 1964-027A

Satellite number: 00802

Remarks: Corona designation changed from "Program 162" to "Program 241." RV-1 separated on orbit 66, midair recovery by Major Wilson on 8 Jun. RV-2 separated on orbit 128, midair recovery on 12 Jun, also by Major Wilson.

Corona flight 80 ("Beagle Hound")

Launch date (time): 13 Jun 1964 (154218.75)

Mission (payload): 9063A, mapping/geodesy (KH-5)

Launch vehicle (number): TAT Agena D (T408/A1606)

Launch pad: Pad 75-1-2

Orbit: Inclined 114.98, period 88.75, perigee 205, apogee 218

Decay date (flight duration): 2 Jun 1965 (354 days)

USAF serial number: 63-8481

Operation number: 3236

International designation: 1964-030A

Satellite number: 00811

Remarks: Argon flight 11. Carried the Starflash 1 geodetic optical beacon as secondary payload. RV separated on orbit 95, midair recovery by Capt. Charles G. Young on 19 Jun.

Corona flight 81 ("Green Door")

Launch date (time): 19 Jun 1964 (231807.22)

Mission (payload): 1007, reconnaissance (KH-4A)

Launch vehicle (number): TAT Agena D (T410/A1609)

Launch pad: Pad 75-1-1

Orbit: Inclined 84.99, period 89.60, perigee 173, apogee 332

Decay date (flight duration): 16 Jul 1964 (27 days)

USAF serial number: 63-8483

Operation number: 3754

International designation: 1964-032A

Satellite number: 00814

Remarks: RV-1 separated on orbit 65, midair recovery by Captain Young on 23 Jun. RV-2 separated on orbit 128, midair recovery by Maj. Edwin R. Bayer on 27 Jun.

Corona flight 82 ("Old Hat")

Launch date (time): 10 Jul 1964 (231504.33)

Mission (payload): 1008, reconnaissance (KH-4A)

Launch vehicle (number): TAT Agena D (T404/A1177)

Launch pad: Pad PALC-1-1

Orbit: Inclined 84.98, period 91.00, perigee 180, apogee 461

Decay date (flight duration): 6 Aug 1984 (7,332 days)

USAF serial number: 63-8477

Operation number: 3491

Corona flight 82 *(continued)*
International designation: 1964-037A
Satellite number: 00828
Remarks: RV-1 separated on orbit 49, midair recovery by Captain Varna-
doe. RV-2 separated on orbit 112, midair recovery by Captain Collins.

Corona flight 83 ("Long Loop")
Launch date (time): 5 Aug 1964 (231535.66)
Mission (payload): 1009, reconnaissance (KH-4A)
Launch vehicle (number): TAT Agena D (T413/A1605)
Launch pad: Pad 75-3-4
Orbit: Inclined 79.99, period 89.35, perigee 175, apogee 307
Decay date (flight duration): 1 Sep 1964 (27 days)
USAF serial number: 63-8486
Operation number: 3042
International designation: 1964-043A
Satellite number: 00846
Remarks: RV-1 separated on orbit 49, midair recovery by Capt. Albert F.
"Al" Muller. RV-2 separated on orbit 128, midair recovery by
Capt. James F. McDonald, Jr.

Corona flight 84 ("Kilo Kate")
Launch date (time): 21 Aug 1964 (154502.37)
Mission (payload): 9064A, mapping/geodesy (KH-5)
Launch vehicle (number): TAT Agena D (T412/A1603)
Launch pad: Pad 75-1-2
Orbit: Inclined 114.96, period 89.15, perigee 219, apogee 232
Decay date (flight duration): 31 Mar 1965 (222 days)
USAF serial number: 63-8485
Operation number: 2739
International designation: 1964-048A
Satellite number: 00861
Remarks: Argon flight 12. Carried the Starflash 1B geodetic optical beacon
as secondary payload. RV separated on orbit 96, midair recovery by
Captain Apaka on 19 Jun.

Corona flight 85 ("Quit Claim")
Launch date (time): 14 Sep 1964 (225322.69)
Mission (payload): 1010, reconnaissance (KH-4A)
Launch vehicle (number): TAT Agena D (T405/A1178)
Launch pad: Pad PALC-1-1
Orbit: Inclined 84.96, period 90.88, perigee 172, apogee 466
Decay date (flight duration): 6 Oct 1964 (22 days)
USAF serial number: 63-8478
Operation number: 3497
International designation: 1964-056A

Satellite number: 00882

Remarks: RV-1 separated on orbit 65, midair recovery by Captain Apaka. RV-2 separated on orbit 144, midair recovery by Major Bayer.

Corona flight 86 ("Solid Pack")

Launch date (time): 5 Oct 1964 (215014.88)

Mission (payload): 1011, reconnaissance (KH-4A)

Launch vehicle (number): TAT Agena D (T421/A1170)

Launch pad: Pad 75-3-4

Orbit: Inclined 79.97, period 90.75, perigee 182, apogee 440

Decay date (flight duration): 26 Oct 1964 (21 days)

USAF serial number: 63-8494

Operation number: 3333

International designation: 1964-061A

Satellite number: 00890

Remarks: RV-1 separated on orbit 65, midair recovery by Captain Varnadoe. RV-2 not ejected, no recovery.

Corona flight 87 ("Moose Horn")

Launch date (time): 17 Oct 1964 (220223.16)

Mission (payload): 1012, reconnaissance (KH-4A)

Launch vehicle (number): TAT Agena D (T418/A1179)

Launch pad: Pad PALC-1-1

Orbit: Inclined 74.99, period 90.59, perigee 189, apogee 416

Decay date (flight duration): 4 Nov 1964 (18 days)

USAF serial number: 63-8491

Operation number: 3559

International designation: 1964-067A

Satellite number: 00911

Remarks: RV-1 separated on orbit 49, midair recovery by Captain Collins. RV-2 separated on orbit 81, water recovery.

Corona flight 88 ("Brown Moose")

Launch date (time): 2 Nov 1964 (213030.45)

Mission (payload): 1013, reconnaissance (KH-4A)

Launch vehicle (number): TAT Agena D (T420/A1173)

Launch pad: Pad 75-3-4

Orbit: Inclined 79.95, period 90.70, perigee 180, apogee 448

Decay date (flight duration): 28 Nov 1964 (26 days)

USAF serial number: 63-8493

Operation number: 5434

International designation: 1964-071A

Satellite number: 00921

Remarks: Both cameras failed on orbit 52. RV-1 separated on orbit 65, midair recovery by Captain McDonald. RV-2 separated on orbit 81, midair recovery by Captain Palmer.

Corona flight 89 ("Verbal Venture")
Launch date (time): 18 Nov 1964 (203554.53)
Mission (payload): 1014, reconnaissance (KH-4A)
Launch vehicle (number): TAT Agena D (T416/A1180)
Launch pad: Pad 75-1-1
Orbit: Inclined 70.02, period 89.71, perigee 180, apogee 339
Decay date (flight duration): 6 Dec 1964 (18 days)
USAF serial number: 63-8489
Operation number: 3660
International designation: 1964-075A
Satellite number: 00930
Remarks: RV-1 separated on orbit 65, midair recovery by Captain Palmer.
    RV-2 separated on orbit 145, midair recovery by Major Bayer.

Corona flight 90 ("Utility Tool")
Launch date (time): 19 Dec 1964 (211016.73)
Mission (payload): 1015, reconnaissance (KH-4A)
Launch vehicle (number): TAT Agena D (T424/A1607)
Launch pad: Pad 75-3-4
Orbit: Inclined 74.95, period 88.74, perigee 166, apogee 258
Decay date (flight duration): 14 Jan 1965 (26 days)
USAF serial number: 63-8497
Operation number: 3358
International designation: 1964-085A
Satellite number: 00961
Remarks: RV-1 separated on orbit 81, midair recovery by Captain Varnadoe.
    RV-2 separated on orbit 175, midair recovery again by Captain Varnadoe.

Corona flight 91 ("Bucket Factory")
Launch date (time): 15 Jan 1965 (210044.13)
Mission (payload): 1016, reconnaissance (KH-4A)
Launch vehicle (number): TAT Agena D (T414/A1608)
Launch pad: Pad 75-3-5
Orbit: Inclined 74.95, period 90.52, perigee 180, apogee 420
Decay date (flight duration): 9 Feb 1965 (25 days)
USAF serial number: 63-8487
Operation number: 3928
International designation: 1965-002A
Satellite number: 00972
Remarks: RV-1 separated on orbit 81, midair recovery by Captain Collins.
    RV-2 separated on orbit 159, midair recovery by Captain Muller.

Corona flight 92 ("Boat Camp")
Launch date (time): 25 Feb 1965 (214454.81)
Mission (payload): 1017, reconnaissance (KH-4A)
Launch vehicle (number): TAT Agena D (T432/A1611)

Launch pad: Pad PALC-1-1
Orbit: Inclined 75.08, period 90.07, perigee 177, apogee 377
Decay date (flight duration): 18 Mar 1965 (21 days)
USAF serial number: 63-9703
Operation number: 4782
International designation: 1965-013A
Satellite number: 01096
Remarks: RV-1 separated on orbit 81, midair recovery by Capt. Douglas
    S. Sliger. RV-2 separated on orbit 145, midair recovery by Captain
    McDonald.

Corona flight 93 ("Paper Route")

Launch date (time): 25 Mar 1965 (211117.54)
Mission (payload): 1018, reconnaissance (KH-4A)
Launch vehicle (number): TAT Agena D (T429/A1612)
Launch pad: Pad 75-3-4
Orbit: Inclined 96.08, period 89.06, perigee 186, apogee 265
Decay date (flight duration): 4 Apr 1965 (10 days)
USAF serial number: 63-9700
Operation number: 4803
International designation: 1965-026A
Satellite number: 01307
Remarks: RV-1 separated on orbit 66, midair recovery by Major Bayer.
    RV-2 separated on orbit 99, midair recovery by Captain Sliger.

Corona flight 94 ("Musk Ox")

Launch date (time): 29 Apr 1965 (214456.53)
Mission (payload): 1019, reconnaissance (KH-4A)
Launch vehicle (number): TAT Agena D (T437/A1614)
Launch pad: Pad PALC-1-1
Orbit: Inclined 85.04, period 91.05, perigee 178, apogee 473
Decay date (flight duration): 26 May 1965 (27 days)
USAF serial number: 63-9708
Operation number: 5023
International designation: 1965-033A
Satellite number: 01330
Remarks: RV-1 separated on orbit 80, midair recovery by Captain
    Varnadoe. RV-2 separated on orbit 143, but was boosted into a higher
    orbit and not recovered.

Corona flight 95 ("Ivy Vine")

Launch date (time): 18 May 1965 (180218.74)
Mission (payload): 1021, reconnaissance (KH-4A)
Launch vehicle (number): TAT Agena D (T438/A1615)
Launch pad: Pad 75-3-4
Orbit: Inclined 75.00, period 88.57, perigee 184, apogee 224

Corona flight 95 *(continued)*
Decay date (flight duration): 15 Jun 1965 (28 days)
USAF serial number: 63-9709
Operation number: 8431
International designation: 1965-037A
Satellite number: 01374
Remarks: RV-1 separated on orbit 81, midair recovery by Major Bayer.
   RV-2 separated on orbit 161, midair recovery by Captain Muller.

Corona flight 96 ("Female Logic")
Launch date (time): 9 Jun 1965 (215816.35)
Mission (payload): 1020, reconnaissance (KH-4A)
Launch vehicle (number): TAT Agena D (T444/A1613)
Launch pad: Pad 75-3-5
Orbit: Inclined 75.07, period 89.94, perigee 176, apogee 362
Decay date (flight duration): 22 Jun 1965 (13 days)
USAF serial number: 63-13216
Operation number: 8425
International designation: 1965-045A
Satellite number: 01396
Remarks: RV-1 separated on orbit 97, midair recovery by Capt. William J.
   "Vip" Vipraio. RV-2 separated on orbit 113, midair recovery by Captain
   Muller.

Corona flight 97 ("Rocky River")
Launch date (time): 19 Jul 1965 (220112.91)
Mission (payload): 1022, reconnaissance (KH-4A)
Launch vehicle (number): TAT Agena D (T446/A1617)
Launch pad: Pad PALC-1-1
Orbit: Inclined 85.05, period 91.00, perigee 182, apogee 464
Decay date (flight duration): 18 Aug 1965 (30 days)
USAF serial number: 63-13218
Operation number: 5543
International designation: 1965-057A
Satellite number: 01457
Remarks: RV-1 separated on orbit 65, midair recovery by Capt. Don P. Olsen.
   RV-2 separated on orbit 144, midair recovery by Capt. Douglas S. Sliger.

Corona flight 98 ("Lights Out")
Launch date (time): 17 Aug 1965 (205957.15)
Mission (payload): 1023, reconnaissance (KH-4A)
Launch vehicle (number): TAT Agena D (T449/A1618)
Launch pad: Pad PALC-1-1
Orbit: Inclined 70.04, period 88.83, perigee 176, apogee 255
Decay date (flight duration): 11 Oct 1965 (55 days)
USAF serial number: 63-13221

Operation number: 7208
International designation: 1965-067A
Satellite number: 01513
Remarks: Forward camera failed. RV-1 separated on orbit 81, midair recovery by Captain Muller. RV-2 separated on orbit 144, midair recovery by Captain Vipraio.

Corona flight 99 ("Word Scramble")
Launch date (time): 2 Sep 1965 (200016.43)
Mission (payload): R&D, radio propagation/ionospheric experiments (Aerospace/Cambridge Research Laboratory, no RV)
Launch vehicle (number): Thor Agena D (T401/A1602)
Launch pad: Pad 75-3-5
Orbit: Failed to orbit
USAF serial number: 62-12398
Operation number: 3373
Remarks: Guidance problem. Destroyed by range safety officer at T+60 sec. Possibly also named "Ivory Nut."

Corona flight 100 ("Nickel Silver")
Launch date (time): 22 Sep 1965 (213114.80)
Mission (payload): 1024, reconnaissance (KH-4A)
Launch vehicle (number): TAT Agena D (T458/A1619)
Launch pad: Pad PALC-1-1
Orbit: Inclined 80.01, period 90.04, perigee 191, apogee 364
Decay date (flight duration): 11 Oct 1965 (19 days)
USAF serial number: 64-17732
Operation number: 7221
International designation: 1965-074A
Satellite number: 01602
Remarks: RV-1 separated on orbit 81, midair recovery by Maj. Dale Palmer. RV-2 separated on orbit 161, midair recovery by Captain McDonald.

Corona flight 101 ("Union Leader")
Launch date (time): 5 Oct 1965 (174557.45)
Mission (payload): 1025, reconnaissance (KH-4A)
Launch vehicle (number): TAT Agena D (T433/A1616)
Launch pad: Pad 75-3-5
Orbit: Inclined 75.05, period 89.75, perigee 203, apogee 323
Decay date (flight duration): 29 Oct 1965 (24 days)
USAF serial number: 63-9704
Operation number: 5325
International designation: 1965-079A
Satellite number: 01615
Remarks: RV-1 separated on orbit 81, midair recovery by Major Bayer. RV-2 separated on orbit 161, midair recovery by Capt. Nicola A. "Nick" Ruscetta.

Corona flight 102 ("High Journey")
Launch date (time): 28 Oct 1965 (211712.71)
Mission (payload): 1026, reconnaissance (KH-4A)
Launch vehicle (number): TAT Agena D (T439/A1620)
Launch pad: Pad PALC-1-1
Orbit: Inclined 74.97, period 90.54, perigee 176, apogee 430
Decay date (flight duration): 17 Nov 1965 (20 days)
USAF serial number: 63-13211
Operation number: 2155
International designation: 1965-086A
Satellite number: 01637
Remarks: RV-1 separated on orbit 81, midair recovery by Olsen. RV-2 separated on orbit 160, midair recovery by Captain Sliger.

Corona flight 103 ("Lucky Fellow")
Launch date (time): 9 Dec 1965 (211019.60)
Mission (payload): 1027, reconnaissance (KH-4A)
Launch vehicle (number): TAT Agena D (T448/A1621)
Launch pad: Pad 75-3-5
Orbit: Inclined 80.04, period 90.72, perigee 183, apogee 437
Decay date (flight duration): 26 Dec 1965 (17 days)
USAF serial number: 63-13220
Operation number: 7249
International designation: 1965-102A
Satellite number: 01816
Remarks: RV-1 separated on orbit 17, midair recovery by Capt. Herbert E. Bronson. RV-2 separated on orbit 33, midair recovery by Captain Vipraio.

Corona flight 104 ("Tall Story")
Launch date (time): 24 Dec 1965 (210615.83)
Mission (payload): 1028, reconnaissance (KH-4A)
Launch vehicle (number): TAT Agena D (T451/A1610)
Launch pad: Pad 75-3-4
Orbit: Inclined 80.01, period 90.83, perigee 178, apogee 446
Decay date (flight duration): 20 Jan 1966 (27 days)
USAF serial number: 63-13223
Operation number: 4639
International designation: 1965-110A
Satellite number: 01866
Remarks: RV-1 separated on orbit 81, midair recovery by Captain Muller. RV-2 separated on orbit 114, midair recovery by Major Palmer.

Corona flight 105 ("Sea Level")
Launch date (time): 2 Feb 1966 (213213.84)
Mission (payload): 1029, reconnaissance (KH-4A)

Launch vehicle (number): TAT Agena D (T450/A1623)
Launch pad: Pad PALC-1-1
Orbit: Inclined 75.05, period 90.64, perigee 185, apogee 425
Decay date (flight duration): 27 Feb 1966 (25 days)
USAF serial number: 63-13222
Operation number: 7291
International designation: 1966-007A
Satellite number: 01968
Remarks: RV-1 separated on orbit 81, midair recovery by Captain Ruscetta.
RV-2 separated on orbit 160, midair recovery by Maj. Don Olsen.

Corona flight 106 ("Easy Chair")
Launch date (time): 9 Mar 1966 (220203.04)
Mission (payload): 1030, reconnaissance (KH-4A)
Launch vehicle (number): TAT Agena D (T452/A1622)
Launch pad: Pad 75-3-4
Orbit: Inclined 75.03, period 90.59, perigee 178, apogee 432
Decay date (flight duration): 29 Mar 1966 (20 days)
USAF serial number: 63-13224
Operation number: 3488
International designation: 1966-018A
Satellite number: 02099
Remarks: RV-1 separated on orbit 81, midair recovery by Maj. Walter
Milam. RV-2 separated on orbit 159, midair recovery by Maj. Albert
Muller.

Corona flight 107 ("Gaping Wound")
Launch date (time): 7 Apr 1966 (220255.17)
Mission (payload): 1031, reconnaissance (KH-4A)
Launch vehicle (number): TAT Agena D (T474/A1627)
Launch pad: Pad PALC-1-1
Orbit: Inclined 75.06, period 89.56, perigee 193, apogee 312
Decay date (flight duration): 26 Apr 1966 (19 days)
USAF serial number: 64-17748
Operation number: 1612
International designation: 1966-029A
Satellite number: 02136
Remarks: RV-1 separated on orbit 113, midair recovery by Major Milam. RV-
2 separated on orbit 177, midair recovery by Captain John E. Cahoon.

Corona flight 108 ("Cargo Net")
Launch date (time): 4 May 1966 (192525.87)
Mission (payload): 1032, reconnaissance (KH-4A)
Launch vehicle (number): TAT Agena D (T465/A1625)
Launch pad: Pad 75-3-5
Orbit: Failed to orbit

Corona flight 108 *(continued)*
USAF serial number: 64-17739
Operation number: 1508
Remarks: Agena failed to separate.

Corona flight 109 ("Short Ton")
Launch date (time): 24 May 1966 (020032.97)
Mission (payload): 1033, reconnaissance (KH-4A)
Launch vehicle (number): TAT Agena D (T469/A1630)
Launch pad: Pad PALC-1-1
Orbit: Inclined 66.04, period 89.00, perigee 179, apogee 271
Decay date (flight duration): 9 Jun 1966 (16 days)
USAF serial number: 64-17743
Operation number: 1778
International designation: 1966-042A
Satellite number: 02181
Remarks: RV-1 separated on orbit 82, midair recovery by Major Bayer.
  RV-2 separated on orbit 178, midair recovery by Captain Ruscetta.

Corona flight 110 ("Game Leg")
Launch date (time): 21 Jun 1966 (213129.88)
Mission (payload): 1034, reconnaissance (KH-4A)
Launch vehicle (number): TAT Agena D (T466/A1626)
Launch pad: Pad 75-3-5
Orbit: Inclined 80.10, period 90.15, perigee 194, apogee 367
Decay date (flight duration): 14 Jul 1966 (23 days)
USAF serial number: 64-17740
Operation number: 1599
International designation: 1966-055A
Satellite number: 02227
Remarks: RV-1 separated on orbit 81, midair recovery by Capt. Joseph
  Modicut. RV-2 separated on orbit 161, midair recovery by Captain
  Vipraio.

Corona flight 111 ("Curly Top")
Launch date (time): 9 Aug 1966 (204603.29)
Mission (payload): 1036, reconnaissance (KH-4A)
Launch vehicle (number): LTTAT Agena D (T506/A1631)
Launch pad: Pad SLC-1W
Orbit: Inclined 100.12, period 89.35, perigee 194, apogee 287
Decay date (flight duration): 11 Sep 1966 (33 days)
USAF serial number: 66-4433
Operation number: 1545
International designation: 1966-072A
Satellite number: 02393
Remarks: First Long-Tank Thrust Augmented Thor (LTTAT) Agena D

launch. RV-1 separated on orbit 115, midair recovery by Maj. Jack H. Wenning. RV-2 separated on orbit 212, midair recovery by Captain Cahoon.

Corona flight 112 ("Big Badge")
Launch date (time): 20 Sep 1966 (211404.96)
Mission (payload): 1035, reconnaissance (KH-4A)
Launch vehicle (number): TAT Agena D (T477/A1628)
Launch pad: Pad SLC-3W
Orbit: Inclined 85.13, period 90.87, perigee 188, apogee 452
Decay date (flight duration): 12 Oct 1966 (22 days)
USAF serial number: 64-17751
Operation number: 1703
International designation: 1966-085A
Satellite number: 02427
Remarks: RV-1 separated on orbit 81, midair recovery by Capt. Richard M. Scofield. RV-2 separated on orbit 160, midair recovery by Captain Bronson.

Corona flight 113 ("Busy Meeting")
Launch date (time): 8 Nov 1966 (195302.49)
Mission (payload): 1037, reconnaissance (KH-4A)
Launch vehicle (number): LTTAT Agena D (T507/A1632)
Launch pad: Pad SLC-1W
Orbit: Inclined 100.09, period 98.42, perigee 172, apogee 318
Decay date (flight duration): 29 Nov 1966 (21 days)
USAF serial number: 66-4434
Operation number: 1866
International designation: 1966-102A
Satellite number: 02537
Remarks: Corona designation changed to "Program 846." RV-1 separated on orbit 66, midair recovery by Captain Vipraio. RV-2 separated on orbit 195, midair recovery by Capt. Jack O. Parker, Jr.

Corona flight 114 ("Long Road")
Launch date (time): 14 Jan 1967 (212821.38)
Mission (payload): 1038, reconnaissance (KH-4A)
Launch vehicle (number): TAT Agena D (T495/A1629)
Launch pad: Pad SLC-3W
Orbit: Inclined 80.07, period 90.13, perigee 180, apogee 380
Decay date (flight duration): 2 Feb 1967 (19 days)
USAF serial number: 65-10613
Operation number: 1664
International designation: 1967-002A
Satellite number: 02642
Remarks: RV-1 separated on orbit 81, midair recovery by Major Wenning. RV-2 separated on orbit 193, midair recovery by Major Schensted.

Corona flight 115 ("Busy Pawnshop")
Launch date (time): 22 Feb 1967 (220215.16)
Mission (payload): 1039, reconnaissance (KH-4A)
Launch vehicle (number): TAT Agena D (T493/A1635)
Launch pad: Pad SLC-3W
Orbit: Inclined 80.03, period 90.12, perigee 180, apogee 380
Decay date (flight duration): 11 Mar 1967 (17 days)
USAF serial number: 65-10611
Operation number: 4750
International designation: 1967-015A
Satellite number: 02686
Remarks: RV-1 separated on orbit 81, midair recovery by Capt. Richard E.
    McDevitt. RV-2 separated on orbit 177, midair recovery by Captain
    Cahoon.

Corona flight 116 ("Giant Banana")
Launch date (time): 30 Mar 1967 (185423.03)
Mission (payload): 1040, reconnaissance (KH-4A)
Launch vehicle (number): TAT Agena D (T501/A1636)
Launch pad: Pad SLC-3W
Orbit: Inclined 85.03, period 89.45, perigee 167, apogee 326
Decay date (flight duration): 17 Apr 1967 (18 days)
USAF serial number: 65-10619
Operation number: 4779
International designation: 1967-029A
Satellite number: 02736
Remarks: RV-1 separated on orbit 81, midair recovery by Maj. Harlan L.
    "Bud" Gurney. RV-2 separated on orbit 145, midair recovery by
    Captain Bronson.

Corona flight 117 ("Busy Banker")
Launch date (time): 9 May 1967 (215042.16)
Mission (payload): 1041, reconnaissance (KH-4A)
Launch vehicle (number): LTTAT Agena D (T508/A1634)
Launch pad: Pad SLC-1E
Orbit: Inclined 85.10, period 94.36, perigee 200, apogee 777
Decay date (flight duration): 13 Jul 1967 (65 days)
USAF serial number: 66-4435
Operation number: 4696
International designation: 1967-043A
Satellite number: 02779
Remarks: RV-1 separated on orbit 96, midair recovery by Captain Scofield.
    RV-2 separated on orbit 215, midair recovery by Captain Modicut.

Corona flight 118
Launch date (time): 16 Jun 1967 (213502.81)
Mission (payload): 1042, reconnaissance (KH-4A)
Launch vehicle (number): LTTAT Agena D (T509/A1633)
Launch pad: Pad SLC-1W
Orbit: Inclined 80.02, period 89.97, perigee 181, apogee 367
Decay date (flight duration): 20 Jul 1967 (34 days)
USAF serial number: 66-4436
Operation number: 3559
International designation: 1967-062A
Satellite number: 02850
Remarks: RV-1, midair recovery by Major Wenning. RV-2, water recovery.

Corona flight 119
Launch date (time): 7 Aug 1967 (214245.48)
Mission (payload): 1043, reconnaissance, radiation measurement
    (KH-4A, S67-3)
Launch vehicle (number): LTTAT Agena D (T510/A——)
Launch pad: Pad SLC-1E
Orbit: Inclined 79.94, period 89.72, perigee 174, apogee 346
Decay date (flight duration): 1 Sep 1967 (25 days)
USAF serial number: 66-4437
Operation number: 4827
International designation: 1967-076A
Satellite number: 02910
Remarks: S67-3 contained a stellar X-ray spectrometer and infrared
    radiometer. RV-1, midair recovery by Capt. Robert J. Larison. RV-2,
    midair recovery by Capt. Edgar H. Pressgrove, Jr.

Corona flight 120
Launch date (time): 15 Sep 1967 (194115.00)
Mission (payload): 1101, reconnaissance (KH-4B)
Launch vehicle (number): LTTAT Agena D (T512/A——)
Launch pad: Pad SLC-1W
Orbit: Inclined 80.07, period 89.95, perigee 150, apogee 389
Decay date (flight duration): 4 Oct 1967 (19 days)
USAF serial number: 66-4439
Operation number: 5089
International designation: 1967-087A
Satellite number: 02946
Remarks: First Corona satellite to carry a KH-4B camera. RV-1, midair
    recovery by Maj. Lester S. McChristian. RV-2, midair recovery by Maj.
    Nicholas Ratiani.

Corona flight 121
Launch date (time): 2 Nov 1967 (213121.34)
Mission (payload): 1044, reconnaissance (KH-4A)
Launch vehicle (number): LTTAT Agena D (T513/A——)
Launch pad: Pad SLC-1E
Orbit: Inclined 81.53, period 90.47, perigee 183, apogee 410
Decay date (flight duration): 2 Dec 1967 (30 days)
USAF serial number: 66-4440
Operation number: 0562
International designation: 1967-109A
Satellite number: 03024
Remarks: RV-1, midair recovery by Captain Pressgrove. RV-2, midair
  recovery by Major Gurney.

Corona flight 122
Launch date (time): 9 Dec 1967 (222541.19)
Mission (payload): 1102, reconnaissance (KH-4B)
Launch vehicle (number): LTTAT Agena D (T514/A——)
Launch pad: Pad SLC-1W
Orbit: Inclined 81.74, period 88.46, perigee 146, apogee 251
Decay date (flight duration): 25 Dec 1967 (16 days)
USAF serial number: 66-4441
Operation number: 1001
International designation: 1967-122A
Satellite number: 03063
Remarks: RV-1, midair recovery by Captain Scofield. RV-2, midair recovery
  by Maj. Paul L. Martin, Jr.

Corona flight 123
Launch date (time): 24 Jan 1968 (222622.36)
Mission (payload): 1045, reconnaissance (KH-4A)
Launch vehicle (number): LTTAT Agena D (T516/A——)
Launch pad: Pad SLC-1E
Orbit: Inclined 81.47, period 88.44, perigee 158, apogee 234
Decay date (flight duration): 27 Feb 1968 (34 days)
USAF serial number: 66-4443
Operation number: 2243
International designation: 1968-008A
Satellite number: 03113
Remarks: RV-1, midair recovery by Maj. Kenneth L. Gilbert. RV-2, midair
  recovery by Captain Pressgrove.

Corona flight 124
Launch date (time): 14 Mar 1968 (220014.75)
Mission (payload): 1046, reconnaissance (KH-4A)
Launch vehicle (number): LTTAT Agena D (T518/A——)
Launch pad: Pad SLC-1E

Orbit: Inclined 82.91, period 89.09, perigee 188, apogee 268
Decay date (flight duration): 10 Apr 1968 (27 days)
USAF serial number: 66-4445
Operation number: 4849
International designation: 1968-020A
Satellite number: 03152
Remarks: RV-1, midair recovery by Captain Modicut. RV-2, midair recovery
  by Capt. Albert R. Kaiser.

Corona flight 125
Launch date (time): 1 May 1968 (213100.68)
Mission (payload): 1103, reconnaissance (KH-4B)
Launch vehicle (number): LTTAT Agena D (T511/A——)
Launch pad: Pad SLC-3W
Orbit: Inclined 83.05, period 88.63, perigee 155, apogee 255
Decay date (flight duration): 15 May 1968 (14 days)
USAF serial number: 66-4438
Operation number: 1419
International designation: 1968-039A
Satellite number: 03228
Remarks: RV-1, midair recovery by Maj. Robert B. Miller. RV-2, midair
  recovery by Major Ratiani.

Corona flight 126
Launch date (time): 20 Jun 1968 (214604.62)
Mission (payload): 1047, reconnaissance (KH-4A)
Launch vehicle (number): LTTAT Agena D (T517/A——)
Launch pad: Pad SLC-1E
Orbit: Inclined 84.99, period 89.75, perigee 193, apogee 326
Decay date (flight duration): 16 Jul 1968 (26 days)
USAF serial number: 66-4444
Operation number: 5343
International designation: 1968-052A
Satellite number: 03296
Remarks: RV-1, midair recovery by Major Gurney. RV-2, midair recovery
  by Maj. Ralph A. Gauthier.

Corona flight 127
Launch date (time): 7 Aug 1968 (213654.62)
Mission (payload): 1104, reconnaissance (KH-4B)
Launch vehicle (number): LTTAT Agena D (T522/A——)
Launch pad: Pad SLC-3W
Orbit: Inclined 82.11, period 88.60, perigee 152, apogee 257
Decay date (flight duration): 27 Aug 1968 (20 days)
USAF serial number: 66-4449
Operation number: 5955
International designation: 1968-065A

Corona flight 127 *(continued)*
Satellite number: 03336
Remarks: RV-1, midair recovery by Captain Scofield. RV-2, midair recovery
   by Major Martin.

Corona flight 128
Launch date (time): 18 Sep 1968 (213122.64)
Mission (payload): 1048, reconnaissance (KH-4A)
Launch vehicle (number): LTTAT Agena D (T524/A——)
Launch pad: Pad SLC-1E
Orbit: Inclined 83.02, period 90.12, perigee 167, apogee 393
Decay date (flight duration): 8 Oct 1968 (20 days)
USAF serial number: 66-4451
Operation number: 0165
International designation: 1968-078A
Satellite number: 03408
Remarks: Forward camera failed. RV-1, midair recovery by Captain Kaiser.
   RV-2, midair recovery by Major Ratiani.

Corona flight 129
Launch date (time): 3 Nov 1968 (213125.22)
Mission (payload): 1105, reconnaissance (KH-4B)
Launch vehicle (number): LTTAT Agena D (T515/A——)
Launch pad: Pad SLC-3W
Orbit: Inclined 82.15, period 88.90, perigee 150, apogee 288
Decay date (flight duration): 23 Nov 1968 (20 days)
USAF serial number: 66-4442
Operation number: 1315
International designation: 1968-098A
Satellite number: 03531
Remarks: RV-1, midair recovery by Captain Modicut. RV-2, midair recovery
   by Major Gauthier.

Corona flight 130
Launch date (time): 12 Dec 1968 (222212.18)
Mission (payload): 1049, reconnaissance (KH-4A)
Launch vehicle (number): LTTAT Agena D (T527/A——)
Launch pad: Pad SLC-3W
Orbit: Inclined 81.02, period 88.67, perigee 169, apogee 248
Decay date (flight duration): 28 Dec 1968 (16 days)
USAF serial number: 66-4454
Operation number: 4740
International designation: 1968-112A
Satellite number: 03604
Remarks: Degraded film. RV-1, midair recovery by Major McChristian.
   RV-2, midair recovery by Captain Pressgrove.

Corona flight 131
Launch date (time): 5 Feb 1969 (215954.25)
Mission (payload): 1106, reconnaissance (KH-4B)
Launch vehicle (number): LTTAT Agena D (T519/A——)
Launch pad: Pad SLC-3W
Orbit: Inclined 81.54, period 88.70, perigee 178, apogee 239
Decay date (flight duration): 24 Feb 1969 (19 days)
USAF serial number: 66-4446
Operation number: 3890
International designation: 1969-010A
Satellite number: 03672
Remarks: Aft camera failed. RV-1, midair recovery by Captain Scofield.
    RV-2, midair recovery by Capt. Robert L. Brenci.

Corona flight 132
Launch date (time): 19 Mar 1969 (213820.07)
Mission (payload): 1050, reconnaissance (KH-4A)
Launch vehicle (number): LTTAT Agena D (T541/A——)
Launch pad: Pad SLC-3W
Orbit: Inclined 83.04, period 88.73, perigee 179, apogee 241
Decay date (flight duration): 24 Mar 1969 (5 days)
USAF serial number: 69-035
Operation number: 3722
International designation: 1969-026A
Satellite number: 03829
Remarks: Agena failed. RV-1, midair recovery by Major Gauthier. RV-2,
    midair recovery by Maj. Miller A. Peeler.

Corona flight 133
Launch date (time): 2 May 1969 (014658.31)
Mission (payload): 1051, reconnaissance (KH-4A)
Launch vehicle (number): LTTAT Agena D (T544/A——)
Launch pad: Pad SLC-3W
Orbit: Inclined 64.97, period 89.54, perigee 179, apogee 326
Decay date (flight duration): 23 May 1969 (21 days)
USAF serial number: 69-037
Operation number: 1101
International designation: 1969-041A
Satellite number: 03914
Remarks: Degraded film. RV-1, midair recovery by Major Miller. RV-2,
    midair recovery by Major Martin.

Corona flight 134
Launch date (time): 24 Jul 1969 (013057.82)
Mission (payload): 1107, reconnaissance (KH-4B)
Launch vehicle (number): LTTAT Agena D (T545/A——)

Corona flight 134 *(continued)*
Launch pad: Pad SLC-3W
Orbit: Inclined 74.98, period 88.49, perigee 178, apogee 220
Decay date (flight duration): 23 Aug 1969 (30 days)
USAF serial number: 69-038
Operation number: 3654
International designation: 1969-063A
Satellite number: 04050
Remarks: Forward camera failed. RV-1, water recovery. RV-2, midair
  recovery by Maj. Robert R. Thornquist.

Corona flight 135
Launch date (time): 22 Sep 1969 (211101.98)
Mission (payload): 1052, reconnaissance (KH-4A)
Launch vehicle (number): LTTAT Agena D (T531/A——)
Launch pad: Pad SLC-3W
Orbit: Inclined 85.03, period 88.83, perigee 178, apogee 253
Decay date (flight duration): 12 Oct 1969 (20 days)
USAF serial number: 68-300
Operation number: 3531
International designation: 1969-079A
Satellite number: 04102
Remarks: Last KH-4A camera flown. RV-1, midair recovery by Maj.
  Edward T. Lynch, Jr. RV-2, midair recovery by Major McChristian.

Corona flight 136
Launch date (time): 4 Dec 1969 (213756.90)
Mission (payload): 1108, reconnaissance (KH-4B)
Launch vehicle (number): LTTAT Agena D (T549/A——)
Launch pad: Pad SLC-3W
Orbit: Inclined 81.48, period 88.61, perigee 159, apogee 251
Decay date (flight duration): 10 Jan 1970 (37 days)
USAF serial number: 69-039
Operation number: 6617
International designation: 1969-105A
Satellite number: 04264
Remarks: RV-1, midair recovery by Captain Pressgrove. RV-2, midair
  recovery by Maj. Richard Bussey.

Corona flight 137
Launch date (time): 4 Mar 1970 (221516.12)
Mission (payload): 1109, reconnaissance (KH-4B)
Launch vehicle (number): LTTAT Agena D (T551/A——)
Launch pad: Pad SLC-3W
Orbit: Inclined 88.02, period 88.76, perigee 167, apogee 257
Decay date (flight duration): 26 Mar 1970 (22 days)

USAF serial number: 69-041
Operation number: 0440
International designation: 1970-016A
Satellite number: 04342
Remarks: RV-1, midair recovery by Major Peeler. RV-2, midair recovery by Major Thornquist.

Corona flight 138
Launch date (time): 20 May 1970 (213510.62)
Mission (payload): 1110, reconnaissance (KH-4B)
Launch vehicle (number): LTTAT Agena D (T555/A——)
Launch pad: Pad SLC-3W
Orbit: Inclined 83.00, period 88.62, perigee 162, apogee 247
Decay date (flight duration): 17 Jun 1970 (28 days)
USAF serial number: 69-045
Operation number: 4720
International designation: 1970-040A
Satellite number: 04405
Remarks: RV-1, midair recovery by Captain Brenci. RV-2, midair recovery by Capt. Bobbie L. Mitchell.

Corona flight 139
Launch date (time): 23 Jul 1970 (012500.61)
Mission (payload): 1111, reconnaissance (KH-4B)
Launch vehicle (number): LTTAT Agena D (T556/A——)
Launch pad: Pad SLC-3W
Orbit: Inclined 60.00, period 90.04, perigee 158, apogee 398
Decay date (flight duration): 19 Aug 1970 (27 days)
USAF serial number: 69-046
Operation number: 4324
International designation: 1970-054A
Satellite number: 04477
Remarks: Unusually low inclination to cover Middle Eastern targets. RV-1, midair recovery by Capt. Marshall A. Eto. RV-2, midair recovery by Lt. Col. William Scott.

Corona flight 140
Launch date (time): 18 Nov 1970 (212849.49)
Mission (payload): 1112, reconnaissance (KH-4B)
Launch vehicle (number): LTTAT Agena D (T552/A——)
Launch pad: Pad SLC-3W
Orbit: Inclined 82.99, period 88.70, perigee 185, apogee 232
Decay date (flight duration): 11 Dec 1970 (23 days)
USAF serial number: 69-042
Operation number: 4992
International designation: 1970-098A

Corona flight 140 *(continued)*
Satellite number: 04721
Remarks: RV-1, midair recovery by Capt. Thomas T. Rauk. RV-2, midair recovery by Maj. John F. Swatek.

Corona flight 141
Launch date (time): 17 Feb 1971 (200430.42)
Mission (payload): 1113, reconnaissance (KH-4B)
Launch vehicle (number): LTTAT Agena D (T537/A———)
Launch pad: Pad SLC-3W
Orbit: Failed to orbit
USAF serial number: 69-033
Operation number: 3297
Remarks: Air-conditioning system in Thor tail failed; turbine oil froze and rocket lost control. Range safety officer destroyed booster at 23.25 sec.

Corona flight 142
Launch date (time): 24 Mar 1971 (210600.44)
Mission (payload): 1114, reconnaissance (KH-4B)
Launch vehicle (number): LTTAT Agena D (T538/A———)
Launch pad: Pad SLC-3W
Orbit: Inclined 81.52, period 88.56, perigee 157, apogee 246
Decay date (flight duration): 12 Apr 1971 (19 days)
USAF serial number: 69-034
Operation number: 5300
International designation: 1971-022A
Satellite number: 05059
Remarks: RV-1, midair recovery by Maj. Maurice G. "Gil" Alford. RV-2, midair recovery by Major Peeler.

Corona flight 143
Launch date (time): 10 Sep 1971 (213256.36)
Mission (payload): 1115, reconnaissance (KH-4B)
Launch vehicle (number): LTTAT Agena D (T567/A———)
Launch pad: Pad SLC-3W
Orbit: Inclined 74.95, period 88.48, perigee 156, apogee 244
Decay date (flight duration): 5 Oct 1971 (25 days)
USAF serial number: 70-012
Operation number: 5454
International designation: 1971-076A
Satellite number: 05468
Remarks: RV-1, midair recovery by Maj. Robert J. "Bobby" Jefferies. RV-2, midair recovery by Capt. Mike Hollomon.

Corona flight 144
Launch date (time): 19 Apr 1972 (214358.54)

Mission (payload): 1116, reconnaissance, radiation measurement (KH-4B, S71-3)

Launch vehicle (number): LTTAT Agena D (T569/A——)

Launch pad: Pad SLC-3W

Orbit: Inclined 81.48, period 88.85, perigee 155, apogee 277

Decay date (flight duration): 12 May 1972 (23 days)

USAF serial number: 70-292

Operation number: 5640

International designation: 1972-032A

Satellite number: 06003

Remarks: S71-3 contained an ion gauge and night-glow detector. RV-1, midair recovery by Lt. Col. James McDonald. RV-2, midair recovery by Maj. Harry V. Boyd.

Corona flight 145

Launch date (time): 25 May 1972 (184100.36)

Mission (payload): 1117, reconnaissance, atmospheric research (KH-4B, S71-5)

Launch vehicle (number): LTTAT Agena D (T571/A1663)

Launch pad: Pad SLC-3W

Orbit: Inclined 96.34, period 89.17, perigee 158, apogee 305

Decay date (flight duration): 4 Jun 1972 (10 days)

USAF serial number: 71-170

Operation number: 6371

International designation: 1972-039A

Satellite number: 06037

Remarks: Last Corona flight; last KH-4B mission. RV-1, midair recovery by Captain Rauk. RV-2, midair recovery by Capt. Donald G. Hard.

Appendix 2
Corona Camera Data

Table 2.1. Total Photographic Coverage by Corona (in millions of square nautical miles)

	Foreign	Domestic	Total
Reconnaissance			
KH-1 to KH-4	106.936	5.628	112.564
KH-4A	195.625	10.295	205.920
KH-4B	183.731	7.563	191.294
KH-6	0.450	insignificant	0.450
Total	486.742	23.486	510.228
Mapping			
KH-4A	26.784	1.504	28.288
KH-4B	26.992	1.692	28.684
KH-5	40.009	2.800	42.809
Total	93.785	5.996	99.781

Data compiled from Appendixes 2, 3, 4, 5, and 7 in Robert A. McDonald, "Corona: Success for Space Reconnaissance, a Look into the Cold War, and a Revolution for Intelligence," *Photogrammetric Engineering & Remote Sensing* (June 1995).

Table 2.2 Corona Camera Statistics

Model	KH-1	KH-2	KH-3	KH-4	KH-4A	KH-4B	KH-5	KH-6
	C	C Prime	C Triple Prime	Mural	J-1	J-3	Argon	Lanyard
Coverage	Mono	Mono	Mono	Stereo	Stereo	Stereo		22 deg
Scan	70 deg	70 deg	70 deg	70 deg	70 deg	70 deg	N/A	
Stereo coverage	N/A	N/A	N/A	30 deg	30 deg	30 deg		
Lens	f/5	f/5	f/5	f/3.5	f/3.5	f/3.5		
	Tessar	Tessar	Tessar	Petzval	Petzval	Petzval		
Focal Length (in)	24	24	24	24	24	24	3	66
Diameter (in)	4.8	4.8	4.8	6.86	6.86	6.86		
Resolution								
Ground (ft)	40	25	12-25	10-25	9-25	6	460	6[1]
Film (lines/mm)	100	100	100	100	120	160	30	160
Coverage (nm)						8.6 x 117	300 x 300	7.5 x 40
Image format (in)						2.18 x 29.8	4.5 x 4.5	4.5 x 25
Film Base	Acetate	Polyester	Polyester	Polyester	Polyester	Polyester		
Missions								
Total	10	10	6	26	52	17	12	3
Successful	1	4	4	20	49	16	6	1
Number of RVs	1	1	1	1	2	2	1	1
Mission series	9000	9000	9000	9000	1000	1100	9000A	8000
Lifetime (days)	1	2-3	1-4	6-7	4-15	19	3-6	2

1. Planned resolution: 2 ft

Appendix 3
Ace List

Table 3. Ace List, August 1960–May 1972

NAME	Number of Recoveries		CORONA MISSIONS
	TOTAL[1]	CORONA	
Maj./Lt. Col. Edwin R. Bayer	12	7	81-2, 85-2, 89-2, 93-1, 95-1, 101-1, 109-1
Capt./Maj. Walter M. Milam	12	6	58, 68, 70, 76-1, 106-1, 107-1
Capt./Maj. Albert F. Muller	8	7	83-1, 91-2, 95-2, 96-2, 98-1, 104-1, 106-2
Capt./Maj. Dale M. Palmer	8	6	65, 69, 88-2, 89-1, 100-1, 104-2
Capt. Richard M. Scofield	8	5	112-1, 117-1, 122-1, 127-1, 131-1
Capt. Jeremiah J. Collins	7	4	76-2, 82-2, 87-1, 91-1
Capt./Lt. Col. James F. McDonald, Jr.	7	5	83-2, 88-1, 92-2, 100-2, 144-1
Capt. Douglas S. Sliger	7	4	92-1, 93-2, 97-2, 102-2
Capt. James E. Varnadoe	7	6	67, 82-1, 86-1, 90-1, 90-2, 94-1
Capt. Albert R. Kaiser	6	2	124-2, 128-1
Maj. Robert B. Miller	6	2	125-1, 133-1
Capt./Maj. Edgar H. Pressgrove, Jr.	6	5	119-2, 121-1, 123-2, 130-2, 136-1
Capt. William J. Vipraio	6	5	96-1, 98-2, 103-2, 110-2, 113-1
Capt./Maj. Jack R. Wilson	6	6	26, 38, 51, 75, 79-1, 79-2
Capt./Maj. Thomas F. Hines	5	5	41, 46, 48, 52, 71-1
Capt. Herbert E. Bronson	5	3	103-1, 112-2, 116-2
Capt./Maj. Harlan L. Gurney	5	3	116-1, 121-2, 126-1
Maj. Lester S. McChristian	5	3	120-1, 130-1, 135-2
Capt. Joseph Modicut	5	4	110-1, 117-2, 124-1, 129-1
Capt./Maj. Warren C. Schensted	5	3	30, 32, 114-2
Maj. Jack H. Wenning	5	3	111-1, 114-1, 118-1

1. "Total" refers to all operational recoveries. These include not only Corona, but also Gambit and Hexagon capsules, ICBM and IRBM warheads, sounding rockets, and balloon payloads. It should be noted that this list only goes to the end of the period of Corona operations. It is presumed that some of the pilots increased their score, while others not on this list later reached "ace" status.

SOURCE: Compiled by Dr. Rick W. Sturdevant of the Space Command History Office, using recovery reports and a notebook listing all midair recoveries.

Notes

1. Toward a New Frontier

1. Albert D. Wheelon, transcribed from tapes of the Corona Seminar, sponsored by the CIA's Center for the Study of Intelligence/Space Policy Institute, held at George Washington University, Washington, D.C., 23–24 May 1995 (hereafter Corona Seminar), tape 4A, 3–13.
2. R. Cargill Hall, "Strategic Reconnaissance in the Cold War from Concept to National Policy, 1945–1955," *Prologue* 28 (Summer 1996): 107–125.
3. Donald E. Welzenbach, "The Anglo-American Origins of Overflying the Soviet Union: The Case of the 'Invisible Aircraft,'" *Seeing Off the Bear: Anglo-American Air Power Cooperation During the Cold War,* ed. Roger G. Miller (Washington, D.C.: Air Force Historical Foundation, 1995), 195–98, 204–5.
4. Frederick I. Ordway III and Mitchell R. Sharpe, *The Rocket Team* (New York: Thomas Y. Crowell, 1979), 271–74.
5. Merton E. Davies and William R. Harris, *RAND's Role in the Evolution of Balloon and Satellite Observation Systems and Related U.S. Space Technology* (Santa Monica, Calif.: RAND, 1988), 6–7.
6. Clarence G. Lasby, *Project Paperclip* (New York: Atheneum, 1971), 101–3.
7. Davies and Harris, *RAND's Role,* 7.
8. "Unhelpful Utterances," *Spaceflight,* June 1971, 316–17.
9. "Preliminary Design of an Experimental World-Circling Spaceship," *Exploring the Unknown,* vol. 1, ed. John M. Logsdon (Washington, D.C.: NASA SP-4407, 1995), 236–44.
10. Davies and Harris, *RAND's Role,* 12–17.
11. Rick W. Sturdevant, "The United States Air Force Organizes for Space: The Operational Quest," *Organizing for the Use of Space: Historical Perspectives on a Persistent Issue,* ed. Roger D. Launius (San Diego: Univelt Incorporated, 1995), 157–58.
12. Jacob Neufeld, *Ballistic Missiles in the United States Air Force, 1945–1960* (Washington, D.C.: Office of Air Force History, 1990), 67.

13. Lasby, *Project Paperclip*, 250.

14. C. B. Moore, letter to author, 27 March 1996; and "Data Report on Four Stratospheric Balloon Flights Made for Photographic Laboratory," 8 September 1950, author's collection.

15. Davies and Harris, *RAND's Role*, 19–21.

16. "To Establish Requirements for Development of a Reconnaissance Capability by Use of Recoverable Free-Balloon," memorandum for record, 3 October 1950, National Archives.

17. "Subject: (Top Secret) Photographic Reconnaissance Balloons," 6 November 1950, National Archives.

18. "Status Report of Project Gopher," memorandum for record, 29 November 1951, National Archives; and C. B. Moore, "Progress Report for January 1952," rough draft of interdepartmental memorandum to G. O. Hagund, 7 February 1952, part IX (Project Gopher).

19. W. W. Rostow, *Open Skies* (Austin: University of Texas Press, 1982), 190–91.

20. "Moby Dick," *History from the Cambridge Research Center* (report), n.d., author's collection.

21. Donald E. Welzenbach, "Observation Balloons and Reconnaissance Satellites," *Studies in Intelligence* 30 (Spring 1986): 22–23.

22. "The Utility of a Satellite Vehicle for Reconnaissance," *Exploring the Unknown*, 245–61.

23. Davies and Harris, *RAND's Role*, 23–31, 44–45.

24. "The Utility of a Satellite Vehicle," 250.

25. Davies and Harris, *RAND's Role*, 35–38.

26. Hall, "Strategic Reconnaissance in the Cold War"; and Davies and Harris, *RAND's Role*, 44.

27. Dino A. Brugioni, interview with the author, 9 March 1996.

28. Jeffrey T. Richelson, *America's Secret Eyes in Space* (New York: Harper & Row, 1990), 61–62.

29. Sturdevant, "Air Force Organizes for Space," 160–61.

30. Davies and Harris, *RAND's Role*, 47–48, 53–55, 57–59.

31. "General Operational Requirement for a Reconnaissance Satellite Weapon System," 15 March 1955 (as revised 26 September 1958), Los Angeles AFB History Office.

32. Kenneth Schaffel, *The Emerging Shield: The Air Force and the Evolution of Continental Air Defense, 1945–1960* (Washington, D.C.: Office of Air Force History, 1991), 98–99, 107, 113, 120, 129–132.

33. Davies and Harris, *RAND's Role*, 48–50.

34. David Holloway, *Stalin and the Bomb* (New Haven: Yale University Press, 1994), 306–10.

35. Dino A. Brugioni, *Eyeball to Eyeball* (New York: Random House, 1991), 8–10.

36. R. Cargill Hall, "The Eisenhower Administration and the Cold War," *Prologue* 27 (Spring 1995): 61–62, 70.

37. Humphrey Wynn, *RAF Nuclear Deterrent Forces* (London: Her Majesty's Stationery Office, 1994), 111–12; and R. Cargill Hall, "Post War Strategic Reconnaissance and the Genesis of Project Corona," draft text, 12–13.

38. Hall, "Strategic Reconnaissance in the Cold War." The first person to meet the damaged RB-47 was the plane's crew chief. He asked, "What the hell kind of seagull did you hit?" Each member of the crew received a pair of Distinguished Flying Crosses for the flight. Certain individuals, pushing a political agenda, have claimed that these overflights were conducted without permission by General LeMay, with the intent of provoking World War III. There is ample evidence that this was not true.

39. Brugioni interview, 9 March 1996.

40. Brugioni, *Eyeball to Eyeball*, 10–11, 17.

41. Richelson, *America's Secret Eyes in Space*, 27–28.

42. Raymond L. Puffer, interview with the author, 29 March 1996.

43. John D. Hardison, *The Megaton Blasters* (Avada, Colo.: Boomerang Books, 1990).

44. Kenneth W. Gatland, "Prelude to the Space Age," *Spaceflight*, November 1982, 386–89.

45. "Studies of a Minimum Orbital Unmanned Satellite of the Earth," *Exploring the Unknown*, 314–24.

46. Andrew Wilson, *The Eagle Has Wings: The Story of American Space Exploration, 1945–1975* (London: British Interplanetary Society, 1982), 9.

47. Constance McLaughlin Green and Milton Lomask, *Vanguard: A History* (Washington, D.C.: NASA SP-4202, 1970), 19–23.

48. Hall, "Eisenhower and the Cold War," 63; and "Summary Minutes of the Eighth Meeting," *Exploring the Unknown*, 295–307.

49. "Draft Statement of Policy on U.S. Satellite Program," *Exploring the Unknown*, 308–10.

50. Davies and Harris, *RAND's Role*, 67–68.

51. Ben R. Rich and Leo Janos, *Skunk Works* (New York: Little, Brown, 1994), 121–22.

52. Hall, "Strategic Reconnaissance in the Cold War."

53. Sergei Khrushchev, interview with R. Cargill Hall and Richard S. Leghorn at Brown University, 5 July 1995.

54. Davies and Harris, *RAND's Role*, 64.

55. Dwayne A. Day, "Corona: America's First Spy Satellite Program," *Quest*, Summer 1995, 9.

56. James W. Plummer, Corona Seminar, tape 2A, 145–82.

57. R. Cargill Hall, "Origins of U.S. Space Policy: Eisenhower, Open Skies, and Freedom of Space," *Exploring the Unknown*, 220, 224–25.

58. Green and Lomask, *Vanguard: A History*, 22–23, 28–29.

59. "Memorandum of Discussion at the 322d Meeting of the National Security Council, May 10, 1957," *Exploring the Unknown*, 324–28.

60. Plummer, Corona Seminar, tape 2A, 168–75.

61. Day, "Corona: America's First Spy Satellite," 10.

62. Davies and Harris, *RAND's Role*, 69–70, 74–75.

63. Richelson, *America's Secret Eyes in Space*, 1–2, 14.

64. Davies and Harris, *RAND's Role*, 78–86; and Walter Levison, interview with the author, 17 April 1996.

65. Day, "Corona: America's First Spy Satellite," 11.
66. Curtis Peebles, *The Moby Dick Project* (Washington, D.C.: Smithsonian Institution Press, 1991).
67. Welzenbach, "Observation Balloons and Reconnaissance Satellites," 23.
68. Peebles, *The Moby Dick Project,* 162–87.
69. Welzenbach, "Observation Balloons and Reconnaissance Satellites," 23. This was not the only Genetrix gondola to be found. In the spring of 1962, a shepherd reported to the RAF Mountain Rescue Service that he had found a "Sputnik" in the Scottish moors. The RAF was originally doubtful, as the reported site was near a wartime crash. When the recovery crew went to the area, however, they found a box-like device with a glass camera port and camera. On its side was a plaque showing the box descending by parachute, being found by a peasant, being taken to town, and the peasant being given a bag of gold. The RAF recovery crew concluded it was a Soviet spacecraft. In fact, it was a Genetrix gondola. The plaque was identical to that placed on the gondola. The Royal Navy base at Evanton used for some of the launches was some fifteen miles to the east.
70. "The American Experience: Spy in the Sky," Public Broadcasting System, March 1996.
71. Kenneth E. Greer, "Corona," *Studies in Intelligence* supplement 17 (Spring 1973): 1.
72. Brackley Shaw, "Origins of the U-2: Interview with Richard M. Bissell Jr.," *Air Power History,* Winter 1989, 21.
73. Donald E. Welzenbach and Nancy Galyean, "Those Daring Young Men and Their Ultra-High-Flying Machines," *Studies In Intelligence* 31 (Fall 1987): 6. Hervey Stockman left the U-2 program in December 1957 and rejoined the Air Force. His first assignment was as an F-102 interceptor pilot. In late December 1966, he began a tour in Vietnam with the 366th Fighter Squadron as an F-4 pilot. During an escort mission on June 11, 1967, his F-4 collided with another F-4. Stockman and his radar operator, Ronald Webb, ejected; the other crew was killed. Stockman and Webb were captured by the North Vietnamese, and spent nearly six years in the "Hanoi Hilton." They were released on March 4, 1973.
74. Jeffrey Richelson, *American Espionage and the Soviet Target* (New York: William Morrow and Co., 1987), 143.
75. Khrushchev interview, 4–5.
76. Brugioni interview, 9 March 1996.
77. Steven J. Zaloga, *Target America* (Novato, Calif.: Presidio Press, 1993), 134–36, 255–56.
78. Ibid., 135–36, 146–47.
79. Khrushchev interview.
80. Timothy Varfolomeyev, "Soviet Rocketry that Conquered Space, Part 1," *Spaceflight,* August 1995, 262.
81. "Correspondence," *Spaceflight,* January 1996, 31.
82. Welzenbach and Galyean, "Those Daring Young Men," 4.

83. Dino A. Brugioni, "The Tyuratam Enigma," *Air Force Magazine*, March 1984, 108–9.
84. Welzenbach and Galyean, "Those Daring Young Men," 4.
85. "Letter: Allen W. Dulles to Donald Quarles," *Exploring the Unknown*, 329.
86. Varfolomeyev, "Soviet Rocketry," 260–61.

2. First Spark

1. Curtis Peebles, "A Traveller in the Night," *Journal of the British Interplanetary Society* 33 (August 1980): 282–86.
2. Robert A. Divine, *The Sputnik Challenge* (Oxford: Oxford University Press, 1993), 33, 39–40, 77–78, 171–78, 180–81.
3. Walter A. McDougall, . . . *the Heavens and the Earth* (New York: Basic Books, 1985), 134.
4. "Briefing on Army Satellite Program" (Carrollton Press, 1977), microfilm, 101B.
5. Peter Pesavento, "U.S. Navy's Untold Story of Space-Related Firsts," and "Secrets Revealed about the Early U.S. Navy Space Program," *Spaceflight*, July 1996, 239–45.
6. Greer, "Corona," *Studies in Intelligence* supplement 17 (Spring 1973): 2–3.
7. Lew Allen, Corona Seminar, tape 1B, 558.
8. John M. Deutch, Corona Seminar, tape 1A, 530.
9. Davies and Harris, *RAND's Role*, 86–89.
10. Central Intelligence Agency, *A Point in Time*, film, ca. 1973, from a declassified audio tape version, author's collection, tape 1A, 200.
11. Richard Garwin, Corona Seminar, tape 2A, 1.
12. Greer, "Corona," 3, 6–7.
13. John McMahon, Corona Seminar, tape 1B, 420.
14. Brian S. Latell, Corona Seminar, tape 5B, 210–24; and Hall, "Post War Strategic Reconnaissance," 34, 53. Another version said a cigar was the source of the name.
15. F. C. E. Oder and Martin Belles, "Corona Program Profile," *The Star* (in-house Lockheed newsletter), 2 June 1995, 2.
16. Greer, "Corona," 4.
17. Plummer, Corona Seminar, tape 2A, 189–207.
18. Greer, "Corona," 3–4.
19. CIA, *A Point in Time*, tape 1A, 310.
20. Levison interview, 17 April 1996.
21. Greer, "Corona," 5–6; and Hall, "Post War Strategic Reconnaissance," 35–37.
22. "USAF Pushes Pied Piper Space Vehicle," *Aviation Week*, 14 October 1957, 26.
23. Greer, "Corona," 6, 8–9.
24. Plummer, Corona Seminar, tape 2A, 232.
25. Robert A. McDonald, "Corona: Success for Space Reconnaissance, a Look into the Cold War, and a Revolution for Intelligence," *Photogrammetric Engineering & Remote Sensing* 61 (June 1995): 720.

26. Greer, "Corona," 7–8.

27. Welzenbach and Galyean, "Those Daring Young Men," 3–4, 6–9, 11–14.

28. Welzenbach, "Observation Balloons and Reconnaissance Satellites," 24–28.

29. Peebles, *The Moby Dick Project,* chap. 7.

30. Greer, "Corona," 6–7.

31. Plummer, Corona Seminar, tape 2A, 207–17; and Oder and Belles, "Corona Program Profile," 2.

32. CIA, *A Point in Time,* tape 1B, 397.

33. Plummer, Corona Seminar, tape 2A, 288–96.

34. Greer, "Corona," 7.

35. Davies and Harris, *RAND's Role,* 95, 97.

36. Divine, *The Sputnik Challenge,* 100–101, 105–6.

37. Hall, "Origins of U.S. Space Policy," 229. One version is that SAMOS stands for "Satellite and Missile Observation System." It has also been claimed that the program was actually named for the Greek island of Samos, and that the press mistakenly printed it as an acronym.

38. Kip D. Cassino, "The Rocket's Red Glare," *Air & Space,* August/September 1995, 22.

39. Greer, "Corona," 9–10, 28.

40. Brugioni interview, 9 March 1996.

41. Harold E. Mitchell, interview with the author, 8 September 1996.

42. Jim Muehlberger, interview with the author, 25 February 1996; and Harold E. Mitchell, letter to the author, 17 September 1996.

43. Greer, "Corona," 11–12.

44. "Spies Above," television documentary, the Arts & Entertainment Network; and "Secret Satellite," television documentary, the Discovery Channel, 1996.

45. "C-119's Reportedly Trying to Catch Nose Cones," *New York Times,* 25 January 1959.

46. John W. Finney, "Pentagon to Fire Heavy Satellites, Animals in Some," *New York Times,* 4 December 1958; and "Defense Plans Satellite Launches on One-a-Month Basis in 1959," *Aviation Week,* 8 December 1958, 31.

47. "Spies Above" and "Secret Satellite."

48. "Polar Sky Spies," *Time,* 15 December 1958, 41–42.

49. Greer, "Corona," 12.

3. The Hard Road to Space

1. "Secret Satellite."

2. Industry Observer, *Aviation Week & Space Technology,* 2 February 1959, 23.

3. Greer, "Corona," 12, 14.

4. "Discoverer Aborted," *Aviation Week & Space Technology,* 2 March 1959, 27.

5. "A Satellite Rocket Fired on West Coast," *New York Times,* 1 March 1959.

6. *Discoverer 1* launch report, author's collection.

7. "Air Force Reports It Is Receiving Signals from Discoverer Satellite," *New York Times,* 2 March 1959.

8. "Signal Reported from Discoverer," *New York Times,* 3 March 1959.

9. Greer, "Corona," 14. Due to the early confusion, one often sees an orbit listed for *Discoverer 1* of 176 by 519 statute miles. This was the orbit announced on March 5, 1959, by the Air Force, based on the erroneous tracking signals.

10. "'Spying' in Space by U.S. Charged," *New York Times,* 6 March 1959.

11. John A. Osmundsen, "Rivalry Is Cited," *New York Times,* 3 March 1959.

12. John W. Finney, "M'Elroy Defends Curbs on Missile," *New York Times,* 3 March 1959.

13. *Discoverer 2* launch report, author's collection.

14. John W. Finney, "Discoverer Shot into Polar Orbit; Recovery Is Aim," *New York Times,* 15 April 1959.

15. John W. Finney, "U.S. Cancels Plan to Catch Capsule," *New York Times,* 15 April 1959.

16. Russell Hawkes, "USAF's Satellite Test Center Grows," *Aviation Week & Space Technology,* 30 May 1960, 58.

17. "Discoverer Capsule Falls in the Arctic; Recovery Is Possible," *New York Times,* 16 April 1959.

18. Richelson, *America's Secret Eyes in Space,* 34; and "Capsule Hunt Halted," *New York Times,* 23 April 1959. The loss of the *Discoverer 2* capsule was the source for Alistair McLean's novel *Ice Station Zebra.* In the story, the Americans and Soviets race to recover a satellite capsule that came down in the Arctic carrying film of U.S. missile silos.

19. Oder and Belles, "Corona Program Profile," 3.

20. "Norway Approves Search," *New York Times,* 17 April 1959.

21. "Capsule Hunt Pressed," *New York Times,* 18 April 1959.

22. Day, "Corona: America's First Spy Satellite," 17.

23. Khrushchev interview, 6–7.

24. Richard Witkin, "4 Mice Prepared for Orbital Effort," *New York Times,* 1 May 1959.

25. "U.S. Rockets 4 Mice; Orbit Is Doubted," *New York Times,* 4 June 1959.

26. *Discoverer 3* launch report, author's collection.

27. Greer, "Corona," 15.

28. Plummer, Corona Seminar, tape 2A, 280.

29. CIA, *A Point in Time,* tape 1A, 410.

30. Greer, "Corona," 17, 24–26.

31. *Discoverer 4* launch report, author's collection.

32. *Discoverer 5* launch report, author's collection.

33. Greer, "Corona," 15; and "Capsule Hope Dims," *New York Times,* 16 August 1959.

34. Marshall Melin, "The 'Unknown' Satellite," *Sky & Telescope,* April 1960, 346.

35. Greer, "Corona," 16.

36. Oder and Belles, "Corona Program Profile," 2.

37. "Satellite Fired into Polar Orbit," *New York Times,* 7 November 1959.

38. William J. Jorden, "Soviet Chief Sees Ordinary People," *New York Times,* 21 September 1959.

39. *Discoverer 7* launch report, author's collection.

40. "Discoverer Failure Caused by Inverter," *Aviation Week & Space Technology,* 16 November 1959, 33. The CIA's Corona history erroneously states that *Discoverer 7* was a launch failure. Presumably, the C camera also failed, but there is no information to confirm this. The Discoverer launch reports cover only the launch, orbital operations, and recovery; there is no mention of the payload.

41. Greer, "Corona," 16; and *Discoverer 8* launch report, author's collection.

42. "Chute Failure Blocks Discoverer Recovery," *Aviation Week & Space Technology,* 30 November 1959, 32.

43. Philip J. Klass, *Secret Sentries in Space* (New York: Random House), 95.

44. Richelson, *America's Secret Eyes in Space,* 37.

45. Greer, "Corona," 16–17.

46. Klass, *Secret Sentries in Space,* 95.

47. Greer, "Corona," 16–17.

48. Leonard Moseley, *Dulles: A Biography of Eleanor, Allen, and John Foster Dulles and Their Family Network* (New York: The Dial Press, 1978), 432.

49. *Discoverer 9* launch report, author's collection.

50. "Discoverer Fails in Rain of Debris," *New York Times,* 20 February 1960; and *Discoverer 10* launch report, author's collection.

51. "Secret Satellite."

52. "Discoverer Project," DoD 36C (Carrollton Press, 1980), Dwight D. Eisenhower Library, Abilene, Kans.

53. "Royalty at Launch," n.d., San Diego Aerospace Museum Discoverer File.

54. Greer, "Corona," 19; and *Discoverer 11* launch report, author's collection.

55. "Summary" and "Program Review: March, April, May 1960," DoD 36C (Carrollton Press, 1980), Eisenhower Library.

56. "Capsule of Discoverer Orbits, Foiling Recovery after Ejection," *New York Times,* 17 April 1960.

57. CIA, *A Point in Time,* tape 1B, 210.

58. Oder and Belles, "Corona Program Profile," 3.

59. Welzenbach and Galyean, "Those Daring Young Men," 15.

60. "Spies in the Sky," Public Broadcasting System.

61. A. J. Goodpaster, memorandum for record, 8 February 1960, Eisenhower Library.

62. Brugioni, *Eyeball to Eyeball,* 43–44.

63. Francis Gary Powers and Curt Gentry, *Operation Overflight* (New York: Holt, Rinehart & Winston, 1970), 139–41.

64. Brugioni, *Eyeball to Eyeball,* 48–49.

65. Oder and Belles, "Corona Program Profile," 3.

66. Greer, "Corona," 17.
67. "Discoverer Project." A minor problem occurred during one of the capsule balloon tests. A Lockheed engineer was checking the tracking beacon before launch. After it had been confirmed that the signals were being received, he put the lid back on the box. The beacon then fell silent. He opened the box back up, and the beacon began transmitting. The engineer closed the lid, and the same thing happened. There was no apparent reason for the failure of the beacon when the lid was closed. Then the engineer looked at the lid. It had an "X" stamped on it. The X was the right size to cancel out the radio signals. Corrections were made and the balloon launch went ahead.
68. Richelson, *America's Secret Eyes in Space,* 39.
69. "13th Discoverer Shot into Orbit," *New York Times,* 11 August 1960.
70. "Discoverer Project."
71. Richard Witkin, "Washington to Hail Retrieved Capsule in Ceremony Today," *New York Times,* 13 August 1960.
72. "Discoverer Project."
73. Mitchell interview.
74. "Frogman First on Scene," *New York Times,* 12 August 1960.
75. McDonald, "Corona: Success for Space Reconnaissance," 689.
76. Greer, "Corona," 20.
77. Richelson, *America's Secret Eyes in Space,* 40–41.
78. Oder and Belles, "Corona Program Profile," 3.
79. "Still Giving Off Signals," *New York Times,* 13 August 1960.
80. "Air Force Shows Prize Capsule," *New York Times,* 14 August 1960.
81. "Ike to View Capsule from 'Lucky 13,'" *Santa Barbara News-Press,* 14 August 1960.
82. Felix Belair, Jr., "Eisenhower Is Given Flag That Orbited the Earth," *New York Times,* 16 August 1960.

4. First Voyages into the Unknown

1. Central Intelligence Agency, "Visual-Talent Coverage of the USSR in Relation to Soviet ICBM Deployment, January 1959–June 1960," 11 July 1960.
2. "List of Highest Priority Targets," COMOR, 18 August 1960, author's collection.
3. R. M. Huffstutler, Corona Seminar, tape 2B, 618.
4. Richard J. Kerr, Corona Seminar, tape 2B, 65–78.
5. Huffstutler, Corona Seminar, tape 2B, 602–11.
6. "New Discoverer Shot into Orbit," *New York Times,* 19 August 1960.
7. "Discoverer Project."
8. Greer, "Corona," 20.
9. "Approximate Track of Mission 9009, Passes 2 through 9" (map), author's collection.

10. Mitchell interview.
11. "'Nervous' Pilot Caught Capsule," *New York Times,* 20 August 1960.
12. Greer, "Corona," 22; and Mitchell interview.
13. "Space Capsule Is Caught in Mid-Air by U.S. Plane on Re-Entry from Orbit," *New York Times,* 20 August 1960. The crew of Pelican 9 was: Capt. Harold E. Mitchell (pilot), Capt. Richmond A. Apaka (copilot), 1st Lt. Robert D. Counts (navigator), Staff Sgt. Arthur P. Hurst (flight engineer), Tech. Sgt. Louis F. Bannick (winch operator), Staff Sgt. Algaene Harmon, Staff Sgt. Wendell King, Airman First Class George W. Donahou, Airman Second Class Lester L. Beale, Jr., and Airman Second Class Daniel R. Hill (loadmasters).
14. "Scientists Check Recovered Cone," *New York Times,* 21 August 1960.
15. CIA, *A Point in Time,* tape 1B, 287–94.
16. "Third Pass Hooked the Discoverer XIV Capsule," *New York Times,* 22 August 1960. There is debate over the final fate of the *Discoverer 14* capsule. According to some published accounts, the capsule was later smashed and thrown into the Pacific. The Air Force Museum, at the author's request, investigated the reports. Dean C. Kallander checked with Col. F. C. E. Oder and Col. Paul E. Northman, who wrote the classified Corona history, and Col. Paul Worthman. Colonel Worthman, in turn, contacted Col. Frank S. Buzard and Col. Charles Murphy. Colonel Murphy was the only person authorized to receive the capsules after they were recovered. He categorically denied the capsules were "bashed," and said they were stored in anticipation of reuse. A small number of Corona capsules were actually reflown later in the program. When the Air Force Museum was given the *Discoverer 14* capsule, they were also given documentation stating it was the capsule. Unless an individual can be found who will state he destroyed *Discoverer 14,* the story seems to be hearsay.
17. Richelson, *America's Secret Eyes in Space,* 43.
18. Dino A. Brugioni, interview with the author, 2 December 1995.
19. Oder and Belles, "Corona Program Profile," 3.
20. "Approximate Track of Mission 9009."
21. Central Intelligence Agency, "Joint Mission Coverage Index: Mission 9009," 18 August 1960.
22. "Approximate Track of Mission 9009."
23. Oder and Belles, "Corona Program Profile," 3.
24. Greer, "Corona," 22.
25. Richelson, *America's Secret Eyes in Space,* 44–46, 61–63.
26. Hall, "Eisenhower and the Cold War," 67–68.
27. "Department of Defense Directive Number TS 5105.23," *Exploring the Unknown,* 373–75.
28. Klass, *Secret Sentries in Space,* 53–54.
29. Zaloga, *Target America,* 194–95.
30. Richelson, *America's Secret Eyes in Space,* 47–48.
31. *Discoverer 15* launch report, author's collection.

32. "Two Launches Highlight Week," *The SAC Missileer,* 16 September 1960, San Diego Aerospace Museum Discoverer File.

33. "Satellite Capsule Sighted, Then Lost," *New York Times,* 16 September 1960.

34. "Declassified Imaging Satellite Systems" (handout at Corona Seminar), author's collection.

35. *Discoverer 16* launch report, author's collection.

36. *Discoverer 17* launch report, author's collection.

37. "Urgent Requirements for Corona and Argon," memorandum from COMOR, 18 August 1960, author's collection.

38. "Drop of Capsule Put Off for Day," *New York Times,* 14 November 1960.

39. "2d Space Capsule Caught in Mid-Air," *New York Times,* 15 November 1960.

40. "Almost Missed Chance," *New York Times,* 15 November 1960.

41. "Capsule Snared; Monkey Shot Near," *Santa Maria Times,* 15 November 1960.

42. "2d Space Capsule Caught."

43. Brugioni interview, 2 December 1995.

44. Greer, "Corona," 24.

45. Jonathan McDowell, "US Reconnaissance Satellite Programs, Part I," *Quest,* Summer 1995, 28–29.

46. Richard Witkin, "Military Chiefs Decry Fund Curb on 'Spy' Satellite," *New York Times,* 5 January 1960.

47. John W. Finney, "Senate May Press for Spy Satellite," *New York Times,* 7 June 1960, and "Senate Unit Raises Spy-Satellite Fund," *New York Times,* 11 June 1960.

48. "SAMOS II Launch," memorandum for the president, 26 January 1961, Declassified Document Reference System, 1981-364B.

49. Richelson, *America's Secret Eyes in Space,* 51–53.

50. Richard Witkin, "SAMOS Satellite Fails First Test," *New York Times,* 12 October 1960.

51. "'Souped Up' Discoverer Launched," *Santa Maria Times,* 7 December 1960.

52. "Twelfth Discoverer Orbited by the U.S.," *New York Times,* 8 December 1960.

53. "U.S. Will Try Today to Regain Capsule," *New York Times,* 9 December 1960.

54. "Defers Capsule Plan," *New York Times,* 9 December 1960.

55. "3rd Space Capsule Caught in Mid-Air," *New York Times,* 11 December 1960.

56. "Sighted at 25,000 Feet," *New York Times,* 10 December 1960.

57. "Capsule Caught in Air; VAFB Ready for No 19," *Santa Maria Times,* 12 December 1960.

58. Greer, "Corona," 24.

59. David S. Doyle, Corona Seminar, tape 2B, 412.

60. Brugioni interview, 2 December 1995.

61. Asif Siddiqi, "Morning Star," *Quest,* Winter 1994, 39, 41, 44–47.

62. James Oberg, "Echoes of the Nedelin Catastrophe," *Air & Space,* December 1990, 76–77.

5. The Kennedy Administration and Corona

1. *Discoverer 19* launch report, author's collection.

2. John A. Byrne, *The Whiz Kids* (New York: Current Doubleday, 1993), 364–66, 372, 394–96.

3. Lawrence Freedman, *The Evolution of Nuclear Strategy* (New York: St. Martin's Press, 1983), 176–78, 181–85, 231, 236.

4. Marion E. Carl and Barrett Tillman, *Pushing the Envelope* (Annapolis, Md.: Naval Institute Press, 1994), 91–92.

5. William Y. Smith, Corona Seminar, tape 3A, 622–30.

6. Richelson, *America's Secret Eyes in Space,* 52.

7. "Pentagon News Blackout," *Aviation Week & Space Technology,* 27 February 1961, 21.

8. "SAMOS II Launch."

9. Bill Becker, "Photo Vehicle Shot into Orbit," *New York Times,* 1 February 1961.

10. Richelson, *America's Secret Eyes in Space,* 68.

11. Greer, "Corona," 24–25.

12. "Appendix 5, Camera Data: Argon & Lanyard," *Photogrammetric Engineering & Remote Sensing* 61 (June 1995): 719.

13. Kenneth Daugherty, Corona Seminar, tape 4B, 417–32.

14. "Urgent Requirements for Corona and Argon."

15. *Discoverer 20* launch report, author's collection; and Greer, "Corona," 25.

16. "Capsule 'Catch' Called Off," *New York Times,* 22 February 1961.

17. *Discoverer 21* launch report, author's collection.

18. *Discoverer 22* launch report, author's collection.

19. *Discoverer 23* launch report, author's collection.

20. *Discoverer 24* launch report, author's collection; and "Attempt to Orbit Discoverer Fails," *New York Times,* 9 June 1961.

21. Anatoli I. Gribkov and William Y. Smith, *Operation Anadyr* (Chicago: edition q, 1994), 86–89.

22. Richelson, *America's Secret Eyes in Space,* 58.

23. Henrik Bering, *Outpost Berlin* (Carol Stream, Ill.: edition q, 1995), 146–47.

24. Curtis Cate, *The Ides of August* (New York: M. Evans & Company, 1978), 128.

25. Gribkov and Smith, *Operation Anadyr,* 84–85, 88–91.

26. John Prados, *The Soviet Estimate* (New York: The Dial Press, 1982), 89, 116–17.

27. Bering, *Outpost Berlin,* 148–49.

28. Bruce Watson, "Shelter-Skelter," *Smithsonian,* April 1994.

29. Cate, *The Ides of August,* 172.

30. Glenn T. Seaborg, *Kennedy, Khrushchev, and the Test Ban* (Berkeley: University of California Press, 1981), 87.
31. Klass, *Secret Sentries in Space,* 61–65.
32. Watson, "Shelter-Skelter."
33. Greer, "Corona," 25; and "Discoverer XXV Retrieved from Orbit," *Aviation Week & Space Technology,* 26 June 1961.
34. "Capsule of Discoverer Is Recovered in Pacific," *New York Times,* 19 June 1961.
35. "3 Airmen Decorated," *New York Times,* 21 June 1961.
36. Doyle, Corona Seminar, tape 2B, 407–28.
37. Central Intelligence Agency, "Strength and Deployment of Soviet Long Range Ballistic Missile Forces," NIE 11-8/1-61, 21 September 1961.
38. James E. Oberg, "The Plesetsk Cosmodrome," *Final Frontier,* May/June 1992.
39. Prados, *The Soviet Estimate,* 119–21; and Robert Berman and Bill Gunston, *Rockets and Missiles of World War III* (New York: Exeter Books, 1983), 23, 83.
40. William Y. Smith, Corona Seminar, tape 3A, 584–93.
41. Klass, *Secret Sentries in Space,* 66–67.
42. William Manchester, *The Glory and the Dream* (New York: Bantam Books, 1974), 913.
43. Richelson, *America's Secret Eyes in Space,* 59–60, 73.
44. Klass, *Secret Sentries in Space,* 69–70.
45. Watson, "Shelter-Skelter"; and Bering, *Outpost Berlin,* 168–71.
46. Smith, Corona Seminar, tape 3A, 584–95.
47. "Discoverer Cone Is Caught in Air," *New York Times,* 10 July 1961.
48. "26th Discoverer Is Shot into Orbit," *New York Times,* 8 July 1961.
49. Greer, "Corona," 25–26.
50. "Capsule Due for Study," *New York Times,* 11 July 1961; and Jack R. Wilson, interview with the author, 5 September 1996.
51. *Discoverer 27* launch report, author's collection.
52. *Discoverer 28* launch report, author's collection.
53. CIA, *A Point in Time,* tape 1A, 319–37.
54. "Appendix 4, Camera Data: Corona," *Photogrammetric Engineering & Remote Sensing* 61 (June 1995): 718.
55. "29th Discoverer Placed in Orbit, Air Force Hopes to Recover It," *New York Times,* 31 August 1961.
56. "Discoverer Going Well," *New York Times,* 1 September 1961.
57. "Satellite Capsule Recovered in Ocean," *New York Times,* 2 September 1961.
58. Greer, "Corona," 26.
59. "Satellite in Orbit, Recovery Planned," *New York Times,* 13 September 1961.
60. "Discoverer Capsule Is Recovered in Air," *New York Times,* 15 September 1961.
61. Thomas F. Hines, interview with the author, 7 September 1996.
62. *Discoverer 31* launch report, author's collection.
63. SAMOS III Fact Sheet, Los Angeles AFB History Office.

64. "SAMOS Fails Test, As Does Nike Zeus," *New York Times,* 10 September 1961.

65. "Satellite Fired in Secret by U.S.," *New York Times,* 23 November 1961.

66. "Moscow Denounces U.S. Space Program," *New York Times,* 7 November 1961.

6. Corona in the Shadows

1. Greer, "Corona," 27.

2. "U.S. Orbits Discoverer," *New York Times,* 14 October 1961; and "Discoverer Capsule Caught over Pacific," *New York Times,* October 1961.

3. *Discoverer 33* launch report, author's collection.

4. *Discoverer 34* launch report, author's collection.

5. Greer, "Corona," 24–25, 27.

6. "3 of 4 U.S. Satellites Launched into Orbit," *New York Times,* 16 November 1961; and "Discoverer Capsule Caught," *New York Times,* 17 November 1961.

7. "Ham-Radio Robot Fired into Orbit," *New York Times,* 13 December 1961.

8. "Capsule Recovered after Record Orbit," *New York Times,* 17 December 1961; and "Discoverer Capsule Taken from Pacific," *New York Times,* 18 December 1961.

9. *Discoverer 37* launch report, author's collection.

10. Greer, "Corona," 27–28; and Wilson interview. The KH-4 series cameras "see" in stereo the same way a person does. The two eyes view a scene from slightly different angles. The brain then combines the two views into a single, three-dimensional image. With the M camera, the area of stereo coverage was 30 degrees (out of the 70-degree scan). Because the two images were taken at a greater angle than by human eyes, the vertical dimension seems exaggerated.

11. Oder and Belles, "Corona Program Profile," 2; and Dwayne A. Day, "Corona: America's First Spy Satellite Program, Part II," *Quest* 4 (Fall 1995): 32–33.

12. Washington Roundup, *Aviation Week & Space Technology,* 3 December 1962, 25.

13. Richelson, *America's Secret Eyes in Space,* 54, 65–75.

14. "U.S. May Put More Wraps on DOD Satellites," *Rockets and Missiles,* 12 February 1962.

15. "Britons Score U.S. on Orbital Secrecy," *New York Times,* 15 March 1962.

16. Program 162 launch reports, author's collection; and Hines interview.

17. "Satellite Fired in Secret," *New York Times,* 5 December 1962.

18. Day, "Corona, Part II," 32–33.

19. McDowell, "US Reconnaissance Satellite Programs, Part I," 28–29.

20. Steven J. Zaloga, *Soviet Air Defence Missiles* (Alexandria, Va.: Jane's Information Group, 1989), 120–21.

21. McDonald, "Corona: Success for Space Reconnaissance," 694, 718–19.

22. Program 162 launch report, 28 February 1963.
23. Program 162 launch report, 18 March 1963.
24. "The U-2's Intended Successor: Project Oxcart, 1956–1968," declassified October 1994, author's collection.
25. Program 162 launch report, 18 May 1963.
26. Program 162 launch report, 30 July 1963.
27. McDonald, "Corona: Success for Space Reconnaissance," 694.
28. Levison interview, 17 April 1996.
29. Greer, "Corona," 29.
30. Zaloga, *Soviet Air Defence Missiles,* 121.
31. Program 162 launch reports.
32. Greer, "Corona," 28.
33. "The U-2's Intended Successor."
34. Smith, Corona Seminar, tape 3A, 575–83.
35. Wynn, *RAF Nuclear Deterrent Forces,* 274–75.
36. Stephen Twigge, "Anglo-American Air Force Collaboration and the Cuban Missile Crisis: A British Perspective," *Seeing Off the Bear,* 210–12, 214–15. The 1962 strike plan allotted two or three nuclear weapons for each target, to ensure it was destroyed. For example, Soviet command and control facilities outside East Berlin would be struck first by a Thor IRBM, then, less than a minute later, by an F-100, and finally by another Thor.
37. Freedman, *The Evolution of Nuclear Strategy,* 234–35.
38. Smith, Corona Seminar, tape 3A, 597.
39. Gribkov and Smith, *Operation Anadyr,* 4, 12–14, 23, 26–27, 40, 54, 104, 128, 130–37, 154–59.
40. Smith, Corona Seminar, tape 3A, 610.
41. Central Intelligence Agency, "Soviet Military Capabilities and Policies, 1962–1967," NIE 11-4-63, 22 March 1963, 3, 4, 20.
42. Central Intelligence Agency, "Main Trends in Soviet Military Policy," NIE 11-4-65, 14 April 1965, 15.
43. "Annex Soviet Strategic Nuclear Forces as Perceived by NIE's, 1962–1975," Report of Team "B" (Washington: Central Intelligence Agency, 1976), 51.
44. CIA, "Soviet Military Capabilities and Policies," 6, 27–30.
45. "Soviet Strategic Nuclear Forces," 51.
46. CIA, "Main Trends in Soviet Military Policy," 13.
47. "Soviet Strategic Nuclear Forces," 52.
48. Lawrence Freedman, *U.S. Intelligence and the Soviet Strategic Threat* (Princeton: Princeton University Press), 104.
49. Prados, *The Soviet Estimate,* 190.
50. John Cobb Cooper, "Self-Defence in Outer Space," *Spaceflight,* September 1962, 164.
51. John Cobb Cooper, "Current Developments in Space Law," *Spaceflight,* July 1963, 136.
52. Klass, *Secret Sentries in Space,* 125–27.
53. Byrne, *The Whiz Kids,* 419–20.

54. Wheelon, Corona Seminar, tape 4A, 454.
55. "The U-2's Intended Successor."
56. Wheelon, Corona Seminar, tape 4A, 220–55, 262–68.
57. Greer, "Corona," 29.
58. Wheelon, Corona Seminar, tape 4A, 295–302.
59. Levison interview, 17 April 1996.
60. Walter Levison, Corona Seminar, tape 2A, 466–85; and "Secret Satellite."
61. Thomas F. Hines, "Events of Mission," ca. 1969, unpublished, author's collection. During the chase and recovery, the crew was too keyed up to give any thought to anything but the task at hand. Afterwards, the tension became apparent. One of the crew handed Hines a cup of coffee; he promptly spilled it. Major Hines was later awarded an Air Medal for the recovery.
62. Edwards Parks, "The Open Gate," *Air & Space,* December 1993/January 1994, 70–73.

7. The Definitive Corona

1. "Camera Data: Corona," 718.
2. CIA, *A Point in Time,* tape 1B, 355.
3. Levison interview, 17 April 1996.
4. Conversations between former Lockheed engineers and the author at the National Air and Space Museum, Washington, D.C., 25 May 1995.
5. Greer, "Corona," 29–31.
6. Program 162 launch report, 23 September 1963.
7. Program 162 launch report, 15 February 1964.
8. Program 162 launch report, 24 March 1964.
9. Program 162 launch report, 27 April 1964.
10. Greer, "Corona," 31–32.
11. "On Trail of Space Device," *New York Times,* 5 August 1964. The capsule from Mission 1005 was not the only debris from Corona flights to be recovered. In April and June 1963, two spherical pressure vessels were found near Broken Hills in New South Wales, Australia. They were traced to the Agenas used on Corona flights 58 (December 14, 1962) and 59 (January 7, 1963). Both had decayed from orbit in January 1963. However, the Mission 1005 capsule represented the most serious compromise of the program, as even in its battered state it was easily identifiable as a Discoverer capsule, and the film roll would make its reconnaissance mission clear.
12. Program 241 launch report, 4 June 1964; and Wilson interview.
13. Program 241 launch report, 2 November 1964.
14. Greer, "Corona," 35.
15. "Appendix 7, Area Coverage," *Photogrammetric Engineering & Remote Sensing* 61 (June 1995): 719.

16. McDowell, "US Reconnaissance Satellite Programs, Part I," table 8; and "Mission Summary (Early Photo Reconnaissance)," *Photogrammetric Engineering & Remote Sensing* 61 (June 1995): 717.

17. Program 241 launch report, 2 September 1965.

18. "Summary Log of Space Launches, 1957–87," *TRW Space Log 1957–1987* (1987), 50, 58.

19. Curtis Peebles, *Guardians* (Novato, Calif.: Presidio Press, 1987), 356–57, 359.

20. Klass, *Secret Sentries in Space,* 193–94.

21. Jonathan McDowell, "US Reconnaissance Satellite Programs, Part II: Beyond Imaging," *Quest,* Winter 1995, 41–42.

22. McDowell, "US Reconnaissance Satellite Programs, Part I," table 8.

23. "Mission Summary (Early Photo Reconnaissance)," 717.

24. McDowell, "US Reconnaissance Satellite Programs, Part I," 29–31.

25. Greer, "Corona," 33–34.

26. Day, "Corona, Part II," 35.

27. Levison interview, 17 April 1996.

28. "Camera Data: Corona," 718.

29. Walter Levison, interview with the author, 13 August 1996.

30. Greer, "Corona," 10, 34–35.

31. Day, "Corona, Part II," 35.

32. Central Intelligence Agency, "KH-4B System Capability Appraisal of Geologic Value for Mineral Resources Exploration," March 1971.

33. McDowell, "US Reconnaissance Satellite Programs, Part II," 41.

34. Lawrence Freedman, *U.S. Intelligence,* 87–90, 111–13.

35. "Soviet Strategic Nuclear Forces," 52.

36. Freedman, *U.S. Intelligence,* 119, 257–59.

37. Freedman, *The Evolution of Nuclear Strategy,* 254–61.

38. Klass, *Secret Sentries in Space,* xv–xvi.

39. Brugioni interview, 9 March 1996.

40. Conversations with former Lockheed engineers at the National Air and Space Museum, 25 May 1995.

41. Levison interview, 17 April 1996.

42. Greer, "Corona," 19.

43. Brugioni interview, 2 December 1995.

44. Muehlberger interview.

45. Jack Schreibman, "AF Nose Cone Catchers Fielding at .950 Average," *Santa Barbara News-Press,* 4 December 1960.

46. Muehlberger interview; and Jim Muehlberger, letter to the author, 16 March 1996.

47. M. J. Ravnitzky, "Catch a Falling Star: Parachute System Lessons Learned During the USAF Space Capsule Mid-Air Recovery Program, 1959–1985," American Institute of Aeronautics and Astronautics Paper 93-1243, 1993.

48. Robert A. Flavell, "Catch a Falling Star: Aerial Recovery of Space Objects," *Air Power History,* Fall 1994, 24.

8. Magic in Their Eyes

1. Dino A. Brugioni, Corona Seminar, tape 2B, 267, 290.
2. Doyle, Corona Seminar, tape 2B, 412.
3. Brugioni, *Eyeball to Eyeball*, 196.
4. Doyle, Corona Seminar, tape 2B, 466–80.
5. Kerr, Corona Seminar, tape 2B, 104.
6. Brugioni, Corona Seminar, tape 2B, 290–302.
7. Doyle, Corona Seminar, tape 2B, 217–29, 484–500.
8. Khrushchev interview.
9. Richelson, *America's Secret Eyes in Space*, 193–94.
10. R. M. Huffstutler, Corona Seminar, tape 3A, 262–70.
11. Doyle, Corona Seminar, tape 3A, 241–50.
12. Brugioni, Corona Seminar, tape 2B, 231.
13. Dino A. Brugioni, interview with the author, 5 August 1995.
14. Brugioni, *Eyeball to Eyeball*, 190–95.
15. Richelson, *America's Secret Eyes in Space*, 76–77.
16. Brugioni, Corona Seminar, tape 2B, 189–230, 358.
17. Doyle, Corona Seminar, tape 2B, 392–430.
18. Brugioni, *Eyeball to Eyeball*, 194–96.
19. Central Intelligence Agency/National Photographic Interpretation Center, "KH-4 Mission 1042-1, 17–22 June 1967," Photographic Intelligence Report, June 1967.
20. Central Intelligence Agency/National Photographic Interpretation Center, "KH-4 Mission 1042-1, 17–22 June 1967, Middle East Edition" and "South China and North Vietnam Edition," Photographic Intelligence Reports.
21. Central Intelligence Agency/National Photographic Interpretation Center, "Probable Solid Propellants Testing Facilities and Associated Explosives Plants in the USSR," Photographic Intelligence Report, December 1963.
22. Huffstutler, Corona Seminar, tape 2B, 548–84.
23. Jerrold L. Schecter and Peter S. Deriabin, *The Spy Who Saved the World* (New York: Charles Scribner's Sons, 1992).
24. Richards J. Heuer, Jr., "Nosenko: Five Paths to Judgment," *Studies in Intelligence* 31 (Fall 1987): 71–101.
25. Central Intelligence Agency, "Soviet Capabilities and Probable Programs in the Guided Missile Field," NIE 11-6-54, 5 October 1954, 1–33.
26. Zaloga, *Soviet Air Defence Missiles*, 26–37.
27. Zaloga, *Target America*, 127–28, 175–78, 252–53.
28. Varfolomeyev, "Soviet Rocketry," 260–61.
29. CIA, NIE 11-8/1-61, 21–27.
30. Andrew J. Goodpaster, Corona Seminar, tape 3A, 440–55.
31. Brugioni, *Eyeball to Eyeball*, 58, 229–30, 523–24, 570.
32. Brugioni interview, 5 August 1995.
33. Christopher Andrew, *For the President's Eyes Only* (New York: Harper Collins, 1995), 309, 311, 313, 320–24.

34. Brugioni interview, 5 August 1995.

35. Brugioni, *Eyeball to Eyeball,* 525–26.

36. Brugioni interview, 5 August 1995. Not all "greetings" were so rude. Troops at a SAM site in East Germany stamped "Merry Christmas" in the snow for an RF-4C reconnaissance plane flying in the Berlin Air Corridor. It is said that U.S. military personnel have also sent similar "greetings" to Soviet reconnaissance satellites. During the Carter Administration, farmers in the Midwest were upset about agricultural policy. One farmer plowed a giant "finger" in his field, while a number of others sent Soviet-style messages in the snow.

9. Top Secret Ruff

1. National Photographic Interpretation Center, "Chronological Development of the Kapustin Yar/Vladimirovka and Tyuratam Missile Test Centers, USSR, 1957 Through 1963," November 1963.

2. CIA, NIE 11-8/1-61.

3. NPIC, "Chronological Development of Kapustin Yar."

4. Charles P. Vick, "Launch Site Infrastructure," *Spaceflight,* January 1996, 28–29.

5. Central Intelligence Agency, "The Soviet Space Program," NIE 11-1-67, 2 March 1967, 2, 9, 11, 18–19.

6. Rob R. Landis, "The N-1 and the Soviet Manned Lunar Landing Program," *Quest,* Winter 1992, 25.

7. Peter Alway, "Capcom," *Quest,* Summer 1995, 2.

8. Vick, "Launch Site Infrastructure," 28–29.

9. Landis, "The N-1," 29–30.

10. James Oberg, "The Moon Race (and Its Coverup) in Hindsight," *Spaceflight,* February 1993, 46–47.

11. CIA, "Joint Mission Coverage Index: Mission 9009."

12. CIA/NPIC, "KH-4 Mission 1042-1."

13. Dino A. Brugioni, "The Unidentifieds," *Studies in Intelligence* 13 (Summer 1969): 1–20.

14. Brugioni, *Eyeball to Eyeball,* chap. 25.

15. Central Intelligence Agency/National Photographic Interpretation Center, "Regional Nuclear Weapons Storage Site Near Berdichev, USSR," May 1963.

16. Central Intelligence Agency/National Photographic Interpretation Center, "Severodvinsk Naval Base and Shipyard 402, Severodvinsk, USSR," November 1964.

17. Willis C. Armstrong, et al., "The Hazards of Single-Outcome Forecasting," *Studies in Intelligence* 28 (Fall 1984): 57–70.

18. Central Intelligence Agency/National Photographic Interpretation Center, "Search for Uranium Mining in the Vicinity of A-ko-su, China," August 1963.

19. Central Intelligence Agency, "The Chances of an Imminent Communist Chinese Nuclear Explosion," SNIE 13-4-64, 26 August 1964.

20. Dino A. Brugioni, "The Art and Science of Photoreconnaissance," *Scientific American* 274 (March 1996): 83.

21. Brugioni, "The Unidentifieds."

22. Brugioni interview, 9 March 1996.

23. Brugioni, "The Art and Science of Photoreconnaissance," 85.

24. Brugioni interview, 9 March 1996.

25. Byrne, *The Whiz Kids*, 434–35, 443–49.

26. "Approximate Coverage of KH-4 Mission, 17–22 June 1967 over South China and North Vietnam" (map), author's collection.

27. CIA/NPIC, "KH-4 Mission 1042-1, 17–22 June 1967, South China and North Vietnam Edition", June 1967.

28. Byrne, *The Whiz Kids*, 449–50.

29. McDowell, "US Reconnaissance Satellite Programs, Part I," tables 8 and 14.

30. CIA/NPIC, "KH-4 Mission 1042-1, 17–22 June 1967, Middle East Edition."

31. Richelson, *America's Secret Eyes in Space*, 97–98.

32. Richard Helms, Corona Seminar, tape 3B, 1–95.

10. Corona's Twilight

1. Freedman, *U.S. Intelligence*, 129–31.

2. Freedman, *The Evolution of Nuclear Strategy*, 335–40, 430–31.

3. Freedman, *U.S. Intelligence*, 153–55.

4. Dino A. Brugioni, interview with the author, 18 August 1996.

5. Helms, Corona Seminar, tape 3B, 92–130.

6. *Soviet Space Programs, 1971–75* (Washington, D.C.: Library of Congress, 1976), 424–29.

7. Khrushchev interview, 6, 11.

8. Day, "Corona, Part II," 32.

9. Freedman, *U.S. Intelligence*, 156–64.

10. McDowell, "US Reconnaissance Satellite Programs, Part I," tables 14 and 16.

11. Philip A. Rowe, Jr., "The Starcatchers," *Air Force Magazine*, June 1995, 74–76.

12. Greer, "Corona," 36.

13. Klass, *Secret Sentries in Space*, 201–2.

14. "Spies Above."

15. Richelson, *Secret Eyes in Space*, 105.

16. Hap Hazard, "Space Shuttle, Comparison: Expendables vs. Shuttle," Navy Space Systems Activities, October 1977, 55. The Hexagon/Big Bird measurements were taken from the internal volume of the Titan IIID shroud.

17. Richelson, *America's Secret Eyes in Space,* 105–31. The idea of a mirror-based reconnaissance system was first developed on the U.S. Air Force's Manned Orbiting Laboratory (MOL). This was a space station project, code named "Dorian," which would operate for 30 days before the two-man crew returned to Earth aboard a modified Gemini spacecraft. The MOL's KH-10 camera was to use a 71-inch mirror. The MOL was to have flown in 1969, but technical problems, and the cost of the Vietnam War, delayed it. President Nixon cancelled the MOL project on June 30, 1969, to make way for the Kennan.
18. Greer, "Corona," 28.
19. Donald G. Hard, interview with the author, 19 August 1996.
20. Freedman, *U.S. Intelligence,* 164–65; and Prados, *The Soviet Estimate,* 221.
21. McDowell, "US Reconnaissance Satellite Programs, Part I," tables 16 and 17.
22. Freedman, *U.S. Intelligence,* 166–67; and Prados, *The Soviet Estimate,* 221.
23. Helms, Corona Seminar, tape 3B, 131.
24. Hard interview.
25. McDonald, "Corona: Success for Space Reconnaissance," 719.
26. Greer, "Corona," 37.

11. The View from 2001

1. James E. Oberg, *Uncovering Soviet Disasters* (New York: Random House, 1988).
2. "Soviets Suffer Setback in Space," *Aviation Week & Space Technology,* 17 November 1969.
3. Smith, Corona Seminar, tape 3A, 632.
4. Wheelon, Corona Seminar, tape 4A, 268.
5. "Soviet Strategic Nuclear Forces."
6. Freedman, *U.S. Intelligence,* 30–37.
7. Armstrong, et al., "The Hazards of Single-Outcome Forecasting."
8. David L. Chandler, "Spy Photos Now Put to Peaceful Uses," *San Diego Union-Tribune,* 28 June 1995. The release of the photos was not an easy process. One major concern was caused by the small percentage of photos taken of the United States. CIA lawyers spent considerable time debating the possibility that someone whose house was in the pictures could claim the CIA was spying on him and then sue. At the Corona seminar, this caused both laughter and groans.
9. William J. Broad, "Spy Satellites Might Shift to Monitoring Earth's Health," *San Diego Union-Tribune,* 29 November 1995.

Index

About the Author

Curtis Peebles is an internationally known aerospace historian. His first article was published in 1977 and his first book in 1983. In 1985 he graduated from California State University, Long Beach, with a B.A. in history. His most recent books are *Watch the Skies,* an examination of the popular beliefs about UFOs, and *Dark Eagles,* on secret aircraft programs. He lives on Palomar Mountain.

The **Naval Institute Press** is the book-publishing arm of the U.S. Naval Institute, a private, nonprofit, membership society for sea service professionals and others who share an interest in naval and maritime affairs. Established in 1873 at the U.S. Naval Academy in Annapolis, Maryland, where its offices remain today, the Naval Institute has members worldwide.

Members of the Naval Institute support the education programs of the society and receive the influential monthly magazine *Proceedings* and discounts on fine nautical prints and on ship and aircraft photos. They also have access to the transcripts of the Institute's Oral History Program and get discounted admission to any of the Institute-sponsored seminars offered around the country.

The Naval Institute also publishes *Naval History* magazine. This colorful bimonthly is filled with entertaining and thought-provoking articles, first-person reminiscences, and dramatic art and photography. Members receive a discount on *Naval History* subscriptions.

The Naval Institute's book-publishing program, begun in 1898 with basic guides to naval practices, has broadened its scope in recent years to include books of more general interest. Now the Naval Institute Press publishes about 100 titles each year, ranging from how-to books on boating and navigation to battle histories, biographies, ship and aircraft guides, and novels. Institute members receive discounts of 20 to 50 percent on the Press's nearly 600 books in print.

Full-time students are eligible for special half-price membership rates. Life memberships are also available.

For a free catalog describing Naval Institute Press books currently available, and for further information about subscribing to *Naval History* magazine or about joining the U.S. Naval Institute, please write to:

Membership Department
U.S. Naval Institute
118 Maryland Avenue
Annapolis, MD 21402-5035
Telephone: (800) 233-8764
Fax: (410) 269-7940
Web address: www.usni.org